Analysis of Financial Statements

ANALYSIS OF FINANCIAL STATEMENTS

LEOPOLD A. BERNSTEIN, Ph.D., C.P.A.

Professor of Accounting
Bernard M. Baruch College
The City University of New York

Revised Edition

DOW JONES-IRWIN
Homewood, Illinois   60430

An expanded version of this text is published by Richard D. Irwin, Inc., under the title *Financial Statement Analysis: Theory, Application, and Interpretation,* third edition.

ISBN 0-87094-494-0

Library of Congress Catalog Card No. 84–71131

Printed in the United States of America

1 2 3 4 5 6 7 8 9 0 K 1 0 9 8 7 6 5 4

Preface

The major objective of this revised edition, as was that of the preceding edition, is to present an up-to-date treatment of the analysis of financial statements as an aid to decision making.

This edition brings into sharper focus the knowledge and skills which are required for the intelligent analysis of financial statements. It reflects a comprehensive updating of authoritative pronouncements on accounting and auditing standards and practices as well as the valuable suggestions of practicing financial analysts, credit analysts, and other users of financial data.

While the analysis of financial statements serves many and varied purposes, its major usefulness is in making investing and lending decisions. Such decisions, and the actions to which they lead, are, of course, at the heart of the free market system.

Investing and lending decisions require the application of thorough analysis to carefully evaluated data. They require, moreover, the ability to forecast—to foresee. Sound information is obtained by an *understanding* of the data from which it is derived as well as by the application of tools of analysis which aid in its extraction and evaluation. Foresight, which is essential to the assessment of opportunity and risk, is also rooted in understanding: understanding of the elements comprising the data and of the factors that can change them. The common denominator is *understanding*. Alfred North Whitehead assured us that foresight can be taught when he wrote: "Foresight depends upon understanding. In practical affairs it is a habit. But the habit of foreseeing is elicited by the habit of understanding. To a large extent, understanding can now be acquired by a conscious effort and it can be taught. Thus the training of foresight is by the medium of understanding."

Thus, the keynote of this work is *understanding*. It focuses on understanding the data which are analyzed as well as the methods by which they are analyzed and interpreted.

Leopold A. Bernstein

v

Contents

1. **Objectives of financial statement analysis, 1**
   The nature of financial analysis. Approaches to the subject: *Objectives of credit grantors. Objectives of equity investors.* Recent developments in investment theory: *Portfolio theory. Evaluation of risk and return. Categories of risk. Components of unsystematic risk. The capital asset pricing model. The efficient market hypothesis. Implications for financial statement analysis. Objectives of management. Objectives of acquisition and merger analysts. Objectives of auditors. Objectives of other interested groups.* Conclusion.

2. **Tools and techniques of financial statement analysis—an overview, 22**
   Basic approaches to financial statement analysis. Reconstruction of business activities and transactions. Importance of the statement of changes in financial position: *Additional analytical functions.* Sources of information. The total information set. The principal tools of analysis: *Comparative financial statements. Index-number trend series. Common-size financial statements. Ratio analysis. Factors affecting ratios. Interpretation of ratios.* Illustration of ratio computations. Market measures. Testing the understanding of relationships: *Specialized tools of analysis.* Building blocks of financial statement analysis. Computer-assisted financial analysis: *1. Data storage, retrieval, and computational ability. 2. Screening large masses of data. 3. A research tool. 4. Specialized financial analyses.* Analytical review of accounting principles—purposes and focus: *Example of importance of accounting assumptions, standards, and determinations: Illustration of a simple investment decision.*
   Appendix 2A: Sources of information on financial and operating ratios.
   Appendix 2B: Financial statements of Alfa, Inc.

3. **Analysis of short-term liquidity, 85**
   Significance of short-term liquidity. Working capital: *Current assets. Current liabilities. Other problem areas in the definition of current assets*

and liabilities. Working capital as a measure of liquidity. Current ratio:
*Limitations of the current ratio. Implications of the limitations to which
the current ratio is subject. The current ratio as a valid tool of analysis.
Measures that supplement the current ratio. Measures of accounts
receivable liquidity.* Average accounts receivable turnover ratio:
Collection period for accounts receivable. Evaluation. Measures of
inventory turnover: *Inventory turnover ratio. Days to sell inventory. The
effect of alternative methods of inventory management.* Current liabilities:
*Differences of the "nature" of current liabilities. Days purchases in
accounts payable ratio.* Interpretation of the current ratio: *Examination
of trend. Interpretation of changes over time. Possibilities of manipulation.
The use of "rules of thumb" standards. The net trade cycle. Valid working
capital standards. The importance of sales. Common-size analysis of
current assets composition. The liquidity index.* Acid-test ratio. Other
measures of short-term liquidity: *Funds flow ratios. Cash flow related
measures.* The concept of financial flexibility. Management's discussion
and analysis: *Projecting changes in conditions or policies.*

4. **Funds flow analysis and financial forecasts, 121**
    Overview of cash flow and funds flow patterns. Short-term cash forecasts:
    *Importance of sales estimates. Pro forma financial statements as an aid
    to forecasting. Techniques of short-term cash forecasting. Differences
    between short-term and long-term forecasts.* Analysis of statements of
    changes in financial position. Illustration of the analysis of statements
    of changes in financial position. The analytically recast statement of
    changes in financial position. Evaluation of the statement of changes
    in financial position. Projection of statements of changes in financial
    position. Illustration of a projection of statements of changes in financial
    position: *The impact of adversity. The funds flow adequacy ratio. Funds
    reinvestment ratio.* Conclusion.

5. **Analysis of capital structure and long-term solvency, 146**
    Key elements in the evaluation of long-term solvency. Importance of
    capital structure. Accounting principles: *Deferred taxes. Long-term
    leases. Off-balance sheet financing. Liabilities for pensions.
    Unconsolidated subsidiaries. Provisions, reserves, and contingent
    liabilities. Minority interests. Convertible debt. Preferred stock.*
    Adjustments to the book value of assets: *Inventories. Marketable
    securities. Intangible assets.* The significance of capital structure. Reasons
    for employment of debt: *The concept of financial leverage. The effect
    of tax deductibility of interest. Other advantages of leverage. Measuring
    the effect of financial leverage.* Measuring the effect of capital structure
    on long-term solvency. Long-term projections—usefulness and
    limitations. Capital structure analysis—common-size statements. Capital
    structure ratios. Total debt to total capital (debt and equity): *Ratio of*

total debt to total equity capital. Long-term debt/equity capital. Confusion in terminology. Short-term debt. Equity capital at market value. Preferred stock within the capital structure. The analytically adjusted ratio of debt to equity. Interpretation of capital structure measures. Measures of assets distribution. Critical importance of "earning power." Measures of earnings coverage: Earnings available to meet fixed charges. Fixed charges to be included. Income tax adjustment of fixed charges. Other elements to be included in fixed charges. Ratio of earnings to fixed charges: Illustration of earnings-coverage ratio calculations. Ratio of earnings to fixed charges—expanded concept of fixed charges. Pro forma computations of coverage ratios. Funds flow coverage of fixed charges: Other useful tests of funds flow relationships. Stability of "flow of funds from operations." Earnings coverage of preferred dividends. Evaluation of earnings-coverage ratios: Importance of earnings variability. Importance of method of computation and of underlying assumptions. Appendix 5A: The rating of debt obligations. Appendix 5B: Ratios as predictors of business failure. Appendix 5C: Illustration of the analytically adjusted debt-to-equity ratio.

6.   **Analysis of return on investment and of asset utilization, 196**
Diverse views of performance. Critieria of performance evaluation. Importance of return on investment (ROI). Major objectives in the use of ROI: An indicator of managerial effectiveness. A measure of enterprise ability to earn a satisfactory ROI. A method of projecting earnings. Internal decision and control tool. Basic elements of ROI: Defining the investment base. Book versus market values in the investment base. Difference between investor's cost and enterprise investment base. Averaging the investment base. Relating income to the investment base. Adjusting the components of the ROI formula: Analysis and interpretation of ROI. Analysis of asset utilization: Evaluation of individual turnover ratios. Use of averages. Other factors to be considered in return on asset evaluation. Return on shareholders' equity. Analysis of return on common stockholders' equity (ROCSE): Equity growth rate. Analysis of financial leverage effects.

7.   **Analysis of results of operations—I, 222**
The significance of income statement analysis. The major objectives of income analysis: What is the relevant net income of the enterprise? Analysis of components of the income statement: Accounting standards used and their implication. Tools of income statement analysis. The analysis of sales and revenues: Major sources of revenue. Financial reporting by diversified enterprises: Reasons for the need for data by significant enterprise segments. Disclosure of "line of business" data. Income statement data. Balance sheet data. Research studies. Statement of Financial Accounting Standards 14. SEC reporting requirements.

Implications for analysis. Stability and trend of revenues. Management's discussion and analysis of financial condition and results of operations. Implications for analysis. Methods of revenue recognition and measurement.

8. **Analysis of results of operations—II, 236**
    Analysis of cost of sales. Gross profit: *Factors in the analysis of gross profit.* Analysis of changes in gross margin. Example of analysis of change in gross margin: *Interpretation of changes in gross margin.* Break-even analysis: *Concepts underlying break-even analysis. Equation approach. Graphic presentation. Contribution margin approach. Pocket calculator problem—additional considerations. Break-even technique— problem areas and limitations. Break-even analysis—uses and their implications. Analytical implications of break-even analysis. The significance of the variable-cost percentage. The significance of the fixed-cost level. The importance of the contribution margin.* Additional considerations in the analysis of cost of sales. Depreciation. Amortization of special tools and similar costs. Maintenance and repairs costs. Other costs and expenses—general: *Selling expenses.* Bad debt expenses: *Future directed marketing costs.* General, administration, financial, and other expenses: *Financial costs. "Other" expenses.* Other income. Income taxes. Analysis of income tax disclosures: *Objectives of the analysis. Analytical steps and techniques. Illustration of income tax analysis of Alfa, Inc. Explaining the tax rate. Focus on pretax earnings.* The operating ratio. Net income ratio: *Statement accounting for variation in net income.*

9. **The evaluation and projection of earnings, 270**
    Objectives of earnings evaluation. Evaluation of the quality of earnings: *The concept of earnings quality. Balance sheet analysis as a check on the validity and quality of reported earnings.* Evaluation of the earnings level and trend: *Factors affecting the level of earnings. The analytical, recasting, and adjustment of income statements. The recasting and adjusting procedure. The adjustment process. Determining the trend of income over the years. Income smoothing and income distortion. Income smoothing and income distortion—some implications for analysis. Extraordinary gains and losses.* The forecasting of earnings: *Can earnings be forecast? SEC disclosure requirements—aid to forecasting. Elements in earnings forecasts. Publication of financial forecasts.* The concept of earnings power: *Earning power time horizon. Adjustment of reported earnings per share.* Monitoring performance and results: *Interim financial statements. APB Opinion 28. SEC interim reporting requirements. Implications for analysis.*

10. **Comprehensive analysis of financial statements, 311**
    The methodology of financial statement analysis. Significance of the

"building block" approach to financial analysis. The earmarks of good financial analysis. Special industry or environmental characteristics. Illustration of a comprehensive analysis of financial statements—Marine Supply Corporation: *Introduction. Financial statements. Additional information. Analysis of short-term liquidity. Cash from operations. Analysis of funds flow. Analysis of capital structure and long-term solvency. Analysis of return on investment. Analysis of asset utilization. Analysis of operating performance. Summary and conclusions.* Uses of financial statement analysis.

Appendix: The auditor's opinion—meaning and significance, 344

Index, 369

1 Objectives of financial statement analysis

THE NATURE OF FINANCIAL ANALYSIS

The process of financial statement analysis consists of the application of analytical tools and techniques to financial statements and data in order to derive from them measurements and relationships that are significant and useful for decision making. Thus, financial statement analysis, first and foremost, serves the essential function of converting *data,* of which, in this age of the computer, there are a bewildering quantity and variety, into useful information, which is always in scarce supply.

The processes of financial analysis can be described in various ways, depending on the objectives to be attained. Thus, financial analysis can be used as a preliminary *screening* tool in the selection of investments or merger candidates. It can be used as a *forecasting* tool of future financial conditions and results. It may be used as a process of *diagnosis* of managerial, operating, or other problem areas. It can serve as a tool in the *evaluation* of management. Above all, financial analysis reduces reliance on pure hunches, guesses, and intuition, and this reduces and narrows the inevitable areas of uncertainty that attend all decision-making processes. Financial analysis does not lessen the need for judgment but rather establishes a sound and systematic basis for its rational application.

APPROACHES TO THE SUBJECT

There are a number of possible approaches to a discussion of the tools and techniques of financial analysis. One way, popularly employed in most books on the subject, is to describe the analysis of specific financial statements, such as balance sheets, without a concurrent emphasis of objectives to be attained. The approach employed here will be to examine the processes of

1

financial statement analysis with emphasis on the major objectives (see Chapter 2, "Building blocks of financial statement analysis") that they are designed to achieve. In order to do this, we turn first to an examination of the information needs and the specific analytical objectives of the most important categories of users of financial data, namely:

Credit grantors.

Equity investors.

Management.

Acquisition and merger analysts.

Auditors.

Other interested groups.

Objectives of credit grantors

Credit grantors are lenders of funds to an enterprise. Funds are lent in many forms and for a variety of purposes.

Trade creditors usually extend very short-term credit. They ship goods or provide services and expect payment within the customary period that forms the terms of trade in their industry. Most trade credit ranges from 30 to 60 days, with cash discounts occasionally allowed for specified earlier payment. The trade creditor does not usually receive interest for an extension of credit. The trade creditor's reward takes the form of the business acquired and the possible profit that flows from it.

An enterprise receives other short-term and longer-term credit or loans from a variety of sources. Short-term credit is often provided by various sources but mainly by banks. Longer-term credit is provided by banks in the form of term loans and by financial institutions, such as insurance companies, through their purchase of bonds or notes or through private placements. Companies also obtain longer-term funds through the public sale of notes or bonds in the securities markets. Leasing and conditional sales are other forms of long-term financing. The sale of convertible, and generally subordinated, bonds combines the borrowing of money with the added feature of an option to the lender to exchange his or her claim for an equity interest should the lender find it profitable to do so. Similarly, the issuance of preferred stock, which is senior to the common equity but junior to debt, combines the fixed reward features of a loan with the absence of definite principal repayment requirements that characterize equity securities.

One outstanding characteristic of all pure credit extension relationships is the fixed nature of the rewards accruing to the credit grantor. Thus, should the enterprise prosper, the credit grantor will still be limited to his or her contractually fixed rate of interest, or to the profit on the goods supplied. However, should the enterprise incur losses or meet other adversities, the credit grantor's principal may be placed in jeopardy. This uneven nature of the lender's risk-reward ratio has a major effect on the lender's point of view and on the manner in which he or she analyzes the possibilities of credit extension.

The difference in the point of view of the lenders as compared to that of the equity investor results in differences in the way they analyze future prospects and in the objectives they seek. The equity investor looks for reward primarily to future prospects of earnings and to changes in those earnings. The credit grantor, on the other hand, is concerned primarily with specific security provisions of his or her loan, such as the fair market value of assets pledged; and for repayment of principal and interest, the credit grantor looks to the existence of resources and the projections of future flows of funds and the reliability and stability of such flows. Lenders differ in their abilities to obtain supplementary financial information from borrowers. Equity investors, as a result of the theoretically unlimited nature of their rewards, may be receptive to highly abstract descriptions of "concepts," potentials, and future probabilities. Lenders, on the other hand, require a more definite link between the projections of the future and the resources already at hand as well as the demonstrated ability to achieve operating results. Thus, credit grantors generally are more conservative in their outlook and approach and rely on financial statement analysis to an even greater extent than do equity investors, for it serves to reassure them regarding the borrower's demonstrated ability to control the flow of funds and to maintain a sound financial condition under a variety of economic and operating circumstances. The more speculative the loan, the more similar are the lender's analytical approaches to those of the equity investor.

The techniques of financial statement analysis used by lenders as well as the criteria of evaluation used by them vary with the term, the security, and the purpose of the loan.

In the case of short-term credit extension, the credit grantor is concerned primarily with the current financial condition, the liquidity of the current assets, and the rate of their turnover. These considerations are covered in Chapter 3.

The evaluation of longer-term loans, which includes the valuation of bonds, requires a far more detailed and forward-looking inquiry and analysis. Such an analysis includes projections of cash flows and fund flows and the evaluation of the longer-term earning power of the enterprise as the ultimate source of assurance of an enterprise's ability to meet the fixed charges arising from its debt as well as from its other commitments under a variety of economic conditions. This subject is examined in Chapter 5.

Since the profitability of an enterprise is a major element in the lender's security, the analysis of profitability is an important criterion to the credit grantor. Profit is viewed as the primary source for interest payments and as a desirable source of principal repayment.

Credit analysis, whether long term or short term, is concerned with capital structure because it has a bearing on risk and on the creditor's margin of safety. The relationship of equity capital to debt is an indicator of the adequacy of equity capital and of the cushion against loss that it provides. This relationship also reflects on the attitude of management toward risk and influences the income coverage of fixed charges.

Lenders, and bankers among them, generally look at asset values in the context of the going-concern assumption. Clearly, the assumption of liquidation would often lead to realizable values of assets that would generally be lower than those stated in accordance with generally accepted accounting principles (GAAP). For this reason, bankers tend to attach very conservative values to fixed and other assets, and to make allowance for all possible future contingencies.

Objectives of equity investors

The equity interest in an enterprise is the supplier of its basic risk capital. The capital is exposed to all the risks of ownership and provides a cushion or shield for the preferred or loan capital that is senior to it. This is why the equity interest is referred to as the *residual* interest. In the course of normal operations as a going concern, this residual interest may receive distributions (dividends) only after the prior claims of senior security holders for bond interest and/or preferred dividends have been satisfied. In liquidation, it has a claim only to what remains *after* the prior claims of creditors and preferred stockholders have been met. Thus, when an enterprise prospers, the equity owners stand to reap all the gains above the fixed amount of senior capital contributors' claims and, conversely, the equity owners will be the first ones to absorb losses should the enterprise flounder.

From the above it is clear that the information needs of equity investors are among the most demanding and comprehensive of all users of financial data. Their interests in an enterprise, of which they own a share, are the broadest because their interest is affected by all aspects and phases of operations, profitability, financial condition, and capital structure.

Common stock valuation. The valuation of common stock is a complex procedure involving, in addition to financial statement analysis, an assessment of such factors as the general state of the economy, industry position, competitive stance, and the quality of management. Since the most thorough and sophisticated analysis and evaluation of equity securities, for the purpose of deciding whether to buy, sell, or hold, are performed by professional security analysts, their point of view will be examined here.

A common stockholder, having no legal claim to a definite dividend or to a capital distribution, looks for three principal rewards from his or her holdings: current dividends, special distributions such as rights, and a market value of the security at a given time in the future that will, hopefully, result in a capital gain. The most important determinant of both dividends and market values is earnings. Current earnings, which are the basic source of dividends and the accumulation of undistributed earnings, as well as the earnings record, current and prospective, are major elements in the determination of the market price of the common stock.

Approaches to common stock valuation.   The basis of most modern stock valuation techniques and models is present value theory. This approach, first set forth in detail by John B. Williams,[1] maintains that the present value of a share of stock is equal to the sum of all dividends expected to be received from it, discounted to the present at an appropriate rate of interest. The difficulty here, of course, as in all other approaches based on this theory, is the estimation of such future distributions.[2] What is clear, however, is the fact that all expected distributions, be they of a current dividend or of a liquidation residual nature, are based largely on earnings and the earning power of assets.

Security valuation models used by security analysts bear out the proposition that earnings, and particularly estimated future earnings, are the most important determinant of the value of common shares.

Graham, Dodd, and Cottle emphasized the importance of earnings as follows:

> The standard method of valuation of individual enterprises consists of capitalizing the expected future earnings and/or dividends at an appropriate rate of return. The average earnings will be estimated for a period running ordinarily between five and ten years.[3]

Most common stock valuation models incorporate earnings growth and earnings payout ratios as factors of prime importance.

The normal procedure in dynamic models is to state the price of a stock as the present value of a growing stream of dividends with each component of this stream discounted at the rate k. One of the best-known dynamic stock valuation models presented in recent years is that by Gordon and Shapiro. Assume that $E(t)$ are the earnings of an enterprise at time t, b is the dividend payout ratio, k is the market discount rate (the cost of capital), and g is the projected annual growth rate in earnings. The valuation formula for the company's justified market price V (intrinsic value) is:

$$V = \frac{bE(t)}{k - g}$$

---

[1] *The Theory of Investment Value* (Cambridge, Mass: Harvard University Press, 1938).

[2] The importance of expected distributions is largely responsible for the focus on cash (or funds) flow. However, so far, most valuation models have not concerned themselves with the purchasing power equivalent of such cash flows, a consideration that looms large in times of price-level changes. Thus, a security represents a contingent claim not only because of the uncertain outcome of future events but also (including here a "riskless" bond) because of an uncertain command over future goods and services.

[3] *Security Analysis* (New York: McGraw-Hill, 1962), p. 435.

The above formula reduces long and awkward statements to more manageable but nevertheless mathematically equivalent terms. It states in effect that the market value V is equal to the current dividend discounted at a rate $k -$ g, i.e.,

$$V = \frac{\text{Current dividend rate}}{\text{Discount rate} - \text{Growth rate}}$$

The elegance and the simplicity of the above formula should not obscure the fact that the most critical element in this or similar approaches to equity valuation is the valid quantification of the variables or inputs themselves. The more conventional approach by practitioners in the field of security analysis is to value a security by multiplying its earnings, which are really a surrogate for present and future dividends, by a *price-earnings ratio*[4] that is usually an imprecise expression of their assessment of external economic factors as well as of the growth prospects, financial strengths, capital structure, and other risk factors associated with the enterprise.

The similarity of the present value models of common stock valuation to the conventional method of bond valuation is quite obvious. In the case of bonds, the value, or proper purchase price, is calculated by discounting each coupon and the ultimate principal repayment to present value at a discount rate equal to the desired yield. In the case of growth stock valuations, the expected dividend corresponds to the bond coupon and the assumed market price of the stock at the model target date corresponds to the repayment of bond principal at maturity date.

The similarity of the bond and stock valuation models under these theories has led Molodovsky and others to construct stock valuation tables that can be used in a fashion similar to the use of bond tables.[5] The formula used by them for the value *(V)* of a stock is:

$$V = D_0 + \frac{D_1}{1 + k} + \frac{D_2}{(1 + k)^2} + \cdots + \frac{D_n}{(1 + k)^n} + \cdots$$

where:

D_0 is the dividend initially.
D_n is the dividend in the nth year.
k is the discount rate, or the desired rate of return.

The model does not include a residual market value of the stock (similar to bond principal to be repaid) because it assumes dividend projections taken out to infinity. With regard to the latter, the authors assure us that because the discount factor becomes so large in the distant future, these increments

---

[4] Expressed in terms of the foregoing Gordon-Shapiro formula, the price-earnings ratio (P/E) can be stated as follows:

$$P/E = \frac{b}{k - g}$$

Thus, for example, if the dividend payout ratio *(b)* changes, so would the P/E ratio.

[5] N. Molodovsky, C. May, and S. Chottiner, "Common Stock Valuation—Principles, Tables, and Application," *Financial Analysts Journal,* March–April 1965.

to value become negligible. It is easy to bring the model closer in form to a bond model by assuming a specified sales price (realization of principal) at a specified date, but that price will itself depend on the application of the foregoing formula.

While we can readily understand why the stock valuation model builders have been attracted by the logic as well as the mathematical elegance of the bond valuation model, we must recognize the important differences that exist between the inputs required by the bond model as opposed to those required by the stock model. The focus on these differences is all the more important since the basic purpose of our discussion in this chapter is to relate the scope and the techniques of financial statement analysis to the purposes that they are designed to serve—in this instance, the valuation of equity securities.

In the case of bond valuation, the bond coupon is known and so is the amount of principal to be repaid at the maturity of the bond. Thus, as we saw in the section dealing with the objectives of credit grantors, the major questions to be considered are the *availability* of funds for the payment of interest and the repayment of principal. While the assessment of the probabilities of such availability of funds does involve the totality of enterprise prospects, the process of estimation is nevertheless less complex than the one involved in arriving at the proper parameters for the stock valuation model.

It should also be noted that there is a basic and important difference in the certainty of results that can be expected from an analysis of debt instruments (such as bonds) and those that can be expected from the analysis of equity securities. In the case of debt instruments, the results of the analysis depend almost entirely on a valid assessment of the borrower's ability to make timely payments of interest and principal. The relationship between analysis and the results achieved are far more complex in the case of equity securities. Thus, no matter how "right" the analyst is in assumptions and forecasts, a major part of the reward of that analysis, i.e., future capital values, depends on the perceptions of others, that is, on buyers agreeing with the analyst's conclusions and seeing things his or her way. No such dependence on validation by the marketplace exists in the case of results to be achieved from the analysis of debt instruments.

This difference, as well as the enormous complexities to which the analysis and evaluation of equity securities are subject, is in large part behind the skepticism with which many practicing security analysts treat those who attempt to compress the market reality into neat, streamlined, and elegant mathematical formulations.

Data required for stock valuation.   Let us now consider the data that are required in order to quantify the factors present in most of the stock valuation models discussed above.

The expected dividend stream in the future is dependent on earnings and dividend payout policy. The latter depends on the company's financial condition, capital structure, and its need for funds both in the present and in the future.

The projection of future earnings (see Chapter 9) is always a complex process subject to varying degrees of uncertainty. The reported earnings must be evaluated and adjusted and, in turn, form the basis for projection. Unlike the bond coupon, which remains constant, the further into the future that earnings are projected, the more conjectural the estimates become.

The size of the discount factor that may properly be used in computing the present value of a future stream of dividends and residual interests depends to a significant extent on the risk involved. The risk reflects such factors as the stability of the industry, the past variability in earnings, and the leverage inherent in its capital structure.

No stock valuation formula has yet been devised and published that has proved to be an accurate forecaster of security market values under all conditions. Perhaps, the factors that bear on the determination of security values are too numerous and too complex for inclusion in a workable formula, and possibly not all such factors can be adequately measured, particularly because of the simplifying assumptions that are introduced in many such models.

Whatever method of stock valuation is used by the security analyst, be it either a simple short-term projection of earnings to be capitalized at a predetermined rate or a complex and sophisticated formula involving elegant mathematical techniques, the results can never reach a higher level of accuracy or be more reliable than the inputs used in such calculations. The reliability and the validity of these inputs, be they earnings projections, expected payout ratios, or various risk factors such as those inherent in capital structure, depend on the quality of the financial statement analysis performed.

The above view was best expressed by Douglas A. Hayes:

> Although the concept that investment results are likely to be heavily related to corporate performance in a long-term sense is generally accepted, some recent contributions to the field have alleged that the implementation methodology should be completely revolutionized. For example, Lerner and Carleton (*A Theory of Financial Analysis,* Harcourt, Brace, and World, Inc. New York: 1966, pp. 3–4) allege that a critical investigation of the past financial statements to reveal potential problems of consistency and comparability of reported income and balance sheet data can be largely discarded because accounting and disclosure standards have improved to the point where the underlying data require no critical review. Moreover, they allege that financial risk factors no longer require appraisal because of the greatly improved stability features of the economy; in lieu thereof, they suggest elegant mathematical techniques to develop the theoretical effects of assumed patterns of various management decisions and economic data on security values.
>
> However, the empirical evidence would suggest that these allegations are seriously in error.[6]

---

[6] "The Dimensions of Analysis: A Critical Review," *Financial Analysts Journal,* September–October 1966.

In short, while the goal of the analyst may be to go forward *from* the figures, a thorough job of the financial analysis requires that he also go *behind* the figures.[7] No present or prospective developments in the field of accountancy justify the assumption that this can be significantly changed in the near future.

RECENT DEVELOPMENTS IN INVESTMENT THEORY

In recent years, the methods and approaches of practicing security analysts have come under repeated challenge by their academic counterparts who have developed a number of theories designed to provide insight into the overall investment process.

Portfolio theory

A pioneering contribution was that of Markowitz who addressed the problem of portfolio construction given analysts' estimates of possible future returns from securities.[8] He demonstrated that both risk and return must be considered, provided a formal framework for quantifying both, and showed how the relationship among security risks and returns could be taken into account in portfolio construction.

He begins with the observation that the future return on a security can be estimated, and he equates risk with the variance of the distribution of returns. Markowitz demonstrated that under certain assumptions there is a linear relationship between risk and return. Using these variables, he provided a framework for deciding how much of each security to hold in constructing a portfolio. The two-dimensional risk-return approach offers the investor an ability to choose in the trade-off between risk and return.

Evaluation of risk and return

The relationship between the risk that must be accepted and the return that may be expected is central to all modern investing and lending decisions. It may seem obvious that the greater the perceived degree of risk of an investment or of a loan, the greater is the required rate of return to compensate for such risk.

Categories of risk

Risk is commonly associated with the uncertainty surrounding the outcome of future events. While many investors and lenders make subjective evalua-

---

[7] Author's note: Women have been analysts and auditors for years, and their numbers are growing. However, in this book, masculine pronouns are often being used for succinctness and are intended to refer to both males and females.

[8] H. Markowitz, "Portfolio Selection," *Journal of Finance,* March 1952, pp. 77–91.

tions of risk, academicians have developed statistical measures of risk that belong to the overall concept known as beta coefficient theory.

Under this theory, the total risk associated with an investment is composed of two elements:

1. *Systematic risk,* which is that portion of total risk attributable to the movement of the market as a whole.
2. *Unsystematic risk,* which is the residual risk that is unique to a specific security.

In the application of the theory, a quantitative expression of systematic risk (known as beta)[9] of one is attributed to the volatility of the market as a whole. The higher a security's beta, the greater will be its expected return. Treasury bills have a beta of zero because they are essentially riskless, i.e., they do not fluctuate with the market. A stock having a beta of 1.20 could rise or fall 20 percent faster than the market, while one having a beta of .90 would on average register market value changes 10 percent less in amplitude than those of the market as a whole. Thus, high beta stocks can expect high returns in a "bull market" and also larger than average declines during a "bear market."

Since by definition, unsystematic risk[10] is the *residual risk* that is unexplained by market movements, no unsystematic risk exists for the market as a whole and almost none exists in a highly diversified portfolio of stocks. Consequently, as portfolios become larger and more diversified, their unsystematic risk will approach zero.

Adherents to this theory hold that the market will not reward those exposing themselves to unsystematic risk that can be removed by proper diversification. They believe that the implication of the theory for common stock investors is to diversify, and if they expect the market to rise, to increase the beta of their portfolios and vice versa. Some experimental studies have indicated that between 30 and 50 percent of an individual stock's price is due to market (systematic) risk and that such influence reaches 85 to 90 percent in a well-diversified portfolio of 30 or more stocks.[11]

It follows that the portfolio manager who does not wish to rely only on market action for returns or who cannot forecast overall market action should

---

[9] Beta indexes are computed by use of regression analysis to relate the historical price movements of a stock to the movements of a general market price index such as the S&P 500 stock index. Alas, because of the ever-changing environment, capital structure, and operations of an enterprise, beta coefficients have exhibited a high degree of instability over time.

[10] A measure of unsystematic risk is alpha, which measures a stock's expected rate of return when the expected market rate of return is zero. Many academicians maintain that the expected alpha for a well-diversified portfolio is zero because the specific business circumstances that give rise to positive and negative alphas tend to cancel out in a portfolio of stocks. Practicing security analysts strive, however, to construct portfolios having positive alphas. In essence, alpha is derived from virtues in a stock that are not recognized by the market, thus resulting in returns above what beta would suggest.

[11] J. B. Cohen, E. D. Zinbarg, and A. Zeikel, *Investment Analysis and Portfolio Management,* 3d ed. (Homewood, Ill.: Richard D. Irwin, 1977), pp. 769–71.

seek nondiversification, i.e., exposure to the amount of unsystematic risk required for achieving the desired rate of return. Such a strategy would emphasize the analysis of individual securities, as discussed in this work, as opposed to overall portfolio risk balancing.

Thus, reaping the rewards of exposure to nonsystematic risk is dependent on an ability to identify undervalued securities and on the proper assessment of their respective risk. (See discussion of efficient market hypothesis later in this chapter.)

Components of unsystematic risk

Those who want to obtain their rewards from exposure to unsystematic or nonmarket risk through the rigorous analysis of individual securities must focus on the various components of such risk. While those components are undoubtedly interrelated and subject to the influence of such elements of systematic risk as overall political, economic, and social factors, they can nevertheless be usefully classified as follows:

Economic risk reflects risks of the overall economic environment in which the enterprise operates including general economic risk (fluctuations in business activity), capital market risk (including changes in interest rates), and purchasing power risk.

Business risk is concerned with the ever-present uncertainty regarding a business enterprise's ability to earn a satisfactory return on its investments as well as with the multitude of cost and revenue factors that enter into the determination of such a return. It includes the factors of competition, product mix, and management ability (see Chapters 6–9).

Financial risk is basically concerned with capital structure and with the ability of an enterprise to meet fixed and senior charges and claims. These factors of short-term liquidity and long-term solvency are discussed in detail in Chapters 3, 4, and 5.

Those who assume, as do beta theorists, that all investors are averse to risk and that they seek to diversify away the specific or unsystematic risks[12] of a security thus exposing themselves only to market risk, must also realize that the historical betas for individual securities have proven quite unstable over time and that consequently such betas seem to be poor predictors of future betas for the same security.[13] Thus, while overall concepts and theories

---

[12] What is often overlooked is that those who seek to diversify away unsystematic risk are also diversifying out a great deal of the rewards that equity investing holds for more aggressive investors.

[13] W. H. Beaver, P. Kettler, and M. Scholes have found that a high degree of association exists between accounting risk measures (such as average payout, asset growth, coverage, etc.) and beta. Thus, these accounting measures of risk may be used in a way that can lead to better forecasts of market determined risk measures (betas) than would be possible using past observed betas. (*The Accounting Review,* October 1970, pp. 654–82.) See also B. Rosenberg and J. Guy, "Prediction of Beta from Investment Fundamentals," *Financial Analysts Journal,* July–August, 1976.

are easier to apply to stock aggregates than to the evaluation of individual stocks, they are at the same time far less reliable and accurate instruments for the achievement of investment results.

Another, and perhaps even more troublesome, question is the assumption of beta theorists that past volatility alone is an acceptable measure of risk without reference to the current price of a security. Is a security that sells significantly *above* its value, as determined by some method of fundamental analysis, no more risky than a security of equal volatility (beta) that sells significantly *below* such fundamentally determined value? We know that paying an excessive price for a stable quality security can amount to as rank a speculation as investing in the most unseasoned of speculative securities.

While market theorists have not yet addressed the above troublesome question, they have addressed the problem of how securities are valued by the market.

The capital asset pricing model

Sharpe[14] and Lintner[15] have extended portfolio theory to a capital asset pricing model (CAPM) that is intended to explain how prices of assets are determined in such a way as to provide greater return for greater risk. This model is based on the assumption that investors desire to hold securities in portfolios that are efficient in the sense that they provide a maximum return for *a given level* of risk. Moreover, the model was derived under the following simplifying assumptions:

1.   That there exists a riskless security.
2.   That investors are able to borrow or lend unlimited amounts at the riskless rate.
3.   That all investors have identical investment horizons and act on the basis of identical expectations and predictions.

Based on these assumptions, it can be shown that when capital markets are in a state of equilibrium, the expected return on an individual security, $E(\tilde{R}_i)$, is related to its systematic risk β_i in the following linear form:

$$E(\tilde{R}_i) = E(\tilde{R}_0) + [E(\tilde{R}_M) - E(\tilde{R}_0)]\beta_i$$

The above formulation states in essence that under conditions of equilibrium, a security's expected return equals the expected return of a riskless security, $E(\tilde{R}_0)$, plus a premium for risk taking. This risk premium consists of a constant, $[E(\tilde{R}_M) - E(\tilde{R}_0)]$, which is the difference between the return expected by the market and the return on a riskless security (such as a

14 W. F. Sharpe, "Capital Asset Prices: A Theory of Market Equilibrium under Conditions of Risk," *Journal of Finance,* September 1964, pp. 425–42.

15 Lintner, "The Valuation of Risky Assets and the Selection of Risky Investments in Stock Portfolios and Capital Budgets," *Review of Economics and Statistics,* February 1965, pp. 13–37.

short-term government bond) multiplied by the systematic risk of the security β_i (its beta) as discussed earlier.

The CAPM thus indicates that the expected return on any particular capital asset consists of two components: (1) the return on a riskless security and (2) a premium for the riskiness of the particular asset computed as outlined above. Thus, under the CAPM, each security has an expected return that is related to its risk. This risk is measured by the security's systematic movements with the overall market, and it cannot be eliminated by portfolio diversification.

It remains for us to consider a related hypothesis that attempts to describe a different property of security prices, i.e., the efficient market hypothesis.

The efficient market hypothesis

Efficient market hypothesis (EMH) deals with the reaction of market prices to financial and other data. The EMH has its origins in the random walk hypothesis that basically states that at any given point in time the size and direction of the next price change is random relative to what is known about an investment at that given time. A derivative of this hypothesis is what is known as the *weak form* of the EMH, which states that current prices reflect fully the information implied by historical price time series. In its *semistrong form,* the EMH holds that prices fully reflect all publicly available information.[16] Moreover, in its *strong form,* the theory asserts that prices reflect *all* information including that which is considered "inside information."

The EMH, in all its terms, has undergone extensive empirical testing with much of the evidence apparently supportive of the weak and semistrong forms of the theory. Lorie and Hamilton[17] for example, present three studies in support of the semistrong form of the hypothesis indicating that:

1. Stock splits do not assure unusual profit for investors.
2. Secondary offerings depress the market price of a stock because such offerings imply that knowledgeable people are selling.
3. Unusual earnings increases are anticipated in the price of the stock before the company's earnings for the year are reported.[18]

None of these findings would, incidentally, clash with the intuition of experienced analysts or seasoned market participants.

---

[16] For one good discussion of this hypothesis, see E. F. Fama, "Efficient Capital Markets: A Review of Theory and Empirical Work," *Journal of Finance,* May 1970, pp. 383–417.

[17] J. H. Lorie and M. T. Hamilton, *The Stock Market: Theories and Evidence* (Homewood, Ill.: Richard D. Irwin, 1973).

[18] See, for example, R. Ball and P. Brown, "An Empirical Evaluation of Accounting Numbers," *Journal of Accounting Research* (Autumn 1968), pp. 159–78; and W. Beaver, "The Informational Content of Annual Earnings Announcements," *Empirical Research in Accounting: Selected Studies,* 1968, University of Chicago, Graduate School of Business 1969, pp. 48–53.

Research supportive of the EMH by accounting scholars on the effect of accounting changes on security prices has found that changes from accelerated to straight-line depreciation for accounting purposes only had no significant effect on stock prices.[19] Another study found that the stock market ignored the effects on income of changes in accounting procedures such as those relating to inventories, depreciation, revenue recognition, and so forth.[20]

Implications for financial statement analysis

The EMH is almost completely dependent on the assumption that competent and well-informed analysts, using tools of analysis such as those described in this book, will constantly strive to evaluate and act upon the ever-changing stream of new information entering the marketplace. And yet the theory's proponents claim that since all that is known is already instantly reflected in market prices, any attempt to gain consistently an advantage by rigorous financial statement analysis is not possible. As H. Lorie and M. T. Hamilton put it, "The most general implication of the efficient market hypothesis is that most security analysis is logically incomplete and valueless."[21]

This position presents an unexplained and unresolved paradox. The thousands of intelligent analysts are assumed to be capable enough to keep our security market efficient through their efforts, but they are not intelligent enough to realize that their efforts can yield no individual advantage. Moreover, should they suddenly realize that their efforts are unrewarded, the market would cease to be efficient.

There are a number of factors that may explain this paradox. Foremost among them is the fact that the entire EMH is built on evidence based on an evaluation of *aggregate*[22] rather than individual investor behavior. The focusing on macro or aggregate behavior results not only in the highlighting of average performance and results but also ignores and masks the results achieved by individual ability, hard work, and ingenuity, as well as by superior timing in acting on information as it becomes available.[23]

---

[19] T. R. Archibald, "Stock Market Reaction to the Depreciation Switch-Back," *The Accounting Review,* January 1972, pp. 22–30.

[20] R. Kaplan and R. Roll, "Accounting Changes and Stock Prices," *The Financial Analysts Journal* (January–February 1973), pp. 48–53; also R. Ball, "Changes in Accounting Techniques and Stock Prices," *Empirical Research in Accounting: Selected Studies,* 1972 (Chicago: Institute of Professional Accounting, Graduate School of Business, University of Chicago, 1974), pp. 1–38.

[21] Lorie and Hamilton, *The Stock Market,* p. 100.

[22] R. J. Chambers put it most effectively: "It is very difficult to escape the conclusion that the whole enterprise of aggregate market analysis with the object of resolving questions about the quality of accounting information is misguided. Men have never advanced their finite knowledge of any subject by attention only to what occurs in the aggregate or on average" (in "Stock Market Prices and Accounting Research," *Abacus,* June 1974, pp. 39–54).

[23] Evidence about superior investment performance by *individuals* is not a matter of public record and is consequently not readily available. But evidence of superior investment performance by portfolio managers is available, one example being *Forbes* magazine's annual "Honor Roll" of consistent long-term superior investment results in both up and down markets.

Few would doubt that important information travels fast. After all, enough is at stake to make it travel fast. Nor is it surprising that the securities markets are rapid processors of information. In fact, using the same type of deductive reasoning as used by the efficient market proponents, we could conclude that the speed and the hardworking efficiency of the market must be evidence that the market participants who make it happen are motivated by substantial rewards.

The reasoning behind the EMH's alleged implication for the usefulness of security analysis fails to recognize the essential difference between information and its proper interpretation. Even if all the information available on a security at a given point in time is impounded in its price, that price may not reflect *value*. It may be under- or overvalued depending on the degree to which an incorrect interpretation or evaluation of the available information has been made by those whose actions determine the market price at a given time.

The work of financial statement analysis is complex and demanding. The spectrum of users of financial statements varies all the way from the institutional analyst who concentrates on only a few companies in one industry to "Aunt Jane" who merely looks at the pictures of an annual report.[24] All act on financial information but surely not with the same insights and competence.

The competent evaluation of "new information" entering the marketplace requires the possession of a prior fund of knowledge, of an information mosaic into which the new information can be fitted, as part of a link in a chain of analytical information, before it can be evaluated and interpreted. Only few have the ability and are prepared to expend the efforts and resources needed to produce such information mosaics, and it is only natural that they would reap the rewards by being able to act both competently and confidently on the new information received. This advantage in timing is all-important in the marketplace.

The vast resources that must be brought to bear on the competent analysis of equity securities have caused some segments of the securities markets to be more efficient than others. Thus, the market for shares of the largest companies is more efficient because many more analysts follow such securities in comparison to those who follow small and lesser-known companies.

The function and purpose of the analysis of equity securities is construed much too narrowly by those who judge its usefulness in an efficient market.[25] While the search for overvalued and undervalued securities is an important function of security analysis, the importance of risk assessment and loss avoidance, in the total framework of investment decision making, cannot be overemphasized. Thus, the prevention of serious investment errors is at least as

---

[24] Comment by G. I. White, CFA, in *Journal of Accountancy,* August 1978, p. 44.

[25] For a more comprehensive discussion of these issues, see the author's article "In Defense of Fundamental Investment Analysis," *Financial Analysts Journal,* January–February 1975, pp. 57–61.

important as the discovery of undervalued securities. Yet, our review of the CAPM and of beta theory earlier in this discussion tends to explain why this important function of analysis is neglected by adherents to these macro models of the security markets. For to some it is a basic premise of these theories that the analysis of unsystematic risk is not worthwhile because that kind of risk taking is not rewarded by the market. They maintain that such risks should be diversified away and that the portfolio manager should look only to systematic or market risk for rewards.[26]

Our basic premise here is that investment results are achieved through the careful study and analysis of *individual* enterprises rather than by an exclusive focus on market aggregates. Our approach in this area is to emphasize the value of fundamental investment analysis not only as a means of keeping our securities markets efficient and our capital markets rational and strong but also as the means by which those investors who, having obtained information, are willing and able to apply knowledge, effort, and ingenuity to its analysis.[27] For those investors, the fruits of fundamental analysis and research, long before being converted to a "public good," will provide adequate rewards. These rewards will not be discernible, however, in the performance of investors aggregated to comprise major market segments, such as mutual funds. Instead, they will remain as individual as the efforts needed to bring them about.

The role of financial statement analysis in the professional decision process leading to the buying, selling, or holding of equity securities has always been the subject of controversy and debate. In times of high speculative market activity, fundamental factors inevitably give way in relative importance to the psychological or technical ones in the overall security appraisal and "valuation" process. The fact that these fundamental factors, based as they are on a concrete analysis of measurable elements, can lead to sounder decisions and to the avoidance of serious judgmental errors will not always prevent their abandonment in favor of the snap decisions that occur in times of speculative frenzy. Nevertheless, the ultimate return of more sober times after periods of speculation and the inevitable corrections of speculative excesses recurringly bring along with them a rediscovery of the virtues of thorough financial analysis as a sound and necessary procedure. In the aftermath of the 1969–70 bear market, David L. Babson urged such a return by stating:

> What we all should do now is to roll up our sleeves and go back to doing what we are paid for—to follow company and industry trends closely, to really dissect balance sheets and to dig into accounting practices—and maybe some

---

[26] A current investment vogue, based on the efficient market adherents' disenchantment with investment results, is the index fund. An index portfolio is merely designed to copy the composition of a market index to such an extent that it will replicate its market performance. Like other schemes that represent mechanical substitutes for analysis and judgment, this too is not likely to satisfy its adherents for too long.

[27] The value of such analysis for other purposes, such as credit evaluation, is not even at issue here.

future Jim Lings, Delbert Colemans and Cortes Randells won't make monkeys out of many of the prestigious firms in our industry again.[28]

The collapse in security values in the early 1970s was, of course, not the first such occurrence that was preceded by a widespread and reckless disregard for fundamentals. It is noteworthy that each generation of analysts has to relearn the lessons so heavily paid for by its predecessors. A. P. Richardson, in an editorial on "The 1929 Stock Market Collapse" published in the *Journal of Accountancy* of December 1929, emphasized this recurring phenomenon of the flight from facts and reason into the world of fancy and wishful thinking:

> The astounding feature of the decline and fall of the stock market in late October and early November was not the fact of descent itself, but the altogether unreasoning consternation which the public in and out of Wall Street displayed. There was nothing at all in the course of events which distinguished the break from its many predecessors. Month after month, even year after year, market prices of securities had climbed to even dizzier heights. Now and then a Jeremiah uttered warning and lament, but the people gave no heed. They thought and consequently dealt in far futures. What a company might earn when the next generation would come to maturity was made the measure of the current value of its stock. In many cases companies whose operations had never yet produced a penny of profit were selected, fortuitously or under artificial stimulation, as a sort of Golconda of the next voyage; and otherwise sane men and women eagerly bought rights of ownership in adventures whose safe return was on the knees of the sea gods. It was not considered enough to look ahead to what was visible. The unseen was the chief commodity. Good stocks, bad stocks and stocks neither good nor bad but wholly of the future rose with almost equal facility, until at last they were sold at prices which seemed to be entirely uninfluenced by the rates of dividend or even by the earnings of the issuing companies. Government bonds and other "gilt-edged" securities were sold at prices nearer the actual interest yield than were the prices of highly speculative stocks to the dividend return or even to the net earnings, past or soon expected, of the companies concerned. Anything was possible when vision was so blurred by success.

Financial statement analysis, while certainly not providing answers to all the problems of security analysis, at least keeps the decision maker in touch with the underlying realities of the enterprise that is investigated. It imposes the discipline of comparing the results already attained with the wide-ranging promises made for the future. As a very minimum, it represents a safeguard against the repetition of the grievous mistakes of judgment recurringly made by investors in time of speculative euphoria.

We have, in this section, examined the needs for information by equity investors. Not all such information can be obtained by means of financial statement analysis nor is the information so obtainable always the most critical

---

[28] "The Stock Market's Collapse and Constructive Aftermath," *The Commercial and Financial Chronicle,* June 4, 1970.

in the determination of security values. However, it should by now be clear to the reader that any rational and systematic approach to the valuation of common stocks must involve the use of quantified data that are mostly the end product of financial statement analysis, evaluation, and interpretation.

Objectives of management

Management's interest in an enterprise's financial condition, profitability, and progress is pervasive and all-encompassing. Management has a number of methods, tools, and techniques available to it in monitoring and keeping up with the ever-changing condition of the enterprise. Financial data analysis is one important type of such methods.

Financial data analysis can be undertaken by management on a continuous basis because it has unlimited access to internal accounting and other records. Such analysis encompasses changes in ratios, trends, and other significant relationships. Ratio change and trend analysis are based on an intelligent, alert, and systematic surveillance of significant relationships in a business situation and the timely detection and interpretation of problem areas by an analysis of changes taking place.

Management's primary objective in utilizing the tools of analysis described in this book is to exercise control over and to view the enterprise in the way important outsiders, such as creditors and investors, view it.

Ratio change and trend analysis make use of the numerous and inevitable relationships and interrelationships among the variables occurring in any business situation. Constant surveillance over the size and amplitude of change in these interrelationships provides valuable clues to important changes in underlying financial and operating conditions. Recognition of such changes and timely action to check adverse trends is the essence of control.

Management derives a number of important advantages from a systematic monitoring of financial data and the basic relationships that they display:

1. There is recognition that no event in a business situation is isolated and that it represents a cause or the effect of a chain of which it is but a link. This approach aims at discovering whether a given event or relationship is the cause or the effect of an underlying situation.

2. There is a recognition that one should not act on an isolated event, but rather by an examination of related changes, one should determine the basic causes of the event. Thus, an event cannot be judged as positive or negative until it has been properly related to other factors that have a bearing on it.

3. Such monitoring prevents management from getting submerged in a maze of facts and figures that in the typical business situation consist of a great variety of factors of varying sizes, velocities of change, and degrees of impact. Instead, it organizes the data and relates them to a pattern of prior experience and external standards.

4. Such monitoring calls for prompt and effective action as the situation unfolds, rather than for *"post mortem"* analyses of causes and effects.

Objectives of acquisition and merger analysts

The valuation of an enterprise in its entirety, for the purpose of purchasing a going concern or for the purpose of assessing the merger of two or more enterprises, represents an attempt to determine economic values, the relative worth of the merging entities, and the relative bargaining strengths and weaknesses of the parties involved. Financial statement analysis is a valuable technique in the determination of economic value and in an assessment of the financial and operating compatibility of potential merger candidates.

The objectives of the acquisition and merger analyst are in many respects similar to those of the equity investor except that the analysis of the acquisition of an entire enterprise must go further and stress the valuation of assets, including intangible assets such as goodwill, and liabilities included in the acquisition or merger plan.

Objectives of auditors

The end product of the financial audit is an expression of opinion on the fairness of presentation of financial statements setting forth the financial conditions and the results of operations of an enterprise. One of the basic objectives of the audit process is to obtain the greatest possible degree of assurance about the absence of errors and irregularities, intentional or otherwise, that if undetected could materially affect the fairness of presentation of financial summarizations or their conformity with generally accepted accounting principles (GAAP).

Financial statement analysis and ratio change and trend analysis represent an important group of audit tools that can significantly supplement other audit techniques such as procedural and validation tests.[29] This is so because errors and irregularities, whatever their source, can, if significant, affect the various financial operating and structural relationships; and the detection and analysis of such changes can lead to the detection of errors and irregularities. Moreover, the process of financial analysis requires of the auditor, and imparts to him, the kind of understanding and grasp of the audited enterprise that indicates the most relevant type of supportive evidence required in his audit work.

The application of financial statement analysis as part of the audit program is best undertaken at the very beginning of the audit because such analysis will often reveal the areas of greatest change and vulnerability, areas to which the auditor will want to direct most of his attention. At the end of the

---

[29] In 1978, the accounting profession formally recognized the importance of analytical audit approaches through issuance of *Statement of Auditing Standards No. 23*, "Analytical Review Procedures."

audit, these tools represent an overall check on the reasonableness of the financial statements taken as a whole.[30]

Objectives of other interested groups

Financial statement analysis can serve the needs of many other user groups. Thus, the Internal Revenue Service can apply tools and techniques of financial statement analysis to the audit of tax returns and the checking of the reasonableness of reported amounts.[31] Various governmental regulatory agencies can use such techniques in the exercise of their supervisory and rate-determination functions.

Labor unions can use the techniques of financial statement analysis to evaluate the financial statements of enterprises with which they engage in collective bargaining. Lawyers can employ these techniques in the furtherance of their investigative and legal work, while economic researchers will find them of great usefulness in their work.

Similarly customers can use such approaches to determine the profitability (staying power) of their suppliers, the returns they earn on capital, and other factors of consequence to them.

CONCLUSION

This chapter has examined the points of view and the objectives of a variety of important users of financial statements. These various objectives determine what aspects of financial statement analysis are relevant to the decision-making process of a particular user. In the chapters that follow, we shall first examine the relationship between financial statement analysis and the accounting framework as well as the tools and techniques of financial statement analysis in general. This will be followed by an examination of the major missions or objectives of financial analysis and the means by which they are accomplished.

QUESTIONS

1. Describe some of the analytical uses to which financial statement analysis can be put.
2. Why are the information needs of equity investors among the most demanding of all users of financial statements?

---

[30] For a more detailed discussion of this subject, see L. A. Bernstein, "Ratio Change and Trend Analysis," *Handbook for Auditors* (New York: McGraw-Hill, 1971).

[31] Among the areas that can be analyzed are questions such as whether (1) the income reported is enough to support exemptions or expenses claimed, (2) the profit margin reported is out of line with that normal for that type of business, (3) the return reported is less than that which can be earned by banking the money, and (4) the changes in net worth support the amounts of reported income.

3. Why is the measurement and evaluation of earning power the key element in the valuation of equity securities?

4. What is the essential difference between a bond valuation model based on the present value of future inflows and a stock valuation model based on the same principles?

5. Differentiate between systematic risk and unsystematic risk and discuss the various components of the latter.

6. Discuss the capital asset pricing model (CAPM) and explain how it deals with the problem of securities valuation by the market.

7. Explain how the efficient market hypothesis (EMH) deals with the reaction of market prices to financial and other data.

8. Explain the concept of the trade-off between risk and return as well as its significance to portfolio construction.

9. Discuss the implications that the CAPM and the EMH present for financial statement analysis.

10. Why is the reliability and the validity of any method of stock valuation, no matter how complete and sophisticated, dependent on the prior performance of a quality analysis of financial statements?

11. Identify clearly three separate factors which have a significant influence on a stock's price-earnings ratio. (CFA)

12. What are the differences in point of view between lenders and equity investors? How do these differences express themselves in the way these two groups analyze financial statements and in the objectives that they seek?

13. *a.* Outline the principal risks inherent in a preferred stock as an investment instrument, relative to a bond or other credit obligation of the same company.
    b. Discuss the various influences of U.S. (or Canadian) income taxation trends on the inherent risks and yields of preferred stocks.
    c. What terms can be included in a preferred stock issue to compensate for its subordination to debt and its relationship to common stock? (CFA)

14. What uses can the management of an enterprise make of financial statement analysis?

15. Of what use can financial statement analysis be to the audit of an enterprise?

2

Tools and techniques of financial statement analysis—an overview

Basic approaches to financial statement analysis

In the first chapter, we examined the various objectives of financial statement analysis as viewed from the point of view of specific user groups. In the performance of an analysis, such objectives can, in turn, be translated into a number of specific questions to which the decision maker needs an answer. Thus, for example, the equity investor may want to know:

1. What has the company's operating performance been over the longer term and over the recent past? What does this record hold for future earnings prospects?
2. Has the company's earnings record been one of growth, stability, or decline? Does it display significant variability?
3. What is the company's current financial condition? What factors are likely to affect it in the near future?
4. What is the company's capital structure? What risks and rewards does it hold for the investor?
5. How does this company compare on the above counts with other companies in its industry?

The banker who is approached with a short-term loan request may look to the financial statements for answers to questions such as the following:

1. What are the underlying reasons for the company's needs for funds? Are these needs truly short term, and if so, will they be self-liquidating?
2. From what sources is the company likely to get funds for the payment of interest and the repayment of principal?
3. How has management handled its needs for short-term and long-term funds in the past? What does this portend for the future?

An important first step in any decision-making process is to identify the most significant, pertinent, and critical questions that have a bearing on the decision. Financial statement analysis does not, of course, provide answers to all such questions. However, each of the questions exemplified above can, to a significant extent, be answered by such analysis.

RECONSTRUCTION OF BUSINESS ACTIVITIES AND TRANSACTIONS

Basic to the analyst's work is the ability to reconstruct the business transactions that are summarized in the financial statements. One can visualize this important skill as the ability to replicate the accountant's work but in reverse order. The flow of the accountant's work is as follows:

⎯⎯⎯⎯⎯⎯ **FLOW OF ACCOUNTANT'S WORK** ⎯⎯⎯⎯⎯⎯⎯⟶

Perception of the reality behind business transactions	GAAP—The framework of accounting for these transactions	Express the transaction in the form of a journal entry	Accumulate transactions in T-accounts	Summarize and classify in the form of financial statements

⟵⎯⎯⎯⎯⎯⎯ **FLOW OF THE ANALYST'S WORK** ⎯⎯⎯⎯⎯⎯

The accountant's effort and skill is first directed to understanding the reality of the transactions or events to be recorded. Next, there must be brought to bear the knowledge of the accounting framework—the generally accepted accounting principals (GAAP) that govern the recording of the transaction, its expression in the form of a journal entry, and its accumulation in accounts. No matter what form data recording and accumulation takes in this electronic age, the basic concepts of the journal entry and the T-account prevail. These, as we shall see, are particularly useful in analytical work. Finally, continuing to be guided by accepted standards of the accounting framework, the accountant summarizes all accounts of a period in the format of financial statements.

The flow of the analyst's work is basically in reverse order. He or she starts with the financial statements made available by the enterprise. The basic task is to recapture, as far as possible, the reality that is imbedded and summarized in these financial statements—the degree to which this is done being dependent on the particular analytical objectives at hand. This analytical process requires that the analyst visualize the journal entries made and that he or she reconstruct, in summary fashion, all or selected accounts in the financial statements. It also requires an understanding of the reality underlying such business transactions as well as a knowledge of the *accounting standards* employed in recording it properly within the accounting framework.

By these means, the analyst will be able to understand the changes in specific balance sheet items, trace the effect of a given transaction or specific accounts, and answer questions such as the following:

- What was the reason for the increase or the decrease in the investment in X Company?
- What effect did the debt refunding have on working capital?
- How much long-term debt was repaid this year?
- What was the effect of income taxes on the financial statements and how much tax was actually paid this year?

The reconstruction of business transactions requires a knowledge of accounting, i.e., the ability to visualize what kind of activities or events will increase or decrease a specific account. It also requires the ability to read carefully and interpret financial statements and related footnotes. Thus, the knowledge of what information can be found in financial statements, where it is to be found, and how to reconstruct transactions, including the making of reasonable assumptions, are important skills in the analysis of financial statements. Generally, in reconstructing transactions, the analyst will work with known information before attempting to deduce unknown facts. The degree of accuracy that can be expected in such reconstructions and the resulting analysis cannot be expected to be nor need it approach the degree of accuracy required in the accounting and recording function.

Throughout this book the T-account will be used as an important analytical tool. The emphasis is not on bookkeeping mechanics but rather on the use of T-account analysis in the reconstruction of transactions. Use of T-account analysis depends on the analyst's ability to express transactions in the form of journal entries.

ILLUSTRATION 1.   The analyst of the financial statements of Alfa, Inc., (see Appendix 2B to this chapter) wants to determine the actual amount of long-term debt paid off in 19x6. This involves the reconstruction and analysis of two accounts. To get all the pertinent information, the analyst must refer to the balances of the long-term debt account in the balance sheet, to details about the "current portion of long-term debt" found in Note 8, and to the statement of changes in financial position. Boldface number references in squares refer to those found in the financial statements of Alfa. Amounts are in thousands of dollars.

Long-Term Debt

(b)	8,080	194,690	Bal. [38]
		58,344 *(a)*	
		244,954	Bal. [38]

(a) Additions to long-term debt (per funds statement [46])
(b) Reduction of long-term debt (per funds statement [55]) transferred to current portion of long-term debt.

Current Portion of Long-Term Debt (included in ⬛32)

Long-term debt paid off (balancing amount)	9,453	8,701 8,080	Bal. (Note 8) Transfer from long-term debt
		7,328	Bal. (Note 8)

Based on the information available, the best estimate of the long-term debt paid off is $9,453. It must be noted that we are dealing here with aggregate (not individual) transactions for 19x6. When there is inadequate information, the analyst may have to combine accounts and transactions and consider them together. Having pinpointed what type of information is lacking, the analyst can develop informed questions for management in order to obtain the desired information that was not disclosed in the financial statements.

The analyst must also know what information is not generally available in financial statements so that he may attempt to secure it. In addition to information such as commitments, lines of credit, and order backlogs, the analyst will also generally not find the details of changes in many important accounts. Thus, for example, a Notes Payable account or a Loan to Officers account may show little or no change in year-end balances but may, in fact, have had significant interim balances that were liquidated during the year.

The analysis and reconstruction of business transactions is an important analytical procedure and will be illustrated throughout this book. Illustrations will be based on the financial statements of Alfa, Inc. (Appendix 2B).

IMPORTANCE OF THE STATEMENT OF CHANGES IN FINANCIAL POSITION

The analytical steps involved in the reconstruction of business transactions often involve use of the statement of changes in financial position (SCFP). For this and other reasons, this statement is of key importance to the analyst. Consequently, the analyst needs to understand how this statement is prepared and how such an understanding can aid in the reconstruction of accounts and transactions. The key to this skill is the ability to visualize what transactions are most likely to affect a given account and where in the financial statements the needed information on such effects can be found.

Additional analytical functions

The following are some additional analytical processes in widespread use:

Direct measurements. Some factors and relationships can be measured directly. For example, the relationship between the debt and the equity of an entity is a direct measurement. Both the amount of debt and that of equity can be measured in absolute terms (i.e., in dollars) and their relationship computed therefrom.

Indirect evidence. Financial statement analysis can provide indirect evidence bearing on important questions. Thus, the analysis of past statements of changes in financial position can offer evidence as to the financial habits of a management team. Moreover, the analysis of operating statements will yield evidence regarding mangement's ability to cope with fluctuations in the level of the firm's business activity. While such indirect evidence and evaluation are often not precise or quantifiable, the data derived therefrom nevertheless possess importance because the effects of almost all managerial decisions, or the lack of them, are reflected in the entity's financial statements.

Predictive functions. Almost all decision questions are oriented towards the future. Thus, an important measure of the usefulness of financial statement analysis tools and techniques is their ability to assist in the prediction of expected future conditions and results.

Comparison. This is a very important analytical process. It is based on the elementary proposition that in financial analysis no number standing by itself can be meaningful, and that it gains meaning only when related to some other comparable quantity. By means of comparison, financial analysis is useful in performing important evaluative, as well as attention-directing and control, functions. Thus, it focuses on exceptions and variations, and saves the analyst the need to evaluate the normal and the expected. Moreover, by means of comparison, selection among alternative choices is accomplished.

Comparison may be performed by using:

1. A company's own experience over the years (i.e., internally derived data);
2. External data, such as industry statistics; or
3. Compiled yardsticks, including standards, budgets, and forecasts.

Historical company data can usually be readily obtained and most readily adjusted for inconsistencies.

Uses of external data. Useful comparison may also be made with external data. The advantages of external data are: (1) they are normally objective and independent; (2) they are derived from similar operations, thus performing the function of a standard of comparison; and (3) if current, they reflect events occurring during an identical period having as a consequence similar business and economic conditions in common.

External information must, however, be used with great care and discrimination. Knowledge of the basis and method of compilation, the period covered, and the source of the information will facilitate a decision of whether the information is at all comparable. At times, sufficient detail may be available to adjust data so as to render them comparable. In any event, a decision on a proper standard of comparison must be made by choosing from those available. Differences between situations compared must be noted. Such differences may be in accounting practices or specific company policies. It must also be borne in mind that the past is seldom an unqualified guide to the future.

SOURCES OF INFORMATION

For basic data on an enterprise and for comparative data of comparable entities in its industry, published financial statements provide the best and most readily available source.

Appendix 2A to this chapter presents a listing of sources of information on financial and operating ratios of various industries as well as sample presentations from these sources. These data, while representing valuable sources for comparison, must be used with care and with as complete a knowledge of the basis of their compilation as is possible to obtain. A realistic and sometimes superior alternative for the analyst is to use as a basis of comparison the financial statements of one or more comparable companies in the same industry. In this way, one can usually have a better command over and comprehension of the data entering into the comparison base.

Annual reports to shareholders contain an ever-expanding amount of information required by either GAAP or by specific SEC requirements.[1]

In addition, company filings with the SEC, such as Registration Statements[2] pursuant to the Securities Act of 1933, supplemental and periodic reports which are required to be filed (such as Forms 8-K, 10-K, 10-Q, 14-K, and 16-K), or proxy statements contain a wealth of information of interest to the analyst.

---

[1] For example, Rule 14c-3 of the Securities Exchange Act of 1934 specifies that annual reports furnished to stockholders in connection with the annual meeting of stockholders include the following financial information: (1) audited financial statements—balance sheets as of the two most recent fiscal years, and statements of income and changes in financial position for each of the three most recent fiscal years; (2) selected quarterly financial data for each quarterly period within the two most recent fiscal years; (3) summary of selected financial data for last five years; (4) management's discussion and analysis of financial condition and results of operations; (5) market price of company's common stock for each quarterly period within the two most recent fiscal years; and (6) segment information.

[2] SEC Regulation S-X, which specifies the form and content of financial statements filed with the Commission, contains numerous requirements for specific disclosures.

THE TOTAL INFORMATION SET

The relative importance of financial statement analysis to the total decision effort can vary significantly. The total information set on which the decision maker draws includes financial as well as other types of information, and the relative importance of each varies from decision to decision. Exhibit 2–1 presents the composition of this information set (or spectrum).

THE PRINCIPAL TOOLS OF ANALYSIS

In the analysis of financial statements, the analyst has available a variety of tools from which he can choose those best suited to his specific purpose. The following principal tools of analysis will be discussed in this chapter:

1. Comparative financial statements.
   a. Year-to-year changes.
2. Index-number trend series.
3. Common-size financial statements.
   ✓a. Structural analysis.
✓4. Ratio analysis.
5. Specialized analyses.
   a. Cash forecasts.
   ✓b. Analysis of changes in financial position.
   c. Statement of variation in gross margin.
   d. Break-even analysis.

The application of these tools as well as other aspects of analysis will be illustrated throughout by means of the financial statements of Alfa, Inc., presented in Appendix 2B. Further examples of tabulations of analytical measures can be found in Chapter 10.

Comparative financial statements

The comparison of financial statements is accomplished by setting up balance sheets, income statements, or statements of changes in financial position (SCFP), side by side, and reviewing the changes that have occurred in individual categories therein from year to year and over the years.

The most important factor revealed by comparative financial statements is *trend*. The comparison of financial statements over a number of years will also reveal the direction, velocity, and the amplitude of trend. Further analysis can be undertaken to compare the trends in related items. For example, a year-to-year increase in sales of 10 percent accompanied by an increase in freight-out costs of 20 percent requires an investigation and explanation of the reasons for the difference. Similarly, an increase of accounts receivable of 15 percent during the same period would also warrant an investigation

Exhibit 2–1: Information set (or spectrum)

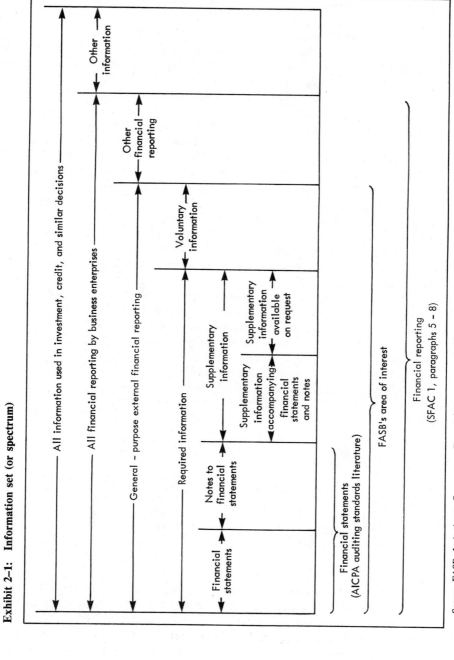

Source: FASB, *Invitation to Comment on Financial Statements and Other Means of Financial Reporting* (Stamford, Conn., 1980), p. 2.

into the reasons for the difference in the rate of increase of sales as against that of receivables.

Year-to-year change. A comparison of financial statements over two to three years can be undertaken by computing the *year-to-year change* in absolute amounts and in terms of percentage changes. Longer-term comparisons are best undertaken by means of *index-number trend series.*

Year-to-year comparisons of financial statements are illustrated in Appendix 2B. When a two- or three-year comparison is attempted, such presentations are manageable and can be understood by the reader. They have the advantage of presenting changes in terms of absolute dollar amounts as well as in percentages. Both have to be considered because the dollar size of the different bases on which percentage changes are computed may yield large percentage changes that are out of proportion to their real significance. For example, in the same financial statements, a 50 percent change from a base figure of $1,000 is far less significant than the same percentage change from a base of $100,000. Thus, reference to the dollar amounts involved is always necessary in order to retain the proper perspective and to reach valid conclusions regarding the relative significance of the changes disclosed by this type of analysis.

The computation of year-to-year changes is a simple matter. However, a few clarifying rules should be borne in mind. When a negative amount appears in the base year and a positive amount in the following year, or vice versa, no percentage change can be meaningfully computed. When an item has a value in a base year and none in the following period, the decrease is 100 percent. Where there is no figure for the base year, no percentage change can be computed. The following summary will illustrate this:

			Change increase (decrease)	
Item	*19x1*	*19x2*	*Amount*	*Per- cent*
Net income (loss).....	$ (4,500)	$ 1,500	$ 6,000	—
Tax expense	2,000	(1,000)	(3,000)	—
Notes payable	—	8,000	8,000	—
Notes receivable	10,000	—	(10,000)	(100)

Comparative financial statements can also be presented in such a way that the cumulative total for the period for each item under study and the average for that period are shown.

The value of comparing yearly amounts with an average covering a number of years is that unusual factors in any one year are highlighted. Averages smooth out erratic or unusual fluctuations in data.

Index-number trend series

When a comparison of financial statements covering more than three years is undertaken, the year-to-year method of comparison may become too cumbersome. The best way to effect such longer-term trend comparisons is by means of index numbers. Such a comparative statement for Alfa, Inc., is illustrated in Appendix 2B.

The computation of a series of index numbers requires the choice of a base year that will, for all items, have an index amount of 100. Since such a base year represents a frame of reference for all comparisons, it is best to choose a year that, in a business conditions sense, is as typical or normal as possible. If the earliest year in the series compared cannot fulfill this function, another year is chosen. In our example of the Alfa, Inc., comparative statements, the year 19x2 was chosen.

As is the case with the computation of year-to-year percentage changes, certain changes, such as those from negative to positive amounts, cannot be expressed by means of index numbers. All index numbers are computed by reference to the base year.

ILLUSTRATION 2.   Assume that in the base year at 12/31/19xA, there is a cash balance of $12,000. Based on an index number of 100 for 19xA, if the cash balance in the following year (at 12/31/19xB) is $18,000, then the index number will be

$$\frac{\$18,000}{\$12,000} \times 100 = 150$$

On 12/31/19xC the cash balance is $9,000, the index will stand at 75 arrived at as follows:

$$\frac{\$9,000}{\$12,000} \times 100 \left(\frac{\text{Balance in current year}}{\text{Balance in base year}} \times 100 \right)$$

It should be noted that when using index numbers, percentage changes cannot be read off directly except by reference to the base year. Thus, the change of the cash balance between 19xA and 19xB is 50 percent (index 150 − index 100), and this can be read off directly from the index numbers. The change from 19xB to 19xC, however, is not 75 percent (150 − 75), as a direct comparison may suggest, but rather 50 percent (i,e., $9,000/$18,000), which involves computing the 19xB to 19xC change by reference to the amount at 19xB. The percentage change can, however, be computed by use of the index numbers only, for example, 75/150 = .5, or a change of 50 percent.

In planning an index-number trend comparison, it is not necessary to include in it all the items in the financial statements. Only the most significant items need be included in such a comparison.

Care should be exercised in the use of index-number trend comparisons because such comparisons have weaknesses as well as strengths. Thus, in trying to assess changes in the current financial condition, the analyst may use to advantage comparative statements of changes in financial position.

On the other hand, the index-number trend comparison is very well suited to a comparison of the changes in the *composition* of working capital items over the years.

The interpretation of percentage changes as well as those of index-number trend series must be made with a full awareness of the effect that the inconsistent application of accounting principles over the years can have on such comparisons. Thus, where possible, such inconsistencies must be adjusted. In addition, the longer the period covered by the comparison, the more distortive are the effects of price-level changes on such comparisons likely to be, and the analyst must be aware of such effects.

One important value of trend analysis is that it can convey to the analyst a better understanding of management's philosophies, policies, and motivations, conscious or otherwise, that have brought about the changes revealed over the years. The more diverse the economic environments covering the periods compared are, the better a picture can be obtained by the analyst of the ways in which the enterprise has weathered its adversities and taken advantage of its opportunities.

Common-size financial statements

In the analysis of financial statements, it is often instructive to find out the proportion that a single item represents of a total group or subgroup. In a balance sheet, the assets as well as the liabilities and capital are each expressed as 100 percent, and each item in these categories is expressed as a percentage of the respective totals. Similarly, in the income statement, net sales are set at 100 percent and every other item in the statement is expressed as a percent of net sales. Since the totals always add up to 100 percent, this community of size has resulted in these statements being referred to as "common size." Similarly, following the eye as it reviews the common-size statement, this analysis is referred to as "vertical" for the same reason that the trend analysis is often referred to as "horizontal" analysis.

Selected common-size statements of Alfa, Inc., are presented in Appendix 2B.

Structural analysis. The analysis of common-size financial statements may best be described as an analysis of the internal structure of the financial statements. In the analysis of a balance sheet, this structural analysis focuses on two major aspects:

1. What are the sources of capital of the enterprise, that is, what is the distribution of equities as between current liabilities, long-term liabilities, and equity capital?
2. Given the amount of capital from all sources, what is the distribution of assets (current, fixed, and other) in which it is invested? Stated differently, what is the mix of assets with which the enterprise has chosen to conduct its operations?

The common-size balance sheet analysis can, of course, be carried further and extended to an examination of what proportion of a subgroup, rather than the total, an item is. Thus, in assessing the liquidity of current assets, it may be of interest to know not only what proportion of total assets is invested in inventories but also what proportion of current assets is represented by this asset.

In the case of the income statement, common-size statement analysis is a very useful tool transcending perhaps in importance the analysis of the balance sheet by such means. This is so because the income statement lends itself very well to an analysis whereby each item in it is related to a central quantum, that is, sales. With some exceptions, the level of each expense item is affected to some extent by the level of sales, and thus it is instructive to know what proportion of the sales dollar is absorbed by the various costs and expenses incurred by the enterprise.

Comparisons of common-size statements of a single enterprise over the years are valuable in that they show the changing proportions of components within groups of assets, liabilities, costs, and other financial statement categories. However, care must be exercised in interpreting such changes and the trend that they disclose. For example, the table below shows the amount of patents and total assets of an enterprise over three years:

	19x3	19x2	19x1
Patents	$ 50,000	$ 50,000	$ 50,000
Total assets	$1,000,000	$750,000	$500,000
Patents as a percentage of total assets	5%	6.67%	10%

While the amount of patents remained unchanged, the increase in total assets made this item a progressively smaller proportion of total assets. Since this proportion can change with either a change in the absolute amount of the item or a change in the total of the group of which it is a part, the interpretation of a common-size statement comparison requires an examination of the actual figures and the basis on which they are computed.

Common-size statements are very well suited to intercompany comparison because the financial statements of a variety of companies can be recast into the uniform common-size format regardless of the size of individual accounts. While common-size statements do not reflect the relative sizes of the individual companies that are compared, the problem of actual comparability between them is a matter to be resolved by the analyst's judgment.

Comparison of the common-size statements of companies within an industry or with common-size composite statistics of that industry can alert the analyst's attention to variations in account structure or distribution, the reasons for which should be explored and understood. A comparison of selected common-size statement items of the Marine Supply Company with similar industry statistics will be found in Chapter 10.

Ratio analysis

Ratios are among the best known and most widely used tools of financial analysis. At the same time, their function is often misunderstood, and consequently their significance may easily be overrated.

A ratio expresses the mathematical relationship between one quantity and another. The ratio of 200 to 100 is expressed as 2:1, or as 2. While the computation of a ratio involves a simple arithmetical operation, its interpretation is a far more complex matter.

To begin with, to be significant, the ratio must express a relationship that has significance. Thus, there is a clear, direct, and understandable relationship between the sales price of an item, on one hand, and its cost, on the other. As a result, the ratio of cost of goods sold to sales is a significant one. On the other hand, there is no a priori or understandable relationship between freight costs incurred and the marketable securities held by an enterprise; and hence, a ratio of one to the other must be deemed to be of no significance.

Ratios are tools of analysis that in most cases provide the analyst with clues and symptoms of underlying conditions. Ratios, properly interpreted, can also point the way to areas requiring further investigation and inquiry. The analysis of a ratio can disclose relationships as well as bases of comparison that reveal conditions and trends that cannot be detected by an inspection of the individual components of the ratio.

Since ratios, like other tools of analysis, are future oriented, the analyst must be able to adjust the factors present in a relationship to their probable shape and size in the future. He must also understand the factors that will influence such ratios in the future. Thus, in the final analysis, the usefulness of ratios is wholly dependent on their intelligent and skillful interpretation. This is, by far, the most difficult aspect of ratio analysis. Let us, by way of example, consider the interpretation of a ratio derived from an area outside that of the business world: In comparing the ratio of gas consumption to mileage driven, A claims to have a superior performance, that is, 28 mpg compared to B's 20 mpg. Assuming that they drove identical cars, the following are factors that affect gas consumption and that will have to be considered before one can properly interpret the ratios and judge whose performance is better:

1. Weight of load driven.
2. Type of terrain (flat versus hilly).
3. City or country driving.
4. Kind of gasoline used.
5. Speed at which cars were driven.

Numerous as the factors that influence gas consumption are, the evaluation of the gas consumption ratio is, nevertheless, a simpler process than the evaluation of most ratios derived from business variables. The reason for this is that the interrelationships of business variables and the factors that affect them are multifaceted and very complex.

Factors affecting ratios

In addition to the internal operating conditions that affect the ratios of an enterprise, the analyst must be aware of the factors, such as general business conditions, industry position, management policies, as well as accounting principles, that can affect them. As far as the latter are concerned, the discussion of accounting principles in this book points up their influence on the measurements on which ratios are based.

Before ratios, or similar measures such as trend indexes or percentage relationships, are computed, the analyst must make sure that the figures entering into their computation are valid and consistent. For example, when inventories are valued on the LIFO basis, under conditions of increasing prices, the current ratio may be understated because LIFO basis inventories may be significantly understated in terms of current value. Similarly, some pension liabilities may be unrecorded and disclosed in footnotes only. Some analysts may wish to recognize these liabilities when computing the debt-to-equity ratio of an enterprise. Care must also be taken to recognize that when such adjustments are made in one ratio, consistency may also require that they be made in other ratios as well. Thus, the omission of the pension liability also means that pension expenses have been understated. As a result, the net income amount used in the computation of certain ratios may require adjustment.

The validity of ratios depends also on the validity of the numbers entering into their computation. Thus, when a company's internal controls are such that the accounting system cannot be relied upon to produce reliable figures, the ratios based on such figures are, of course, also unreliable. It is widely believed that such was the situation in the case of W. T. Grant Co. in the years immediately preceding the giant retailer's bankruptcy.

Interpretation of ratios

Ratios should always be interpreted with great care since factors affecting the numerator may correlate with those affecting the denominator. Thus, for example, it is possible to improve the ratio of operating expenses to sales by reducing costs that act to stimulate sales. If the cost reduction consequently results in a loss of sales or share of market, such a seeming improvement in profitability may, in fact, have an overall detrimental effect on the future prospects of the enterprise and must be interpreted accordingly.

It should also be recognized that many ratios have important variables in common with other ratios, thus tending to make them vary and be influenced by the same factors. Consequently, there is no need to use all available ratios in order to diagnose a given condition.

Ratios, like most other relationships in financial analysis, are not significant in themselves and can be interpreted only by comparison with (1) past ratios of the same enterprise, or (2) some predetermined standard, or (3) ratios of other companies in the industry. The range of a ratio over time is also significant as is the trend of a given ratio over time.

ILLUSTRATION OF RATIO COMPUTATIONS

A great many ratios can be developed from the multitude of items included in an enterprise's financial statements. Some ratios have general application in financial analysis, while others have specific uses in certain circumstances or in specific industries. Listed below are some of the more significant ratios that have general applicability to most business situations. They are grouped by major objectives of financial analysis, and the data used to illustrate their computation are taken from the financial statements of Alfa, Inc. (see Appendix 2B):

Major categories of ratios	Method of computation	Alfa, Inc., ratio for 19x6
Short-term liquidity ratios:		
Current ratio	$\dfrac{\text{Current assets}}{\text{Current liabilities}} = \dfrac{406,784\ \boxed{26}^{(a)}}{185,376\ \boxed{35}} =$	2.19
Acid test ratio	$\dfrac{\text{Cash + Cash equivalents + Receivables}}{\text{Current liabilities}} = \dfrac{18,802\ \boxed{22} + 179,652\ \boxed{23}}{185,376\ \boxed{35}} =$	1.07
Days sales in receivables (collection period)	$\dfrac{\text{Accounts receivable}}{\text{Credit sales} \div 360} = \dfrac{179,652\ \boxed{23}}{1,251,088\ \boxed{1} \div 360} =$	51 days
Inventory turnover	$\dfrac{\text{Cost of goods sold}}{\text{Average inventory during period}} = \dfrac{840,043\ \boxed{2}}{163,771\ \boxed{24} + 192,543\ \boxed{24} \div 2} =$	4.72
Capital structure and long-term solvency ratios:		
Total debt to total capital[(b)]	$\dfrac{\text{Current liabilities + Long-term liabilities}}{\text{Equity capital + Total liabilities}} = \dfrac{185,376\ \boxed{35} + 285,216\ \boxed{36} + \boxed{37} + \boxed{38}}{331,080\ \boxed{40} + 470,592\ (\text{Total numerator})} =$	.59
Long-term debt to equity capital . .	$\dfrac{\text{Long-term debt}}{\text{Equity capital}} = \dfrac{35,404\ \boxed{36} + 4,858\ \boxed{37} + 244,954\ \boxed{38}}{331,080} =$	.86
Times interest earned[(b)]	$\dfrac{\text{Income before interest and taxes}}{\text{Interest}} = \dfrac{25,368\ \boxed{8} + 18,504\ \boxed{5}}{18,504} =$	2.37
Return-on-investment ratios:		
Return on total assets	$\dfrac{\text{Net income + Interest expense }(1 - \text{Tax rate})^{(c)}}{\text{Average total assets}} = \dfrac{19,139\ \boxed{16} + 18,440\ (\boxed{5} - \boxed{6})(1 - .48)}{(738,469\ \boxed{31} + 801,672\ \boxed{31}) \div 2} =$	3.7%

Major categories of ratios	*Method of computation*	*Alfa, Inc., ratio for 19x6*
Return on equity capital	$\dfrac{\text{Net income}}{\text{Average equity capital}} = \dfrac{19{,}139 \ \boxed{16}}{321{,}713 \ \boxed{40} + 331{,}080 \ \boxed{40} \div 2} =$	5.9%
Operating performance ratios:		
Gross margin ratio	$\dfrac{\text{Gross profit (margin)}}{\text{Sales}} = \dfrac{411{,}045 \ (\boxed{1} - \boxed{2})}{1{,}251{,}088 \ \boxed{1}} =$	32.9%
Operating profits to sales	$\dfrac{\text{Operating profit}}{\text{Sales}} = \dfrac{43{,}808 \ (\boxed{1} - \boxed{2} - \boxed{3} - \boxed{4})}{1{,}251{,}088 \ \boxed{1}} =$	3.5%
Pretax income to sales	$\dfrac{\text{Pretax income}}{\text{Sales}} = \dfrac{25{,}368 \ \boxed{8}}{1{,}251{,}088 \ \boxed{1}} =$	2.0%
Net income to sales	$\dfrac{\text{Net income}}{\text{Sales}} = \dfrac{19{,}139 \ \boxed{16}}{1{,}251{,}088 \ \boxed{1}} =$	1.5%
Asset-utilization ratios:		
Sales to cash	$\dfrac{\text{Sales}}{\text{Cash}} = \dfrac{1{,}251{,}088 \ \boxed{1}}{18{,}802 \ \boxed{22}} =$	66.54
Sales to accounts receivables	$\dfrac{\text{Sales}}{\text{Accounts receivable}} = \dfrac{1{,}251{,}088 \ \boxed{1}}{179{,}652 \ \boxed{23}} =$	6.96
Sales to inventories	$\dfrac{\text{Sales}}{\text{Inventories}} = \dfrac{1{,}251{,}088 \ \boxed{1}}{192{,}543 \ \boxed{24}} =$	6.50
Sales to working capital	$\dfrac{\text{Sales}}{\text{Working capital}} = \dfrac{1{,}251{,}088 \ \boxed{1}}{221{,}408 \ (\boxed{26} - \boxed{35})} =$	5.65
Sales to fixed assets	$\dfrac{\text{Sales}}{\text{Fixed assets}} = \dfrac{1{,}251{,}088 \ \boxed{1}}{273{,}645 \ \boxed{29}} =$	4.57

Sales to total assets .... $\dfrac{\text{Sales}}{\text{Total assets}} = \dfrac{1{,}251{,}088 \; \boxed{1}}{801{,}672 \; \boxed{31}} =$ 1.56

Market measures:

Price-earnings ratio .... $\dfrac{\text{Market price}}{\text{Earnings per share}} = \dfrac{14^{(a)}}{1.50 \; \boxed{18}} =$ 9.3

Earnings yield .... $\dfrac{\text{Earnings per share}}{\text{Market price}} = \dfrac{1.50 \; \boxed{18}}{14^{(a)}} =$ 10.7%

Dividend yield .... $\dfrac{\text{Dividends per share}}{\text{Market price per share}} = \dfrac{1.00 \; \boxed{19}}{14^{(a)}} =$ 7.1%

Dividend payout ratio .... $\dfrac{\text{Dividends per share}}{\text{Primary earnings per share}} = \dfrac{1.00 \; \boxed{19}}{1.55 \; \boxed{17}} =$ 64%

---

[a] Key references are to financial statements of Alfa, Inc.
[b] These are simpler versions of more elaborate ratios discussed in Chapter 5.
[c] Using the marginal (corporate) tax rate.
[d] Average for last quarter of 19x6 $\boxed{70}$.

Each of the above five major areas of objectives of financial statement analysis will be examined in this book; and therein the computation, use, and interpretation of the ratios listed under each category as well as other ratios will be examined in detail and thoroughly discussed.

MARKET MEASURES

Analysts and investors use a variety of measures to evaluate the price and yield behavior of securities. The *price-earnings ratio* measures the multiple at which the market is capitalizing the earnings per share of a company at any given time. The *earnings yield* is the inverse of the price-earnings ratio and represents the income-producing power of a share of common stock at the current price. The *dividend yield* is the return accruing to an investor on a share of stock based on the current dividend rate and current price. Thus, part of the earned yield may be distributed as dividends and the balance retained in the business. The *dividend payout ratio* measures the proportion of earnings that is currently paid out as common stock dividends.

TESTING THE UNDERSTANDING OF RELATIONSHIPS

The following is an example of an exercise designed to test the reader's understanding of various intra- and interstatement ratios and relationships.

ILLUSTRATION 3.   Given the following information, we are to complete the balance sheet below:

Cash
Accounts receivable
Inventory .... $ 50
Building
Land
Current liabilities
Common stock
Retained earnings   100

Assets — Liabilities = $600.
Stockholders equity = 3 × debt.
The carrying amount of land is two thirds of that of the building.
Acid-test ratio = 1.25.
Inventory turnover based on cost of goods sold is 15.
Gross profit is 44 percent of the cost of goods sold.
There are 20 days sales in accounts receivable.
The determination of the balance sheet that follows is based on the steps described below:

Cash	$190	Current liabilities	$200
Accounts receivable.....	60	Common stock	500
Inventory	50	Retained earnings	100
Buildings	300		$800
Land	200		
	$800		

STEP 1:

Assets − Liabilities = $600
Stockholders equity = 600
Retained earnings   = 100 (as given)
Common stock   = 500

STEP 2:

Equity = 3 × debt
$\qquad$ 3 × current liabilities (which are the total debt) = $600
$\qquad$ Add current liabilities 200
$\qquad$ So total assets equal $800

Step 3:

Acid test = 1.25

$$\frac{\text{Cash} + \text{Accounts receivable}}{\$200} = 1.25$$

Hence,
$\qquad$ Cash + Accounts receivable = $250

STEP 4:

Inventory + Buildings + Land = $550 [i.e., Total assets − (Cash + A/R)]
$\qquad$ Buildings + Land = $500 (since inventory is given at $50)
Land = ⅔ of building; thus, if x = carrying amount of building
$\qquad$ $x + ⅔ x = 500 $\qquad$ $x = 300 (building)
$\qquad$ Land = $500 − $300 = $200

STEP 5:

$$\frac{\text{Cost of goods sold (CGS)}}{\text{Inventory}} = \text{Inventory turnover; } \frac{\text{CGS}}{\$50} = 15$$

Cost of goods sold = $750 $\quad$ Gross profit, 44% of $750 = $330

STEP 6:

Cost of goods sold + Gross profit ($750 + $330) = Sales = $1,080

$$\text{Amount of sales per day } \frac{\$1,080}{360} = \$3$$

Accounts receivable = 20 days sales = 20 × $3 = $60
Cash = $250 − Accounts receivable ($60) = $190

Specialized tools of analysis

In addition to the multipurpose tools of financial statement analysis that we discussed above, such as trend indexes, common-size statements, and ratios, the analyst has at his or her disposal a variety of special-purpose tools. These tools focus on specific financial statements or segments of such statements, or they can address themselves specifically to the operating conditions of a particular industry, for example, occupancy-capacity analysis in the hotel, hospital, or airline industries. These special-purpose tools of analysis include cash forecasts, analyses of changes in financial position, statements of variation in gross margin, and break-even analyses.

BUILDING BLOCKS OF FINANCIAL STATEMENT ANALYSIS

Whatever approach to financial statement analysis the analyst takes and whatever methods are used, he or she will always have to examine one or more of the important aspects of an enterprise's financial condition and results of its operations. All such aspects, with perhaps the exception of the most specialized ones, can be found in one of the following six categories:

1. Short-term liquidity.
2. Funds flow.
3. Capital structure and long-term solvency.
4. Return on investment.
5. Operating performance.
6. Assets utilization.

Each of the above categories and the tools used in measuring them will be discussed in greater depth later in this book. In this way, the financial analysis required by any conceivable set of objectives may be structured by examining any or all of the above areas in any sequence and with any degree of relative emphasis called for by circumstances. Thus, these six areas of inquiry and investigation can be considered as building blocks of financial statement analysis.

COMPUTER-ASSISTED FINANCIAL ANALYSIS

The major emphasis throughout this book is on the application of thoughtful and logical analysis upon carefully evaluated and verified data. Financial statement analysis does, however, involve a significant amount of work of a computational nature as well as numerous logical steps that can be preplanned and programmed. It is in these areas that the financial analyst can utilize computers to great advantage.

The modern electronic computer has a remarkable facility for performing complex computations with great speed. Moreover, it can perform these computations, comparisons, and other logical steps for long periods of time without exhaustion and once properly programmed will do them without error. In today's environment, when business complexity has outstripped our ability to grasp it and when our ability to generate information has outrun our ability to utilize it, the computer can render vital assistance.

The intelligent use of the computer's formidable capabilities in financial analysis depends, however, on thorough understanding of the limitations to which this powerful tool is subject. Thus, the computer lacks the ability to make intuitive judgments or to gain insights, capabilities that are essential to a competent and imaginative financial analysis.

There is nothing that the computer can do that a competent analyst armed with a calculator cannot do. On the other hand, the speed and the capabilities of modern computers are such that to accomplish what they can do would require so many hours of work as to render most such efforts uneconomical or unfeasible. Computers have thus automated some of the statistical and analytical steps that were previously done manually.

The stored data bases on which computer assisted security analysis often relies do not include all the information that is needed to adjust accounting data in order to render it comparable or in order to make the data conform to the analyst's specific needs. This is particularly true for the following reasons:

1. The data banks generally lack information on accounting policies and principles employed by a given enterprise. This information is essential to an interpretation of the data and to its comparison to other data.
2. Footnotes and other explanatory or restrictive information usually found in individual enterprise reports containing the financial statements are also generally not available in any meaningful detail.
3. Lack of retroactive adjustments because the necessary data are often not available.
4. Errors and omissions may occur when large masses of financial data are processed on a uniform basis for purposes of inclusion in the data base.
5. The aggregation of dissimilar or noncomparable data results in a loss of vital distinctions and thus reduces its meaning and its value for analysis.

Given an understanding of the capabilities as well as the limitations to which the computer is subject, the following are the more significant uses that can be made of this important tool in the broad area of financial analysis:

1. Data storage, retrieval, and computational ability

A machine-accessible comprehensive data base is essential to the use of the computer in most phases of security and credit analysis. The ability of the computer to store vast amounts of data and to afford access to them is one of its important capabilities. Another is the ability to sift these data, to manipulate them mathematically, and to select from among them in accordance with set criteria, as well as to constantly update and modify them. Moreover, the ability of computers to perform computations (of ratios etc.) is almost unlimited.

A large commercially available data base comprising financial information on many hundreds of corporations covering 20 or more years is available from COMPUSTAT, a service of Standard & Poor's Corporation. Another important data base is that provided by Value Line. Many other specialized data bases and time-sharing services are available from various sources and those include the AICPA time-sharing program library.

2. Screening large masses of data

The computer can be used to screen for specified criteria as a means of selecting investment opportunities and for other purposes. A variation of these techniques consists of "filtering" data in accordance with a set of preselected criteria (e.g., certain sales levels, returns, growth rates, financial characteristics, etc.)

3. A research tool

The computer can be used as a research tool for uncovering characteristics of and relationships between data on companies, industries, the market behavior, and the economy.

4. Specialized financial analyses

The computer can be an input tool for financial analysis in credit extension and security analysis.

A. Financial analysis in credit extension.
  1. Storage of facts for comparison and decision making.
  2. Projection of enterprise cash requirements under a variety of assumptions.
  3. Projection of financial statements under a variety of assumptions showing the impact of changes on key variables. Known as *sensitivity analysis,* this technique allows the user to explore the effect of systematically changing a given variable repeatedly by a predetermined amount.
  4. The introduction of probabilistic inputs. The data can be inserted as probability distributions, either normally shaped or skewed, or random probability distributions otherwise known as Monte Carlo trials.

B. Security analysis.
  1. Calculations based on past data.
  2. Trend computations.
      —Simple.
      —Regression analysis.
  3. Predictive models.
  4. Projections and forecasts.
  5. Sensitivity analysis.
  6. Complex probabilistic analysis.

Given an understanding of the capabilities of the modern electronic computer, as well as the limitations to which it is subject, the financial analyst will find in it an important tool that promises to grow in importance as new applications to which it can be put are perfected in the future.

ANALYTICAL REVIEW OF ACCOUNTING PRINCIPLES— PURPOSES AND FOCUS

Throughout this book we are concerned with accounting standards used in the preparation of financial statements. The purpose always is to examine the variety of standards that can be applied to similar transactions and circumstances, as well as the latitude that is possible in the interpretation and application of these standards in practice. Thus, the focus is on an understanding of accounting standards as well as on an appreciation of the impact that the application of these standards may have on the reported financial condition and results of operations of an enterprise. Such possible impact must be appreciated and understood before any intelligent analysis can be undertaken or any useful and meaningful comparison is made. To obtain a fuller understanding of accounting principles, the reader will, in some instances, find it advisable to consult specialized accounting texts.[3]

Example of importance of accounting assumptions, standards, and determinations: Illustration of a simple investment decision

The importance of standards and assumptions in accounting determinations can perhaps be best illustrated and understood within the framework of an exceedingly simple example of a business situation. Let us assume that the owner of an apartment building has found an interested buyer. How should the price be set? How should the buyer gain confidence in the soundness and profitability of such investment at a given price?

The first question is the method to be followed in arriving at a fair value of the building. While many approaches are possible, such as comparable current values, reproduction costs, and so forth, let us settle here on the most widely accepted method for the valuation of income-producing properties as well as other investments: the capitalization of earnings. If earning power is the major consideration, then the focus must be on the income statement. The prospective buyer is given the following income statement:

184 EAGLE STREET APARTMENT HOUSE
Income Statement
For the Year Ending December 31, 19x9

Revenue:	
Rental revenue	$46,000
Garage rentals	2,440
Other income from washer and dryer concession	300
Total revenue	48,740

[3] See, for example, Part II of this author's comprehensive volume "Financial Statement Analysis" 3d ed, Richard D. Irwin.

Expenses:

Real estate taxes	$4,900	
Mortgage interest	2,100	
Electricity and gas	840	
Water	720	
Superintendent's salary	1,600	
Insurance	680	
Repairs and maintenance	2,400	13,240
Income before depreciation		35,500
Depreciation		9,000
Net income*		$26,500

* Income taxes are excluded from consideration here because they depend on the owner's tax status.

The first questions the prospective buyer will want to ask himself about the foregoing income statement are these:

1. Can I rely on the fairness of presentation of the income statement?
2. What adjustments have to be made so as to obtain a net income figure that can be used with confidence in arriving at a proper purchase price?

In our society, the most common way of gaining assurance about the fairness of presentation of financial statements is to rely on the opinion of an independent certified public accountant. This professional is assumed to perform a skillful audit and to satisfy himself that the financial statements do accurately portray the results of operations and the financial position, in accordance with principles that are generally accepted as proper and useful in the particular context in which they are applied. Such an auditor is also presumed to understand that someone like our prospective buyer will rely on his opinion in reaching a decision on whether to buy and at what price. In the Appendix, we will explore in more detail the function of the auditor and what his opinion means to the user of financial statements.

Our prospective buyer's second question is far more complex. The auditor's opinion relates to the income statement as representing fairly the net income for the year ended December 31, 19x9. That in no way means that this is *the* relevant figure to use in arriving at a valuation of the apartment building. Nor would an auditor ever claim that his opinion is directed at the relevance of financial statement figures to any particular decision. Let us then examine what information our buyer will need and what assumptions will have to be made in order to arrive at a figure of net income that can be used in setting the value of the apartment building.

Rental income. Does the $46,000 figure represent 100 percent occupancy during the year? If so, should an allowance be made for possible vacancies? What are rental trends in the area? What would rents be in five years? In 10 years? Are demand factors for apartments in the area going to stay stable, improve, or deteriorate? The aim, of course, is to come nearest to that figure of yearly rental income that approximates a level that, on the average, can be expected to prevail over the forseeable future. Prior years' data will be useful in judging this.

Real estate taxes.   Here the trend of taxes over the years is an important factor. That in turn depends on the character of the taxing community and revenue and expense trends within it.

Mortgage interest.   This expense is relevant to the buyer only if he or she assumes the existing mortgage. Otherwise the interest cost that will be incurred as a result of new financing will have to be substituted.

Utilities.   These expenses must be scrutinized with a view to ascertaining whether they are at a representative level of what can be expected to prevail.

Superintendent's salary.   Is the pay adequate to secure acceptable services? Can the services of superintendent be retained?

Insurance.   Are all forseeable risks insured for? Is the coverage adequate?

Repairs and maintenance.   These expenses must be examined over a number of years in order to determine an average or representative level. Is the level of expenses such that it affords proper maintenance of the property or is the expense account "starved" so as to show a higher net income?

Depreciation.   This figure is not likely to be relevant to the buyer's decision unless his cost approximates that of the seller. If the cost to the buyer differs, then depreciation will have to be computed on that cost using a proper method of depreciation over the useful life of the building, so as to recover the buyer's original cost.

The buyer must also ascertain whether any expenses that he will be properly expected to incur are omitted from the above income statement. Additional considerations concern the method of financing this acquisition and other costs related thereto.

It should be understood that most of the above questions will have to be asked and properly answered even if the auditor issues an unqualified opinion on the financial statements. Thus, for example, while generally accepted accounting principles (GAAP) require that insurance expense include accruals for the full year, they are not concerned with the adequacy of insurance coverage or of the maintenance policy, or the superintendent's pay, or with expected, as opposed to actual, revenues or expense levels.

If one views the many complex questions and problems that arise in the attempt to analyze this very simple income statement for decision-making purposes, one can begin to grasp the complexities involved in the analysis of the financial statements of a sizable, modern business enterprise.

It is clear that essential to an intelligent analysis of such statements is an appreciation of what financial statements do portray as well as what they do not or cannot portray. As we have seen, there are items that properly belong in such statements and there are items that, because of an inability to quantify them or to determine them objectively, cannot be included.

Those items that properly belong in the financial statements should be presented therein in accordance with principles of accounting that enjoy general acceptance. The wide variety of standards that are "acceptable" as well as the even greater variety in the ways in which they can be applied in practice make it imperative that the user of financial statements be fully aware of these possibilities and their implications. The following chapters will explore this important area.

The example of the apartment house buyer illustrates the obvious fact that despite their limitations, financial statements and presentations are indispensible to the decision-making process. While the potential buyer could not use the income statement without obtaining more information and making further assumptions and adjustments, he would not have had any basis for his decision without it. Had he not received one, he would have had to make one up without utilization of the objectivity and the benefit of the experience of actual transactions over a period of time. Thus, in most cases, the interpretation of historical financial statements represents the essential first step in the decision-making process.

APPENDIX 2A

SOURCES OF INFORMATION ON FINANCIAL
AND OPERATING RATIOS

A good way to achieve familiarity with the wide variety of published financial and operating ratios available is to classify them by the type of source that collects or compiles them. The specific sources given under each category are intended to exemplify the type of material available. These are by no means complete lists:

Professional and commercial organizations

Dun & Bradstreet, Inc., Business Economics Division, New York, N.Y.
Key Business Ratios. Important operating and financial ratios in 190 lines.
Selected operating expense figures for many retailing, wholesaling, manufacturing lines, as well as for contract construction; service/transportation/communication; finance/insurance/real estate; agriculture/forestry/fishing; mining.
Cost-of-Doing Business Series. Typical operating ratios for 185 lines of business, showing national averages. They represent a percentage of business receipts reported by a representative sample of the total of all federal tax returns.

Moody's Investor Service, New York, N.Y.

Moody's Manuals contain financial and operating ratios on individual companies covered.

National Cash Register Company. *Expenses in Retail Businesses.* Biennial.

Operating ratios for 35 lines of retail business, as taken from trade associations and other sources including many from *Barometer of Small Business.*

Robert Morris Associates. *Annual Statement Studies.*

Financial and operating ratios for about 300 lines of business—manufacturers, wholesalers, retailers, services, and contractors—based on information obtained from member banks of RMA. Data is broken down by company size.

Standard & Poor's Corporation

Industry Surveys in two parts: (1) Basic Analysis and (2) Current Analysis contains many industry and individual company ratios.

Analysts Handbook. "Composite corporate per share data—by industries," for over 90 industries. Statistics and percentages cover 13 components, including sales, operating profits, depreciation, earnings dividends, and the like.

Industry Surveys. Basic data on 36 important industries, with financial comparisons of the leading companies in each industry. Includes a "Basic Analysis" for each, revised annually. A "Current Analysis" is published quarterly for each industry. A monthly "Trends and Projections" includes tables of economic and industry indicators.

Almanac of Business and Industrial Financial Ratios by Leo Troy. Prentice-Hall, Englewood Cliffs, N.J.

A compilation of corporate performance ratios (operating and financial). The significance of these ratios is explained. All industries are covered in the study, each industry is subdivided by asset size.

The federal government

Small Business Administration

Publications containing industry statistics:

Small Marketers Aid.

Small Business Management Series.

Business Service Bulletins.

U.S. Department of Commerce

Census of Business—Wholesale Trade—Summary Statistics. Monthly Wholesale Trade Report. Ratio of operating expenses to sales.

Department of the Treasury

Statistics of Income, Corporation Income Tax Returns. Operating Statistics based on income tax returns.

Federal Trade Commission—Securities and Exchange Commission.

Quarterly Financial Report for Manufacturing, Mining and Trade Corporations. Contains operating ratios and balance sheet ratios as well as the balance sheet in ratio format.

U.S. Internal Revenue Service

Source Book: Statistics of Income: Corporation Income Tax Returns. Washington, D.C. Annual. "Balance sheet, income statement, tax and investment credit items by major and minor industries, broken down by size of total assets."

Statistics of Income: Corporation Income Tax Returns. Washington, D.C.: U.S. Government Printing Office. Annual. Balance sheet and income statement statistics from a sample of corporate returns. Includes tables by major industry, by asset size, and so on. Includes historical summaries.

Sources of specific industry ratios

Many retail and wholesale trade associations compile and publish periodic ratio statistics. Very few manufacturing associations compile ratios that they make available to the public; and so for most manufacturing industries one must rely on general sources.

American Meat Institute. *Annual Financial Review of the Meat Packing Industry.* Washington, D.C. Includes operating ratios.

Bank Operating Statistics. Federal Deposit Insurance Corporation. Annual.

Institute of Real Estate Management. Experience Exchange Committee. *A Statistical Compilation and Analysis of Actual (year) Income and Expenses Experienced in Apartment, Condominium and Cooperative Building Operation.* Annual.

Discount Merchandiser. *The True Look of the Discount Industry.* June issue each year. Includes operating ratios.

National Electrical Contractors Association. *Operation Overhead.* Annual.

National Farm & Power Equipment Dealers Association. *Cost of Doing Business Study.* Annual.

National Retail Hardware Association. *Lumber/Building Material Financial Report.* Indianapolis. Annual.

Journal of Commercial Bank Lending. "Analysis of Year End Composite Ratios of Installment Sales Finance and Small Loan Companies."

Harris, Kerr, Forster & Company. *Trends in the Hotel-Motel Business.* Annual.

National Association of Music Merchants. *Merchandising and Operating Statistics.* New York. Annual.

National Decorating Products Association. *NDPA'S Annual Cost of Doing Business Survey.* St. Louis. Taken from *Decorating Retailer,* e.g., September 1980 issue.

National Office Products Association. *NOPA Dealers Operating Results.* Alexandria, Va. Annual.

Restaurant Industry Operations Report for the United States. Washington, D.C.: National Restaurant Association in cooperation with Laventhol & Horwath. Annual.

Bibliographies

Robert Morris Associates. *Sources of Composite Financial Data—A Bibliography.* 4th ed. N.Y., 1976, 29 pp.

An annotated list of sources, with an index by specific industry at front.

Sanzo, Richard. *Ratio Analysis for Small Business.* 4th ed. Washington, D.C., 1977. 66 pp. (U.S. Small Business Administration, Small Business Management Series, No. 20).

"Sources of Ratio Studies," pp. 22–35, lists the industries covered by basic sources such as D & B, Robert Morris Associates; also the names of trade associations that have published ratio studies.

APPENDIX 2B

This appendix contains the financial statements of Alfa, Inc., which are adapted from the published financial statements of a large company engaged in the processing of food products, production of raw cane sugar, merchandising, hospitality, and financial and asset management services.

The purpose of this appendix is to provide an illustration of the contents of a modern and comprehensive set of financial statements which will be referred to throughout the text for purposes of illustration and as a basis for problems. For ease of reference, the most important captions have been identified by key numbers.

Exhibit 2B-1

ALFA, INC., AND CONSOLIDATED SUBSIDIARIES
Statement of Income
Year Ended December 31

(All Dollars Reported in Thousands)

		19x6	19x5	19x4	19x3	19x2
1	Revenues (Notes, 2, 3, 4 and 6)	$1,251,088	$1,133,817	$1,147,288	$880,396	$694,958
	Costs And Expenses:					
2	Cost of sales	840,043	730,280	691,077	569,348	441,858
3	Selling, general and administrative	343,023	296,893	285,310	238,957	196,671
4	Depreciation and amortization	24,214	21,158	22,008	16,973	14,398
5	Interest (Note 6)	18,504	16,319	25,054	18,859	11,092
6	Interest capitalized	(64)	—	(3,267)	(1,287)	(463)
7	Total	1,225,720	1,064,650	1,020,182	842,850	663,556
8	**Income Before Income Taxes**	25,368	69,167	127,106	37,546	31,402
9	Income Taxes (Note 7)	7,600	33,000	65,006	13,640	10,858
10	Income From Consolidated Continuing Operations	17,768	36,167	62,100	23,906	20,544
11	Net Income Of Nonconsolidated Finance Subsidiaries	1,371	2,329	2,068	3,609	3,095
12	**Income From Continuing Operations**	19,139	38,496	64,168	27,515	23,639
13	Income (Loss) From Discontinued Operations (Note 3)	—	(1,000)	(7,325)	(957)	657
14	Income Before Cumulative Effect On Prior Years of Accounting Changes	19,139	37,496	56,843	26,558	24,296
15	Cumulative Effect On Prior Years Of Accounting Changes ($36,647 less income taxes of $19,240) (Note 2)	—	(17,407)	—	—	—
16	**Net Income (Notes 2, 3 and 4)**	$ 19,139	$ 20,089	$ 56,843	$ 26,558	$ 24,296

17 Primary Earnings Per Share (Note 10):

Income from continuing operations	$ 1.55	$ 3.25	$ 5.57	$ 2.40	$ 2.06
Income (loss) from discontinued operations	—	(.08)	(.63)	(.08)	.06
Cumulative effect on prior years of accounting changes	—	(1.47)	—	—	—
Net income	$ 1.55	$ 1.70	$ 4.94	$ 2.32	$ 2.12

18 Fully Diluted Earnings Per Share (Note 10):

Income from continuing operations	$ 1.50	$ 3.04	$ 5.14	$ 2.28	$ 1.97
Income (loss) from discontinued operations	—	(.07)	(.58)	(.08)	.05
Cumulative effect on prior years of accounting changes	—	(1.33)	—	—	—
Net income	$ 1.50	$ 1.64	$ 4.56	$ 2.20	$ 2.02

19 Cash Dividends Per Common Share

	$ 1.00	$ 1.00	$ .70	$ .64	$ .60

20 Pro Forma Amounts (giving retroactive effect to accounting changes; Note 2):

Revenues	—	$1,133,817	$1,114,937	$877,831	—
Income from continuing operations	—	38,496	48,801	25,475	—
Net income	—	37,496	41,476	24,518	—
Primary earnings per share:					
Income from continuing operations	—	3.25	4.24	2.29	—
Net income	—	3.17	3.61	2.21	—

21

ALFA, INC., AND CONSOLIDATED SUBSIDIARIES
Management's Analysis of the Statement of Income (Note 2)
(Unaudited)

(All Dollars Reported in Thousands)

	Increase (decrease) over prior year	
	19x6	19x5
Revenues		
Food	$ 76,928	$ 9,670
Agriculture	(51,248)	(81,467)
Retail	25,959	26,183
Distribution	42,558	34,404
Hospitality	22,743	9,062
Asset Management	98	(11,355)
Corporate investments	233	32
Total increase (decrease) in revenues	117,271	(13,471)
Cost Of Sales		
Food	55,664	(1,876)
Agriculture	264	8,277
Retail	13,766	12,800
Distribution	37,193	28,745
Hospitality	2,704	(299)
Asset Management	172	(8,444)
Total increase in cost of sales	109,763	39,203

For 19x6, revenues increased 10% and both cost of sales and expenses increased 15% over 19x5. Food Group revenues for 19x6 were up 56% over the prior year, including 34% relating to businesses acquired during the year. Volume increases accounted for the other 22% as selling prices remained relatively unchanged. Cost of food product sales increased 62% and expenses increased 44% over 19x5. Sugar prices for 19x6 were 31% lower than the prior year. Sugar sold was down 8% because fewer acres were harvested and yields were lower than 19x5. As a result of increased volume and prices, retail sales and cost of sales for 19x6 were 8% higher than 19x5 and expenses were 9% higher. Distribution sales were 10% ahead of the prior year primarily as a result of businesses acquired and new branches opened. Cost of sales was up 11% and expenses were up 14%, which resulted in lower contribution to earnings for the Distribution Group in 19x6 compared to 19x5. Hospitality revenues for 19x6 increased 19% over the prior year primarily as a result of new hotels, increased rates and occupancy. Hospitality costs and expenses increased 17% over 19x5. Interest costs for 19x6 were 13% higher than 19x5, principally because of increased borrowings.

For 19x5, revenues decreased 1%, cost of sales increased 6% and expenses increased 2% over 19x4. Food Group revenues for 19x5 were 8% over the prior year primarily as a result of increased selling prices. Cost of food product sales was slightly lower and expenses were 6% higher than 19x4. Sugar prices for 19x5 were 35% lower than the prior year. Sugar sold increased 18% primarily because more acres were harvested. Agriculture Group costs and expenses for 19x5 were up 6% over the prior year. Retail sales for 19x5 were 9% higher than 19x4, including 3% for new stores (net of closed stores). Cost of retail sales for 19x5 increased 8% as gross margins improved over 19x4 and expenses increased 9%. Distribution sales for 19x5 were 9% ahead of the prior year primarily because of businesses acquired and new branches opened. Cost of sales was up 9% and expenses were up 12% over 19x4. Hospitality revenues for 19x5 increased 8% over the prior year primarily as a result of new hotels and restaurants. Hospitality costs and expenses increased 7% over 19x4. Interest expense was 25% lower than 19x4, primarily as a result of lower borrowings during 19x5.

Expenses

Food	14,524	2,018
Agriculture	723	(2,558)
Retail	10,764	9,647
Distribution	7,282	5,509
Hospitality	15,632	7,898
Asset Management	(283)	(9,598)
Accounting change for deferred preopening expenses (Note 2)		(3,205)
Corporate	544	1,022
Interest	2,121	(5,468)
Total increase in expenses	51,307	5,265
Decrease In Income Before Income Taxes	(43,799)	(57,939)
Decrease In Income Taxes (Note 7)	(25,400)	(32,006)
Decrease In Income From Consolidated Continuing Operations	(18,399)	(25,933)
Increase (Decrease) In Net Income Of Nonconsolidated Finance Subsidiaries	(958)	261
Decrease In Income From Continuing Operations	(19,357)	(25,672)
Discontinued Operations (Note 3)	1,000	6,325
Cumulative Effect On Prior Years Of Accounting Changes (Note 2)	17,407	(17,407)
Total Decrease in Net Income	(950)	(36,754)
Net Income Prior Year	20,089	56,843
Net Income Current Year	**$ 19,139**	**$ 20,089**

Exhibit 2B–2

ALFA, INC., AND CONSOLIDATED SUBSIDIARIES
Balance Sheet

(All Dollars Reported in Thousands)

ASSETS

		December 31	
		19x6	*19x5*
Current Assets:			
22	Cash (Note 8)	$ 18,802	$ 20,677
23	Receivables—less allowance for doubtful receivables of $5,010 and $4,465 (Note 5)	179,652	158,056
24	Inventories (Notes 2 and 5)	192,543	163,771
25	Prepaid expenses	15,787	17,543
26	Total current assets	406,784	360,047
Investments:			
27	Nonconsolidated finance subsidiaries (Note 13)	32,443	31,072
28	Other (Note 5)	23,053	22,377
29	**Property, Plant And Equipment**—less accumulated depreciation and amortization of $174,932 and $156,959 (Note 5)	273,645	253,580
30	**Other Assets** (Note 5)	65,747	71,393
31	Total	$801,672	$738,469

LIABILITIES

Current Liabilities:

32	Notes payable and current portion of long-term debt (Note 8) .... **$ 34,028**	$ 38,951
33	Accounts payable and accrued expenses (Note 8) **127,144**	118,868
34	Income taxes—including deferred taxes of $21,556 and $19,155 .... **24,204**	27,993
35	Total current liabilities **185,376**	185,812
36	**Deferred Income Taxes** **35,404**	31,883
37	**Other Deferred Credits** **4,858**	4,371
38	**Long-Term Debt (Note 8)** **244,954**	194,690
39	**Commitments and Contingent Liabilities (Notes 11, 12 and 14)**	
40	**Stockholders' Equity (Note 9)** **331,080**	321,713
	Total **$801,672**	$738,469

STOCKHOLDERS' EQUITY

	Preferred Stock—authorized 5,000,000 shares of no par value:		
	$2.50 cumulative convertible (involuntary liquidation value, $1,523) shares issued and outstanding, 38,076 .... **$ 610**	$ 610
	Series B $1.00 cumulative convertible (involuntary liquidation value, $23,183) shares outstanding, 927,308 and 927,322 .... **14,330**	14,330
40	Common Stock—authorized 20,000,000 shares of no par value; shares outstanding, 11,723,774 and 11,243,734 .... **90,138**	90,088
	Excess of Equity Over Cost Of Subsidiary Companies At Dates Of Acquisitions (no change during the five years ended December 31, 19x6) **11,171**	11,171
	Earnings Reinvested—$31,000 available for cash dividends under most restrictive terms of indebtedness agreements **214,954**	205,637
	Cost of Treasury Shares (6,667 Series B preferred shares) .... **(123)**	(123)
	Total **$331,080**	$321,713

Exhibit 2B–3

ALFA, INC., AND CONSOLIDATED SUBSIDIARIES
Statement of Changes in Financial Position
Year Ended December 31

(All Dollars Reported in Thousands)

		19x6	19x5	19x4	19x3	19x2
	Sources:					
	Internally generated funds:					
41	Net income	$ 19,139	$ 20,089	$ 56,843	$ 26,558	$ 24,296
42	Depreciation and amortization	24,383	21,579	22,508	17,423	14,766
43	Deferred income taxes—noncurrent portion	3,521	207	223	5,983	5,962
44	Less undistributed income of non-consolidated domestic subsidiaries	(1,439)	(2,042)	(3,994)	(2,637)	(2,153)
45	Total from operations	45,604	39,833	75,580	47,327	42,871
46	Additions to long-term debt	58,344	16,323	31,698	73,476	51,563
47	Decrease in noncurrent receivables	7,886	—	—	—	—
48	Issuance of capital stock for businesses acquired	2,494	2,228	871	46	10,725
49	Property sales and retirements:					
	Sale—leaseback financing	—	853	9,827	25,272	8,580
	Other	3,409	7,824	9,616	8,866	8,986
50	Decrease in deferred charges	—	—	8,086	—	—
51	Other—net	—	618	—	181	24
	Total	117,737	67,679	135,678	155,168	122,749

Applications:

Property additions:

52 Businesses acquired	6,683	1,620	57	436	7,757
53 Existing businesses	41,174	41,094	56,661	59,628	63,165
54 Increase in noncurrent receivables	—	3,380	3,343	5,935	1,298
55 Reduction of long-term debt	8,080	24,092	26,633	31,789	26,080
56 Cash dividends on capital stock	12,266	11,989	8,664	7,971	7,448
57 Increase in investment in nonconsolidated finance subsidiaries	—	—	—	1,303	8,638
58 Increase in deferred charges	1,972	1,070	—	1,861	5,036
59 Other—net	389	—	189	—	—
Total	70,564	83,245	95,547	108,923	119,422
60 **Increase (Decrease) In Working Capital**	$ 47,173	$(15,566)	$ 40,131	$ 46,245	$ 3,327

Represented By:

Current assets—increase (decrease):

61 Cash and marketable securities	$ (1,875)	$ 645	$ 12,967	$ 3,646	$ (1,806)
62 Receivables	21,596	(51,453)	49,721	36,783	34,530
63 Inventories	28,772	3,953	14,332	37,139	16,887
64 Prepaid expenses	(1,756)	6,414	1,670	691	1,473
Change in current assets	46,737	(40,441)	78,690	78,259	51,084

Current liabilities—increase (decrease):

65 Notes payable and current portion of long-term debt	(4,923)	13,298	(26,446)	15,535	20,134
66 Accounts payable and accrued expenses	8,276	(5,676)	12,432	17,325	31,087
Current income taxes:					
67 Currently payable	(6,190)	(12,832)	21,670	(87)	(4,614)
68 Deferred	2,401	(19,665)	30,903	(759)	1,150
Change in current liabilities	(436)	(24,875)	38,559	32,014	47,757
60 **Increase (Decrease) In Working Capital**	$ 47,173	$(15,566)	$ 40,131	$ 46,245	$ 3,327

ALFA, INC., AND CONSOLIDATED SUBSIDIARIES
Statement of Earnings Reinvested
Year Ended December 31

	19x6	19x5	19x4	19x3	19x2
(All Dollars Reported in Thousands)					
Balance, Beginning of Year	**$205,637**	$196,582	$147,613	$129,043	$106,801
Minor Businesses Pooled (prior years not restated)	**2,444**	955	790	(17)	5,394
Net Income	**19,139**	20,089	56,843	26,558	24,296
Cash Dividends Declared:					
$2.50 Preferred	**(95)**	(95)	(95)	(95)	(124)
$1.00 Series B Preferred	**(927)**	(927)	(926)	(933)	(934)
Common (per share: $1.00, $1.00, 70¢, 64¢ and 60¢)	**(11,244)**	(10,967)	(7,643)	(6,943)	(6,390)
Balance, End of Year	**$214,954**	$205,637	$196,582	$147,613	$129,043

69

60

Exhibit 2B–5

70

ALFA, INC., AND CONSOLIDATED SUBSIDIARIES
Quarterly Financial Data
(Unaudited)

	Common (1)	$2.50 preferred (1)	$1.00 Series B preferred (1)	Revenues (2)	Net income (2)	Earnings per share (2)
19x6				$1,251,088	$19,139	$1.55
1st Quarter	$19⅞-14⅞	$ 25	$14¼-11¾	264,769	4,554	.37
2nd Quarter	18½-15⅛	28-25	13 -11½	312,276	6,970	.57
3rd Quarter	16⅝-14⅝	No Trades	12½-11	330,558	3,589	.29
4th Quarter	15 -13	No Trades	12 -11⅛	343,485	4,026	.32
19x5				$1,133,817	$20,089	$1.70
1st Quarter	$22 -15⅝	No Trades	$13⅞-10⅞	246,748	(7,159)	(.61)
2nd Quarter	21 -16⅝	No Trades	14 -11½	278,024	9,217	.78
3rd Quarter	18⅝-15¼	$ 26	12⅞-11⅛	302,184	9,606	.81
4th Quarter	15¾-13¾	No Trades	11⅞-11	306,861	8,425	.72

(1) Quarterly high and low stock price ranges. Alfa's common stock is registered on the New York, Pacific, and Honolulu Stock Exchanges. The $2.50 preferred stock is registered on the Honolulu Stock Exchange and the $1.00 Series B preferred stock is registered on the Pacific Stock Exchange.

(2) 19x6 restated for December pooling of interests. First Quarter 19x5 includes cumulative effect on prior years of accounting changes which reduced net income $17,407 or $1.47 per share. Fourth Quarter 19x5 includes discontinued operations which reduced net income $1,000 or $.08 per share.

ALFA, INC., AND CONSOLIDATED SUBSIDIARIES
Notes to Financial Statements
(All Dollars Reported in Thousands)

1. Accounting Policies: The accounting policies of Alfa, Inc., considered significant to understanding its financial statements are:

Consolidation: Alfa's consolidated financial statements include the accounts of all domestic subsidiaries except Alfa Financial, Inc., and its subsidiaries, Alfa Credit Corporation and its subsidiaries and an insurance company organized in 19x3 to provide Alfa and its subsidiaries with certain insurance. Significant intercompany transactions and balances are eliminated. Investments in common stock of nonconsolidated subsidiaries are accounted for by the equity method.

Sugar revenues: Alfa sells its sugar to California and Hawaiian Sugar Company (C and H), a nonprofit agricultural cooperative. Sugar revenues are accrued at the time of sale to C and H based on C and H's estimated net return (sales proceeds less costs and expenses including estimates for unsold sugar held by C and H). Estimated profits from Alfa's share of C and H's unsold sugar are deferred until sales are ultimately made by C and H to its customers; estimated losses based on current sales prices and estimated expenses are charged against income currently. Amounts withheld by and added to the capital of C and H are accounted for as an additional investment in C and H (see Note 2).

Leased department sales: In accordance with industry practice, revenues of retail operations include leased department sales.

Real property sales: Income from sales of real property is recognized when cash received as a percentage of total sales price is at least 10% for residences, 25% for raw land and 20% for other real property, collection of the balance of the sales price is reasonably assured and risks of ownership have passed to the buyer.

Pension plans: Alfa and its subsidiaries have pension plans covering substantially all full-time employees. Substantially all pension costs, including prior service costs amortized over 30 years or less, are funded as accrued.

Research, development and preopening costs: Such costs are charged to expense as incurred. Prior to 19x4, preopening costs, including initial operating losses, were deferred and amortized over three years (see Note 2).

Excess of cost over equity of subsidiary companies at dates of acquisition: Such excess relates principally to businesses acquired prior to 1970 which will not be amortized until, in the opinion of management, diminution in value is expected.

Income taxes: Federal income tax returns are filed on a consolidated basis. Income taxes are reduced by investment tax credits using the flow-through method. Deferred income taxes are provided on items (principally depreciation, installment sales and uncollected sugar revenues) recorded in different periods for tax than for financial reporting purposes.

Earnings per share: Primary earnings per share are based on the average number of outstanding shares of common stock and common stock equivalents (preferred stock and dilutive stock options). Fully diluted earnings per share also assume the conversion of the Company's convertible debentures and elimination of related interest expense (after applicable income taxes).

Inventories: All inventories are stated at the lower of cost or market. The cost of certain processed food, raw material and supply inventories is determined using the last-in, first-out (LIFO) inventory method. The costs of other inventories are determined princi-

71

pally by the first-in, first-out or average methods. Merchandise inventories in retail stores are determined by the retail method, which involves pricing individual items at current selling prices and reducing such amounts by the application of departmental mark-up ratios to the lower of average cost or market.

Growing crops: In accordance with Hawaii sugar industry practice, all costs of growing sugarcane (which has a growing cycle of approximately two years) are charged to expense in the year incurred.

Investments: Investments in partnerships, joint ventures and common stock of nonconsolidated affiliates over which Alfa exercises significant influence are accounted for by the equity method. Other investments are stated at cost or estimated realizable value if less than cost.

Property, plant and equipment: Property is stated at cost. In order to include all applicable costs, interest on funds borrowed for construction of buildings costing over $1,000 is capitalized during the construction period. Depreciation is provided using the straight-line method over the estimated economic lives for financial reporting purposes and accelerated methods as permitted for income tax purposes. The principal lives used for financial reporting purposes are 20–40 years for land improvements, 25–40 years for buildings, 3–18 years for machinery and equipment, and the term of the lease if less than the aforementioned lives for leasehold improvements. Maintenance and repairs are charged to operations. Renewals and betterments are capitalized. When properties are retired or otherwise disposed of in the normal course of business, the original cost, reduced by any salvage realized, is charged to accumulated depreciation, with no gain or loss reflected in income. Gains or losses on specifically identified abnormal retirements are reflected in income.

Excess of equity over cost of subsidiary companies at dates of acquisition: The excess of equity over cost of businesses acquired prior to 19w9, which is not being amortized to income, is presented separately in stockholders' equity. Similar excesses arising since 19w9 have not been significant.

Stock options: No accounting entries are made when stock options are granted. When options are exercised, proceeds are credited to common stock.

2. Accounting Changes: Under new accounting methods adopted in 19x5, (a) estimated sugar profits are deferred until sales are ultimately made by C and H to its customers, (b) investment in C and H is stated at equity and (c) retail purchase discounts are deferred until sales are made to customers. Consistent with the change to the equity method, Alfa's net income of prior years has been restated to include its share of operating profits and losses reported by C and H. Such amounts include C and H's antitrust litigation settlement which C and H charged to the years covered by the litigation, 19w9–19x4 (see Note 12).

As shown in the following tabulation, net income for 19x5 would have been $1,140 or $.10 per share higher if (a) Alfa had not adopted the new accounting methods which it considers preferable and (b) its share of estimated future withholdings by C and H had been charged to 19x5 expenses instead of to the years covered by the litigation (see Note 12):

	Increased (Decreased)	
	Amount	*Per Share*
Sugar profits deferred at year-end	$ 1,603	$ .14
C and H litigation charge	(1,285)	(.11)
Retail purchase discounts deferred	822	.07
Total	$ 1,140	$ .10

72

63

Alfa's five sugar companies sell their sugar to C and H. Prior to 19x5, Alfa's investment in C and H was carried at cost and sugar revenues ($55,000, $68,000, $209,000 and $130,000 for the four years ended December 31, 19x5) were accrued at the time of sale to C and H based on C and H's estimated net return (sales proceeds, including estimates for unsold sugar of C and H less costs, expenses and withholdings for capital reserves). Since 1951, C and H has increased its capital principally through retaining in certain years a small portion of members' revenues from the sale of sugar. Alfa's interest in such capital reserves was not completely identified until September 19x5 when it was advised by C and H of its allocation.

Prior to 19x4, sugar prices remained relatively stable primarily because the domestic sugar industry was covered by the Sugar Act of 1948, as amended. This Act expired on December 31, 19x4 and no substitute legislation has been enacted to date. In 19x4, sugar prices increased to historic highs and have since declined substantially. The change in method of accounting for sugar profits was made because proceeds from the sale of C and H unsold sugar cannot be estimated accurately during periods of severely fluctuating sugar prices. The equity method for Alfa's investment in C and H is more consistent with its new method of accounting for sugar profits.

Prior period financial statements have been restated for the change to the equity method of accounting for the investment in C and H. Such restatement increased (decreased) previously reported net income as follows: 19x4 $920, 19x3 $(464), 19x2 $(448) and years prior $4,562.

Alfa also changed its method of accounting for retail purchase discounts. Previously, purchase discounts were treated as revenue when received. Such discounts are now included in income when the related merchandise is sold.

The cumulative effect on earnings reinvested at the beginning of 19x5 resulting from the changes in accounting for sugar revenues ($16,585 or $1.40 per share) and retail purchase discounts ($822 or $.07 per share) has been included in the accompanying financial statements as a charge against 19x5 net income. Pro forma amounts in the statements of income for 19x5, 19x4 and 19x3 include the effect of applying the new accounting methods retroactively. The effect on periods prior to 19x3 is not material.

Alfa's 19x4 net income was reduced $7,634 ($.66 per share) as a result of changes made in 19x4 to preferable accounting methods as set forth below:

In 19x4, Alfa adopted the last-in, first-out (LIFO) method for pricing Lamb-Weston's processed food, raw material and supply inventories. Previously, average, first-in, first-out (FIFO) or identified cost methods were used for pricing these inventories. The effect of the change was to reduce 19x4 net income by $6,112 ($.53 per share). There is no effect on prior years since the ending inventory previously reported for 19x3 is the beginning inventory in 19x4 for LIFO purposes.

Prior to September 30, 19x4, preopening expenses and initial operating losses incurred during the first six months after opening new department stores and hotels were deferred and amortized over three years. As of September 30, 19x4, the unamortized balances were charged to expense. This change in estimate effected by a change in accounting principle reduced 19x4 net income $1,522 ($.13 per share). Since September 30, 19x4, such costs have been charged to operations as incurred.

3. Unusual Items: On November 15, 19x4, Alfa decided to discontinue operations of its Wilhelm Foods division and since that date has been in the process of disposing of the division's assets. Wilhelm's remaining assets, totaling $4,123 at December 31, 19x6 and consisting principally of receivables and property, are expected to be sold in 19x7. During 19x5 and 19x4 provisions of $2,083 and $1,700, respectively, before income taxes were made for anticipated losses on sale of assets and from operations during phase-out periods. Such losses aggregated $427 in 19x6 and $2,713 in 19x5. Wilhelm's revenues were $5,952 in 19x6, $30,499 in 19x5, $67,741 in 19x4, $68,755 in 19x3 and $54,264 in 19x2. Operating results of Wilhelm are included as discontinued operations in the statement of income and are after income taxes (credits) of $1,448, $(1,048), $(7,722) and $(1,083) for the four years ended December 31, 19x5.

In 19x5, regulatory authorities disapproved the 19x3 sale of Alfa Credit Corporation to a bank. Primarily as a result of operating losses since the sale in 19x3, Alfa charged 19x6, 19x5 and 19x4 net income $260 ($.02 per share), $674 ($.06 per share) and $2,168 ($.19 per share), respectively. Alfa expects to sell Alfa Credit Corporation in 19x7.

In 19x4, Alfa charged net income $1,853 ($.16 per share) for losses expected to be incurred in connection with the planned liquidation of mobile home parks and disposal of certain other property in California.

In 19x3, net income was reduced $703 ($.06 per share) for costs incurred in connection with the final closing of the Rhodes-WAY mass merchandising stores in that year. 19x2 net income was reduced $3,221 ($.28 per share) by store operating losses and inventory write-downs in anticipation of such closings.

Alfa's 19x3 net income also included gains of $2,100 ($.18 per share) from the sale of one of Alfa's food processing plants. Net income also included gains of $1,824 ($.16 per share) in 19x3 and $1,573 ($.14 per share) in 19x2 from the sale of surplus property formerly used by Construction Materials Hawaii, Inc. (CMH), a subsidiary of Alfa.

4. Business Acquisitions: As of April 1, 19x3, Alfa acquired a 20-branch drug wholesaling business. The acquisition was accounted for as a purchase and, accordingly, its operations are included only from date of acquisition. Had its operations been included for the entire 19x3 fiscal year, Alfa's revenues and net income for that year would have been $900,521 and $26,734 ($2.33 per share), respectively.

On April 1, 19x2, Alfa Mortgage Corporation, a subsidiary of Alfa Financial, Inc. (a wholly-owned nonconsolidated finance subsidiary of Alfa, Inc.), acquired Commonwealth, Inc., a mortgage banking company, for $11,500 in cash.

Alfa acquired CMH under a Plan of Arrangement approved by the Federal District Court of Honolulu on August 9, 19x2. CMH, Alfa's former Construction Materials Division, was sold to Telecheck International, Inc. in 19x0.

Alfa has had additional acquisitions each of the years from 19x2 through 19x6, none of which has been material.

65

Notes to Financial Statements *(continued)*

75 5. Supplemental Assets Information:

	December 31	
	19x6	19x5
Receivables:		
Trade accounts	$154,659	$140,900
California and Hawaiian Sugar Company—estimated market value for Alfa's share of unsold sugar held by C and H, less cash advances and deferred sugar profits of $3,375 in 19x5 ($6,622 less than cost in 19x6)	17,648	13,875
Trade notes	12,355	7,746
Allowance for doubtful receivables	(5,010)	(4,465)
Total	$179,652	$158,056
Inventories:		
Retail	$ 57,063	$ 53,735
Distribution	74,193	67,379
Food—net of LIFO reserves of $8,443 and $10,763	42,837	26,091
Real property development projects	8,598	6,383
Other	9,852	10,183
Total	$192,543	$163,771
Other investments:		
At equity:		
California and Hawaiian Sugar Company (Note 2)	$ 14,824	$ 14,824
Other nonconsolidated domestic subsidiaries	2,167	2,099
Other—principally joint ventures	4,957	4,604
At cost or less	1,105	850
Total	$ 23,053	$ 22,377

	December 31	
	19x6	19x5
Property, plant and equipment (about $77,000 and $71,000 pledged as collateral for mortgage and other loans):		
Land	$ 20,471	$ 20,858
Real estate improvements	85,875	82,223
Buildings	91,081	81,258
Machinery and equipment	234,418	215,359
Construction in progress	16,732	10,841
Total	448,577	410,539
Less accumulated depreciation and amortization	174,932	156,959
Total	$273,645	$253,580
Other assets:		
Excess of cost over equity of subsidiary companies at dates of acquisition prior to 1970	$ 22,010	$ 22,010
Noncurrent notes receivable	31,792	39,678
Land held for future property development	2,694	2,426
Deferred charges	9,251	7,279
Total	$ 65,747	$ 71,393
Growing crops not included in the balance sheet—estimated	$ 50,000	$ 46,000
Less applicable income taxes	26,000	24,000
Net addition to stockholders' equity if growing crop costs were deferred until harvest rather than expensed in the year incurred	$ 24,000	$ 22,000

76 6. Supplemental Income and Expense Information:

	19x6	19x5	19x4	19x3	19x2
Leased department sales	$ 44,897	$ 39,246	$ 33,975	$ 31,621	$ 33,532
77 Inventories entering into cost of sales (Note 2):					
Beginning of year	163,771	159,818	145,486	108,347	91,460
End of year	192,543	163,771	159,818	145,486	108,347
Maintenance and repairs*	19,602	17,630	13,412	8,120	6,770
78 Taxes, other than income taxes	26,983	23,484	19,486	18,793	13,288
79 Advertising	16,006	14,055	12,413	9,611	8,668
80 Research and development costs	1,442	1,892	1,291	1,317	1,261
Net deferral (amortization) of preopening expense and initial operating losses of new department stores and hotels (Note 2)	—	—	(3,149)	(808)	1,800
81 Interest expense:					
Long-term debt	14,883	12,727	16,437	13,627	7,675
Short-term borrowings	3,621	3,592	8,617	5,232	3,417
Total charged to income	18,504	16,319	25,054	18,859	11,092
82 Increase (decrease) in net income resulting from capitalizing interest	(47)	(75)	1,482	603	218

* Excluding maintenance and repairs of Agriculture Group subsidiaries which are not practicable to segregate.

7. Supplemental Income Tax Information:

	19x6	19x5	19x4	19x3	19x2
83 Income taxes:					
Computed federal tax at statutory rate	$11,437	$30,176	$55,592	$17,356	$14,441
%	48	48	48	48	48
84 Benefit for income taxable at capital gains rate	(782)	(818)	(1,610)	(3,115)	(2,670)
%	(3.3)	(1.3)	(1.4)	(8.7)	(8.9)
85 Investment tax credits	(4,311)	(2,734)	(1,618)	(1,483)	(1,898)
%	(18.1)	(4.3)	(1.4)	(4.1)	(6.3)
86 Other—net	(284)	76	1,352	(508)	(334)
%	(1.2)	.1	1.2	(1.4)	(1.1)
87 Reported federal income tax	6,060	26,700	53,716	12,250	9,539
%	25.4	42.5	46.4	33.8	31.7
88 State income taxes	1,540	6,300	11,290	1,390	1,319
Total	$ 7,600	$33,000	$65,006	$13,640	$10,858

	Year ended December 31				
	19x6	19x5	19x4	19x3	19x2
Current					
Federal	$ 5,139	$45,392	$28,870	$ 8,063	$ 6,367
Less investment tax credits	(4,311)	(2,734)	(1,618)	(1,483)	(1,898)
State	850	9,800	5,739	788	725
Total	1,678	52,458	32,991	7,368	5,194
Deferred Federal and State:					
Excess tax depreciation	3,818	2,447	1,922	1,733	2,488
Net deferral of profits on installment sales	(192)	257	1,931	4,939	2,691
Uncollected sugar revenues	1,965	(22,682)	29,642	—	—
Net deferral (amortization) of preopening expenses and initial operating losses	—	520	(1,636)	(404)	900
Other—net	331	—	156	4	(415)
Total	5,922	(19,458)	32,015	6,272	5,664
Total	$ 7,600	$33,000	$65,006	$13,640	$10,858

Left margin markers: 89, 90, 91, 92, 93, 94

8. Supplemental Liabilities and Debt Information:

	December 31	
	19x6	19x5
Accounts Payable and Accrued Expenses:		
Accounts payable—trade	$ 77,143	$ 71,754
Accrued compensation	17,663	16,142
Accrued interest	5,445	4,894
Alfa Financial, Inc.	656	2,208
Other	26,237	23,870
Total	$127,144	$118,868
Notes Payable and Current Portion of Long-Term Debt:		
Banks—average rate 6¼% and 8½%	$ 26,200	$ 25,250
Commercial paper—average rate 5% and 6¼%	35,500	30,000
Current portion of long-term debt	7,328	8,701
Less interim borrowings included in long-term debt	(35,000)	(25,000)
Total	$ 34,028	$ 38,951

	December 31	
	19x6	19x5
Notes Payable, Including Interim Borrowing in Long-Term Debt:		
Highest month-end borrowings	$ 72,250	$ 71,850
Average borrowings outstanding during the year	42,000	38,250
Weighted average interest on borrowings outstanding during the year	6⅛%	7⅜%
Unused bank credit at December 31 (also available for commercial paper support):		
Bank lines	11,800	37,750
Revolving credit	60,000	35,000
Standby credit at December 31 (available for commercial paper support)	—	20,000

Alfa utilizes commercial paper and bank lines of credit for its daily cash requirements. The Company intends to refinance certain short-term borrowings by issuance of the additional $35,000 of long-term notes described below. Accordingly, this amount has been classified as long-term.

In connection with its bank lines of credit Alfa has informally agreed to maintain average compensating balances based on available lines of credit. Such balances averaged about $6,000 during 19x6 and $7,000 during 19x5.

	December 31	
	19x6	19x5
Long-Term Debt—Less Current Portion Notes and mortgage loans:		
5% Notes due 19x8–19y2	$ 11,803	$ 13,503
7½% Notes due 19x8–19z2	22,500	22,500
8⅜% Notes due 19x8–19z3	48,750	48,750
8¾% Notes due 19x9–19y4	10,000	10,000
9½% Notes due 19y1–19z6	40,000	—
Mortgage loans average rate 7½% and 7%, due 19x8–2004	13,860	15,884
Interim borrowings to be refinanced by long-term loan	35,000	25,000
Other, average rate 8%, due 19x8–19z7	12,955	8,967
Total	194,868	144,604
Convertible subordinated debentures		
5% due 19y9	15,086	15,086
5¼% due 19z4	35,000	35,000
Total	50,086	50,086
Total	$244,954	$194,690

Annual maturities of long-term debt in the next five years are as follows:

19x7	$ 7,328
19x8	7,380
19x9	10,571
19y0	10,211
19y1	15,298

Under the revolving credit agreement with certain banks, Alfa may borrow up to $60,000 and may convert any such loans outstanding prior to September 3, 19x7 into five-year term loans with interest at ½% above prime rate.

On June 22, 19x6, Alfa issued $40,000 of its 9½% notes and agreed to issue an additional $35,000 on or about February 1, 19x7. These notes are due on July 1, 19z6, with annual installments of $4,690 required from July 1, 19y1.

95 **9. Capital Stock:** Changes in outstanding capital stock during 19x6 and 19x5 are summarized as follows:

	Increase (Decrease)			
	19x6		19x5	
	Shares	*Amount*	*Shares*	*Amount*
Preferred Series B				
Conversions to common	(14)	$ —	—	$ —
Common:				
Acquisition of businesses	480,000	$ 50	283,841	$ 1,273
Stock options exercised:				
Previously unissued shares	—	—	1,876	25
Treasury shares (option price lower than cost)	—	—	1,999	(48)
Stock performance unit plan	32	—	21	—
Preferred stock conversions	8	—	—	—
Total	480,040	$ 50	287,737	$ 1,250

Shares of common stock were reserved as follows:

	December 31	
	19x6	*19x5*
Outstanding stock options	98,721	133,835
Future stock option grants	113,879	138,129
Conversion of 19y9 debentures (initial conversion price $35.7143)	422,698	422,698
Conversion of 19z4 debentures (initial conversion price $43.67)	801,465	801,465
Conversion of $2.50 cumulative convertible preferred stock (1.2 for 1) (redeemable at $40 per share)	45,691	45,691
Conversion of Series B $1.00 cumulative convertible preferred stock (.5897 for 1) (redeemable at $25 per share) ..	546,834	546,842
Total	2,029,288	2,088,660

10. Earnings Per Share: The calculation of primary and fully diluted earnings per share follows (shares in thousands):

	Year ended December 31				
	19x6	19x5	19x4	19x3	19x2
Primary earnings per share:					
Average number of common shares outstanding during year	**11,724**	11,240	10,914	10,850	10,785
Average number of preferred shares outstanding during year converted into equivalent common shares:					
$2.50 series	—	46	46	49	66
Series B	—	547	547	548	551
Average number of dilutive stock options outstanding during year, less common shares which could be purchased from proceeds on exercise	**2**	4	4	13	70
Total average number of primary shares	**11,726**	11,837	11,511	11,460	11,472
Net income (19x6 after preferred dividends)	**$18,117**	$20,089	$56,843	$26,558	$24,296
Primary earnings per share	**$ 1.55**	$ 1.70	$ 4.94	$ 2.32	$ 2.12
Fully diluted earnings per share:					
Total average number of primary shares	**11,726**	11,837	11,511	11,460	11,472
Average debentures outstanding during the year converted into equivalent common shares	**1,224**	1,224	1,224	1,224	1,224
Additional dilutive stock options	**—**	—	2	—	2
Total average number of fully diluted shares	**12,950**	13,061	12,737	12,684	12,698
Net income (19x6 after preferred dividends)	**$18,117**	$20,089	$56,843	$26,558	$24,296
Interest expense on debentures for year, less applicable income taxes	**1,284**	1,245	1,265	1,297	1,296
Adjusted net income	**$19,401**	$21,334	$58,108	$27,855	$25,592
Fully diluted earnings per share	**$ 1.50**	$ 1.64	$ 4.56	$ 2.20	$ 2.02

11. Leased Properties: Alfa operates in various leased facilities which are not included in its balance sheet. Most of the major leases provide for renewal options and some provide for minimum rentals plus additional payments based on revenues or profits. Rent expense is summarized as follows:

71

	19x6	19x5	19x4	19x3	19x2
Financing leases:					
Minimum and fixed	$16,050	$14,116	$11,489	$ 9,359	$ 7,628
Additional	2,716	2,170	1,754	2,179	1,479
Other leases over one year:					
Minimum and fixed	11,866	10,120	10,850	9,407	8,261
Additional	9,128	9,680	12,622*	5,699	4,120
Property taxes, insurance and other charges on above leases	3,986	3,455	3,110	2,772	3,772
Short-term leases	3,529	2,992	3,758	2,450	3,439
Total	$47,275	$42,533	$43,583	$31,866	$28,699

* Increase principally due to percentage rental on land leased for sugar operations

Financing leases include those which cover 75% or more of the economic life of the property or have terms which assure the lessor full recovery of the fair market value of the property plus a reasonable return. If financing leases had been capitalized and expenses included interest and depreciation over the lease terms instead of fixed rents, Alfa's consolidated net income would have been reduced by $1,900 for 19x6, $1,600 for 19x5, $1,210 for 19x4, $882 for 19x3 and $766 for 19x2.

[98] Minimum rental commitments and the present value of lease obligations with remaining terms of one year or more at December 31, 19x6 follow:

	Financing	Other	Total
Minimum rental commitments:			
Year ending December 31:			
19x7	$ 16,361	$ 11,762	$ 28,123
19x8	16,159	11,521	27,680
19x9	16,349	10,875	27,224
19y0	16,098	10,324	26,422
19y1	15,918	9,537	25,455
Five years ending December 31:			
19y6	76,819	40,393	117,212
19z1	71,691	29,115	100,846
19z6	67,673	16,024	83,697
19z7 and thereafter (in total)	137,025	10,358	147,383
Total	$434,093	$149,949	$584,042

[99]

	Financing	Other	Total
By major categories of properties:			
Land	$ 18,867	$ 52,602	$ 71,469
Buildings	408,475	97,112	505,587
Machinery and equipment	6,751	235	6,986
Total	$434,093	$149,949	$584,042
Present value of minimum rental commitments:			
Land	$ 5,038	$ 23,920	$ 28,958
Buildings	157,213	55,916	213,129
Machinery and equipment	4,959	41	5,000
Total	$167,210	$ 79,877	$247,087
Discount rates:			
Range	3.1-12.0%	3.4-10.4%	3.1-12.0%
Average	8.0%	7.9%	8.0%

100

12. Contingent Liabilities: Contingent liabilities of the Company at December 31, 19x6 included a guaranty of a $8,960 mortgage loan of the Waikiki Beachcomber, a 50% joint venture which owns a 500-room hotel operated by Alfa (this loan is also guaranteed by UAL, Inc., a corporation with substantial net worth) and guarantees of loans totaling $38,450 including nonconsolidated subsidiaries of $25,640.

In December 19x4, C and H was named as one of several defendants, including five other sugar refiners, for alleged participation in regional conspiracies to fix refined sugar prices and to restrain the sale of refined sugar in violation of the Sherman Anti-

trust Act. A proposed settlement of the above litigation made in 19x5 is expected to be approved by most of the private claimants. In providing for the settlement, C and H charged each member's allocated capital in C and H in proportion to their respective sugar production during the years covered by the litigation. Alfa's portion of the settlement, net of applicable income taxes, was $429 for 19x4, $462 for 19x3, $447 for 19x2 and $1,232 for prior years.

Alfa is involved in various matters of litigation and other claims. Based on opinions of legal counsel, management is of the opinion that Alfa's liability, if any, when ultimately determined will not have a material adverse effect on Alfa's financial statements.

101

13. Nonconsolidated Finance Subsidiaries: A condensed balance sheet and related condensed statement of income of Alfa Financial, Inc., and subsidiaries follow:

CONDENSED BALANCE SHEET

	December 31	
	19x6	19x5
Assets:		
Cash	$ 6,880	$ 10,759
Receivables, less unearned finance charges and allowance for losses	223,937	219,635
Real property developments	20,590	23,578
Other assets	23,698	27,987
Total	$275,105	$281,959
Liabilities:		
Notes payable banks*—average rate 6¼% and 7¼%	$ 97,809	$109,269
Notes payable other—average rate 6½% and 8¼%	22,440	15,646
Investment certificates—average rate 7% and 8%	81,609	92,083
Accounts payable, income taxes and other liabilities	10,175	12,579
Long-term debt—average rate 8¾% and 8¼%	30,629	21,310
Stockholder's Equity (including undistributed earnings of $19,263 and $17,892; $12,561 available for dividends*)	32,443	31,072
Total	$275,105	$281,959

102

CONDENSED STATEMENT OF INCOME

103

	19x6	19x5
Revenues	$ 43,860	$ 41,284
Costs and Expenses:		
Interest	15,917	17,990
Other costs and expenses	25,526	18,843
Income taxes	1,046	2,122
Net Income	$ 1,371	$ 2,329

* In connection with certain borrowings, Alfa, Inc., has agreed to maintain Alfa Financial, Inc.'s net worth and working capital at certain minimum levels. During 19x6 and 19x5, these levels were adequate by a reasonable margin.

104

	December 31	
Bank borrowing arrangements of Alfa Financial, Inc.:	19x6	19x5
Highest month-end borrowings	$116,400	$127,000
Average borrowings outstanding during the year	87,000	108,600
Weighted average interest rate on borrowings outstanding during the year	7%	8%
Unused short-term bank credit lines at December 31	6,200	50,700

Note. The above does not include Alfa, Inc.'s investment in Alfa Credit Corporation (see Note 3).

Notes to Financial Statements *(continued)*

In connection with its bank lines of credit Alfa Financial Inc., has informally agreed to maintain average compensating balances based on available lines of credit. Such balances averaged about $20,000 during 19x6 and $22,000 during 19x5.

14. Pension and Compensation Plans: Alfa has various formal pension plans which cover most full-time employees and provide benefits based on length of service and compensation levels. Pension expense, including amortization of prior service costs, totaled $7,500, $7,000, $6,600, $5,100, and $3,300 for the years ended December 31, 19x6 through 19x2, respectively. Based on most recent actuarial valuations (December 31, 19x5) vested benefits exceeded the fair value of plan assets by $19,300 and unfunded prior service costs totaled $32,500. Alfa's pension plans substan-

During 19x6, subsidiaries of Alfa Financial, Inc., made construction loans totaling $13,100 to affiliated real property development joint ventures. Interest and loan fees are charged consistent with market conditions at the time such loans are originated.

tially meet the requirements of the Employee Retirement Income Security Act of 1974 and compliance with the Act is not expected to have a substantial effect on future pension expense.

Under Alfa's stock option plans, options to purchase up to 113,879 shares of common stock at December 31, 19x6 were available for future grants at not less than market prices. Options become exercisable in increments during periods from one to five years subsequent to date of grant. No stock options were granted during 19x6 and 19x5. Other stock option information is summarized as follows:

	Number of shares	Option price			Market price at date of transaction		
		Per share			Per share		
		From	To	Total	From	To	Total
Options outstanding December 31:							
19x6	98,721	$12.63	$41.00	$2,742			
19x5	133,835	12.63	41.00	3,628			
Options exercisable December 31:							
19x6	66,921	12.63	41.00	1,802	$13.25	$25.75	$1,194
19x5	66,334	12.63	41.00	1,737	13.25	38.75	1,218
Options which became exercisable:							
19x6	30,124	12.63	41.00	806	13.25	19.38	465
19x5	35,182	12.63	41.00	931	13.88	20.50	604
Options exercised:							
19x6	—	—	—	—	—	—	—
19x5	3,875	12.63	16.25	50	18.13	20.25	71

Alfa has granted certain officers and key employees units under its stock performance unit plan. Each unit has an assigned value equal to the market value of one share of Alfa's common stock on the award date. The benefits are payable (in cash, common stock or a combination of both) in 25% annual increments based on the excess (if any) of the market price of Alfa's common stock on the payment date over the market price on the award date, adjusted for cash dividends between the award and payment dates.

At December 31, 19x6, units outstanding totaled 105,606 at an average value per unit of $16.44. Expenses under this plan totaled $15 for 19x6, $19 for 19x5, $75 for 19x4 and $191 for 19x2 (there was no expense in 19x3).

Prior to 19x5, certain officers participated in an executive bonus plan which was discontinued when base salaries were increased to include the bonus. Such bonuses totaled $397 for 19x4, $342 for 19x3 and $348 for 19x2.

Exhibit 2B-6

106

ALFA, INC., AND CONSOLIDATED SUBSIDIARIES
Five-Year Summary of Revenues
and Contributions of Operating Groups

(All Dollars Reported in Thousands)

	19x6		19x5		19x4		19x3		19x2	
	Amount	%	Amount	%	Amount	%	Amount	%	Amount	%
Revenues:										
Food processing	$ 304,249	24%	$ 278,569	25%	$ 350,366	30%	$172,845	20%	$134,934	20%
Food[2]	215,118	17	138,190	12	128,520	11	95,674	11	72,139	11
Agriculture[2]	89,131	7	140,379	13	221,846	19	77,171	9	62,795	9
Merchandising	786,354	63	717,837	63	657,250	57	573,449	65	430,409	62
Retail[2]	335,296	27	309,337	27	283,154	25	276,857	31	241,389	35
Distribution	451,058	36	408,500	36	374,096	32	296,592	34	189,020	27
Hospitality	141,865	11	119,122	10	110,060	10	94,690	11	85,681	12
Asset Management[3]	17,770	2	17,672	2	29,027	3	34,045	4	20,055	3
Corporate	850	—	617	—	585	—	636	—	505	—
Other[4]	—	—	—	—	—	—	4,731	—	23,374	3
Total	$1,251,088	100%	$1,133,817	100%	$1,147,288	100%	$880,396	100%	$694,958	100%
Contribution:[1]										
Food processing	$ 12,393	23%	$ 57,888	60%	$ 135,546	85%	$ 27,555	41%	$ 11,847	22%
Food[2]	22,017	40	15,277	16	5,749	4	14,323	21	8,403	16
Agriculture[2]	(9,624)	(17)	42,611	44	129,797	81	13,232	20	3,444	6
Merchandising	20,592	38	21,080	21	17,194	11	10,234	15	23,714	44
Retail[2]	8,453	16	7,024	7	3,288	2	129	—	15,992	30
Distribution	12,139	22	14,056	14	13,906	9	10,105	15	7,722	14
Hospitality	13,961	25	9,554	10	8,091	5	6,852	10	6,877	13
Asset Management[2&3]	7,749	14	8,580	9	2,425	1	21,535	32	15,280	29
Other[4]	—	—	—	—	(3,205)	(2)	1,277	2	(4,129)	(8)
Total	54,695	100%	97,102	100%	160,051	100%	67,453	100%	53,589	100%

107

Less Unallocated Expenses:

Corporate—net	8,420	8,109	7,119	5,531	5,799
Interest expense	18,440	16,319	21,787	17,572	10,629
Income taxes[1]	8,696	34,178	66,977	16,835	13,522
Income From Continuing Operations	19,139	38,496	64,168	27,515	23,639
Income (Loss) From Discontinued Operations	—	(1,000)	(7,325)	(957)	657
Income Before Cumulative Effect Of Accounting Changes	19,139	37,496	56,843	26,558	24,296
Cumulative Effect Of Accounting Changes ($36,647, less income taxes of $19,240)	—	(17,407)	—	—	—
Net Income	$ 19,139	$ 20,089	$ 56,843	$ 26,558	$ 24,296
Average Net Assets Employed[5]	$ 625,845	$ 592,934	$ 592,520	$524,983	$438,977
Market Data:					
Common stock price range	19⅞-13	22-13¾	21⅜-12⅝	31⅜-11	39¾-25
Price-earnings ratio range[6]	13-8	13-8	4-3	14-5	19-12
Book value per share at year-end	$ 26.13	$ 26.42	$ 26.16	$ 21.96	$ 20.36
Pro Forma Amounts Assuming The New Accounting Method For Sugar Profits Is Applied Retroactively:					
Agriculture: Revenues	$ —	$ 140,379	$ 189,495	$ 74,606	$ —
Contribution	$ —	$ 42,611	$ 97,446	$ 10,667	$ —

[1] Income before unallocated corporate expenses, interest expense and income taxes. Income taxes include those of nonconsolidated finance subsidiaries and $50 in 19x6 and $944 credit in 19x5 for Alfa Credit Corporation.

[2] See Notes 2 and 3 to Financial Statements for accounting changes and unusual items.

[3] Asset Management includes financial service operations which are conducted through nonconsolidated subsidiaries and, for such operations, contribution is after interest expense but before unallocated corporate expenses and income taxes. Revenues of these subsidiaries are not included because equity and net income is reported separately in Alfa's financial statements. Includes Alfa, Inc.'s temporary investment in Alfa Credit Corporation which had losses of $210 in 19x6, $1,420 in 19x5, and $4,565 in 19x4. See Notes 3 and 13 to Financial Statements.

[4] Includes RhodesWAY gain on sale of Construction Materials Hawaii, Inc., surplus property and accounting change for deferred preopening expenses. (See Notes 2 and 3 to Financial Statements.)

[5] 13-month average of total assets (excluding cash) less accounts payable, accrued expenses and other deferred credits.

[6] Common stock price range divided by primary earnings per share.

Exhibit 2B–7

ALFA, INC., AND CONSOLIDATED SUBSIDIARIES
Ten-Year Financial Summary

(All Dollars and Shares Reported in Thousands)

	19x6	19x5	19x4	19x3	19x2	19x1	19x0	19w9	19w8	19w7
Revenues originally reported*	$1,251,088	$1,133,817	$1,147,288	$949,151	$749,222	$574,116	$406,725	$303,326	$205,321	$145,881
Add pooled businesses	—	—					50,317	45,586	50,008	80,960
Less discontinued operations	—	—	—	(68,755)	(54,264)	—	—	—	—	—
Revenues as restated	1,251,088	1,133,817	1,147,288	880,396	694,958	574,116	457,042	348,912	255,329	226,841
Income from continuing operations	19,139	38,496	64,168	27,515	23,639	19,134	16,550	13,781	10,873	6,906
Extraordinary items and discontinued operations	—	(18,407)	(7,325)	(957)	657	—	—	213	—	1,835
Net income	19,139	20,089	56,843	26,558	24,296	19,134	16,550	13,994	10,873	8,741
Earnings per share:										
Primary**										
Income from continuing operations	1.55	3.25	5.57	2.40	2.06	1.88	1.74	1.59	1.28	.83
Net income	1.55	1.70	4.94	2.32	2.12	1.88	1.74	1.62	1.28	1.05
Fully diluted**—Net income	1.50	1.64	4.56	2.20	2.02	1.79	1.65	1.55	1.28	1.05
Cash dividends per common share**	1.00	1.00	.70	.64	.60	.58	.53	.53	.49	.47

Financial position—as
originally reported:

Working capital	221,408	174,235	189,801	149,670	103,425	101,098	69,165	72,722	43,842	38,443
Property—net	273,645	253,580	241,122	226,355	217,852	179,262	148,436	112,270	78,195	74,332
Total assets	801,672	738,469	749,824	659,246	559,940	451,925	347,171	290,506	176,464	160,564
Long-term debt	244,954	194,690	202,459	197,394	155,707	130,224	128,246	96,871	35,974	40,145
Stockholders' equity	331,080	321,713	306,765	259,354	240,308	212,457	144,486	127,632	102,108	82,052
Return on year-end stockholders' equity	5.8%	6.2%	18.2%	10.4%	10.3%	9.2%	9.8%	9.0%	8.1%	7.6%
Common shares outstanding at end of year	11,724	11,244	10,956	10,852	10,837	10,308	5,071	4,777	4,276	2,466

* Includes changes in Alfa's equity in California and Hawaiian Sugar Co. and excludes equity in net income of nonconsolidated finance subsidiaries.
** Adjusted for stock dividends and splits.

[109]

Auditors' Opinion

To the Stockholders and Directors of Alfa, Inc.:

We have examined the balance sheet of Alfa, Inc. and its consolidated subsidiaries as of December 31, 19x6 and the related statements of income, earnings reinvested, and changes in financial position for the five years ended December 31, 19x6. Our examination was made in accordance with generally accepted auditing standards, and accordingly included such tests of the accounting records and such other auditing procedures as we considered necessary in the circumstances.

In our opinion, such financial statements present fairly the financial position of Alfa, Inc., and its consolidated subsidiaries at December 31, 19x6 and 19x5 and the results of their operations and the changes in their financial position for the five years ended December 31, 19x6, in conformity with generally accepted accounting principles consistently applied during the period except for the changes in accounting methods in 19x5 and 19x4, with which we concur, described in Note 2 to the financial statements.

Simon, Pure & Co.
Honolulu, Hawaii
January 19, 19x7

ALFA, INC., AND CONSOLIDATED SUBSIDIARIES
Five-Year Summary of Revenues
and Contributions of Operating Groups

(All Dollars Reported in Thousands)

	19x6		19x5		19x4		19x3		19x2	
	Amount	%	Amount	%	Amount	%	Amount	%	Amount	%
Revenues:										
Food processing	$ 304,249	24%	$ 278,569	25%	$ 350,366	30%	$172,845	20%	$134,934	20%
Food	215,118	17	138,190	12	128,520	11	95,674	11	72,139	11
Agriculture	89,131	7	140,379	13	221,846	19	77,171	9	62,795	9
Merchandising	786,354	63	717,837	63	657,250	57	573,449	65	430,409	62
Retail	335,296	27	309,337	27	283,154	25	276,857	31	241,389	35
Distribution	451,058	36	408,500	36	374,096	32	296,592	34	189,020	27
Hospitality	141,865	11	119,122	10	110,060	10	94,690	11	85,681	12
Asset Management	17,770	2	17,672	2	29,027	3	34,045	4	20,055	3
Corporate	850	—	617	—	585	—	636	—	505	—
Other	—	—	—	—	—	—	4,731	—	23,374	3
Total	$1,251,088	100%	$1,133,817	100%	$1,147,288	100%	$880,396	100%	$694,958	100%
Contribution:										
Food processing	$ 12,393	23%	$ 57,888	60%	$ 135,546	85%	$ 27,555	41%	$ 11,847	22%
Food	22,017	40	15,277	16	5,749	4	14,323	21	8,403	16
Agriculture	(9,624)	(17)	42,611	44	129,797	81	13,232	20	3,444	6
Merchandising	20,592	38	21,080	21	17,194	11	10,234	15	23,714	44
Retail	8,453	16	7,024	7	3,288	2	129	—	15,992	30
Distribution	12,139	22	14,056	14	13,906	9	10,105	15	7,722	14
Hospitality	13,961	25	9,554	10	8,091	5	6,852	10	6,877	13
Asset Management	7,749	14	8,580	9	2,425	1	21,535	32	15,280	29
Other	—	—	—	—	(3,205)	(2)	1,277	2	(4,129)	(8)
Total	54,695	100%	97,102	100%	160,051	100%	67,453	100%	53,589	100%

Less Unallocated Expenses:

Corporate—net	**8,420**	8,109	7,119	5,531	5,799
Interest expense	**18,440**	16,319	21,787	17,572	10,629
Income taxes	**8,696**	34,178	66,977	16,835	13,522
Income From Continuing Operations	**19,139**	38,496	64,168	27,515	23,639
Income (Loss) From Discontinued Operations	—	(1,000)	(7,325)	(957)	657
Income Before Cumulative Effect Of Accounting Changes	**19,139**	37,496	56,843	26,558	24,296
Cumulative Effect Of Accounting Change ($36,647, less income taxes of $19,240)	—	(17,407)	—	—	—
Net Income	**$ 19,139**	$ 20,089	$ 56,843	$ 26,558	$ 24,296

Pro Forma Amounts Assuming The New Accounting Method For Sugar Profits Is Applied Retroactively:

Agriculture: Revenues	$ —	$ 140,379	$ 189,495	$ 72,875	$ —
Contribution	$ —	$ 42,611	$ 97,446	$ 8,936	$ —

Exhibit 2B–9

ALFA, INC.
Analysis of the Results of Operations
Common-Size Income Statement

	19x6	19x5	19x4	19x3	19x2
Revenues	100.00%	100.00%	100.00%	100.00%	100.00%
Costs and expenses:					
Cost of sales	67.14%	64.40%	60.23%	64.68%	63.58%
Selling, general, and administrative	27.42	26.19	24.87	27.14	28.30
Depreciation and amortization	1.94	1.87	1.92	1.93	2.07
Interest	1.48	1.44	2.18	2.14	1.60
Interest capitalized	(.01)	—	(.28)	(.15)	(.07)
Total	97.97%	93.90%	88.92%	95.74%	95.48%
Income before taxes	2.03%	6.10%	11.08%	4.26%	4.52%
Income taxes	(.61)	(2.91)	(5.67)	(1.54)	(1.56)
Income from consolidated continuing operations	1.42%	3.19%	5.41%	2.72%	2.96%
Net income of nonconsolidated finance subsidiaries	.11	.21	.18	.41	.45
Income from continuing operations	1.53%	3.40%	5.59%	3.13%	3.41%
Income (loss) from discontinued operations	—	(.09)	(.64)	(.11)	.09
Income before cumulative effect on prior years of accounting changes	1.53%	3.31%	4.95%	3.02%	3.50%
Cumulative effect on prior years of accounting changes	—	(1.54)	—	—	—
Net income	1.53%	1.77%	4.95%	3.02%	3.5%

Exhibit 2B–10

ALFA, INC.
Analysis of the Results of Operations
Trend Analysis (assuming 19x2 base year)

	19x6	19x5	19x4	19x3	19x2
Revenues	180	163	165	127	100
Costs and expenses:					
Cost of sales	190	165	156	129	100
Selling, general, and					
administrative	174	151	145	122	100
Depreciation and amortization	168	147	153	118	100
Interest	167	147	226	170	100
Interest capitalized	14	—	706	278	100
Total	185	160	154	127	100
Income before income taxes	81	220	405	120	100
Income taxes	70	304	599	126	100
Income from consolidated continuing					
operations	86	176	302	116	100
Net income of nonconsolidated					
subsidiaries	44	75	67	117	100
Income from continuing operations	81	163	271	116	100
Income (loss) from discontinued					
operations	—	—	—	—	—
Income before cumulative effect					
on prior years of accounting					
changes	79	154	234	109	100
Cumulative effect on prior years					
of accounting changes	—	—	—	—	—
Net income	79	82	234	109	100

QUESTIONS

1. Compare the flow of the analyst's work in reconstructing business transactions to that of the accountant's work. How does such reconstruction of accounts contribute to the analysis of financial statements?

2. As a potential investor in a common stock, what information would you seek? How do you get such information?

3. The president of your client company approached you, the financial officer of a local bank, for a substantial loan. What could you do?

4. What, in broad categories, are some of the approaches utilized by the financial analyst in diagnosing the financial health of a business?

5. How useful is a comparative financial analysis? How do you make useful comparison?

6. What are some of the precautions required of a financial analyst in his comparative analytical work?

7. Give four broad categories of analysis tools.

8. Is the trend of the past a good predictor of the future? Give reasons for your argument.

9. Which is the better indicator of significant change—the absolute amount of change or the change in percentage? Why?

10. What conditions would prevent the computation of a valid percentage change? Give an example.

11. What are some of the criteria to be used in picking out a base year in an index number comparative analysis?

12. What information can be obtained from trend analysis?

13. What is a common-size financial statement? How do you prepare one?

14. What does a common-size financial statement tell about an enterprise?

15. Do all ratios have significance? Explain.

16. What are some of the limitations of ratio analysis?

17. Give five ratios that can be prepared by use of balance sheet figures only.

18. Give five ratios that can be prepared by use of income statement data only.

19. Give seven ratios that require data from both the balance sheet and the income statement.

20. Give four examples of special-purpose analytical tools commonly utilized by the financial analyst.

21. What are the steps generally taken by the financial analyst in his work? What do these steps achieve?

22. Identify and explain two significant limitations associated with ratio analysis of financial statements. (CFA)

23. What are some of the principal uses of computers in investment analysis? (CFA)

24. What are the most important limitations or disadvantages to the application of computers to security analysis? (CFA)

3

Analysis of short-term liquidity

SIGNIFICANCE OF SHORT-TERM LIQUIDITY

The short-term liquidity of an enterprise is measured by the degree to which it can meet its short-term obligations. Liquidity implies the ready ability to convert assets into cash or to obtain cash. The short term is conventionally viewed as a time span up to a year, although it is sometimes also identified with the normal operating cycle of a business, that is, the time span encompassing the buying-producing-selling and collecting cycle of an enterprise.

The importance of short-term liquidity can best be gauged by examining the repercussions that stem from a lack of ability to meet short-term obligations.

Liquidity is a matter of degree. A lack of liquidity may mean that the enterprise is unable to avail itself of favorable discounts and is unable to take advantage of profitable business opportunities as they arise. At this stage, a lack of liquidity implies a lack of freedom of choice as well as constraints on management's freedom of movement.

A more serious lack of liquidity means that the enterprise is unable to pay its current debts and obligations. This can lead to the forced sale of long-term investments and assets and, in its most severe form, to insolvency and bankruptcy.

To the owners of an enterprise, a lack of liquidity can mean reduced profitability and opportunity or it may mean loss of control and partial or total loss of the capital investment. In the case of owners with unlimited liability, the loss can extend beyond the original investment.

To creditors of the enterprise, a lack of liquidity can mean delay in collection of interest and principal due them or it can mean the partial or total loss of the amounts due them.

Customers as well as suppliers of goods and services to an enterprise can also be affected by its short-term financial condition. Such effects may take the form of inability of the enterprise to perform under contracts and the loss of supplier relationships.

From the above description of the significance of short-term liquidity it can be readily appreciated why the measures of such liquidity have been accorded great importance. For, if an enterprise cannot meet its current obligations as they become due, its continued existence becomes doubtful and that relegates all other measures of performance to secondary importance if not to irrelevance. In terms of the framework of objectives discussed in Chapter 1, the evaluation of short-term liquidity is concerned with the assessment of the unsystematic risk of the enterprise.

While accounting determinations are made on the assumption of indefinite continuity of the enterprise, the financial analyst must always submit the validity of such assumption to the critical test of the enterprise's liquidity and solvency.

One of the most widely used measures of liquidity is working capital. In addition to its importance as a pool of liquid assets that provides a safety cushion to creditors, net working capital is also important because it provides a liquid reserve with which to meet contingencies and the ever-present uncertainty regarding an enterprise's ability to balance the outflow of funds with an adequate inflow of funds.

WORKING CAPITAL

The basic concept of working capital is relatively simple. It is the excess of current assets over current liabilities. That excess is sometimes referred to as *net working capital* because some businessmen consider current assets as working capital. A working capital deficiency exists when current liabilities exceed current assets.

The importance attached by credit grantors, investors, and others to working capital as a measure of liquidity and solvency has caused some enterprises, desiring to present their current condition in the most favorable light, to stretch to the limit the definition of what constitutes a current asset and a current liability. For this reason, the analyst must use his own judgment in evaluating the proper classification of items included in working capital.

Current assets

Current assets include cash and other assets that are reasonably expected to be realized in cash or sold or consumed during the normal operating cycle of the business or within one year if the operating cycle is shorter than one year. Current liabilities include those expected to be satisfied by either the use of assets classified as current in the same balance sheet or the creation of other current liabilities, or those expected to be satisfied within a relatively short period of time, usually one year. [APB *Statement 4*, par. 198.]

The general rule about the ability to convert current assets into cash within a year is subject to important qualifications. The most important qualification relates to the operating cycle. The operating cycle comprises the average time span intervening between the acquisition of materials and services entering the production or trading process to the final realization in cash of the proceeds from the sale of the enterprise's products. This time span can be quite extended in industries that require a long inventory holding period (e.g., tobacco, distillery, and lumber) or those that sell on the installment plan. Whenever no clearly defined operating cycle is evident, the arbitrary one-year rule continues to prevail.

The most common categories of current assets are:

1. Cash.
2. Cash equivalents (i.e., temporary investments).
3. Accounts and notes receivable.
4. Inventories.
5. Prepaid expenses.

Cash is, of course, the ultimate measure of a current asset since current liabilities are paid off in cash. However, earmarked cash held for specific purposes, such as plant expansion, should not be considered as current. Compensating balances under bank loan agreements cannot, in most cases, be regarded as "free" cash. SEC FRR No. 1 Sec. 203 requires the disclosure of compensating balance arrangements with the lending banks as well as the segregation of such balances.

Cash equivalents represent temporary investments of cash in excess of current requirements made for the purpose of earning a return on these funds.

The analyst must be alert to the valuation of such investments. Equity investments are now accounted for in accordance with *SFAS 12.* Debt securities may still be carried above market if management views a decline as merely "temporary" in nature. Similarly, the "cash equivalent" nature of securities investments may sometimes be stretched quite far.

The mere ability to convert an asset to cash is not the sole determinant of its current nature. It is the intention and normal practice that govern. Intention is, however, not always enough. Thus, the cost of fixed assets that are intended for sale should be included in current assets only if the enterprise has a contractual commitment from a buyer to purchase the asset at a given price within the following year or the following operating cycle.

An example where the above principle was not followed is found in the 1970 annual report of International Industries. In this report, the company carries as a current asset $37.8 million in "Real estate held for sale." A related footnote explains that "the company intends to sell this real estate during the ensuing operating cycle substantially at cost under sale-and-lease-back agreements, however, prevailing economic conditions may affect its ability to do so."

This is an obvious attempt to present a current position superior to the one the company can justifiably claim. Without the inclusion of real estate, the company's current ratio would have dropped to 1.1 (with working capital at about $3 million) as against a current ratio, based on reported figures, of 1.8 and a working capital of $40.3 million.

This reinforces the ever-recurring message in this text that the analyst cannot rely on adherence to rules or accepted principles of preparation of financial statements, but instead must exercise eternal vigilance in his use of ratios and all other analytical measures that are based on such statements. If anything, attempts by managements to stretch the rules in order to present a situation as better than it really is should serve as an added warning of potential trouble and risk.

Accounts receivable, net of provisions for uncollectible accounts, are current unless they represent receivables for sales, not in the ordinary course of business, which are due after one year. Installment receivables from customary sales usually fall within the operating cycle of the enterprise.

The financial analyst must continuously be alert to the valuation as well as validity of receivables, particularly in cases such as those where "sales" are made on consignment or are subject to the right of return.

Receivables from affiliated companies or from officers and employees can be considered current only if they are collectible in the ordinary course of business within a year or, in the case of installment sales, within the operating cycle.

Inventories are considered current assets except in cases where they are in excess of current requirements. Such excess inventories, which should be shown as noncurrent, must be distinguished from inventories, such as tobacco, which require a long aging cycle. The variations in practice in this area are considerable, as the following illustrations will show, and should be carefully scrutinized by the analyst.

ILLUSTRATION 1. National Fuel Gas Company (prospectus dated July 23, 1969) shows a current as well as a noncurrent portion of gas stored underground and explains this as follows:

"Included in property, plant, and equipment as gas stored underground—noncurrent is $18,825,232 at April 30, 1969, the cost of the volume of gas required to maintain pressure levels for normal operating purposes at the low point of the storage cycle. The portion of gas in underground storage included in current assets does not exceed estimated withdrawals during the succeeding two years."

ILLUSTRATION 2. Some trucking concerns include the tires on their trucks as current assets, presumably on the theory that they will be used up during the normal operating cycle.

The analyst must pay particular attention to inventory valuation. Thus, for example, the inclusion of inventories at LIFO can result in a significant understatement of working capital.

Prepaid expenses are considered current, not because they can be converted into cash but rather because they represent advance payments for services and supplies that would otherwise require the current outlay of cash.

Current liabilities

Current liabilities are obligations that would, generally, require the use of current assets for their discharge or, alternatively, the creation of other current liabilities. The following are current liabilities most commonly found in practice:

1. Accounts payable.
2. Notes payable.
3. Short-term bank and other loans.
4. Tax and other expense accruals.
5. Current portion of long-term debt.

The foregoing current liability categories are usually clear and do not require further elaboration. However, as is the case with current assets, the analyst cannot assume that they will always be properly classified for his purposes. Thus, for example, current practice sanctions the presentation as noncurrent of current obligations that are expected to be refunded. The degree of assurance of the subsequent refunding is mostly an open question that in the case of adverse developments may well be resolved negatively as far as the enterprise is concerned.

SEC FRR No. 1 Sec. 203 has expanded significantly the disclosure requirements regarding short-term bank and commercial paper borrowing. *SFAS 6* established criteria for the balance sheet classification of short-term obligations that are expected to be refinanced.

The analyst must also be alert to the possibility of presentations designed to present the working capital in a better light than warranted by circumstances.

ILLUSTRATION 3. Penn Central Company excluded the current maturities of long-term debt from the current liability category and included it in the "long-term debt" section of the balance sheet. In 1969, this treatment resulted in an excess of current assets over current liabilities of $21 million, whereas the inclusion of current debt maturities among current liabilities would have resulted in a working capital *deficit* of $207 million. (The subsequent financial collapse of this enterprise is now a well-known event.)

The analyst must also ascertain whether all obligations, regarding which there is a reasonably high probability that they will have to be met, have been included as current liabilities in computing an effective working capital figure. Two examples of such obligations follow:

1. The obligation of an enterprise for notes discounted with a bank where the bank has full recourse in the event the note is not paid when due

is generally considered a contingent liability. However, the likelihood of the contingency materializing must be considered in the computation of working capital. The same principle applies in case of loan guarantees.

2.   A contract for the construction or acquisition of long-term assets may call for substantial progress payments. Such obligations for payments are, for accounting purposes, considered as commitments rather than liabilities, and hence are not found among the latter. Nevertheless, when computing the excess of liquid assets over short-term obligations such commitments may have to be recognized.

Other problem areas in the definition of current assets and liabilities

An area that presented a problem of classification but that has now been settled in favor of consistency is that of deferred tax accounting. Thus, if an asset (e.g., installment accounts receivable) is classified as current, the related deferred tax arising from differences in treatment between book and tax return must be similarly classified.

Current deferred tax debits are no more true current assets than current deferred tax credits are real current liabilities. While these are the result of present generally accepted methods of accounting for taxes (now under review), the resulting debits do not necessarily represent expected means of payment nor do the resulting credits necessarily represent obligations currently due.

Many concerns that have fixed assets as the main "working assets," such as, for example, trucking concerns and some leasing companies, carry as current, prospective receipts from billings out of which their current equipment purchase obligations must be met. Such treatments, or the absence of any distinction between current and noncurrent on the balance sheet, as is the case with real estate companies, some contractors, banks, and insurance companies, are attempts by such concerns to convey to the reader their "special" financing and operating conditions that, they claim, make the current versus noncurrent distinction inapplicable and that have no parallel in the regular trading or industrial concern.

Some of these "special" circumstances may indeed be present, but they do not necessarily change the relationship existing between current obligations and the liquid funds available, or reasonably expected to become available, to meet them. It is to this relationship that the analyst, faced with the task of evaluating liquidity, must train his attention.

Working capital as a measure of liquidity

The popularity of working capital as a measure of liquidity and of short-term financial health is so widespread that it hardly needs documentation. Credit grantors compute the relationship between current assets and current liabilities; financial analysts measure the size of the working capital of enterprises they analyze; government agencies compute aggregates of working capital of corporations; and most published balance sheets distinguish between current and noncurrent assets and liabilities. Moreover, loan agreements and bond indentures often contain stipulations regarding the maintenance of minimum working capital levels.

The absolute amount of working capital has significance only when related to other variables such as sales, total assets, and so forth. It is at best of limited value for comparison purposes and for judging the adequacy of working capital. This can be illustrated as follows:

	Company A	Company B
Current assets	$300,000	$1,200,000
Current liabilities	100,000	1,000,000
Working capital	200,000	200,000

While both companies have an equal amount of working capital, a cursory comparison of the relationship of current assets to current liabilities suggests that Company A's current condition is superior to that of Company B.

CURRENT RATIO

The above conclusion is based on the ratio of current assets to current liabilities. It is 3:1 ($300,000/$100,000) for Company A and 1.2:1 ($1,200,000/$1,000,000) for Company B. It is this ratio that is accorded substantial importance in the assessment of an enterprise's current liquidity.

Some of the basic reasons for the widespread use of the current ratio as a measure of liquidity are obvious:

1. It measures the degree to which current assets cover current liabilities. The higher the amount of current assets in relation to current liabilities, the greater the assurance that these liabilities can be paid out of such assets.
2. The excess of current assets over current liabilities provides a buffer against losses that may be incurred in the disposition or liquidation of the current assets other than cash. The more substantial such a buffer is, the better for creditors. Thus, the current ratio measures the margin of safety available to cover any possible shrinkage in the value of current assets.
3. It measures the reserve of liquid funds in excess of current obligations that is available as a margin of safety against uncertainty and the random shocks to which the flows of funds in an enterprise are subject. Random shocks, such as strikes, extraordinary losses, and other uncertainties, can temporarily and unexpectedly stop or reduce the inflow of funds.

What is not so obvious, however, is the fact that the current ratio, as a measure of liquidity and short-term solvency, is subject to serious theoretical as well as practical shortcomings and limitations. Consequently, before we embark on a discussion of the uses of the current ratio and related measures of liquidity, these limitations must be thoroughly understood.

Limitations of the current ratio

The first step in our examination of the current ratio as a tool of liquidity and short-term solvency analysis is to examine the components that are normally included in the ratio shown in Exhibit 3–1.

Exhibit 3–1

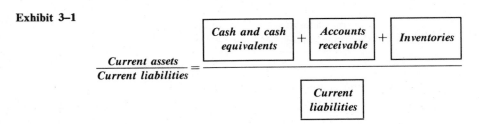

Disregarding, for purposes of this evaluation, prepaid expenses and similar unsubstantial items entering the computation of the current ratio, we are left with the above four major elements that make up this ratio.

Now, if we define liquidity as the ability to balance required cash outflows with adequate inflows, including an allowance for unexpected interruptions of inflows or increases in outflows, we must ask: Does the relationship of these four elements at a given point in time—

1. Measure and predict the pattern of future fund flows?
2. Measure the adequacy of future fund inflows in relation to outflows?

Unfortunately, the answer to these questions is mostly negative. The current ratio is a static or "stock" concept of what resources are available at a given moment in time to meet the obligations at that moment. The existing reservoir of net funds does not have a logical or causative relationship to the future funds that will flow through it. And yet it is the future flows that are the subject of our greatest interest in the assessment of liquidity. These flows depend importantly on elements *not* included in the ratio itself, such as sales, profits, and changes in business conditions. To elaborate, let us examine more closely the four elements of the ratio.

Cash and cash equivalents   The amount of cash held by a well-managed enterprise is in the nature of a precautionary reserve, intended to take care of short-term imbalances in cash flows. For example, in cases of a business downturn, sales may fall more rapidly than outlays for purchases and expenses. Since cash is a nonearning asset and cash equivalents are usually low-yielding securities, the investment in such assets is kept at a safe minimum. To conceive of this minimum balance as available for payment of current debts would require the dropping of the going-concern assumption underlying accounting statements. While the balance of cash has some relation to the existing level of activity, such a relationship is not very strong nor does it contain predictive implications regarding the future. In fact, some enterprises may use cash substitutes in the form of open lines of credit that, of course, do not enter at all into the computation of the current ratio.

The important link between cash and solvency in the minds of many is due to the well-known fact that a shortage of cash, more than any other factor, is the element that can clinch the insolvency of an enterprise.

Accounts receivable The major determinant of the level of accounts receivable is sales. The size of accounts receivable in relation to sales is governed by terms of trade and credit policy. Changes in receivables will correspond to changes in sales though not necessarily on a directly proportional basis.

When we look at accounts receivable as a source of cash, we must, except in the case of liquidation, recognize the revolving nature of the asset with the collection of one account replaced by the extension of fresh credit. Thus, the level of receivables per se is not an index to future net inflows of cash.

Inventories As is the case with accounts receivable, the main determinant of the size of inventories is the level of sales, or expected sales, rather than the level of current liabilities. Given that the level of sales is a measure of the level of demand then, scientific methods of inventory management (economic order quantities, safe stock levels, and reorder points) generally establish that inventory increments vary not in proportion to demand but vary rather with the *square root* of demand.

The relationship of inventories to sales is further accented by the fact that it is sales that is the one essential element that starts the conversion of inventories to cash. Moreover, the determination of future cash inflows through the sale of inventories is dependent on the profit margin that can be realized because inventories are generally stated at the lower of *cost* or market. The current ratio, while including inventories, gives no recognition to the sales level or to profit margin, both of which are important elements entering into the determination of future cash inflows.

Current liabilities The level of current liabilities, the safety of which the current ratio is intended to measure, is also largely determined by the level of sales.

Current liabilities are a source of funds in the same sense that receivables and inventories tie up funds. Since purchases, which give rise to accounts payable, are a function of the level of activity (i.e., sales), these payables vary with sales. As long as sales remain constant or are rising, the payment of current liabilities is essentially a refunding operation. There again the components of the current ratio give little, if any, recognition to these elements and their effects on the future flow of funds. Nor do the current liabilities that enter into the computation of the current ratio include prospective outlays, such as commitments under construction contracts, loans, leases, or pensions, all of which affect the future outflow of funds.

Implications of the limitations to which the current ratio is subject

There are a number of conclusions that can be reached on the basis of the foregoing discussion:

1. Liquidity depends to some extent on cash or cash equivalents balances and to a much more significant extent on prospective cash flows.
2. There is no direct or established relationship between balances of working capital items and the pattern that future cash flows are likely to assume.
3. Managerial policies directed at optimizing the levels of receivables and inventories are oriented primarily towards efficient and profitable assets utilization and only secondarily at liquidity.[1]

Given these conclusions, which obviously limit the value of the current ratio as an index of liquidity, and given the static nature of this ratio and the fact that it is composed of items that affect liquidity in different ways, we may ask why this ratio enjoys such widespread use and in what way, if any, it can be used intelligently by the analyst.

The most probable reasons for the popularity of the current ratio are evidently the simplicity of its basic concept, the ease with which it can be computed, and the readiness with which data for it can be obtained. It may also derive its popularity from the credit grantor's, and especially the banker's, propensity to view credit situations as conditions of last resort. They may ask themselves: "What if there were a complete cessation of funds inflow? Would the current assets then be adequate to pay off the current liabilities?" The assumption of such extreme conditions is, of course, not always a useful way of measuring liquidity.

To what use can the intelligent analyst put the current ratio?

Let it first be said that the analyst who wishes to measure short-term liquidity and solvency will find cash flow projections and pro forma financial statements to be the most relevant and reliable tools to use. This involves

---

[1] The nature of the business is also a factor. In the case of many electric utilities, current liabilities exceed current assets because the prompt payment by utility customers enables the utilities to pay off their obligations on time. In other words, utility current assets get converted into cash faster than current obligations must be met. As an added example from another field, Fair Lanes, a bowling lanes operator, obviously does not sell on credit and thus has no receivables. It also carries no inventories of any consequences. Consequently, it has during most of its 50-year existence operated with a working capital deficiency. With almost all of its current assets in cash, it has no problem meeting current obligations.

obtaining information that is not readily available in published financial statements and it also involves the need for a great deal of estimation. This area of analysis will be discussed in the next chapter.

The current ratio as a valid tool of analysis

Should the analyst want to use the current ratio as a static measure of the ability of current assets to satisfy the current liabilities, he will be employing a different concept of liquidity from the one discussed above. In this context, liquidity means the readiness and speed with which current assets can be converted to cash and the degree to which such conversion will result in shrinkage in the stated value of current assets.

It is not our purpose here to discredit the current ratio as a valid tool of analysis but rather to suggest that its legitimate area of application is far less wide than popularly believed.

Defenders of this, the oldest and best known of financial ratios, may say that they are aware of the multitude of limitations and inconsistencies of concept outlined above but that they will "allow" for them in the evaluation of the ratio. A careful examination of these limitations suggests that such process of "allowing" for such limitations is well nigh impossible.

The best and most valid way to use this ratio is to recognize its limitations and to restrict its use to the analytical job it can do, that is, measuring the ability of *present* current assets to discharge *existing* current liabilities and considering the excess, if any, as a liquid surplus available to meet imbalances in the flow of funds and other contingencies. This should be done with an awareness of the fact that the test envisages a situation of enterprise liquidation,[2] whereas in the normal, going-concern situation current assets are of a revolving nature, for example, the collected receivable being replaced with a newly created one, while the current liabilities are essentially of a refunding nature, that is, the repayment of one is followed by the creation of another.

Given the analytical function of the current ratio, as outlined above, there are two basic elements that must be measured before the current ratio can form the basis for valid conclusions:

1. The quality of the current assets and the nature of the current liabilities that enter the determination of the ratio.
2. The rate of turnover of these assets and liabilities, that is, the average time span needed to convert receivables and inventories into cash and the amount of time that can be taken for the payment of current liabilities.

---

[2] It should be realized that the circumstances leading to bankruptcy or liquidation will have an effect on how much the amounts realized on asset dispositions will shrink. They will, for example, be likely to shrink more severely if the liquidation is caused by overall adverse industry conditions than if caused by specific difficulties such as poor management or inadequate capitalization.

To measure the above, a number of ratios and other tools have been devised, and these can enhance the use of the current ratio as an analytic tool.

Measures that supplement the current ratio

The most liquid of current assets is, of course, cash, which is the standard of liquidity itself. A close second to cash is "temporary investments" that are usually highly marketable and relatively safe temporary repositories of cash. These are, in effect, considered as "cash equivalents" and usually earn a modest return.

Cash ratios. The proportion that cash and cash equivalents constitute of the total current assets group is a measure of the degree of liquidity of this group of assets. It is measured by the cash ratio that is computed as follows:

$$\frac{\text{Cash} + \text{Cash equivalents}}{\text{Total current assets}}$$

Evaluation. The higher the ratio, the more liquid is the current asset group. This, in turn, means that with respect to this cash and cash equivalents component there is a minimal danger of loss in value in case of liquidation and that there is practically no waiting period for conversion of these assets into usable cash.

APB Opinion 18 generally requires the carrying of investments, representing an interest of 20 percent or higher, at underlying equity. This is, of course, neither cost nor, necessarily, market value. While such substantial positions in the securities of another company are not usually considered cash equivalents, *should* they nevertheless be so considered, their market value would be the most appropriate figure to use in the computation of liquidity ratios.

As to the availability of cash, the analyst should bear in mind possible restrictions that may exist with respect to the use of cash balances. An example is so-called compensating balances that banks extending credit expect their customers to keep. While such balances can be used, the analyst must nevertheless assess the effect on a company's credit standing and credit availability, as well as on its banking connection, of a breach of the tacit agreement not to draw on the compensating cash balance.

Two additional factors bearing on the evaluation of cash ratios should be mentioned. One is that modern computerized cash management methods have led to more efficient uses of cash by corporations and this has led to lower levels of cash needed for ordinary operations. The other is that open lines of credit and other standby credit arrangements are effective substitutes for cash balances and should be so considered.

An additional ratio that measures cash adequacy should be mentioned. The cash to current liabilities ratio is computed as follows:

$$\frac{\text{Cash} + \text{Cash equivalents}}{\text{Current liabilities}}$$

It measures how much cash is available to pay current obligations. This is a severe test that ignores the refunding nature of current liabilities. It supplements the cash ratio discussed above in that it measures cash availability from a somewhat different point of view.

To view the cash ratio as a further extension of the acid-test ratio (see below) would, except in extreme cases, constitute a test of short-term liquidity too severe to be meaningful. Nevertheless, the importance of cash as the ultimate form of liquidity should never be underestimated. The record of business failures provides many examples of insolvent companies, possessing sizable noncash assets, current and noncurrent, and no cash to pay debts or to operate with.

Measures of accounts receivable liquidity

In most enterprises that sell on credit, accounts and notes receivable are a significant part of working capital. In assessing the quality of working capital and of the current ratio, it is important to get some measure of the quality and the liquidity of the receivables.

Both the quality[3] and liquidity of accounts receivable are affected by their rate of turnover. By quality is meant the likelihood of collection without loss. An indicator of this likelihood is the degree to which receivables are within the terms of payment set by the enterprise. Experience has shown that the longer receivables remain outstanding beyond the date on which they are due, the lower is the probability of their collection in full. Turnover is an indicator of the age of the receivables, particularly when it is compared with an expected turnover rate that is determined by credit terms granted.

The measure of liquidity is concerned with the speed with which accounts receivables will, on average, be converted into cash. Here again turnover is among the best measures to use.

AVERAGE ACCOUNTS RECEIVABLE TURNOVER RATIO

The receivable turnover ratio is computed as follows:

$$\frac{\text{Net sales on credit}}{\text{Average accounts receivable}}$$

---

[3] The validity of the collection claim is also one aspect of quality. Thus, the analyst must be alert to problems that can arise from "sales" on consignment or those with right of return.

The quickest way for an external analyst to determine the average accounts receivable is to take the beginning receivables of the period, add the ending receivables, and divide the sum by two. The use of monthly or quarterly sales figures can lead to an even more accurate result. The more widely sales fluctuate, the more subject to distortion this ratio is, unless the receivables are properly averaged.

Notes receivable arising from normal sales should be included in the accounts receivable figure in computing the turnover ratio. Discounted notes receivable that are still outstanding should also be included in the accounts receivable total.

The sales figure used in computing the ratio should be that of credit sales only, because cash sales obviously do not generate receivables. Since published financial statements rarely disclose the division between cash and credit sales, the external analyst may have to compute the ratio under the assumption that cash sales are relatively insignificant. If they are not insignificant, then a degree of distortion may occur in the ratio. However, if the proportion of cash sales to total sales remains relatively constant, the year-to-year comparison of changes in the receivables turnover ratio may nevertheless be validly based.

The average receivables turnover figure indicates how many *times,* on average, the receivables revolve, that is, are generated and collected during the year.

For example, if sales are $1,200,000 and beginning receivables are $150,000 while year-end receivables are $250,000, then receivable turnover is computed as follows:

$$\frac{\$1,200,000}{(\$150,000 + \$250,000) \div 2} = \frac{\$1,200,000}{\$200,000} = 6 \text{ times}$$

While the turnover figure furnishes a sense of the speed of collections and is valuable for comparison purposes, it is not directly comparable to the terms of trade that the enterprise normally extends. Such comparison is best made by converting the turnover into days of sales tied up in receivables.

Collection period for accounts receivable

This measure, also known as *days sales in accounts receivable,* measures the number of days it takes, on average, to collect accounts (and notes) receivable. The number of days can be obtained by dividing the average accounts receivable turnover ratio discussed above into 360, the approximate round number of days in the year. Thus,

$$\text{Collection period} = \frac{360}{\text{Average accounts receivable turnover}}$$

Using the figures of the preceding example, the collection period is:

$$\frac{360}{6} = 60 \text{ days}$$

An alternative computation is to first obtain the average daily sales and then divide the *ending gross* receivable balance by it.

$$\text{Accounts receivable} \div \frac{\text{Sales}}{360}$$

The result will differ from the foregoing computation because the average accounts receivable turnover figure uses *average* accounts receivable, while this computation uses *ending* accounts receivable only; it thus focuses specifically on the latest accounts receivable balances. Using the figures from our example, the computation is:

$$\text{Average daily sales} = \frac{\text{Sales}}{360} = \frac{\$1,200,000}{360} = \$3,333$$

$$\frac{\text{Accounts receivable}}{\text{Average daily sales}} = \frac{\$250,000}{\$3,333} = 75 \text{ days}$$

Note that if the collection period computation would have used ending receivables rather than *average* receivables turnover, the identical collection period, that is, 75 could have been obtained as follows:

$$\frac{\text{Sales}}{\text{Accounts receivable (ending)}} = \frac{\$1,200,000}{\$250,000} = 4.8 \text{ times}$$

$$\frac{360}{\text{Receivables turnover}} = \frac{360}{4.8} = 75 \text{ days}$$

The use of 360 days is arbitrary because while receivables are outstanding 360 days (used for computational convenience instead of 365), the sales days of the year usually number less than 300. However, consistent computation of the ratio will make for valid period to period comparisons.

Evaluation

Accounts receivable turnover rates or collection periods can be compared to industry averages or to the credit terms that are generally granted by the enterprise.

When the collection period is compared with the terms of sale allowed by the enterprise, the degree to which customers are paying on time can be assessed. Thus, if the average terms of sale in the illustration used above are 40 days, then an average collection period of 75 days reflects either some or all of the following conditions:

1. A poor collection job.
2. Difficulty in obtaining prompt payment from customers in spite of diligent collection efforts.
3. Customers in financial difficulty.

The first conclusion calls for remedial managerial action, while the last two reflect particularly on both the quality and the liquidity of the accounts receivable.

An essential analytical first step is to determine whether the accounts receivable are representative of company sales activity. Significant receivables may, for example, be lodged in the captive finance company of the enterprise. In that case, the bad debt provision may also relate to receivables not on company books.

It is always possible that an *average* figure is not representative of the receivables population it represents. Thus, it is possible that the 75-day average collection period does not represent an across-the-board payment tardiness on the part of customers but is rather caused by the excessive delinquency of one or two substantial customers.

The best way to investigate further an excessive collection period is to *age* the accounts receivable in such a way that the distribution of each account by the number of days past due is clearly apparent. An aging schedule in a format such as given below will show whether the problem is widespread or concentrated:

Accounts receivable aging schedule

		Days past due			
	Current	0–30	31–60	61–90	Over 90
Accounts receivable					

The age distribution of the receivables will, of course, lead to better in-formed conclusions regarding the quality and the liquidity of the receivables as well as the kind of action that is necessary to remedy the situation. Another dimension of receivables classification is by quality ratings of credit agencies such as Dun & Bradstreet.

Notes receivable deserve the particular scrutiny of the analyst because while they are normally regarded as more negotiable than open accounts, they may be of poorer quality than regular receivables if they originated as an extension device for an unpaid account rather than at the inception of the original sale.

In assessing the quality of receivables, the analyst should remember that a significant conversion of receivables into cash, except for their use as collat-eral for borrowing, cannot be achieved without a cutback in sales volume. The sales policy aspect of the collection period evaluation must also be kept in mind. An enterprise may be willing to accept slow-paying customers who provide business that is, on an overall basis, profitable; that is, the profit on sales compensates for the extra use by the customer of the enterprise funds. This circumstance may modify the analyst's conclusions regarding the *quality* of the receivables but not those regarding their *liquidity*.

In addition to the consideration of profitability, an enterprise may extend more liberal credit in cases such as (1) the introduction of a new product, (2) a desire to make sales in order to utilize available excess capacity, or (3) special competitive conditions in the industry. Thus, the relationship between the level of receivables and that of sales and profits must always be borne in mind when evaluating the collection period. The trend of the collection period over time is always important in an assessment of the quality and the liquidity of the receivables.

Another trend that may be instructive to watch is that of the relationship between the provision for doubtful accounts and gross accounts receivable. The ratio is computed as follows:

$$\frac{\text{Provision for doubtful accounts}}{\text{Gross accounts receivable}}$$

An increase in this ratio over time may indicate management's conclusion that the collectibility of receivables has deteriorated. Conversely, a decrease of this ratio over time may lead to the opposite conclusion or may cause the analyst to reevaluate the adequacy of the provision for doubtful accounts.

Measures of accounts receivable turnover are, as we have seen in this section, important in the evaluation of liquidity. They are also important as measures of asset utilization, a subject that will be covered in more detail in Chapter 6.

MEASURES OF INVENTORY TURNOVER

Inventories represent in many cases a very substantial proportion of the current asset group. This is so for reasons that have little to do with an enterprise's objective of maintaining adequate levels of liquid funds. Reserves of liquid funds are seldom kept in the form of inventories. Inventories represent investments made for the purpose of obtaining a return. The return is derived from the expected profits that may result from sales. In most businesses, a certain level of inventory must be kept in order to generate an adequate level of sales. If the inventory level is inadequate, the sales volume will fall to below the level otherwise attainable. Excessive inventories, on the other hand, expose the enterprise to expenses such as storage costs, insurance and taxes, as well as to risks of loss of value through obsolescence and physical deterioration. Moreover, excessive inventories tie up funds that can be used more profitably elsewhere.

Due to the risk involved in holding inventories as well as the fact that inventories are one step further removed from cash than receivables (they have to be sold before they are converted into receivables), inventories are normally considered the least liquid component of the current assets group. As is the case with most generalizations, this is not always true. Certain staple items, such as commodities, raw materials, standard sizes of structural steel, etc., enjoy broad and ready markets and can usually be sold with little effort, expense, or loss. On the other hand, fashion merchandise, specialized components, or perishable items can lose their value rapidly unless they are sold on a timely basis.

The evaluation of the current ratio, which includes inventories in its computation, must include a thorough evaluation of the quality as well as the liquidity of these assets. Here again, measures of turnover are the best overall tools available for this purpose.

Inventory turnover ratio

The inventory turnover ratio measures the average rate of speed with which inventories move through and out of the enterprise.

Computation. The computation of the average inventory turnover is as follows:

$$\frac{\text{Cost of goods sold}}{\text{Average inventory}}$$

Consistency of valuation requires that the cost of goods sold be used because, as is the case with inventories, it is stated principally at *cost*. Sales, on the other hand, normally include a profit. Although the cost of goods sold figure is now disclosed in most published income statements, the external analyst is still occasionally confronted with an unavailability of such a figure. In such a case, the sales figure must be substituted. While this results in a theoretically less valid turnover ratio, it can still be used for comparison and trend development purposes, especially if used consistently and when sharp changes in profit margins are not present.

The average inventory figure is most readily obtained as follows:

$$\frac{\text{Opening inventory} + \text{Closing inventory}}{2}$$

Further refinement in the averaging process can be achieved, where possible and necessary, by averaging quarterly or monthly inventory figures.

When an inventory turnover ratio is computed in order to evaluate the *level* of inventory at a certain date, such as the year-end inventory, the inventory figure in the denominator should be the figure as of that date rather than an average inventory figure.

Before a turnover ratio is computed, the analyst must carefully examine the composition of the inventory figure and make adjustments, such as those from LIFO to FIFO, etc.

Days to sell inventory

Another measure of inventory turnover that is also useful in assessing purchasing policy is the required number of *days to sell inventory*. The computation that follows, that is,

$$\frac{360 \text{ days}}{\text{Average inventory turnover}}$$

measures the number of days it takes to sell the average inventory in a given year, and an alternative computation

$$\frac{\text{Ending inventory}}{\text{Cost of average day's sales}}$$

measures the number of days that are required to sell off the ending inventory, assuming the given rate of sales where the

$$\text{Cost of an average day's sales} = \frac{\text{Cost of goods sold}}{360}$$

Example of computations

Sales	$1,800,000
Cost of goods sold	1,200,000
Beginning inventory	200,000
Ending inventory	400,000

$$\text{Inventory turnover} = \frac{\$1,200,000}{(\$200,000 + \$400,000) \div 2} = \frac{\$1,200,000}{\$300,000} = 4 \text{ times}$$

$$\text{Number of days to sell average inventory} = \frac{360}{4} = 90 \text{ days}$$

Alternatively the computation based on ending inventory is as follows:

Step 1:

$$\frac{\text{Cost of goods sold}}{360} = \frac{\$1,200,000}{360} = \$3,333 \text{ (cost of average day's sales)}$$

Step 2:

$$\frac{\text{Ending inventory}}{\text{Cost of average day's sales}} = \frac{\$400,000}{\$3,333} = 120 \text{ days}$$

Interpretation of inventory turnover ratios. The current ratio computation views its current asset components as sources of funds that can, as a means of last resort, be used to pay off the current liabilities. Viewed this way, the inventory turnover ratios give us a measure of the quality as well as of the liquidity of the inventory component of the current assets.

The quality of inventory is a measure of the enterprise's ability to use it and dispose of it without loss. When this is envisaged under conditions of forced liquidation, then recovery of cost is the objective. In the normal course of business, the inventory should, of course, be sold at a profit. Viewed from this point of view, the normal profit margin realized by the enterprise assumes importance because the funds that will be obtained, and that would theoretically be available for payment of current liabilities, will include the profit in addition to the recovery of cost. In both cases, costs of sale will reduce the net proceeds.

In practice, a going concern cannot use its investment in inventory for the payment of current liabilities because any drastic reduction in normal inventory levels will surely cut into the sales volume.

A rate of turnover that is slower than that experienced historically, or that is below that normal in the industry, would lead to the preliminary conclusion that it includes items that are slow moving because they are obsolete, in weak demand, or otherwise unsalable. Such conditions do, of course, cast doubt on the feasibility of recovering the cost of such items.

Further investigation may reveal that the slowdown in inventory turnover is due to a buildup of inventory in accordance with a future contractual commitment, in anticipation of a price rise, in anticipation of a strike or shortage, or for any number of other reasons that must be probed into further.

A better evaluation of inventory turnover can be obtained from the computation of separate turnover rates for the major components of inventory such as (1) raw materials, (2) work in process, and (3) finished goods. Departmental or divisional turnover rates can similarly lead to more useful conclusions regarding inventory quality. One should never lose sight of the fact that the total inventory turnover ratio is an aggregate of widely varying turnover rates of individual components.

The biggest problem facing the external analyst who tries to compute inventory turnover ratios by individual product components is obtaining the necessary detailed data. This is, at present, rarely provided in published financial statements.

The turnover ratio is, of course, also a gauge of liquidity in that it conveys a measure of the speed with which inventory can be converted into cash. In this connection, a useful additional measure is the conversion period of inventories.

Conversion period of inventories.   This computation adds the collection period of receivables to the days needed to sell inventories in order to arrive at the time interval needed to convert inventories into cash.

Using figures developed in our examples of the respective ratios above, we get:

	Days
Days to sell inventory	90
Days to collect receivables....................	60
Total conversion period of inventories	150

It would thus normally take 150 days to sell inventory on credit and to collect the receivables. This is a period identical to the *operating cycle* that we discussed earlier in this chapter.

The effect of alternative methods of inventory management

In evaluating the inventory turnover ratio, the analyst must be alert to the influence that alternative accounting principles have on the determination of the ratio's components. It is obvious that the use of the LIFO method of inventory valuation may render both the turnover ratios as well as the current ratio practically meaningless. Information is usually found in published financial statements that enable the analyst to adjust the unrealistically low LIFO inventory valuation occurring in times of rising price levels so as to render it useful for inclusion in turnover ratio or the current ratio. Even if two companies employ LIFO cost methods for their inventory valuation computation of their ratios, using such inventory figures may nevertheless not be comparable because their respective LIFO inventory pools (bases) may have been acquired in years of significantly different price levels. The inventory figure enters the numerator of the current ratio and also the denominator because the inventory method utilized affects the income tax liability.

The analyst must also bear in mind that companies using the so-called natural year may have at their year-end an unrepresentatively low inventory level and that this may increase the turnover ratio to unrealistically high levels.

Prepaid expenses are expenditures made for benefits that are expected to be received in the future. Since most such benefits are receivable within a year or within an enterprise's operating cycle, they will conserve the outlay of current funds.

Usually, the amounts included in this category are relatively small compared to the size of the other current assets, and consequently no extensive discussion of their treatment is needed here. However, the analyst must be aware of the tendency of managements of enterprises with weak current positions to include in prepaid expenses deferred charges and other items of dubious liquidity. Such items must consequently be excluded from the computation of working capital and of the current ratio.

CURRENT LIABILITIES

In the computation of working capital and of the current ratio, current liabilities are important for two related reasons:

1. A basic objective of measuring the excess of current assets over current liabilities is to determine whether the latter are covered by current assets and what margin of safety is provided by the excess of such assets over current liabilities.
2. Current liabilities are deducted from current assets in arriving at the net working capital position.

In the computation of the current ratio, the point of view adopted towards current liabilities is *not* one of a continuing enterprise but rather of an enterprise in liquidation. This is so because in the normal course of operations, current liabilities are not paid off but are rather of a refunding nature. As long as the sales volume remains stable, purchases will also remain at a stable level, and that in turn will cause current liabilities to remain level. Increasing sales, in turn, will generally result in an increasing level of current liabilities. Thus, it can be generally stated that the trend and direction of sales is a good indication of the future level of current liabilities.

In assessing the quality of the current ratio, the nature of the current liabilities must be carefully examined.

Differences in the "nature" of current liabilities

Not all liabilities represent equally urgent and forceful calls for payment. At one extreme we find liabilities for taxes of all kinds that must be paid promptly regardless of current financial difficulties. The powers of collection of federal and local government authorities are as well known as they are powerful.

On the other hand, current liabilities to suppliers with whom the enterprise has a long-standing relationship and who depend on, and value, the enterprise's business are of a very different degree of urgency. Postponement and renegotiation of such debts in times of financial stringency are both possible and are commonly found.

The "nature" of current liabilities in terms of our present discussion must be judged in the light of the degree of urgency of payment that attaches to them. It should be understood that if fund inflows from current revenues are viewed as sources of funds available for the payment of current liabilities, then labor costs and other current fund-requiring costs and expenses have a first call on sales revenues and that trade bills and other liabilities can be paid only after such recurring outlays have been met. This dynamic aspect of funds flow will be examined more closely in the chapter that follows.

The analyst must also be aware of unrecorded liabilities that may have a claim to current funds. Examples of these are purchase commitments and obligations under pensions and leases. Moreover, under long-term loan acceleration clauses, a failure to meet current installments of long-term debt may render the entire debt due and payable, that is, cause it to become current.

Days purchases in accounts payable ratio

A measure of the degree to which accounts payable represent current rather than overdue obligations can be obtained by calculating the *days purchases in accounts payable ratio*. This ratio is computed as follows:

$$\frac{\text{Accounts payable}}{\text{Purchases per day*}} = \text{Days purchases in accounts payable}$$

* Computed: Purchases/360.

The difficulty that the external analyst will encounter in computing this ratio is that normally purchases are not separately disclosed in published financial statements. For retailers a rough approximation of the amount of purchases can be obtained by adjusting the cost of goods sold figure for depreciation and other nonfund requiring charges as well as for changes in inventories. However, the cost of goods sold figure may contain significant cash charges, and this may reduce the validity of a computation that contains such an approximation of purchases.

INTERPRETATION OF THE CURRENT RATIO

In the foregoing sections, we have examined the means by which the quality and the liquidity of the individual components of the current ratio is measured. This evaluation is, of course, essential to an overall interpretation of the current ratio as an indicator of short-term liquidity and financial strength.

The analyst must, however, exercise great care if he wants to carry the interpretation of the current ratio beyond the conclusion that it represents an excess of current resources over current obligations as of a given point in time.

Examination of trend

An examination of the trend of the current ratio over time can be very instructive. Two tools of analysis are useful here. One is known as *trend analysis,* where the components of working capital as well as the current ratio would be converted into an index to be compared over time. The other is *common-size analysis,* by means of which the *composition* of the current asset group is examined over time. A historical trend and common-size comparison over time, as well as an intra-industry comparison of such trends, can also be instructive to financial analysts.

Interpretation of changes over time

Changes in the current ratio over time must, however, be interpreted with great care. They do not automatically imply changes in liquidity or operating results. Thus, for example, in a prosperous year an increased liability for taxes may result in a lowering of the current ratio. Conversely, during a business contraction, current liabilities may be paid off while there may be a concurrent involuntary accumulation of inventories and uncollected receivables causing the ratio to rise.

In times of business expansion, which may reflect operating successes, the enterprise may suffer from an expansion in working capital requirements, otherwise known as a prosperity squeeze with a resulting contraction of the current ratio. This can be seen in the following example:

	Year 1	Year 2
Current assets	$300,000	$600,000
Current liabilities	100,000	400,000
Working capital	$200,000	$200,000
Current ratio	3:1	1.5:1

As can be seen from the above example, a doubling of current assets, accompanied by a quadrupling of current liabilities and an unchanged amount of working capital will lead to a halving of the current ratio. This is the effect of business expansion unaccompanied by an added capital investment. Inflation can have a similar effect on a business enterprise in that it will lead to a substantial increase in all current items categories.

Possibilities of manipulation

The analyst must be aware of the possibilities of year-end manipulation of the current ratio, otherwise known as window dressing.

For example, towards the close of the fiscal year, the collection of receivables may be pressed more vigorously, advances to officers may be called in for temporary repayment, inventory may be reduced to below normal levels, and normal purchases may be delayed. Proceeds from these steps can then be used to pay off current liabilities. The effect on the current ratio of the reduction of current liabilities through the use of current assets can be seen in the following example:

	Payoff of $50,000 in liabilities	
	Before	After
Current assets	$200,000	$150,000
Current liabilities	100,000	50,000
Current ratio	2:1	3:1

The accounting profession, sensing the propensity of managements to offset liabilities against assets, has strengthened its prohibitions against offsets by restricting them strictly to situations where the legal right to offset exists.

To the extent possible, the analyst should go beyond year-end measures and should try to obtain as many interim readings of the current ratio as possible, not only in order to guard against the practice of window dressing described above but also in order to gauge the seasonal changes to which the ratio is exposed. The effect of a strong current ratio in December on an assessment of current financial condition may be considerably tempered if it is discovered that at its seasonal peak in July the enterprise is dangerously close to a serious credit squeeze.

The use of "rules of thumb" standards

A popular belief that has gained considerable currency is that the current ratio can be evaluated by means of *rules of thumb*. Thus, it is believed that if the current ratio is 2:1 (or 200 percent), it is sound and anything below that norm is bad while the higher above that figure the current ratio is, the better.

This rule of thumb may reflect the lender's, and particularly the banker's, conservatism. The fact that it is down from the norm of 2.5:1 prevailing at the turn of the century may mean that improved financial reporting has reduced this size of the "cushion" that the banker and other creditors would consider as the minimum protection they need.

What the 2:1 standard means is that there are $2 of current assets available for each dollar of current liabilities or that the value of current assets can, on liquidation, shrink by 50 percent before it will be inadequate to cover the current liabilities. Of course, a current ratio much higher than 2:1, while implying a superior coverage of current liabilities, may also mean a wasteful accumulation of liquid resources which do not "carry their weight" by earning an appropriate return for the enterprise.

It should be evident by now that the evaluation of the current ratio in terms of rules of thumb is a technique of dubious validity. This is so for two major reasons:

1. As we have learned in the preceding sections, the quality of the current assets, as well as the composition of the current liabilities that make up this ratio, are the most important determinants in an evaluation of the quality of the current ratio. Thus, two companies that have identical current ratios may nevertheless be in quite different current financial condition due to variations in the quality of the working capital components.

2. The need of an enterprise for working capital varies with industry conditions as well as with the length of its own particular *net trade cycle*.

The net trade cycle

An enterprise's need for working capital depends importantly on the relative size of its required inventory investment as well as on the relationship between the credit terms it receives from its suppliers as against those it must extend to its customers.

ILLUSTRATION 4.   Assume a company shows the following data at the end of 19x1:

Sales for 19x1	$360,000
Receivables	40,000
Inventories	50,000
Accounts payable	20,000

The following tabulation measures the company's cash cycle in terms of days:

$$\text{Sales per day } \frac{\$360,000}{360} = \$1,000$$

Number of days sales in—	Days
Accounts receivable	40
Inventories	50
Total trade cycle	90
Less: Accounts payable	20
Net trade cycle	70

From the above we can see that the company is keeping 50 days of sales in inventory and that it receives only 20 sales days of trade credit while it must extend 40 sales days of credit to its customers. Obviously, the higher the *net trade cycle* a company has the larger its investment in working capital is likely to be. Thus, in our above example, if the company could lower its investment in inventories by 10 sales days, it could lower its investment in working capital by $10,000. A similar result can be achieved by increasing the number of days sales in accounts payable by 10.

It should be noted that for the sake of simplicity and uniformity, the net trade cycle computation uses number of *days sales* as a common factor. This does introduce, however, a degree of distortion because while receivables can be related directly to sales, inventories are more logically related to cost of goods sold and accounts payable to purchases. This distortion will, however, not normally be large enough to invalidate the tool for analytical and comparison purposes and the degree of distortion will depend on factors such as the profit margin.

The working capital requirements of a supermarket with its high inventory turnover and low outstanding receivables are obviously lower than those of a tobacco company with its slow inventory turnover.

Valid working capital standards

Comparison with industry current ratios as well as analyses of working capital requirements such as the net trade cycle analysis described above can lead to far more valid conclusions regarding the adequacy of an enterprise's working capital than can a mechanical comparison of its current ratio to the 2:1 rule of thumb standard.

The amount of working capital needed by an enterprise is importantly determined by industry conditions and practices. In recent years, the average industrial company needed about 15 cents of working capital for every dollar of sales. But averages can be misleading, and therefore it is best to focus on specific industry conditions and standards as cases for comparison.

The importance of sales

In an assessment of the overall liquidity of current assets, the trend of sales is an important factor. Since it takes sales to convert inventory into receivables or cash, an uptrend in sales indicates that the conversion of inventories into more liquid assets will be easier to achieve than when sales remain constant. Declining sales, on the other hand, will retard the conversion of inventories into cash.

Common-size analysis of current assets composition

The composition of the current asset group, which can be analyzed by means of common-size statements, is another good indicator of relative working capital liquidity.

Consider, for example, the following comparative working capital composition:

	Year 1		Year 2	
Current assets:				
Cash	$ 30,000	30%	$ 20,000	20%
Accounts receivable	40,000	40	30,000	30
Inventories	30,000	30	50,000	50
Total current assets	$100,000	100%	$100,000	100%

From the simple illustration above it can be seen, even without the computation of common-size percentages, that the liquidity of the current asset group has deteriorated in year 2 by comparison with year 1. However, the use of common-size percentage comparisons will greatly facilitate the evaluation of comparative liquidity, regardless of the size of the dollar amounts involved.

The liquidity index

The measurement of the comparative liquidity of current assets can be further refined through the use of a *liquidity index*. The construction of this index (first suggested by A. H. Finney) can be illustrated as follows:

Using the working capital figures from the common-size computation above, and assuming that the conversion of inventories into accounts receivable takes 50 days on average and that the conversion of receivables into cash takes an average of 40 days, the index is computed as follows:

Year 1

	Amount	×	$\begin{array}{c}\textit{Days removed}\\\textit{from cash}\end{array}$	=	$\begin{array}{c}\textit{Product}\\\textit{dollar-days}\end{array}$
Cash	$ 30,000		—		—
Accounts receivable	40,000		40		1,600,000
Inventories	30,000		90		2,700,000
Total	$100,000 *(a)*				4,300,000 *(b)*

$$\text{Liquidity index} = \frac{b}{a} = \frac{4,300,000}{\$100,000} = \underline{\underline{43}}$$

Year 2

	Amount	×	$\begin{array}{c}\textit{Days removed}\\\textit{from cash}\end{array}$	=	$\begin{array}{c}\textit{Product}\\\textit{dollar-days}\end{array}$
Cash	$ 20,000		—		—
Accounts receivable	30,000		40		1,200,000
Inventories	50,000		90		4,500,000
Total	$100,000				5,700,000

$$\text{Liquidity index} = \frac{5,700,000}{\$100,000} = \underline{\underline{57}}$$

The computation of the respective liquidity indexes for the years 1 and 2 tells what we already knew instinctively in the case of this simple example, that is, that the liquidity has deteriorated in year 2 as compared to year 1.

The liquidity index must be interpreted with care. The index is in itself a figure without significance. It gains its significance only from a comparison between one index number and another as a gauge of the period to period change in liquidity or as a company to company comparison of relative liquidity. Increases in the index signify a deterioration in liquidity while decreases signify changes in the direction of improved liquidity. The index that is expressed in days is a weighing mechanism and its validity depends on the validity of the assumptions implicit in the weighing process.

An additional popular technique of current ratio interpretation is to submit it to a somewhat sterner test.

ACID-TEST RATIO

This test is the acid-test ratio, also known as the *quick ratio* because it is assumed to include the assets most quickly convertible into cash.

The acid-test ratio is computed as shown in Exhibit 3–2.

The omission of inventories from the acid-test ratio is based on the belief that they are the least liquid component of the current asset group. While this is generally so, we have seen in an earlier discussion in this chapter that this is not always true and that certain types of inventory can be more liquid than are slow-paying receivables. Another reason for the exclusion of inventories is the belief, quite often warranted, that the valuation of inventories normally requires a greater degree of judgment than is required for the valuation of the other current assets.

Exhibit 3–2

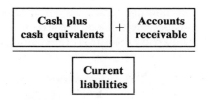

Since prepaid expenses are usually insignificant in relation to the other current assets, the acid-test ratio is sometimes computed simply by omitting the inventories from the current asset figure.

The interpretation of the acid-test ratio is subject to most of the same considerations which were discussed regarding the interpretation of the current ratio. Moreover, the acid-test ratio represents an even sterner test of an enterprise's liquidity than does the current ratio, and the analyst must judge by himself what significance to his conclusions the total omission of inventories, as a source of current funds, is.

OTHER MEASURES OF SHORT-TERM LIQUIDITY

The static nature of the current ratio that measures the relationship of current assets to current liabilities, at a given moment in time, as well as the fact that this measure of liquidity fails to accord recognition to the great importance that funds or cash flows play in an enterprise's ability to meet its maturing obligations has led to a search for more dynamic measures of liquidity.

Funds flow ratios

Funds flow ratios relate obligations to funds (working capital) generated by operations that are available to meet them. These resources do consequently not include funds from nonoperating sources such as borrowing or the sale of fixed assets.

One such ratio relates current liabilities to the funds from operations for the year:

$$\frac{\text{Funds provided by operations}}{\text{Current liabilities}}$$

This is a measure of how many times current liabilities are covered by the funds flow of the year just elapsed. It is, of course, backward looking while current liabilities as of a certain date must be paid out of *future,* rather than past, funds flow. Nevertheless, in the absence of drastic changes in conditions, the latest yearly funds flow represents at least a good basis for an estimate of the next period's funds flow.

Importance of nonfund items in net income. Since the conversion of income into funds flow depends on the size of the net *nonfund* items included in it, a useful comparison measure is the relationship between the net nonfund items in income and net income. The computation of this ratio is as follows:

$$\frac{\text{Net nonfund items in income}}{\text{Net income}}$$

The higher the relationship of net nonfund requiring items to net income, the greater the funds flow is in relation to reported net income and, thus, the higher the funds flow will be in relation to a given net income figure. An example of the computation of the *net nonfund items* follows:

Depreciation	$3,500,000
Depletion	1,200,000
Patent amortization	400,000
Deferred income taxes	2,800,000
Total nonfund charges	7,900,000
Less: Unremitted earnings of	
foreign subsidiaries	2,100,000
Net nonfund requiring items	$5,800,000

If net income is $58,000,000, the net nonfund items ratio is as follows:

$$\frac{\$5,800,000}{\$58,000,000} = .1, \text{ or } 10 \text{ percent}$$

This means that funds flow will normally be expected to approximate 110 percent of net income.

Cash flow related measures

Since liabilities are paid with cash rather than funds (i.e., working capital), the relationship of cash provided by operations to current liabilities is even more significant than the relationship of working capital provided by operations to total liabilities.

A ratio, which focuses on cash expense of the year and measures how many days of expenses the most liquid current assets could finance, assuming that all other cash inflows were to suddenly dry up, can be computed as follows:

$$\frac{\text{Cash + Cash equivalents + Receivables}}{\text{Year's cash expense}}$$

Like the acid-test ratio, the sternness of this test is such that its usefulness must be carefully weighed by the analyst.

THE CONCEPT OF FINANCIAL FLEXIBILITY

In addition to the tools of analysis of short-term liquidity with which we have dealt here and which lend themselves to quantification, there are important qualitative considerations that also have an important bearing on the short-term liquidity of an enterprise. These can be usefully characterized as depending on the financial flexibility of an enterprise.

Financial flexibility is characterized by the ability of an enterprise to take steps to counter unexpected interruptions in the flow of funds for reasons however unexpected. It means the ability to borrow from a variety of sources, to raise equity capital, to sell and redeploy assets, and to adjust the level and the direction of operations in order to meet changing circumstances.

The capacity to borrow depends on numerous factors and is subject to rapid change. It depends on profitability, stability, relative size, industry position, asset composition, and capital structure. It depends, moreover, on such external factors as credit market conditions and trends.

The capacity to borrow is important as a source of funds in time of need for funds and is also important when an enterprise must roll over its short-term debt. Prearranged financing or open lines of credit are more reliable sources of funds in time of need than is potential financing.

Other factors that bear on the assessment of the financial flexibility of an enterprise are the ratings of its commercial paper, bonds, and preferred stock; restrictions on the sale of its assets; the degree to which expenses are of a discretionary nature as well as the ability to respond quickly to changing conditions such as strikes, shrinking demand, or the cessation of sources of supply.

Financial flexibility is also important in the assessment of long-term solvency (see Chapter 5).

MANAGEMENT'S DISCUSSION AND ANALYSIS

Within the framework of its new Integrated Disclosure System, the SEC now requires an expanded management discussion and analysis of Financial

Condition and Results of Operations. The "Financial Condition" portion of that discussion requires a discussion of liquidity factors—including known trends, demands, commitments, or uncertainties likely to have a material impact on the enterprise's ability to generate adequate amounts of cash. If a material deficiency in liquidity is identified, management must discuss the course of action it has taken or proposes to take in order to remedy the deficiency. In addition, internal and external sources of liquidity as well as any material unused sources of liquid assets must be identified and described.

Excerpts from Rohr Industries 1981 management discussion will convey a notion of the types of areas covered:

> Working capital requirements are expected to increase substantially in future years, with the anticipated reduction of investments in the older programs in future years more than offset by requirements of the "new generation" programs which either are or will be entering the production stage. The sums required for working capital and other purposes have been, and will continue to be, difficult to determine, but the Corporation estimates that such additional requirements for funds cumulatively could approximate a range of $42 million to $98 million during the three fiscal years ending July 31, 1984. The actual amount will depend on a number of key factors, the most significant of which are: the ability to obtain significantly increased advances from customers by renegotiating existing contracts to help finance working capital needs; the amount of internally generated funds; the ability to reduce the continued heavy inflow of materials and to improve program inventory turnover ratios to historical levels; the level of deliveries on older programs and on "new generation" programs presently under contract; bank interest rates; various levels of participation in and payment terms of certain additional aircraft programs; continued improvement in production efficiencies; the ability to meet technical and production problems (particularly as may be encountered in new programs); and the level of capital facilities expenditures. In addition, this range assumes the Corporation is able to defer for two years the $18.7 million repayments of bank debt presently scheduled for fiscal 1983, and to defer subsequent scheduled payments. The actual amount of these future requirements for funds could change significantly as the various assumptions and estimates involved in analyzing these factors are changed over time. . . . The Corporation anticipates that it will require substantial additional financing to meet the above-described needs, as the Corporation does not expect to be able to generate sufficient funds from operations to provide all of the necessary working capital and other funds required by the introduction of the "new generation" programs currently under contract or to provide for further sums for future new programs in which the Corporation may participate.

Financial analysts should benefit significantly from a careful analysis and evaluation of such required management discussion and analysis (see also Chapter 7).

Projecting changes in conditions or policies

It is possible and often very useful to trace through the effects of changes in conditions and/or policies on the funds or cash resources of an enterprise.

ILLUSTRATION 5.   Assume that the Foresight Company has the following account balances at December 31, 19x1:

	Debit	Credit
Cash	$ 70,000	
Accounts receivable	150,000	
Inventory	65,000	
Accounts payable		$130,000
Notes payable		35,000
Accrued taxes		18,000
Fixed assets	200,000	
Accumulated depreciation		43,000
Capital stock		200,000

The following additional information is available for 19x1:

Sales	$750,000
Cost of sales	520,000
Purchases	350,000
Depreciation	25,000
Net income	20,000

The company anticipates a growth of 10 percent in sales for the coming year. All corresponding revenue and expense items are also expected to increase by 10 percent, except for depreciation which will remain the same. All expenses are paid in cash as they are incurred during the year. The 19x2 ending inventory will be $150,000. By the end of 19x2, the company expects to have a notes payable balance of $50,000 and no balance in the accrued taxes account. The company maintains a minimum cash balance of $50,000 as a managerial policy.
   I.   Assume that the company is considering a change in credit policy so that the ending accounts receivable balance will represent 90 days of sales. What impact will this change have on the company's cash balance? Will it have to borrow?
      This can be computed as follows:

Cash, January 1, 19x2		$ 70,000
Accounts receivable, January 1, 19x2 ..	$150,000	
Sales	825,000	
	975,000	
Less: Accounts receivable,		
December 31, 19x2	206,250 [(a)]	768,750
Total cash available		838,750

Explanation:
[(a)] $825,000 \times \dfrac{90}{360} = \$206,250.$

Cash disbursements:

Accounts payable, January 1, 19x2 ..	$130,000		
Purchases	657,000 [(b)]		
	787,000		
Accounts payable, December 31, 19x2	244,000 [(c)]	543,000	
Notes payable, January 1, 19x2	35,000		
Notes payable, December 31, 19x2 ..	50,000	(15,000)	
Accrued taxes		18,000	
Cash expenses [(d)]		203,500	749,500
			89,250
Cash balance desired			50,000
Cash excess			$ 39,250

[(b)] 19x2 cost of sales*: $520,000 \times 1.1 = $572,000

Ending inventory (given)	150,000
Goods available for sale	722,000
Beginning inventory	65,000
Purchases	$657,000

* Which excludes depreciation.

[(c)] $\text{Purchases} \times \dfrac{\text{Old accounts payable}}{\text{Old purchases}} = \$657,000 \times \dfrac{\$130,000}{\$350,000}$

$= \$244,000$

[(d)]

Gross profit ($825,000 − $572,000)		$253,000
Less: Net income	$24,500*	
Depreciation	25,000	49,500
Other cash expenses		$203,500

* 110 percent of $20,000 (19x1 N.I.) + 10 percent of $25,000 (19x1 depreciation).

II. What would the effect be if the change, instead of as in I, is to an *average* accounts receivable turnover of 4?

We compute this as follows:

Excess cash balance as computed above		$39,250
Change from an *ending* to an *average* accounts receivable turnover will increase year-end accounts receivable balance to:		

$\dfrac{\$825,000}{4} = \$206,250 \times 2$

$= \$412,500 - \$150,000 = \dots\dots$ \quad $262,500$ [(e)]

Less: Accounts receivable balance as above (I)	206,250	56,250 (cash decrease)
Cash required to borrow		$17,000

[(e)] $\dfrac{\text{Sales}}{\text{Average A/R turnover}} = \text{Average A/R};$
$\text{Ending A/R} = [(\text{Average A/R}) \times 2] - \text{Beginning A/R}$

III. Assuming that in addition to the conditions prevailing in II above, suppliers require the company to pay within 60 days, what would be the effect on the cash balance?

The computation is as follows:

Cash required to borrow (from II above) .... $ 17,000

Ending accounts payable (I above) $244,000

Ending accounts payable under 60-day payment

$$= \text{Purchases} \times \frac{60}{360} = \$657,000 \times \frac{60}{360} = \dots\dots\dots \quad 109,500$$

Additional disbursements required 134,500

Cash to be borrowed $151,500

QUESTIONS

1. Why is short-term liquidity so significant? Explain from the viewpoint of various parties concerned.

2. The concept of working capital is simple, that is, the excess of current assets over current liabilities. What are some of the factors that make this simple computation complicated in practice?

3. What are cash equivalents? How should an analyst value them in his analysis?

4. Can fixed assets be included in current assets? If so, explain the situation under which the inclusion may be allowed.

5. Some installment receivables are not collectible within one year. Why are they included in current assets?

6. Are all inventories included in current assets? Why or why not?

7. What is the theoretical justification for including prepaid expenses in current assets?

8. The company under analysis has a very small amount of current liabilities, but the long-term liabilities section shows a significant balance. In the footnote to the audited statements, it is disclosed that the company has a "revolving loan agreement" with a local bank. Does this disclosure have any significance to you?

9. Some industries are subject to peculiar financing and operating conditions that call for special consideration in drawing the distinction between what is *current* and what is *noncurrent.* How should the analyst recognize this in his evaluation of working capital?

10. Your careful computation of the working capitals of Companies A and B reveals that both have the same amount of working capital. Are you ready to conclude that the liquidity position of both is the same?

11. What is the current ratio? What does it measure? What are the reasons for its widespread use?

12. The holding of cash generally does not yield a return. Why does an enterprise hold cash at all?

13. Is there a relationship between the level of inventories and that of sales? Are inventories a function of sales? If there is a functional relationship between the two, is it proportional?

14. What are the major objectives of management in determining the size of inventory and receivables investment?

15. What are the theoretical limitations of the current ratio as a measure of liquidity?

16. If there are significant limitations attached to the current ratio as a measure of liquidity, what is the proper use of this tool?

17. What are cash ratios? What do they measure?

18. How do we measure the "quality" of various current assets?

19. What does the average accounts receivable turnover measure?

20. What is the collection period for accounts receivable? What does it measure?

21. A company's collection period is 60 days this year as compared to 40 days last year. Give three or more possible reasons for this change.

22. What is an accounts receivable aging schedule? What is its use in the analysis of financial statements?

23. What are the repercussions to an enterprise of (a) overinvestment or (b) underinvestment in inventories?

24. What problems would you expect to encounter in an analysis of a company using the LIFO inventory method in an inflationary economy? What effects do the price changes have (a) on the inventory turnover ratio and (b) on the current ratio?

25. Why does the "nature" of the current liabilities have to be analyzed in assessing the quality of the current ratio?

26. An apparently successful company shows a poor current ratio. Explain the possible reasons for this.

27. What is *window dressing?* Is there any way to find out whether the financial statements are window dressed or not?

28. What is the rule of thumb governing the expected size of the current ratio? What dangers are there in using this rule of thumb mechanically?

29. Describe the importance which the sales level plays in the overall current financial condition and liquidity of the current assets of an enterprise.

30. What is the liquidity index? What significance do the liquidity index numbers have?

31. What do cash flow ratios attempt to measure?

32. In addition to the tools of analysis of short-term liquidity that lend themselves to quantification, there are important qualitative considerations that also have an important bearing on the short-term liquidity of an enterprise. What are such considerations? And what are the SEC disclosure requirements that would help financial analysts in this regard?

33. What is the importance of projecting the effects of changes in conditions or policies on the cash resources of an enterprise?

4 Funds flow analysis and financial forecasts

The preceding chapter examined the various measures that are derived from past financial statement data and that are useful in the assessment of short-term liquidity. The chapter that follows will focus on the use of similar data in an evaluation of longer-term solvency. The limitations to which these approaches are subject are due mainly to their static nature, that is, to their reliance on status reports, as of a given moment, of claims against an enterprise and the resources available to meet these claims.

An important and, in many cases, superior alternative to such static measures of conditions prevailing at a given point in time is the analysis and projection of more dynamic models of cash and funds flow. Such models use the present only as a starting point, and while building on reliable patterns of past experience, utilize the best available estimates of future plans and conditions in order to forecast the future availability and disposition of cash or working capital.

OVERVIEW OF CASH FLOW AND FUNDS FLOW PATTERNS

Before we examine the methods by means of which funds flow projections are made, it would be useful to get a thorough understanding of the nature of funds flow. Exhibit 4–1 presents a diagram of the flow of funds through an enterprise.

The flow of funds diagram focuses on two concepts of funds: cash and working capital (also known as funds).

Cash (including cash equivalents) is the ultimate liquid asset. Almost all decisions to invest in assets or to incur costs require the immediate or eventual use of cash. This is why managements focus, from an operational point of view, on *cash* rather than on working capital. The focus on the latter represents

121

Exhibit 4–1: Flow of funds through an enterprise

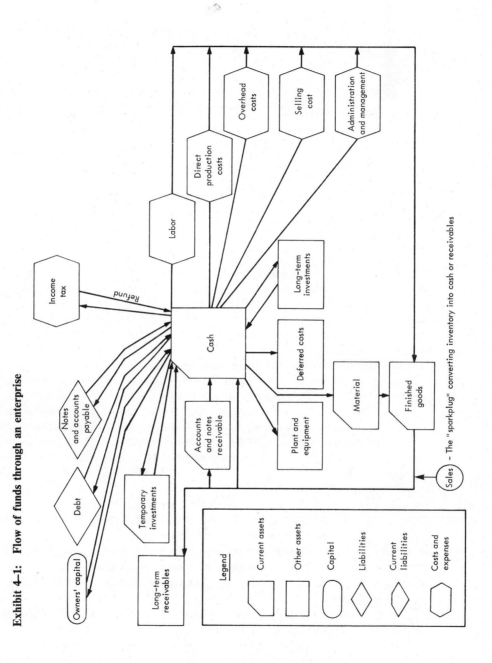

Sales – The "sparkplug" converting inventory into cash or receivables

Legend

Current assets

Other assets

Capital

Liabilities

Current liabilities

Costs and expenses

122

mainly the point of view of creditors who consider as part of the liquid assets pool other assets, such as receivables and inventories, which are normally converted into cash within a relatively short time span.

Careful examination of the flows depicted in Exhibit 4–1 should contribute greatly to the reader's understanding of the importance of liquid funds in an enterprise as well as the factors which cause them to be converted into assets and costs. The following factors and relationships are worthy of particular note:

> Since the diagram focuses on cash and funds flows only, assets, liabilities, and other items that are not directly involved, such as prepayments and accruals, as well as the income account are not included in it. Some flows are presented in simplified fashion for an easier understanding of relationships. For example, accounts payable are presented as direct sources of cash, whereas in reality they represent a temporary postponement of cash payment for the acquisition of goods and services.

> It is recognized that the holding of cash provides no return or a very low return and that in times of rising price levels, cash as a monetary asset is exposed to purchasing power loss. However, these considerations aside, the holding of this most liquid of assets represents, in a business sense, the lowest exposure to risk. Management must make the decision to invest cash in assets or costs, and such a conversion increases risk because the certainty of ultimate reconversion into cash is less than 100 percent. There are, of course, a variety of risks. Thus, the risk involved in a conversion of cash into temporary investments is lower than the risk involved in committing cash to long-term, long-payout assets such as plant, machinery, or research costs. Similarly, the investment of cash in a variety of assets and costs for the creation and marketing of a new product involves serious risk regarding the recovery in cash of amounts so committed. The short-term liquidity as well as the long-term solvency of an enterprise depend on the recovery and realizability of such outlays.

> The inflow and outflow of cash (or funds) are highly interrelated. A failure of any part of the system to circulate can affect the entire system. A cessation of sales affects the vital conversion of finished goods into receivables or cash and leads, in turn, to a drop in the cash reservoir. Inability to replenish this reservoir from sources such as owners' capital, debt, or accounts payable (upper left-hand corner of diagram) can lead to a cessation of production activities that will result in a loss of future sales. Conversely, the cutting off of expenses, such as for advertising and marketing, will slow down the conversion of finished goods into receivables and cash. Longer-term blockages in the flows may lead to insolvency.

> The diagram clarifies the interrelationship between profitability, income, and cash flow. The only real source of funds from operations is sales.

When finished goods, which for the sake of simplicity represent the accumulation of *all* costs and expenses in the diagram, are sold, the profit margin will enhance the inflow of liquid funds in the form of receivables and cash. The higher the profit margin, the greater the accretion of these funds.

Income, which is the difference between the cash and credit sales and the cost of goods sold, can have a wide variety of effects on cash flow. For example, the costs that flow from the utilization of plant and equipment or from deferred charges generally do not involve the use of current funds. Similarly, as in the case of land sales on long-term installment terms, the creation of long-term receivables through sales reduces the impact of net income on cash flow. It can be readily seen that adding back depreciation to net income creates a very crude measure of cash flow.

The limitation of the cash flow concept can be more clearly seen. As cash flows into its reservoir, management has a *degree* of discretion as to where to direct it. This discretion depends on the amount of cash already committed to such outlays as dividends, inventory accumulation, capital expenditures, or debt repayment. The total cash inflow also depends on management's ability to tap sources such as equity capital and debt. With respect to noncommitted cash, management has, at the point of return of the cash to the reservoir, the discretion of directing it to any purpose it deems most important. It is this noncommitted cash flow segment that is of particular interest and importance to financial analysts.

Under present accounting conventions, certain cash outlays, such as those for training or sales promotion, are considered as business (period) costs and are not shown as assets. These costs can, nevertheless, be of significant future value in either the increasing of sales or in the reduction of costs.

SHORT-TERM CASH FORECASTS

In the measurement of short-term liquidity, the short-term cash forecast is one of the most thorough and reliable tools available to the analyst.

Short-term liquidity analysis is of particular interest to management in the financial operations of an enterprise and to short-term credit grantors who are interested in an enterprise's ability to repay short-term loans. The security analyst will pay particular attention to the short-term cash forecast when an enterprise's ability to meet its current obligations is subject to substantial doubt.

Realistic cash forecasts can be made only for relatively short time spans. This is so because the factors influencing the inflows and outflows of cash are many and complex and cannot be reliably estimated beyond the short term.

Importance of sales estimates

The reliability of any cash forecast depends very importantly on the forecast of sales. In fact, a cash forecast can never reach a higher degree of reliability than the sales forecast on which it is based. Except for transactions involving the raising of money from external sources or the investment of money in long-term assets, almost all cash flows relate to and depend on sales.

The sales forecast involves considerations such as:

1. The past direction and trend of sales volume.
2. Enterprise share of the market.
3. Industry and general economic conditions.
4. Productive and financial capacity.
5. Competitive factors.

These factors must generally be assessed in terms of individual product lines that may be influenced by forces peculiar to their own markets.

Pro forma financial statements as an aid to forecasting

The reasonableness and feasibility of short-term cash forecasts can be checked by means of pro forma financial statements. This is done by utilizing the assumptions underlying the cash forecast and constructing, on this basis, a pro forma statement of income covering the period of the forecast and a pro forma balance sheet as at the end of that period. The ratios and other relationships derived from the pro forma financial statements should then be checked for feasibility against historical relationships that have prevailed in the past. Such relationships must be adjusted for factors that it is estimated will affect them during the period of the cash forecast.

Techniques of short-term cash forecasting

ILLUSTRATION 1. The Prudent Corporation has recently introduced an improved product that has enjoyed excellent market acceptance. As a result, management has budgeted sales for the six months ending June 30, 19x1, as follows:

	Estimated sales
January	100,000
February	125,000
March	150,000
April	175,000
May	200,000
June	250,000

The cash balance at January 1, 19x1, is $15,000, and the treasurer foresees a need for additional funds necessary to finance the sales expansion. He has obtained a commitment from an insurance company for the sale to them of long-term bonds as follows:

> April . . . . . $50,000 (less $2,500 debt costs)
> May   60,000

He also expects to sell real estate at cost: $8,000 in May and $50,000 in June. In addition, equipment with an original cost of $25,000 and a book value of zero was to be sold for $25,000 cash in June.

The treasurer considers that in the light of the expanded sales volume the following minimum cash balances will be desirable:

> January $20,000
> February   25,000
> March   27,000
> April, May, and June   30,000

He knows that during the next six months he will not be able to meet his cash requirements without resort to short-term financing. Consequently, he approaches his bank and finds it ready to consider his company's needs. The loan officer suggests that in order to determine the cash needs and the sources of funds for loan repayment, the treasurer prepare a cash forecast for the six months ending June 30, 19x1, and pro forma financial statements for that period.

The treasurer, recognizing the importance of such a forecast, proceeded to assemble the data necessary to prepare it.

The pattern of receivables collections based on experience was as follows:

Collections	Percent of total receivable
In month of sale	40
In the second month	30
In the third month	20
In the fourth month	5
Write-off bad debts	5
	100

On the basis of this pattern and the expected sales, the treasurer constructed Schedule A shown in Exhibit 4–2.

An analysis of past cost patterns resulted in the estimates of cost and expense relationships for the purpose of the cash forecast (Schedule B) shown in Exhibit 4–3.

It was estimated that all costs in Schedule B (exclusive of the $1,000 monthly depreciation charge) would be paid for in cash in the month incurred,

Exhibit 4–2

SCHEDULE A
Estimates of Cash Collections
For the Months January–June, 19x1

	January	February	March	April	May	June
Sales	$100,000	$125,000	$150,000	$175,000	$200,000	$250,000
Collections:						
1st month—40% ..	40,000	50,000	60,000	70,000	80,000	100,000
2d month—30% ..		30,000	37,500	45,000	52,500	60,000
3d month—20% ..			20,000	25,000	30,000	35,000
4th month—5% ..				5,000	6,250	7,500
Total cash						
collections ...	40,000	80,000	117,500	145,000	168,750	202,500
Write-offs—5%				5,000	6,250	7,500

Exhibit 4–3

SCHEDULE B
Cost and Expense Estimates for Six Months
Ending June 30, 19x1

Materials	30% of sales
Labor	25% of sales
Manufacturing overhead:	
Variable	10% of sales
Fixed	$48,000 for six months (including $1,000 of depreciation per month)
Selling expenses	10% of sales
General and administrative expenses:	
Variable	8% of sales
Fixed	$7,000 per month

Exhibit 4–4

SCHEDULE C
Pro Forma Schedule of Cash Payments for Materials Purchases
For the Months January–June 19x1

	January	February	March	April	May	June
Materials purchased						
during month*	$40,000	$38,000	$43,000	$56,000	58,000	$79,000
Payments:						
1st month—50%	20,000	19,000	21,500	28,000	29,000	39,500
2d month—50%		20,000	19,000	21,500	28,000	29,000
Total payments	$20,000	$39,000	$40,500	$49,500	$57,000	$68,500

* These reconcile with material costs and changes in inventories.

except for material purchases that are to be paid 50 percent in the month of purchase and 50 percent in the following month. Since the product is manufactured to specific order, no finished goods inventories are expected to accumulate.

The raw materials inventory at the end of each month for the period January to June 19x1 is expected to be as follows: $67,000, $67,500, $65,500, $69,000, $67,000, and $71,000, respectively. Raw materials inventory on January 1, 19x1, was $57,000.

Schedule C (Exhibit 4–4) shows the pattern of payments of accounts payable (for materials).

Exhibit 4–5

THE PRUDENT CORPORATION
Cash Forecast
For the Months January–June 19x1

	January	February	March
Cash balance—beginning	$15,000	$20,000	$ 25,750
Add: Cash receipts:			
Collections of accounts receivable			
(Schedule A)...............	40,000	80,000	117,500
Proceeds from sale of real estate .			
Proceeds from additional			
long-term debt			
Proceeds from sale of			
equipment			
Total cash available	$ 55,000	$100,000	$143,250
Less: Disbursements:			
Payments for:			
Materials purchases			
(Schedule C)	20,000	39,000	40,500
Labor	25,000	31,250	37,500
Fixed factory overhead	7,000	7,000	7,000
Variable factory overhead	10,000	12,500	15,000
Selling expenses	10,000	12,500	15,000
General and administrative	15,000	17,000	19,000
Taxes.....................			
Purchase of fixed assets		1,000	1,000
Total disbursements	87,000	120,250	135,000
Tentative cash balance (negative)...	(32,000)	(20,250)	8,250
Minimum cash balance required ...	20,000	25,000	27,000
Additional borrowing required ...	52,000	46,000	19,000
Repayment of bank loan			
Interest paid on balance out-			
standing at rate of ½ per			
month*			
Ending cash balance	$ 20,000	$ 25,750	$ 27,250
Loan balance	$ 52,000	$ 98,000	$117,000

  * Interest is computed at the rate of ½ percent per month and paid on date of repayment which occurs at month end. Loan is taken out at beginning of month.

Equipment costing $20,000 will be bought in February for notes payable that will be paid off, starting that month, at the rate of $1,000 per month. The new equipment will not be fully installed until sometime in August 19x1.

Exhibit 4–5 presents the cash forecast for the six months ending June 30, 19x1, based on the data given above. Exhibit 4–6 presents the pro forma income statement for the six months ending June 30, 19x1. Exhibit 4–7 presents the actual balance sheet of The Prudent Corporation as at January 1, 19x1, and the pro forma balance sheet as at June 30, 19x1.

The financial analyst should examine the pro forma statements critically and submit to feasibility tests the estimates on which the forecasts are based. The ratios and relationships revealed by the pro forma financial statements

April	May	June	Six-month totals
$ 27,250	$ 30,580	$ 30,895	$ 15,000
145,000	168,750	202,500	753,750
	8,000	50,000	58,000
47,500	60,000		107,500
		25,000	25,000
$219,750	$267,330	$308,395	$959,250
49,500	57,000	68,500	274,500
43,750	50,000	62,500	250,000
7,000	7,000	7,000	42,000
17,500	20,000	25,000	100,000
17,500	20,000	25,000	100,000
21,000	23,000	27,000	122,000
		19,000	19,000
1,000	1,000	1,000	5,000
157,250	178,000	235,000	912,500
62,500	89,330	73,395	46,750
30,000	30,000	30,000	30,000
—	—	—	117,000
30,000	58,000	29,000	(117,000)
1,920	435	145	2,500
$ 30,580	$ 30,895	$ 44,250	$ 44,250
$ 87,000	$ 29,000	—	—

Exhibit 4–6

THE PRUDENT CORPORATION
Pro Forma Income Statement
For the Six Months Ending June 30, 19x1

Source of estimate

Sales	$1,000,000	Based on sales budget (page 125)
Cost of sales:		
Materials	300,000	Schedule B
Labor	250,000	Schedule B
Overhead	148,000	Schedule B
	698,000	
Gross profit	302,000	
Selling expense	100,000	Schedule B
Bad debts expense	18,750	Schedule A
General and administrative		
expense	122,000	Schedule B
Total	240,750	
Operating income	61,250	
Gain on sale of equipment.....	25,000	
Interest expense	(2,500)	Exhibit 4–5, footnote
Income before taxes	83,750	
Income taxes	38,050	30% of first $25,000; 52% of balance. Pay ½ in June and accrue balance.
Net income	$ 45,700	

should be analyzed and compared to similar ratios of the past in order to determine whether they are reasonable and feasible of attainment. For example, the current ratio of The Prudent Corporation increased from 2.6 on January 1, 19x1, to 3.2 in the pro forma balance sheet as of June 30, 19x1. During the six months ended June 30, 19x1, a pro forma return on average equity of almost 16 percent was projected. Many other significant measures of turnover, common-size statements, and trends can be computed. The reasonableness of these comparisons and results must be assessed. They can help reveal serious errors and inconsistencies in the assumptions that underlie the projections and thus help strengthen confidence in their reliability.

Differences between short-term and long-term forecasts

The short-term cash forecast is, as we have seen, a very useful and reliable aid in projecting the state of short-term liquidity. Such a detailed approach is, however, only feasible for the short term, that is, up to about 12 months.

Exhibit 4–7

THE PRUDENT CORPORATION
Balance Sheets

	Actual *January 1, 19x1*		*Pro forma* *June 30, 19x1*	
Assets				
Current assets:				
Cash	$ 15,000		$ 44,250	
Accounts receivable (net)	6,500		234,000	
Inventories—raw materials	57,000		71,000	
Total current assets		$ 78,500		$349,250
Real estate	58,000		—	
Fixed assets	206,400		201,400	
Accumulated depreciation	(36,400)		(17,400)	
Net fixed assets		228,000		184,000
Other assets		3,000		3,000
Deferred debt expenses				2,500
Total assets		$309,500		$538,750
Liabilities and Equity Capital				
Current liabilities:				
Accounts payable	2,000		41,500	
Notes payable	28,500		43,500	
Accrued taxes	—		19,050	
Total current liabilities		$ 30,500		$104,050
Long-term debt	15,000		125,000	
Common stock	168,000		168,000	
Retained earnings	96,000		141,700	
		279,000		434,700
Total liabilities and equity capital		$309,500		$538,750

Beyond this time horizon the uncertainties become so great as to preclude detailed and accurate cash forecasts. Instead of focusing on collections of receivables and on payments for labor and materials, the longer-term estimates focus on projections of net income and on other sources and uses of funds. Over the longer term, the emphasis on cash becomes less important, and the estimation process centers on funds, that is, working capital. Over the short term, the difference between cash and other working capital assets is significant. Over the longer term, however, the distinction between cash, receivables, and inventories becomes less significant because the conversion period of these assets to cash is not significant relative to the period encompassed by the longer term. In other words, if the trade cycle is 90 days long, such a period is not as significant in a 3-year forecast as it is in relation to a 6 or 12 months' span. The further we peer into the future, the broader are the financial statement categories that we must estimate and the less detailed can the data behind the estimates be.

The projection of future statements of changes in financial position (SCFPs) is best begun with an analysis of prior year funds statements. To these data can then be added all available information and estimates about the future needs for funds and the most likely sources of funds needed to cover such requirements.

ANALYSIS OF STATEMENTS OF CHANGES IN FINANCIAL POSITION

We shall now focus on the analysis of the SCFP paying particular attention to the value of such an analysis to a projection of future funds flows.

In any analysis of financial statements, the most recent years are the most important because they represent the most recent experience. Since there is an inherent continuity in business events, it is this latest experience that is likely to have the greatest relevance to the projection of future results. So it is with the SCFP.

It is important that the analyst obtain SCFPs for as many years as possible. This is particularly important in the case of an analysis of this statement since the planning and execution of plant expansions, of modernization schemes, of working capital increases as well as the financing of such activities by means of short-term and long-term debt and by means of equity funds is an activity that is likely to encompass many years. Thus, in order for the analyst to be able to assess management's plans and their execution, SCFPs covering a number of years must be analyzed. In this way, a more comprehensive picture of management's financial habits can be obtained and an assessment of them made.

Because conditions vary so greatly from enterprise to enterprise, only a few useful generalizations regarding the thrust of such analysis are possible.

The analyst must first establish what the major sources of funds over the years were and what the major uses were to which these funds were put. A common-size analysis of the funds statements will aid in this year-to-year comparison. Detailed funds statements often tend to obscure the major sources and uses of funds. In assessing overall trends and practices, it is best to cumulate the major sources and uses over a span of years, such as 5 or 10, because single fiscal periods are too short for purposes of reaching meaningful conclusions. Thus, for example, the financing of a major capital expansion may be accomplished years before it is in full swing.

In evaluating sources and uses of funds, the analyst should focus on questions such as these:

- Has the enterprise been able to finance fixed asset *replacements* from internally generated funds? Historical-cost as well as current-cost depreciation may be useful in this assessment. Many companies do not provide adequate information to enable the analyst to distinguish between replacement and capacity expansion.
- How have expansion and business acquisitions been financed?
- To what extent is the enterprise dependent on outside financing? How frequently is it required, and what form does it take?
- What does the company's need for funds and its access to funds suggest as implications for its dividend policy?

When funds are defined as working capital, further analysis is required in order to focus on cash. Thus, the changes in receivables, inventories, payables, and accruals will have to be analyzed and a determination made whether they affect operations so that funds are converted to cash focus.

ILLUSTRATION OF THE ANALYSIS OF STATEMENTS OF CHANGES IN FINANCIAL POSITION

In this illustration, we shall analyze the statements of changes in financial position of Alfa, Inc. (see Appendix 2B), covering the five-year period ending December 31, 19x6. Exhibit 4–8 presents these statements in common-size format.

During the five-year period the major sources of funds of Alfa were (dollars in millions): operations 251, long-term debt (115 net of debt reductions), and property sales 82. The major uses were property additions 278 and cash dividends 48 which resulted in a net addition to working capital of 121. During this period, operations as a percentage of total sources fluctuated from a low of 30.5 percent in 19x3 to a high of 58.9 percent in 19x5. The preceding year, 19x4, was by far the most profitable year in this period. In 19x5, Alfa not only used up more than its funds from operations to invest in long-term assets but it also reduced its working capital by $15.5 million in order to repay debt and raise cash dividends to a new high level. That level of dividends required 17.7 percent of total sources compared to only 6.4 percent in the previous year. The higher absolute level of dividends was maintained in 19x6.

Over the five-year period, funds from operations did not cover property additions and thus dividends were in effect financed by either long-term debt or property sales.

Over the five-year period, Alfa's addition of $121 million to working capital was necessitated by the growth in the volume of its business. Cash increased by only $13.4 million over this period while receivables grew by $91.1 million and inventories by $100.5 million. Accounts payable and accrued expenses grew by $63.3 million. The reasons for the company's failure to use more

Exhibit 4–8

◆ ALFA, INC.

Common-Size Statement of Changes in Financial Position
For the Five Years Ended December 31, 19x6

	19x6	19x5	19x4	19x3	19x2
Sources:					
Internally generated funds:					
Net income	16.2%	29.7%	41.9%	17.1%	19.8%
Depreciation and amortization	20.7	31.9	16.6	11.2	12.0
Deferred income taxes—					
noncurrent portion	3.0	.3	.1	3.9	4.9
Less undistributed income of					
unconsolidated domestic					
subsidiaries	(1.2)	(3.0)	(2.9)	(1.7)	(1.8)
Total from operations	38.7	58.9%	55.7%	30.5	34.9%
Additions to long-term debt	49.6	24.1	23.4	47.4	42.0
Decrease in noncurrent					
receivables	6.7	—	—	—	—
Issuance of capital stock for					
businesses acquired	2.1	3.3	.6	—	8.8
Property sales and retirements:					
Sale-and-leaseback financing	—	1.3	7.2	16.3	7.0
Other	2.9	11.5	7.1	5.7	7.3
Decrease on deferred charges					
Other net	—	.9	6.0	.1	—
Total	100.0%	100.0%	100.0%	100.0%	100.0%
Applications:					
Property additions:					
Businesses acquired	5.7%	2.4%	—	.3%	6.3%
Existing businesses	35.0	60.7	41.8%	38.4	51.4

Increase in noncurrent receivables	—	5.0	2.5	3.8	1.1
Reduction of long-term debt	6.8	35.6	19.6	20.5	21.2
Cash dividends on capital stock	10.4	17.7	6.4	5.1	6.1
Increase in investment in non-consolidated finance subsidiaries	—	—	—	.9	7.1
Increase in deferred charges	1.7	1.6	—	1.2	4.1
Other—net	.3	—	.1	—	—
Total	59.9	123.	70.4	70.2	97.3
Increase (decrease) in working capital	40.1%	(23.0)%	29.6%	29.8%	2.7%

Represented by:

Current assets—increase (decrease):					
Cash and marketable securities	(4.0)%	4.1%	32.3%	7.9%	(54.3)%
Receivables	45.8	(330.5)	123.9	79.5	1037.9
Inventories	61.0	25.4	35.7	80.3	507.5
Prepaid expenses	(3.7)	41.2	4.2	1.5	44.3
Change in current assets	99.1	(259.8)	196.1%	169.2%	1535.4
Current liabilities—increase (decrease):					
Notes payable and current portion of long-term debt	(10.4)	85.4	(65.9)	33.6	605.2
Accounts payable and accrued expenses	17.5	(36.5)	31.0	37.4	934.4
Current income taxes:					
Currently payable	(13.1)	(82.4)	54.0	(.2)	(138.7)
Deferred	5.1	(126.3)	77.0	(1.6)	34.5
Change in current liabilities	(.9)	(159.8)	96.1	69.2	435.4
Increase (decrease) in working capital	100.0%	(100.0)%	100.0%	100.0%	100.0%

trade credit are not clear. As discussed above, this net investment in working capital was financed mostly by debt. The company did not resort to equity financing during this period.

A forecast of future SCFPs would have to take into consideration all above discussed trends that the enterprise has exhibited, such as those relating to income, the elements that convert it to sources of funds from operations, fixed assets additions, the relationship of sales to growth in working capital and possibly to sources of funds provided by operations as well. The size of nonfund adjustments, such as depreciation, depends on future depreciation policies and equipment acquisitions. The latter as well as write-off methods to be used for tax purposes will in turn determine the size of the deferred tax adjustments. The more we know about factors such as these the more reliable the forecast will be.

THE ANALYTICALLY RECAST STATEMENT OF CHANGES IN FINANCIAL POSITION

The analysis of the SCFP can often be facilitated by recasting the statement to a form that differs from that in which it was presented by the company. Exhibit 4–9 illustrates such a recasting of Alfa, Inc.'s SCFP (see Appendix 2B) for two years. Often the analysis will require the recasting of the statements for a longer period.

The recasting of Alfa's SCFP is illustrative of the types of adjustments and rearrangements that can be effected—others are possible depending on circumstances and on analytical objectives. The major changes in this recasting are a switch to a cash focus and the deduction from "cash from operations" of the best available estimate of the current (replacement) cost of long-term assets used up in the profit-directed activities of the period. Thus, capital expenditures are subdivided into replacement of long-lived assets used in operations with the balance being designated as expansion and/or improvement.

A review of the analytically recast SCFP reveals that compared to 19x5, 19x6 had a substantial ($33.5 million) adjusted outflow of cash for operations. As a result, this outflow, the dividends, investments in long-lived assets as well as required debt repayments, all had to be financed in 19x6 by a substantial issuance ($58 million) of long-term debt as well as by depleting cash by almost $2 million.

EVALUATION OF THE STATEMENT OF CHANGES IN FINANCIAL POSITION

The foregoing example of an analysis of the SCFP illustrates the variety of information and insights that can be derived. Of course, the analysis of

Exhibit 4–9

ALFA, INC.
Analytically Recast SCFP (Cash Focus)
(in thousands)

	19x6	19x5
Sources:		
Cash from operations	$ 9,365 [a]	$42,746
Replacement of long-term assets used		
up in operations	42,860 [b]	37,450 [b]
Adjusted cash from operations	(33,495)	5,296
Dispositions of:		
Property, plant, and equipment	3,409 49 †	8,677
Debt sources of funds:		
Short term	— 65	13,298
Long term	58,344 46	16,323
Equity sources of funds:		
Common	2,494 48	2,228
Preferred		
Miscellaneous other*	51	618
Total sources	30,752	46,440
Uses:		
Acquisition and/or improvement of:		
Property, plant, and equipment	4,997 [c]	5,264 [d]
Other assets	1,972 54 + 58	4,450
Repayment of debt (net):		
Short term	4,923 65	—
Long term	8,080 55	24,092
Dividends paid:		
On common	11,244 69	10,967
On preferred	1,022 69	1,022
Miscellaneous other*	389 59	—
Total uses	32,627	45,795
Net change in cash and		
cash equivalents	$(1,875) 61	$ 645

    * Nonmaterial items can be aggregated.

    † Refers to key numbers in Alfa, Inc.'s financial statements (Appendix 2B).

    [a] Assuming that decrease in noncurrent receivables 41 represents operating receipts.

    [b] Current cost depreciation as reported by management. (Information available from *SFAS 33* data.

    [c] Property additions: Items 52 + 53 = $47,857 minus [b] above or $42,860 = $4,997 which is assumed to represent capital improvements and/or expansion.

    [d] Property additions: Items 52 + 53 = $42,714 minus [b] above or $37,450 = $5,264 which is assumed to represent capital improvement and/or expansion.

SCFPs is to be performed within the framework of an analysis of all the financial statements, and thus the conclusion reached from an analysis of one statement may be strengthened and corroborated by an analysis of the other financial statements.

There are some useful generalizations that can be made regarding the value of the analysis of the SCFP to the financial analyst.

This statement enables the analyst to appraise the quality of management decisions over time, as well as their impact on the results of operations and financial condition of the enterprise. When the analysis encompasses a longer period of time, the analyst can evaluate management's response to the changing economic conditions as well as to the opportunities and the adversities which invariably present themselves.

Evaluation of the SCFP analysis will indicate the purposes to which management chose to commit funds, where it reduced investment, the source from which it derived additional funds, and to what extent it reduced claims against the enterprise. Such an analysis will also show the disposition of earnings over the years, as well as how management has reinvested the internal fund inflow over which it had discretion. The analysis will also reveal the size and composition of funds from operations, as well as their pattern and degree of stability.

As depicted in Exhibit 4–1 earlier in this chapter, the circulation of funds in an enterprise involves a constant flow of funds and their periodic reinvestment. Thus, funds are invested in labor, material, and overhead costs as well as in long-term assets, such as inventories and plant and equipment, which join the product-cost stream at a slower rate. Eventually, by the process of sales, these costs are converted back into accounts receivable and into cash. If operations are profitable, the funds recovered will exceed the amounts invested, thus augmenting the funds inflow or cash flow. Losses have, of course, the opposite effect.

What constitutes funds inflow, or cash flow, as it is often more crudely referred to, is the subject of considerable confusion. Generally, the funds provided by operations, that is, net income adjusted for nonfund requiring or supplying items, is an index of management's ability to redirect funds away from areas of unfavorable profit opportunity into areas of greater profit potential. However, not all the funds provided by operations may be so available because of existing commitments for debt retirement, stock redemption, equipment replacement, and dividend payments. Nor are funds provided by operations the only potential cash inflows, since management can avail itself of external sources of capital in order to bolster its funds inflow. The components of the "sources of funds from operations" figure hold important clues to the stability of that source of funds. Thus, for example, depreciation is a more stable element in the total than net income itself in that it represents a recovery by the enterprise of the investment in fixed assets out of selling prices even before a profit is earned.

In evaluating the SCFP, the analyst will judge a company's quality of earnings by the impact that changes in economic and industry conditions have on its flow of funds. The statement will also reveal nonfunds generating income that may have a bearing on the evaluation of earnings quality.

If in his estimates of future earnings potential the analyst foresees a need for additional capital, his analysis of the funds statement will be directed towards a projection of the source from which these funds will be obtained, and what dilution of earnings per share, if any, this will involve.

The analysis and evaluation of the SCFP is, as the foregoing discussion suggests, an important early step in the projection of future SCFPs.

PROJECTION OF STATEMENTS OF CHANGES IN FINANCIAL POSITION

No thorough model of an enterprise's future results is complete without a concurrent forecast of the size of funds needed for the realization of the projections in the model as well as an assessment of the possible sources from which such funds can be derived.

If a future expansion of sales and profits is forecast, the analyst must know whether the enterprise has the "financial horsepower" to see such an expansion through by means of internally generated funds and, if not, where the required funds are going to come from.

The projection of the SCFP will start with a careful estimate of the expected changes in each individual category of assets and the funds that will be derived from or required by such changes. Some of the more important factors to be taken into consideration follow:

1. The net income expected to be generated by future results will be adjusted for nonfund items, such as depreciation, depletion, deferred income taxes, and nonremitted earnings of subsidiaries and investees, in order to arrive at estimates of funds provided by operations.
2. Sources of funds from disposals of assets, sales of investments, and the sale of stocks and bonds will be estimated.
3. The needs for working capital will be arrived at by estimating the required level of the individual working capital items such as cash, receivables, and inventories and reducing this by the expected levels of payables. There is usually a relationship between incremental sales and the corresponding increment in required working capital amounts.
4. Expected capital expenditures will be based on the present level of operations as compared with productive capacity, on an estimate of the future level of activity implied by the profit projections, as well as on current replacement cost data.
5. Mandatory debt retirement and desirable minimum levels of dividend payments will also be estimated.

ILLUSTRATION OF A PROJECTION OF STATEMENTS OF CHANGES IN FINANCIAL POSITION

Based on the financial statements of Alfa, Inc. (see Appendix 2B), and on the preceding analysis we will prepare a forecast of the SCFPs of Alfa for 19x7 and 19x8 based on the following assumptions:

Forecast (in thousands)	19x8	19x7
Sources of funds:		
Undistributed income of nonconsolidated domestic subsidiaries	$ (2,000)	$ (1,500)
Issuance of capital stock for businesses acquired	2,000	2,500
Property sales and retirements		
Sale-and-leaseback financing	9,000	8,000
Other	4,000	3,500
Other—net	—	300
Applications of funds:		
Property additions:		
Businesses acquired	5,000	7,000
Existing businesses	50,000	45,000
Increase in noncurrent receivables	3,300	3,000
Cash dividends on capital stock	14,000	13,000
Increase in deferred charges	2,500	2,000
Other—net	400	—
Increase in investments in nonconsolidated finance subsidiaries	7,400	7,300
Other projections:		
Revenues	1,500,000	1,350,000

Assumptions

The remaining sources and uses of funds will be estimated based on the following assumptions:

1. Net income in 19x7 and 19x8 will be at a level representing the average percentage of net income to revenues as prevailed in the five-year period ended December 31, 19x6.
2. Depreciation and amortization in 19x7 and 19x8 will bear the same relationship to net income as have the average depreciation and amortization over the five-year period 19x2–x6 borne to average net income over the same period.
3. Deferred income taxes—noncurrent portion—will be in 19x7 at a level that reflects the relationship of total five-year deferred taxes (noncurrent) to total five-year net income. It will change in 19x8 by the percentage change that 19x8 net income bears to 19x7 net income.

4. Additions to long-term debt in 19x7 and 19x8 will be at the level needed to meet the needed year-end working capital. The assumed year-end working capital needs will be at a level that is measured by the ratio of working capital to revenues reflecting the working capital to revenue ratio that prevailed in 19x6.

    Exhibit 4–10 presents the projected SCFPs for Alfa, Inc., for 19x7 and 19x8.

Some assumptions in the above projections may be considered as somewhat mechanical. They are presented here merely for purposes of illustration. In practice, more refined relationships may be calculated on the basis of detailed studies of past relationships.

The impact of adversity

The projected SCFP is useful not only in estimating the funds implications of future expansion and opportunity but also in assessing the impact on the enterprise of sudden adversity.

A sudden adversity, from the point of view of its impact on the flow of funds, will usually manifest itself in a serious interruption in the inflow of funds. This can be brought about by such events as recessions, strikes, or the loss of a major customer or market. In this context, a projection of the SCFP would be a first step in the assessment of the defensive posture of an enterprise. The basic question to which such an analysis is directed is this: what can the enterprise do; and what resources, both internal and external, can it marshal to cope with a sudden and serious reduction in the inflow of funds?

The strategies and alternatives available to an enterprise faced with such adversities are ably examined and discussed in a work by Professor Donaldson. Dr. Donaldson defines financial mobility as the capacity to redirect the use of financial resources in response to new information about the company and its environment.[1] This concept is related to that of "financial flexibility" discussed in the preceding chapter.

The projected sources and uses of funds statement is an important tool in the assessment of the resources available to meet such "new information" as well as in planning the changes in financial strategy which this may require.

To the prospective credit grantor such an approach represents an excellent tool in the assessment of risk. In estimating the effects of, for example, a recession, on the future flow of funds he can trace through not only the potential shrinkage in cash inflows from operations but also the effects of such shrinkage on the uses of funds and on the sources from which they can be derived.

---

[1] Gordon Donaldson, *Strategy for Financial Mobility* (Boston: Graduate School of Business Administration, Harvard University, 1969).

Exhibit 4–10

ALFA, INC.
Projected Statement of Changes in Financial Position
(in thousands)

	19x8	19x7
Sources:		
Internally generated funds:		
Net income [a]	$ 43,500	$ 39,150
Depreciation and amortization [b]	29,798	26,818
Deferred income taxes—noncurrent		
portion [c]	4,693	4,228
Less undistributed income of		
nonconsolidated domestic subsidiaries [d]	(2,000)	(1,500)
Total from operations	75,991	68,696
Additions to long-term debt—net [f]	18,159	11,846
Issuance of capital stock for businesses		
acquired [d]	2,000	2,500
Property sales and requirements:		
Sale-and-leaseback financing [d]	9,000	8,000
Other [d]	4,000	3,500
Other—net [d]		300
Total	109,150	94,842
Applications:		
Property additions:		
Businesses acquired [d]	5,000	7,000
Existing businesses [d]	50,000	45,000
Increase in noncurrent receivables [d]	3,300	3,000
Cash dividends on capital stock [d]	14,000	13,000
Increase in investment in nonconsolidated		
finance subsidiaries [d]	7,400	7,300
Increase in deferred charges [d]	2,500	2,000
Other—net [d]	400	
Total	82,600	77,300
Increase (decrease) in working		
capital [c]	$ 26,550	$ 17,542
Working capital at year-end [e]	$265,500	$238,950

[a] Average percent of net income to revenues in 19x2–x6 $= \dfrac{\text{Total net income}}{\text{Total revenues}} =$ $\dfrac{\$146,925}{\$5,107,547} = 2.9$ percent.

Net income for 19x7 $= \$1,350,000 \times .029 = \$39,150$
Net income for 19x8 $= \$1,500,000 \times .029 = \$43,500$

[b] Average percent of depreciation and amortization to net income in 19x2–x6 $= \dfrac{\text{Total depreciation and amortization}}{\text{Total net income}} = \dfrac{\$100,659}{\$146,925} = 68.5$ percent.

Depreciation and amortization for 19x7 $= \$39,150 \times .685 = \$26,818$
Depreciation and amortization for 19x8 $= \$43,500 \times .685 = \$29,798$

[c] Average percent of deferred income taxes (noncurrent portion) to net income in 19x2–19x6 $= \dfrac{\text{Total deferred taxes—noncurrent}}{\text{Total net income}} = \dfrac{\$15,896}{\$146,925} = 10.8$ percent.

Exhibit 4–10 (*concluded*)

Deferred income taxes—noncurrent for 19x7 = $39,150 × .108 = $4,228

Percent change of 19x8 net income to 19x7 net income $= \dfrac{\$43,500}{\$39,150} = 1.11$

Deferred taxes noncurrent for 19x8 = $4,228 × 1.11 = $4,693

(d) Given.

(e) Percentage of year-end working capital to revenues in 19x6 $= \dfrac{\$221,408}{\$1,251,087} = .177$.

Yearend working capital in 19x7 = $1,350,000 × .177 = $238,950
Yearend working capital in 19x8 = $1,500,000 × .177 = $265,500
Increase in working capital in 19x7 = $238,950 − $221,408 = *$17,542*
Increase in working capital in 19x8 = $265,500 − $238,950 = *$26,550*

(f) Amounts needed to balance the statements.

The funds flow adequacy ratio

The purpose of this ratio is to determine the degree to which an enterprise generated sufficient funds from operations to cover capital expenditures, net investment in inventories, and cash dividends. To remove cyclical and other erratic influences, a five-year total is used in the computation of the ratio, thus:

$$\frac{\text{Five-year sum of sources of funds from operations}}{\begin{array}{c}\text{Five-year sum of capital expenditures, inventory}\\\text{additions, and cash dividends}\end{array}}$$

The investment in the other important working capital item, receivables, is omitted on the theory that it can be financed primarily by short-term credit, i.e., growth in payables, and so forth.

A ratio of 1 indicates that an enterprise has covered its needs based on attained levels of growth without the need for external financing. To the degree that the ratio falls below 1, internally generated funds may be inadequate to maintain dividends and current operating growth levels. This ratio may also reflect the effect of inflation on the fund requirements of an enterprise. The reading of this, like any other ratio, can provide no definitive answers and is only a pointer to further analysis and investigation. The ratio for Alfa, Inc., (see Appendix 2B) for the five years ending 19x6 is:

$$\frac{\$251,215\,(a)}{\$278,275\,(b) + \$101,083\,(c) + 48,338\,(d)} = \underline{\underline{.59}}$$

From statement of changes in financial position— five years sum of:

(a) Funds from operations—item 45 .
(b) Property additions—items 52 and 53 .
(c) Inventories—item 63 .
(d) Cash dividends—item 56 .

This ratio indicates that for the five years ending in 19x6 Alfa's funds from operations fell far short of covering the three items in the denominator of the ratio.

Funds reinvestment ratio

This ratio is useful in measuring the percentage of the investment in assets, which is being retained and reinvested in the enterprise for the replacement of assets and for growth in operations. The formula is:

$$\frac{\text{Funds provided by operations} - \text{Dividends}}{\text{Gross plant} + \text{Investment} + \text{Other assets} + \text{Working capital}}$$

A reinvestment rate of 8 to 10 percent is considered generally to be at a satisfactory level. The ratio for Alfa, Inc. (Appendix 2B), for 19x6 is:

$$\frac{\$45,604^{(e)} - \$12,266^{(f)}}{\$448,577^{(g)} + \$55,496^{(h)} + \$65,747^{(i)} + \$221,408^{(j)}} = 4.2 \text{ percent}$$

(e) Funds from operations—item 45.
(f) Cash dividends—item 56.
(g) Gross property, plant, and equipment item 29.
(h) Investments items 27 + 28.
(i) Other assets—item 30.
(j) Total current assets 26 − Total current liabilities 35.

Alfa's funds reinvestment ratio for 19x6 is a rather low 4.2 percent that compares to the corresponding ratio of 3.9 percent in 19x5.

CONCLUSION

In the assessment of future liquidity, the use of cash forecasts for the short term and of projected SCFPs for the longer term represent some of the most useful tools available to the financial analyst. In contrast to ratio measures of liquidity, these tools involve a detailed examination of sources and uses of cash or funds. Such examination and estimation processes can be subjected to feasibility tests by means of pro forma statements and to the discipline inherent in the double-entry accounting system.

QUESTIONS

1. What is the primary difference between funds flow analysis and ratio analysis? Which is superior and why?

2. "From an operational point of view, management focuses on cash rather than working capital." Do you agree with the statement? Why or why not?

3. What is the relationship between inflows and outflows of cash?

4. Why is the short-term cash forecast important to the financial analyst?

5. What is the first step to be taken in preparing a cash forecast, and what considerations are required in such a step?

6. What are pro forma financial statements? How are they utilized in conjunction with funds flow projections?

7. What are the limitations of short-term cash forecasts?

8. If the usefulness of a short-term cash forecast is limited, what analytical approach is available to the financial analyst who wants to analyze future flows of working capital?

9. What questions will the analyst focus on in evaluating sources and uses of funds?

10. What useful information do you, as a financial analyst, expect to get from the analysis of past SCFPs (funds statement)?

11. What would a forecast of future SCFPs have to take into consideration?

12. What are the differences between short-term and long-term financial forecasts?

13. What analytical function does the common-size SCFP serve?

14. Why is a projected SCFP necessary when you have historical data which are based on actual performance?

15. If actual operations are seriously affected by unforeseen adversities, would a projected SCFP still be useful?

16. "Cash flow per share" is sometimes used in common stock analysis in the same fashion as *earnings per share*. In financial analysis, shouldn't the former be used more often than the latter? Explain. (CFA)

5 Analysis of capital structure and long-term solvency

The financial strength and stability of a business entity and the probability surrounding its ability to weather random shocks and to maintain its solvency in the face of adversity are important measures of risk associated with it. This evaluation of risk is critical because, as discussed in Chapter 1, the equity investor as well as the lender require returns that are commensurate with the levels of risk that each assumes. This and the preceding two chapters deal with the evaluation of the financial strength and viability of enterprises within different time frames.

KEY ELEMENTS IN THE EVALUATION OF LONG-TERM SOLVENCY

The process of evaluation of long-term solvency of an enterprise differs markedly from that of the assessment of short-term liquidity. In the latter, the time horizon is short and it is often possible to make a reasonable projection of funds flows. It is not possible to do this for the longer term, and thus the measures used in the evaluation of longer-term solvency are less specific but more all-encompassing.

There are a number of key elements involved in the evaluation of the long-term solvency of an enterprise. The analysis of capital structure is concerned with the types of capital funds used to finance the enterprise, ranging from "patient" and permanent equity capital to short-term funds that are a temporary, and, consequently, a much more risky source. There are different degrees of risk associated with the holding of different types of assets. Moreover, assets represent secondary[1] sources of security for lenders ranging from

---

[1] When lending to going concerns, lenders should regard the liquidation of assets for the purpose of recovery of principal and interest as a measure of last resort and as an undesirable source of funds to rely on at the time credit is granted.

loans secured by specific assets to assets available as general security to unsecured creditors.

On a long-term basis, earnings and earning power (which implies the recurring ability to generate cash in the future) are some of the most important and reliable indications of financial strength available. Earnings are the most desirable and reliable sources of funds for the longer-term payment of interest and repayment of principal. As a surrogate for funds generated by operations, earnings are the yardstick against which the coverage of interest and other fixed charges is measured. Moreover, a reliable and stable trend of earnings is one of the best assurances of an enterprise's ability to borrow in times of funds shortage and its consequent ability to extricate itself from the very conditions that lead to insolvency.

In addition to general measures of financial strength and long-term solvency, lenders rely on the protection afforded by loan covenants or the pledges of specific assets as security. All loan covenants define default and the legal remedies available when it occurs in order to give the lender the right to step in at an early stage. Most are designed to alert the lender to the deterioration in such key measures of financial health as the current ratio and the debt-to-equity ratio, against the issuance of further debt, or to ensure against the disbursement of resources through the payments of dividends above specified levels or through acquisitions. Of course, there can be no prohibition against operating losses, a core problem attending most cases of deterioration in financial condition. Thus, the existence of protective provisions cannot substitute for alertness and a continuous monitoring of the financial condition of an enterprise in which long-term funds are at risk.[2]

The vast amount of public and private debt outstanding has led to standardized approaches to its analysis and evaluation. By far the most important is the rating of debt securities by rating agencies that is discussed in Appendix 5A to this chapter. Appendix 5B examines the use of ratios as predictors of failure.

In this chapter, we shall examine in further detail the tools and the measures available for the analysis of long-term solvency.

IMPORTANCE OF CAPITAL STRUCTURE

The capital structure of an enterprise consists basically of equity funds and debt. It is measured in terms of the relative magnitude of the various

---

[2] Lenders have learned that senior positions in the debt hierarchy do not always afford in practice the security they seem to afford in theory. Thus, subordinated debt is not akin to capital stock because subordinated creditors have a voice in determining whether a debtor should be rescued or be thrown into bankruptcy. This interdependence between junior and senior lenders has led some to the belief that one might as well buy the highest yielding obligation of an enterprise since any situation serious enough to affect the value of the junior security is likely to affect the senior security as well.

Exhibit 5-1:   Asset distribution and capital structure of an enterprise

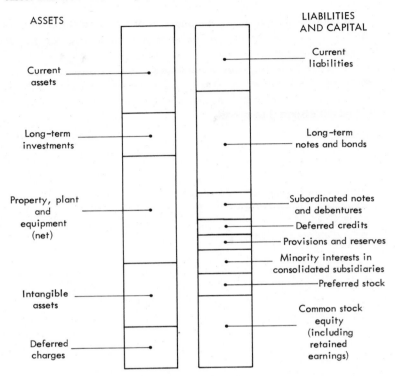

sources of funds of the enterprise. The inherent financial stability of an enterprise and the risk of insolvency to which it is exposed are importantly dependent on the sources of its funds as well as on the type of assets it holds and the relative magnitude of such asset categories. Exhibit 5-1 presents an example of the distribution of assets of an enterprise and the sources of funds used to finance their acquisition. It is evident from the diagram in Exhibit 5-1 that within the framework of equality prevailing between assets and liabilities plus capital, a large variety of combinations of assets and sources of funds used to finance them is possible.

ACCOUNTING PRINCIPLES

The amounts at which liabilities and equity accounts are shown on the financial statements are governed by the application of GAAP. The analyst must keep these principles in mind when analyzing the capital structure and its effect on long-term solvency. While it can be stated, as a broad generalization, that the accounting principles governing the measurement of liabilities and equities do not affect the analysis of financial statements as importantly as do those governing the measurement of assets, the importance of the former are quite important to our present topic.

The relationship between liabilities and equity capital, the two major sources of capital in an enterprise, is always an important factor entering into the assessment of long-term solvency. Thus, an understanding of their nature is essential to the analyst. There are liabilities that are not fully reflected in the balance sheet, and there are accounts whose accounting classification as debt or equity should not be automatically accepted by the analyst. The proper decision of how to classify or deal with these depends on a thorough understanding of their nature and/or the particular conditions of issue to which they are subject. The discussion that follows highlights some important analytical considerations.

Deferred taxes

Most deferred credits, such as bond premiums, represent allocation accounts designed primarily to aid in the measurements of income. They do not present an important problem of analysis and are relatively insignificant in size. Deferred income items, such as subscription income received in advance, represent an obligation for future service and are, as such, clearly liabilities.

One type of deferred credit that is generally much more sizable, and consequently much more important, is *deferred income taxes*. This account is not a liability in the usual sense because the government does not have a definite short-term or even longer-term claim against the enterprise. Nevertheless, this account does represent the aggregate exhaustion in tax deductibility of assets and other items, over and above that recorded for book purposes, and this means that at some time in the future the deferred tax account will be used to reduce the higher income tax expense that corresponds to *increased* tax liabilities. Even if the likelihood of the deferred tax account "reversing" in the foreseeable future is quite good, there still remains the question of whether the time-adjusted present value of such future expected "reversals" should not be used instead of the nominal face value amount of the deferred credit. After all, most other liabilities on the balance sheet are carried at present value. The higher the interest rates (cost of debt) applicable to an entity are, the more significant is the impact of discounting to present value.

To the analyst, the important question here is whether to treat the deferred tax account as a liability, as an equity item, or as part debt and part equity. The decision depends on the nature of the deferral, the past experience with the account (e.g., has it been constantly growing?), and the likelihood of future "reversal."

In making his judgment, the analyst must recognize that under normal circumstances, deferred tax liabilities will reverse, i.e., become payable, only when a firm shrinks in size. Generally, a shrinkage in size is attended by losses rather than by taxable income. In such circumstances, the drawing down of the deferred tax account is more likely to involve credits to tax loss carry-forwards or carry-backs, rather than to the Cash account.

To the extent that such future "reversal" is only a remote possibility, as is the case with timing differences due to accelerated depreciation, the deferred credit should be viewed as a source of funds of such long-term nature as to be classifiable as equity. On the other hand, if the possibility of a "drawing down" of the deferred tax account in the foreseeable future is quite strong, then the account, or a part of it, is more in the nature of a long-term liability.[3] In classifying the deferred tax account as between debt and equity, the analyst must be guided by considerations such as the ones discussed above. Current deferred taxes relate to some corresponding current asset or liability and should generally not be reclassified.

When the analyst decides to classify deferred tax credits as equity (either in whole or in part), the following *analytical* entry is appropriate:

Deferred Income Taxes—Current* X
Deferred Income Taxes—Noncurrent* .... Y
    Owners' Equity ....   Z

    * As applicable.

Long-term leases

Under *SFAS 13,* most financing of long-term noncancelable leases must be shown as debt. While *SFAS 13* has tightened the rules considerably, companies can still find ways around them by the way leases are written and by other means. If the analyst concludes that leases that are not capitalized by the reporting entity should be capitalized, he can, for analytical purposes, book them as follows:

Leasehold Assets X
    Liabilities under Long-Term Leases ....   Y

Off-balance sheet financing

SFAS 13 has significantly curtailed one of the most significant and widely used methods of off-balance sheet financing. However, in trying to determine

---

[3] H. C. Herring and F. A. Jacobs in "The Expected Behavior of Deferred Tax Credits," *Journal of Accountancy,* August 1976, argue that statistically the probability of the deferred tax accounting reversing is quite good.

the total debt to which an entity is subject, the analyst must be aware that some managements will attempt to understate debt and that new methods of doing this are constantly tried. Chapter 7 contains a discussion of recent methods in use such as "take or pay contracts," "sales" of receivables, and inventory repurchase agreements. A careful reading of footnotes and of management comments along with inquiries of management can shed light on the existence of such practices.

Liabilities for pensions

Analysts should generally regard an excess of vested pension benefits over pension plan assets as an *unfunded vested pension liability* (UVPL), even though presently accepted accounting standards do not regard them as liabilities. While we favor focusing on this amount as the unrecorded liability, two other elements deserve consideration. If we take a liquidating point of view then, if 30 percent of shareholders' equity is lower than the UVPL, it should be substituted as the pension liability because in liquidation a company's liability for pensions is limited to 30 percent of net worth. The other element deserving consideration is the case when the unfunded past or prior service costs (UPSC) exceed the UVPL. If we adopt the going-concern point of view, then we can regard the larger of the two amounts as an unrecorded interest-bearing pension liability, and this is a reasonable point of view.[4] The amount of the unfunded prior service cost is not easily or readily obtainable.

The analyst will adjust for the unrecorded pension liability by reducing stockholders' equity to reflect the charges to income that would have been made all along in recording the obligation. However, recognition should be given to the fact that when pension costs will ultimately be funded, they will be tax deductible and that consequently a future tax benefit also arises. Thus, the *analytical* entry to record a pension liability of $1,000 is as follows:[5]

Stockholders' Equity 540
Deferred Taxes* (balance sheet account
  for future tax benefits assuming a
  46 percent tax rate) 460
  Long-Term Pension Liability* 1,000

* Since the future tax benefit will be realized at the same time that the pension liability will be discharged analytically, one can be netted against the other thus creating a net liability of $540.

---

[4] Two articles that ably discuss these issues are P. J. Regan, "Credit Ratings and Pension Costs," *Financial Analysts Journal,* March–April 1979; and D. A. Lasman and R. L. Weil, "Adjusting the Debt-Equity Ratio," *Financial Analysts Journal,* September–October, 1978.

[5] Another point of view in making this adjustment, one of doubtful validity in our opinion, is to debit an asset instead of stockholders' equity with $1,000 on the assumption that the pension obligation gives rise to substantial future benefits in the form of higher morale and increased productivity.

Unconsolidated subsidiaries

It is important to remember that the preferred method of presenting the financial statements of a parent and its subsidiary is in consolidated format. This is also the preferred method from the analyst's point of view for most analytical purposes, although separate financial statements of the consolidated entities are necessary in some cases, such as when the utilization of assets of a subsidiary (e.g., an insurance company or a bank) is not subject to the full discretion of the parent.

Information on unconsolidated subsidiaries may also be important because bondholders of such subsidiaries can look only to the latter's assets as security for their bonds. Moreover, bondholders of the parent company (particularly holding companies) may derive a significant portion of their fixed-charge coverage from the dividends of the unconsolidated subsidiaries. Yet, in the event of the subsidiary's bankruptcy, the parent bondholders may be in a junior position to the bondholders of the subsidiary.

When the financial statements of a finance subsidiary are not consolidated with the parent, consolidation may be undertaken as an analytical adjustment as follows:

Subsidiary's Assets* X
    Subsidiary's Liabilities* .... Y
    Parent's Investment in Subsidiary .... Z

    * Using as much detail as is needed or is available.

If the subsidiary has unrecorded lease or pension liabilities, they too may be consolidated for purposes of analysis.

Provisions, reserves, and contingent liabilities

Provisions such as for guarantees and warranties represent obligations to offer future service and should be classified as such. Generally speaking, reserves created by charges to income may also be considered as liabilities. However, general contingency reserves or reserves for very indeterminate purposes (most of which are now prohibited by *SFAS 5*) should not be considered as genuine liabilities.

The analyst must make a judgment regarding the probability of commitments or contingencies becoming actual liabilities and should then treat these items accordingly. Thus, guarantees of indebtedness of subsidiaries or others that are likely to become liabilities should be treated as such.

Minority interests

Minority interests in consolidated financial statements represent the ownership interests of minority shareholders of the subsidiaries included in the consolidated group. These are not liabilities similar in nature to debt because they have neither mandatory dividend payment nor principal repayment requirements. Capital structure measurements concentrate on the mandatory payments aspects of liabilities. From this point of view, minority interests are more in the nature of outsider's claim to a portion of the equity or an offset representing their proportionate ownership of assets.[6]

Convertible debt

Convertible debt is generally classified among liabilities. However, if the conversion terms are such that the only reasonable assumption that can be made is that the debt will be converted into common stock, then it may be classified as equity for purposes of capital structure analysis.

Preferred stock

Most preferred stock entails no absolute obligation for payment of dividends or repayment of principal, possessing thus the characteristics of true equity. However, preferred stock with a fixed maturity or stock subject to sinking fund requirements should, from an analytical point of view, be considered as debt.

Preferred stock with mandatory redemption requirements is akin to debt and should be considered as such by the financial analyst.

ADJUSTMENTS TO THE BOOK VALUE OF ASSETS

Because the owners' equity of an enterprise is measured by the excess of total assets over total liabilities, any analytical revision of asset book values (i.e., amounts at which assets are shown in the financial statements) will also result in a change in the amount of the owners' equity. For this reason, in assessing capital structure, the analyst must decide whether or not the book value amounts of assets are realistically stated. The following are examples of the need for possible adjustments. Different or additional adjustments may be needed depending on circumstances.

Inventories

Inventories carried at LIFO are generally understated in times of rising prices. The amount by which inventories computed under FIFO (which are closer to replacement cost) exceed inventories computed under LIFO is now disclosed. So is the current cost of inventories under *SFAS 33*. These financial disclosures should enable the analyst to adjust inventory amounts and the

---

[6] Minority interests are shown at book value. Thus, if the analyst wants to assess what the parent company would have to pay in order to acquire the minority interest, market rather than book values will be the determining factor.

corresponding owners' equity amounts (after tax) to more realistic current costs or values.

Marketable securities

Marketable securities are generally stated at cost that may be below market value. Using parenthetical or footnote information, the analyst can make an analytical adjustment increasing this asset to market value and owners' equity (after tax) by an equal amount.

Intangible assets

Intangible assets and deferred items of dubious value that are included on the asset side of the balance sheet have an effect on the computation of the total equity of an enterprise. To the extent that the analyst cannot evaluate or form an opinion on the present value or future utility of such assets, they may be excluded from consideration thereby reducing the amount of equity capital (after tax) by the amounts at which such assets are carried. However, the arbitrary exclusion of all intangible assets from the capital base is an unjustified exercise in overconservatism.

The foregoing discussion related to the evaluation and the classification of debt and equity accounts. Let us now turn to an examination of the significance of capital structure in financial analysis.

THE SIGNIFICANCE OF CAPITAL STRUCTURE

The significance of capital structure is derived, first and foremost, from the essential difference between debt and equity.

The equity is the basic risk capital of an enterprise. Every enterprise must have some equity capital that bears the risk to which it is inevitably exposed. The outstanding characteristic of equity capital is that it has no guaranteed or mandatory return that must be paid out in any event and no definite timetable for repayment of the capital investment. Thus, capital that can be withdrawn at the contributor's option is not really equity capital and has, instead, the characteristics of debt.[7] From the point of view of an enterprise's stability and exposure to the risk of insolvency, the outstanding characteristic of equity capital is that it is permanent, can be counted on to remain invested in times of adversity, and has no mandatory requirement for dividends. It is such funds that an enterprise can most confidently invest in

---

[7] For example, during the financial crisis that befell many brokerage houses in the late 1960s, it was discovered that much "equity" capital that was thought to lend strength to the enterprise and additional security to customers and creditors was in effect subject to withdrawal by owners. At the sign of real trouble, these owners withdrew their capital, thus compounding the financial problems even more.

long-term assets and expose to the greatest risks. Their loss, for whatever reason, will not necessarily jeopardize the firm's ability to pay the fixed claims against it.

Both short-term and long-term debt, in contrast to equity capital, must be repaid. The longer the term of the debt and the less onerous its repayment provisions, the easier it will be for the enterprise to service it. Nevertheless, it must be repaid at certain specified times regardless of the enterprise's financial condition; and so must interest be paid in the case of most debt instruments. Generally, the failure to pay principal or interest will result in proceedings under which the common stockholders may lose control of the enterprise as well as part or all of their investment. Should the entire equity capital of the enterprise be wiped out by losses, the creditors may also stand to lose part or all of their principal and interest due.

It can be readily appreciated that the larger the proportion of debt in the total capital structure of an enterprise, the higher the resulting fixed charges and repayment commitments and the greater the probability of a chain of events leading to an inability to pay interest and principal when due.

To the investor in the common stock of an enterprise, the existence of debt represents a risk of loss of his investment, and this is balanced by the potential of high profits arising from financial leverage. Excessive debt may also mean that management's initiative and flexibility for profitable action will be stifled and inhibited.

The creditor prefers as large a capital base as possible as a cushion that will shield him against losses that can result from adversity. The smaller the relative capital base, or conversely, the larger the proportionate contribution of funds by creditors, the smaller is the creditors' cushion against loss and consequently the greater their risk of loss.

While there has been a considerable debate, particularly in academic circles, over whether the *cost of capital* of an enterprise varies with different capital structures, that is, with various mixes of debt and equity, the issue seems significantly clearer from the point of view of outsiders to the enterprise, such as creditors or investors, who must make decisions on the basis of conditions as they are. In the case of otherwise identical entities, the creditor exposes himself to greater risk if he lends to the company with 60 percent of its funds provided by debt (and 40 percent by equity capital) than if he lends to a similar company that derives, say, only 20 percent of its funds from debt.

Under the Modigliani-Miller thesis, the cost of capital of an enterprise in a perfect market is, except for the tax deductibility of interest, not affected by the debt-to-equity relationship.[8] This is so, they assert, because each individual stockholder can inject, by use of personally created leverage, his own

---

[8] F. Modigliani and M. Miller, "The Cost of Capital, Corporation Finance and the Theory of Investment," *American Economic Review,* June 1958, pp. 261–97.

blend of risk into the total investment position. Thus, under this theory, the advantage of debt will be offset by a markdown in a company's price-earnings ratio.

The degree of risk in an enterprise, as judged by the outside prospective investor is, however, a given; and our point of view, as well as our task here, is to measure the degree of risk residing in the capital structure of an enterprise.

REASONS FOR EMPLOYMENT OF DEBT

In addition to serving as an inflation hedge, a primary reason for the employment of debt by an enterprise is that up to a certain point, debt is, from the point of view of the ownership, a less expensive source of funds than equity capital. This is so for two main reasons:

1. The interest cost of debt is fixed,[9] and thus, as long as it is lower than the return that can be earned on the funds supplied by creditors, this excess return accrues to the benefit of the equity.
2. Unlike dividends, which are considered a distribution of profits, interest is considered an expense and is, consequently, tax deductible.

A further discussion of these two main reasons follows.

The concept of financial leverage

Financial leverage means the use in the capital structure of an enterprise of debt that pays a fixed return. Since no creditor or lender would be willing to put up loan funds without the cushion and safety provided by the owners' equity capital, this borrowing process is also referred to as "trading on the equity," that is, utilizing the existence of a given amount of equity capital as a borrowing base.

In Exhibit 5–2, a comparison is made of the returns achieved by two companies having identical assets and earnings before interest expense. Company X derives 40 percent of its funds from debt while Company Y has no debt. In year 1, when the average return on total assets is 10 percent, the return on the stockholders' equity of Company X is 13.3 percent. This higher return is due to the fact that the stockholders benefited from the excess return on total assets over the cost of debt. For Company Y, the return on equity always equals the return on total assets. In year 2, the return on total assets of Company X was equal to the interest cost of debt and, consequently, the effects of leverage were neutralized. The results of year 3 show that leverage is a double-edged sword. Thus, when the return on total assets

---

[9] Except for debt subject to variable interest rates.

Exhibit 5–2: Trading on the equity—results under different earning assumptions (dollars in thousands)

	Assets	Debt payable	Stock-holders' equity	Income before interest and taxes	10 percent debt interest	Taxes[a]	Net income	Net income + (Interest) × (1 – Tax rate)	Return on Total assets[b]	Return on Stock-holders' equity[c]
Year 1:										
Company X	$1,000,000	$400,000	$ 600,000	$200,000	$40,000	$ 80,000	$ 80,000	$100,000	10.0%	13.3%
Company Y	1,000,000	—	1,000,000	200,000	—	100,000	100,000	100,000	10.0	10.0
Year 2:										
Company X	1,000,000	400,000	600,000	100,000	40,000	30,000	30,000	50,000	5.0	5.0
Company Y	1,000,000	—	1,000,000	100,000	—	50,000	50,000	50,000	5.0	5.0
Year 3:										
Company X	1,000,000	400,000	600,000	50,000	40,000	5,000	5,000	25,000	2.5	.83
Company Y	1,000,000	—	1,000,000	50,000	—	25,000	25,000	25,000	2.5	2.5

[a] Assuming a 50 percent tax rate.

[b] $\dfrac{\text{Net income} + \text{Interest} (1 - .50)}{\text{Total assets}}$.

[c] $\dfrac{\text{Net income}}{\text{Stockholders' equity}}$.

157

falls below the cost of debt, Company X's return on the equity is lower than that of debt-free Company Y.

The effect of tax deductibility of interest

The second reason given for the advantageous position of debt is the tax deductibility of interest as opposed to the distribution of dividends. This can be illustrated as follows:

Assume the facts given in Exhibit 5–2 for year 2, and that the operating earnings of Company X and Company Y, $60,000 for each, are both of equal quality.[10] The results of the two companies can be summarized as follows:

	Company X	Company Y
Income before interest and taxes	$200,000	$200,000
Interest (10% of $400,000)	40,000	
Income before taxes	160,000	200,000
Taxes	80,000	100,000
Net Income	80,000	100,000
Add back interest paid to bondholder	40,000	
Total return to security holders (debt and equity)	$120,000	$100,000

Disregarding leverage effects that are neutral in the above example, even if the return on assets is equal to the interest rate, the total amount available for distribution to the bondholders and stockholders of Company X is $20,000 higher than the amount available for the stockholders of Company Y. This is due to the lower total tax liability to which the security holders of Company X are subject.

It should be borne in mind that the value of the tax deductibility of interest is dependent on the existence of sufficient earnings. However, unrecovered interest charges can be carried back and carried forward as part of tax loss carry-overs permitted by law.

Other advantages of leverage

In addition to the advantages accruing to equity stockholders from the successful employment of financial leverage and the tax deductibility of interest expenses, a sound longer-term debt position can result in other advantages to the equity owner. A rapidly growing company can avoid earnings dilution

---

[10] The concept of the quality of earnings is discussed in Chapter 9.

through the issuance of debt. Moreover, if interest rates are headed higher, all other things being equal, a leveraged company paying fixed interest rates will be more profitable than its nonleveraged competitor. There is, moreover, a financial benefit from advantageously placed debt because debt capital is not always available to an enterprise and the capacity to borrow may disappear should adverse operating results occur. Finally, in times of inflation, monetary liabilities will result in price-level gains.

Measuring the effect of financial leverage

The effect of leverage on operating results is positive when the return on the equity capital exceeds the return on total assets. This difference in return isolates the effect that the return on borrowed money has on the return on the owner's capital. As was seen in the example in Exhibit 5–2, leverage is positive when the return on assets is higher than the cost of debt. It is negative when the opposite conditions prevail. The terms *positive* and *negative* are not used here in the strict algebraic sense.

The effect of financial leverage can be measured by the following formula:

$$\text{Financial leverage index} = \frac{\text{Return on common equity}}{\text{Return on total assets}}$$

Using the data in Exhibit 5–2, we compute the financial leverage indexes of Company X for years 1, 2, and 3 as follows:

Financial leverage index

$$\text{Year 1:} \quad \frac{13.3}{10.0} = 1.33$$

$$\text{Year 2:} \quad \frac{5.0}{5.0} = 1$$

$$\text{Year 3:} \quad \frac{.083}{2.5} = .033$$

In year 1, when the return on equity exceeded that on total assets, the index at 1.4 was positive. In year 2, when the return on equity equaled that on total assets, the index stood at 1 reflecting a neutralization of financial leverage. In year 3, the index, at .07, was way below 1.0, thus indicating the very negative effect of financial leverage in that year. The subject of return on investment is discussed in Chapter 6.

The financial leverage index for Alfa, Inc. (Appendix 2B), for 19x6 is calculated as follows:

$$\frac{\text{Return on common equity}}{\text{Return on total assets}} = \frac{5.82\%}{3.73\%} = \underline{\underline{1.56}}$$

with both returns calculated as follows:

Return on common equity:

$$\frac{\$19,139^{(a)} - \$1,022^{(b)}}{(\$331,080^{(c)} - \$14,940^{(d)}) + (\$321,713^{(c)} - \$14,940^{(d)}) \div 2} = \underline{\underline{5.82}} \text{ percent}$$

Return on total assets:

$$\frac{\$19,139^{(a)} + \$18,440^{(e)}(1 - .48)^{(f)}}{(\$801,672 + \$738,469) \div 2^{(g)}} = \underline{\underline{3.73}} \text{ percent}$$

(a) Net income (item $\boxed{16}$).
(b) Preferred dividends (from statement of earnings reinvested—item $\boxed{69}$).
(c) Total stockholders' equity (item $\boxed{40}$). We accept here the company's classification of "Excess of Equity Over Cost of Subsidiary Companies at Dates of Acquisition" as part of equity. After 1970, these amounts have to be amortized to income.
(d) Sum of two issues of preferred stock (item $\boxed{40}$).
(e) Net interest expense = Item $\boxed{5}$ − Item $\boxed{6}$.
(f) 1 − Marginal tax rate.
(g) Average total assets $\boxed{31}$.

MEASURING THE EFFECT OF CAPITAL STRUCTURE ON LONG-TERM SOLVENCY

From the foregoing discussion it is clear that the basic risk involved in a leveraged capital structure is the risk of running out of cash under conditions of adversity.

Debt involves a commitment to pay fixed charges in the form of interest and principal repayments. While certain fixed charges can be postponed in times of cash shortage, those associated with debt cannot be postponed without adverse repercussion to the ownership and also to the creditor groups.

Another important repercussion of excessive debt is a loss of financing flexibility, i.e., the ability to raise funds particularly in adverse capital markets.

LONG-TERM PROJECTIONS—USEFULNESS AND LIMITATIONS

If a shortage of cash required to service the debt is the most adverse possibility envisaged, then the most direct and most relevant measure of risk inherent in the leveraged capital structure of an enterprise would be a projection of future cash resources and flows that would be available to meet these cash requirements. These projections must assume the worst set of economic conditions that are likely to occur, since this is the most realistic and useful test of safety from the creditor's point of view. If only prosperous and normal times are to be assumed, then the creditor would not need his preferred position and would be better off with an equity position where the potential rewards are higher.

In Chapter 4, we concluded that detailed cash flow projections can be reliably made only for the short term. Consequently, they are useful only in the measurement of short-term liquidity.

The statement of changes in financial position (SCFP) can be projected over a relatively longer term because such a projection is far less detailed than a projection of cash flows. However, as we saw in the discussion of such projections in the preceding chapter, this lack of detail as well as the longer time horizon reduces the reliability of such projections.

The short term is understood to encompass, generally, a period of up to one year. The longer term, however, is a much wider ranging period. Thus, it may include a solvency analysis with respect to a three-year term loan, or it may encompass the evaluation of risk associated with a 30-year bond issue. Meaningful projections covering the period over which the interest and principal of the term loan will be paid can still reasonably be made. However, a 30-year projection of funds flow covering the bond issue would be an unrealistic exercise. For this reason, longer-term debt instruments often contain sinking fund provisions that act to reduce the uncertain time horizon, and stipulations of additional security in the form of specific assets pledged as collateral. Moreover, they often contain provisions requiring the mainte-nance of minimum working capital levels or restrictions on the payment of dividends, all of which are designed to ensure against a deterioration in the financial ratios prevailing at the time the bonds are issued. They cannot, of course, prohibit adverse operating results.

Desirable as funds flow projections may be, their use for the extended longer term is severely limited. For this reason, a number of measures of long-term solvency have evolved that are more static in nature and are based on measures of capital structure as well as on asset and earnings coverage tests. These measures will be considered below.

CAPITAL STRUCTURE ANALYSIS—COMMON-SIZE STATEMENTS

A simple measure of financial risk in an enterprise is the composition of its capital structure. This can be done best by constructing a common-size statement of the liabilities and equity section of the balance sheet as shown in Exhibit 5–3.

An alternative way of analyzing capital structure with common-size per-centages would be to focus only on the longer-term capital funds by excluding the current liabilities from total funds.

The advantage of a common-size analysis of capital structure is that it presents clearly the relative magnitude of the sources of funds of the enterprise, a presentation that lends itself readily to a comparison with similar data of other enterprises.

Exhibit 5–3:   Liabilities and equity section—with common-size percentages

Current liabilities	$ 428,000	19.0%
Long-term debt	500,000	22.2
Equity capital:		
Preferred stock	400,000	17.8
Common stock	800,000	35.6
Paid-in capital	20,000	.9
Retained earnings	102,000	4.5
Total equity capital	1,322,000	58.8
Total liabilities and equity capital	$2,250,000	100.0%

A variation of the approach of analyzing capital structure by means of common-size or component percentages is to analyze it by means of ratios.

CAPITAL STRUCTURE RATIOS

The basic ratio measurements of capital structure relate the various components of the capital structure to each other or to their total. Some of these ratios in common use are explained below.

TOTAL DEBT TO TOTAL CAPITAL (DEBT AND EQUITY)

The most comprehensive ratio in this area is that which measures the relationship between *total debt* (i.e., Current liabilities + Long-term debt + any other form of liability determined by the analyst to be debt, such as obligations under capitalized leases) to *total capital* that in addition to total debt includes the stockholders' equity (inclusive of preferred stock). The ratio can thus be expressed as

$$\frac{\text{Total debt}}{\text{Total capital}} \text{ as defined above}$$

and can also be expressed as debt as a percentage of total capitalization (rather than the ratio of one to the other).

The 19x6 debt to total capital ratio for Alfa, Inc. (Appendix 2B), is computed as follows (dollars in millions):

$$\frac{\$186^{(a)} + \$35^{(b)} + \$5^{(c)} + \$245^{(d)} + \$167^{(e)}}{\$331^{(f)} + \$638^{(g)}} = \frac{\$638}{\$969} = \underline{\underline{.66}}$$

   [a] Total current liabilities (item |35|).
   [b] Deferred income taxes (item |36|), assumed here to be liabilities.
   [c] Other deferred credits (item |37|).
   [d] Long-term debt (item |38|).
   [e] Present value of long-term financing lease obligations (item |99|). *SFAS 13* requires capitalization and inclusion among balance sheet liabilities.
   [f] Stockholder's equity (item |40|) including "negative goodwill" as classified by company.
   [g] Total debt (total numerator).

The result can be expressed as a ratio of .66 or as debt being 66 percent of Alfa's total capital (Debt + Equity).

Ratio of total debt to total equity capital

An alternate measure of the relationship of debt to capital sources is the ratio of total debt (as defined above) to total equity capital only. Thus:

$$\frac{\text{Total debt}}{\text{Total stockholders' equity}}$$

This ratio for 19x6 for Alfa, Inc., is computed as follows:

$$\frac{\$638^*}{\$331^*} = \underline{\underline{1.93}}$$

* See above
for derivation.

This ratio means that Alfa's total debt is 1.93 times its equity capital or that the company borrowed from all sources $1.93 for every dollar of equity capital it has.

A reciprocal measure of the above is:

$$\frac{\text{Total stockholders' equity}}{\text{Total debt}}$$

For Alfa, $\frac{\$331}{\$638} = \underline{\underline{.52}}$, and this can be interpreted from the creditor's point of view as meaning that every dollar of debt is backed by only 52 cents of equity capital. This also clarifies the fact that the owners have a smaller stake in the enterprise than do all creditors. The creditors have, conversely, $1.52 in assets (at book value) backing up each dollar claim. This relationship ignores, of course, prior, senior, or specific claims some creditors may have as compared to others.

Long-term debt/equity capital

This ratio measures the relationship of long-term debt to equity capital.[11] A ratio in excess of 1∶1 indicates a higher long-term debt participation as compared to equity capital. This ratio is the familiar debt-to-equity ratio that is computed as follows:

$$\frac{\text{Long-term debt}}{\text{Equity capital}}$$

For Alfa, the 19x6 long-term debt to stockholders' equity ratio is computed as follows:

---

[11] The term *long-term debt* usually includes *all* liabilities that are not current.

$$\frac{\$638^{(a)} - \$186^{(b)}}{\$331^{(c)}} = \underline{\underline{1.37}}$$

(a) Total debt.
(b) Total current liabilities.
(c) Stockholders' equity.
(For derivation of amount,
see above.)

Confusion in terminology

Analysts must be aware that in this area, as in many others, the popular name of a ratio may not convey precisely its meaning and, hence, the method of its computation. Before any measure or ratio is used, care must be taken that the method of its computation is thoroughly understood.

Short-term debt

The ratio of debt that matures over the short term to total debt is an important indicator of the short-run funds and financing needs of an enterprise. Short-term debt, as opposed to maturing long-term debt or sinking fund requirements, is often an indicator of enterprise reliance on bank financing. Moreover, short-term debt is subject to frequent changes in interest rates.

Equity capital at market value

Accounting principles in current use place primary emphasis on historical costs rather than on current values. Since the shareholders' capital is the residual of assets minus liabilities, this accounting can result in equity capital book value figures that are far removed from realistic market values.

One method of correcting this flaw in the stated equity capital amounts, particularly when they enter importantly into the computation of many of the ratios that we have considered above, is to restate them by converting the assets from historical cost to current market values. This may be particularly important in the case of natural resource companies whose book values greatly understate the market value of their assets.

Although SEC disclosure requirements affecting certain companies will provide analysts with some replacement cost data, we are still far from having complete market values available.

One way of overcoming the problem of giving recognition to market values is to compute the equity capital at current (or some kind of average) market value of the stock issues that comprise it. On the assumption that the valuation placed by the market on the equity capital recognizes the current values of assets and their earning power, this amount can then be used in the computation of the various debt-to-equity ratios.

A serious objection to this method is that stock prices fluctuate widely and may, particularly in times of overspeculation, not be representative of "true" values at a given moment. However, this argument can be countered with considerable evidence that the judgment of the marketplace is most of the time superior to that of other judgmental processes and that use of average market prices would solve the problem of temporary aberrations. Thus, the use of equity capital figures computed at current, or at average, market values has much to commend it. Being more realistic, they can improve the ratio measurements in which they are used and can provide a more realistic measure of the asset cushion that bondholders can count on.[12]

A persistent trend of equity at book value that is in excess of equity at market value can be interpreted as a sign of financial weakness and of restricted financial capability, such as the capability to sell equity capital or even raise new debt capital.

One important advantage of earnings-coverage ratios, as will be seen in the subsequent discussion of this subject, is that they are based on the earning power of assets rather than on the amount at which they are carried in the financial statements. Market values do, of course, give recognition to such earning power of an entity's assets. In that sense, ratio measures, such as debt-to-equity ratios, that use equity capital amounts at market value, are more consistent with earnings-coverage ratios than are ratios using historical book values.

Using Alfa, Inc.'s (see Appendix 2B) average common stock market price for 19X6 (item ⟨107⟩ bottom) we can compute ($ millions):

$$\frac{\text{Total debt}}{\text{Common equity at market value} + \text{Preferred equity at book value}} =$$

$$\frac{638^*}{(11{,}723{,}774 \text{ shares} \times \$16.50) + .610 + 14.330} = \frac{638^*}{208} = \underline{\underline{3.08}}$$

* See preceding derivation of amount.

Comparing the above ratio with the corresponding 1.93 ratio computed at book value we can conclude that due to the market's low evaluation of Alfa's stock (average $16.50 price vs. 26.13 of book value) the market value based Debt/Equity ratio is far worse than the book value computed ratio. This low market evaluation can be interpreted as a negative factor in Alfa's financial strength, and in its ability to sell equity shares.

---

[12] B. Graham, D. L. Dodd, and S. Cottle in their *Security Analysis,* 4th ed. (New York: McGraw-Hill, 1962), p. 361, suggest that the ratio of

$$\frac{\text{Market value of junior equity}}{\text{Par value of bonds}}$$

should not be less than .5 and can be used to corroborate earnings coverage measures. It would not be prudent to have to assume, they maintain, that the junior equity is undervalued by the market.

PREFERRED STOCK WITHIN THE CAPITAL STRUCTURE

Within the total stockholders' equity, preferred stock holds a preferential position with a prior claim on assets ahead of the common stock. Thus, it is instructive to compute the ratio of preferred stock to total stockholders' equity which is done as follows:

$$\frac{\text{Preferred stock at stated value (or liquidating value if higher)}}{\text{Total stockholders' equity}}$$

Alfa, Inc.'s (see Appendix 2B) 19x6 ratio is calculated as follows (dollars in millions):

$$\frac{\$1.5^{(a)} + \$23.2^{(b)}}{\$331.1^{(c)}} = 7.46 \text{ percent}$$

See item 40.
(a) $2.50 cumulative convertible preferred at liquidation value.
(b) Series B $1 cumulative convertible preferred at liquidation value.
(c) Total stockholders' equity.

Analytically, the excess of liquidation over stated values ($1.5 − $.6) + ($23.2 − $14.3) that is added to the preferred equity should be charged to retained earnings, i.e., the common equity.

The above computation shows the preferred stock to constitute 7.46 percent of the total shareholders' equity.

The analyst must also consider how to treat preferred stock that is subject to mandatory redemption requirements. While such stock is akin to a liability more than to equity, it must be recognized that a failure to meet the redemption requirements may not have as disastrous a result on the entity's status as would a failure to meet a sinking fund requirement of debt.

THE ANALYTICALLY ADJUSTED RATIO OF DEBT TO EQUITY

In our earlier discussion of the elements that enter into an entity's capital structure, we concluded that there are many types of analytical adjustments that the analyst may wish to make to the published financial data in computing debt-to-equity ratios.[13] An illustration of the computation of the analytically adjusted debt-to-equity ratio is given in Appendix 5C.

---

[13] For an excellent discussion of such adjustments, see Lasman and Weil, "Adjusting the Debt-Equity Ratio."

INTERPRETATION OF CAPITAL STRUCTURE MEASURES

The common-size and ratio analyses of capital structure, which have been examined above, are all measures of risk inherent in the capital structure of an enterprise. The higher the proportion of debt, the larger the fixed charges of interest and debt repayment, the greater the likelihood of insolvency during protracted periods of earnings decline or other adversities.

One obvious value of these measures is that they serve as screening devices. Thus, when the ratio of debt-to-equity capital is relatively small, say, 10 percent or less, there is normally no need to be concerned with this aspect of an enterprise's financial condition; and the analyst may well conclude that he can spend his time better by directing his attention to the more critical areas revealed by analysis.

Should an examination of the debt-to-equity ratios reveal that debt is indeed a significant factor in the total capitalization, then further analysis is necessary. Such an analysis will encompass many aspects of an enterprise's financial condition, results of operations, and future prospects.

An analysis of short-term liquidity is always important because before the analyst starts to assess long-term solvency he has to be satisfied about the short-term financial survival of the enterprise. Chapter 3 examines the analysis of short-term liquidity, and the analyst will use the tools discussed there to assess the situation and also to relate the size of working capital to the size of long-term debt. Loan and bond indenture covenants requiring the maintenance of minimum working capital ratios attest to the importance attached to current liquidity in ensuring the long-term solvency of an enterprise.

Additional analytical steps of importance will include an examination of debt maturities (as to size and spacing over time), interest costs, and other factors that have a bearing on the risk. Among those, the earnings stability of the enterprise and its industry as well as the kind of assets its resources are invested in are also important factors.

MEASURES OF ASSETS DISTRIBUTION

The type of assets an enterprise employs in its operations should determine to some extent the sources of funds used to finance them. Thus, for example, it is customarily held that fixed and other long-term assets should not be financed by means of short-term loans. In fact, the most appropriate source of funds for investment in such assets is equity capital, although debt also has a place in such financing especially in industries such as utilities that generally enjoy stable revenue sources. On the other hand, working capital, and particularly seasonal working capital needs, can be appropriately financed by means of short-term credit. The ratio of working capital to long-term debt should generally not fall below 1, and in most industries that are affected by the business cycle, a ratio below 1.5 to 2 may indicate weakness and vulnerability.

In judging the risk exposure of a given capital structure, the asset composition is one of the important factors to consider. This asset composition is best measured by means of common-size statements of the asset side of the balance sheet. For example, Exhibit 5–4 shows the common-size asset section of the balance sheet whose liabilities and equity section was presented in Exhibit 5–3.

Exhibit 5–4:   Assets section—with common-size percentages

Current assets:		
Cash	$ 376,000	16.7%
Accounts receivable (net)	425,000	18.9
Merchandise inventory	574,000	25.5
Total current assets	1,375,000	61.1
Investments	268,000	11.9
Land, property, and equipment (net)	368,000	16.4
Intangibles	239,000	10.6
Total assets	$2,250,000	100.0%

Judging *only* by the distribution of assets and the related capital structure, it would appear that since a relatively high proportion of assets is current (61 percent), a 41 percent debt and current liabilities position (see Exhibit 5–3) is not excessive. Other considerations and measurements may, however, change this conclusion.

Asset coverage is an important element in the evaluation of long-term solvency. Assets of value provide protection to holders of debt obligations both because of their earning power and because of their liquidation value. Additionally, they represent the bases on which an enterprise can obtain the financing that may be required to tide it over a period of financial stringency.

The relationship between asset groups and selected items of capital structure can also be expressed in terms of ratios.

Fixed assets equity capital is a ratio that measures the relationship between long-term assets and equity capital. A ratio in excess of 1:1 means that some of the fixed assets are financed by means of debt.

Net tangible assets as a percentage of long-term debt is a measure of asset coverage of long-term obligations. It excludes assets of doubtful realizability or value and represents a measure of safety of debt based on liquidation of assets.

Total obligations to total net tangible assets (including net working capital) is another useful measure of the relationship between debt and the entity's investment in operating assets. An analysis of the property backing enjoyed by creditors is likely to be most useful in the case of companies, such as those in the natural resource field, where book values may be significantly understated.

If the financial structure ratios are such that they require further analysis, one of the best means for further investigation are tests that measure an enterprise's ability to service its debt requirements out of earnings. This is the area we shall turn to next.

CRITICAL IMPORTANCE OF "EARNING POWER"

One conclusion of our discussion of debt-to-equity ratios was that a major usefulness of these measurements lies in their function as a screening device, that is, a means of deciding whether the apparent risk inherent in the capital structure of an enterprise requires further investigation and analysis. An important limitation of the measurements of debt-to-equity relationships is that they do not focus on the availability of funds or cash flows that are necessary to service the enterprise's debt. In fact, as a debt obligation is repaid, the debt-to-equity ratio tends to improve whereas the yearly amount of cash needed to pay interest and sinking fund requirements may remain the same or may even increase, as, for example, in the case of level payment debt or loans with "balloon" repayment provisions.

The long-term creditor must in the final analysis rely on the enterprise's earning power as the most reliable source of interest and principal repayments. While a highly profitable enterprise can in the short run be illiquid because of the composition of its assets, earning power is in the long run the only reliable source of liquidity and of borrowing capacity.

MEASURES OF EARNINGS COVERAGE

Earnings-coverage ratios measure directly the relationship between debt related fixed charges and the earnings available to meet these charges.[14] The concept of the basic earnings coverage of fixed-charges ratio is simple:

$$\frac{\text{Earnings available to meet fixed charges}}{\text{Fixed charges (as defined)}}$$

While the concept behind this measurement is simple and straightforward, its practical implementation is complicated by the problem of defining what should be included in "earnings" and in "fixed charges."

Earnings available to meet fixed charges

It should be borne in mind that net income determined under the principles of accrual accounting is not the same thing as sources of funds provided

---

[14] Fixed-charges-coverage ratios represent important inputs in bond rating decisions. Bond indentures often specify that minimum levels of this ratio must be maintained before additional debt can be issued.

by operations. Specifically, certain items of income, such as undistributed earnings of subsidiaries and controlled companies or sales on extended credit terms, do not create funds, that is, working capital. Similarly, certain expenses such as depreciation, amortization, depletion, and deferred income tax charges do not require the outlay of current funds. On the other hand, it should be borne in mind that a parent company can determine the dividend policy of a controlled subsidiary.

Fixed-debt charges are paid out of current funds rather than out of net income. Thus, the analyst must realize that an unadjusted net income figure may not be a correct measure of funds available to meet fixed charges.

Since fixed charges are paid off with cash, a clarification is needed as to why we accept here working capital as a surrogate for cash. The reason is that over the longer term the conversion period of current assets into cash becomes relatively insignificant. Thus, even if the conversion period of inventories into receivables, and ultimately into cash, is 120 days, this period is not significant compared with the longer-term period over which the fixed charges of debt must be paid.

The use of net income as an approximation of funds provided by operations may, in some instances, be warranted while in others it may significantly overstate or understate the amount actually available for the servicing of debt. Thus, the soundest approach to this problem lies not in generalizations but rather in a careful analysis of the nonfund generating items included in income as well as the nonfund requiring expenses charged to that income. Thus, for example, in considering depreciation as a nonfund requiring expense, the analyst must realize that over the long run an enterprise must replace its plant and equipment.

The problem of determining the amount of income to be included in fixed-charges-coverage ratios requires consideration of a number of additional factors:

1. *The treatment of extraordinary gains and losses.* As pointed out in the more comprehensive discussion of this subject in Chapter 9, extraordinary gains and losses enter into the determination of longer-term average earnings power. As such they must be recognized as a factor that may, over the longer term, contribute to or reduce the funds available to pay fixed charges. Any computation of earnings-coverage ratios utilizing average earnings figures must recognize the existence of extraordinary gains and losses over the years. This is particularly true of earnings-coverage ratios where what we measure is the risk of loss of sources of funds used for payment of fixed charges.

2. *Preferred dividends* need not be deducted from net income because the payment of such dividends is not mandatory. However, in consolidated financial statements, preferred dividends of a subsidiary whose income is consolidated must be deducted because they represent a charge that has priority over the distribution of earnings to the parent.

3. Earnings that are attributed to *minority interests* are usually deducted from net income available for fixed charges even though minority shareholders

can rarely enforce a cash claim under normal operating conditions. An exception arises where the consolidated subsidiary has fixed charges. In such instances, the coverage ratio should be computed on the basis of earnings before deducting minority interests.

If a subsidiary with a minority interest has a loss, the credit in the income statement that results from the minority's share in the loss should be excluded from consolidated earnings for purposes of the coverage ratio computation. The parent would, in most cases, meet fixed-charges obligations of its subsidiary to protect its own credit standing, whether or not legally obligated to do so.

4. *The impact of income taxes* on the computation of earnings-coverage ratios should always be carefully assessed. Since interest is a tax-deductible expense, it is met out of pretax income. Thus, the income out of which interest payments are met is pretax income. On the other hand, preferred dividends or sinking fund payments are not tax deductible and must be paid out of aftertax earnings.

5. *Add-back of fixed charges.* In order to determine the amount of pretax earnings available to meet specific fixed charges, those fixed charges that were deducted in arriving at pretax earnings must be added back to pretax income in the numerator of the ratio.

6. *The level of income* used in the computation of earnings-coverage ratios deserves serious consideration. The most important consideration here is: what level of income will be most representative of the amount that will actually be available in the *future* for the payment of debt-related fixed charges? An average figure of earnings from continuing operations encompassing the entire range of the business cycle, and adjusted for any known factors that may change it in the future, is most likely to be the best approximation of the average source of funds from future operations that can be expected to become available for the payment of fixed charges. Moreover, if the objective of the earnings-coverage ratio is to measure the creditor's maximum exposure to risk, then the proper earnings figure to use is that achieved at the low point of the enterprise's business cycle.

Fixed charges to be included

Having considered the amount of earnings that should be included in the earnings coverage, we shall now turn to an examination of the types of fixed charges that are generally includable in the computation of this ratio.

1. Interest incurred

Interest incurred is the most direct and most obvious fixed charge that arises from the incurrence of indebtedness. Interest expense includes the amortization of deferred bond discount and premium. The bond discount and issue expenses represent the amount by which the par value of the bond indebtedness exceeded the proceeds from the bond issue. As such, the discount amortization represents an addition to the stated interest expense. The amortization of bond issue premium represents the reverse situation, and thus results in a reduction of interest expense over the period of amortization.[15]

If low coupon bonds have only a short period to run before maturity and it is likely that they will have to be refinanced with higher coupon bonds, it may be appropriate to incorporate in fixed charges the expected higher interest costs.

Interest on income bonds must, at best, be paid only as earned. Consequently, it is not a fixed charge from the point of view of the holder of fixed-interest securities. It must, however, be regarded as a fixed charge from the point of view of the income bond issuer.

2. Capitalized interest

SFAS 34 requiring the capitalization of certain interest costs has greatly increased the practice of interest capitalization. Care must be taken to arrive at proper amounts in both the numerator and the denominator of the fixed-charges-coverage ratio.

Let us clarify where interest can be found in the income statement and the terminology that relates to it. Interest that the enterprise pays or is obligated to pay during a period is referred to as *interest incurred*. This is the amount we focus on as being covered by earnings. Interest incurred that is not expensed but rather charged to some asset account is *interest capitalized*. Interest incurred less interest capitalized equals *interest expensed*. Since interest that is expensed is that which enters into the determination of pretax income, it should be added back to the pretax income found in the numerator of the ratio. The denominator of the ratio will, however, include as a fixed-charge interest incurred whether capitalized or not.

Interest capitalized in one period will find its way into the income statement in the form of costs such as depreciation or amortization. Such amortized interest that was previously capitalized must be added back to pretax income.[16] In effect, failure to add back such interest results in including earnings in the numerator *after* some interest costs rather than *before* interest, with a resulting understatement of the fixed-charges-coverage ratio. Since the FASB has not required the disclosure of the amount of previously capitalized interest that is amortized in a given period, analysts can obtain these amounts through voluntary disclosure by companies or they can sometimes derive them from other disclosures such as those relating to deferred taxes.

---

[15] Bond discount and premium amortization, which are usually relatively insignificant in amount, do not, strictly speaking, require a current outlay of funds. They represent cost or income item allocations over the term of the loan.

[16] SEC regulations require that different methods of computation apply to rate-regulated public utilities. In their case, the allowance for funds used during construction shall be added to gross income but not deducted from interest expense. Utilities may not add to earnings the amount of previously capitalized interest amortized during the period.

3. Interest implicit in lease obligations

In an analysis of liabilities we must consider the present status of accounting recognition of leases as financing devices. *SFAS 13* requires the capitalization of most financing leases.

When a lease is capitalized, the interest portion of the lease payment is designated as such on the income statement while most of the balance is usually considered as repayment of the principal obligation. A problem arises, however, when the analyst feels that certain leases that should have been capitalized are not so treated in the financial statements. The issue here actually goes beyond the pure accounting question of whether capitalization is, or is not, appropriate. It stems rather from the fact that a long-term lease represents a fixed obligation that must be given recognition in the computation of the earnings-coverage ratio. Thus, even long-term leases that, from an accounting theory point of view, need not be capitalized may be considered as including fixed charges that have to be included in the coverage ratio computation.[17]

The problem of extracting the interest portion of long-term lease payments is not a simple one. The external analysts can possibly obtain the implicit interest rate of financing leasing from an examination of the more extensive disclosure now available on the subject. Otherwise a rough rule of thumb, such as that interest represents one third of rentals, originally suggested by Graham and Dodd, may have to be used.[18] The SEC, which had used this rule, no longer accepts it automatically and insists on a more reliable estimate of the portion of rentals that represent interest.[19] "Delay rentals" in the extractive industries represent payment for the privilege of deferring the development of properties and, being in the nature of not regularly recurring compensation to owners, are not considered as rentals includable in the earnings-coverage ratio.

As with the offsetting of interest income against interest expense, the general rule is that rental income should not be offset against rental expense when determining fixed charges. An exception is made, however, where the rental income represents a direct reduction in rental expense.

4. Preferred stock dividend requirements of majority-owned subsidiaries

These are considered fixed charges because they have priority over the distribution of earnings to the parent. Items that would be or are eliminated in consolidation should not be considered fixed charges.

---

[17] In the discussion preceding the release of its 1982 revised regulations concerning the computation of the fixed-charges-coverage ratio, the SEC has reemphasized that "some long-term leases may narrowly miss the criteria for a capital lease but still have the characteristics of a financing transaction. The Commission does not believe that the presence of an interest factor is dependent upon the rental contract extending over any given period of time."

[18] Graham, Dodd, and Cottle, *Security Analysis,* p. 344. (This rule was developed in a previous edition of this book.)

[19] SEC *Accounting Series Release 155* (now superseded), as well as discussion preceding the SEC's release of revised rules concerning the computation of the ratio in 1982.

Income tax adjustment of fixed charges

Fixed charges that are not tax deductible must be tax adjusted. This is done by increasing them by an amount equivalent to the income tax that would be required to obtain an aftertax income sufficient to cover such fixed charges. The above preferred stock dividend requirement is one example of such nontax-deductible fixed charge. The following adjustment is made to compute the "grossed-up" amount:

$$\frac{\text{Preferred stock dividend requirements}}{1 - \text{Income tax rate}}$$

The tax rate to be used should be based on the relationship of the provision for income tax expense applicable to income from continuing operations to the amount of pretax income from continuing operations, i.e., the company's normal effective tax rate.

Other elements to be included in fixed charges

The foregoing discussions concerned the determination of fixed financing charges, that is, interest and the interest portion of lease rentals. These are the most widely used measures of "fixed charges" included in conventional fixed-charges-coverage ratios such as that required by the SEC which we adopt as the standard required computation.

However, if the purpose of this ratio is to measure an enterprise's ability to meet fixed commitments that if unpaid could result in repercussions ranging all the way from financial embarrassment to insolvency, there are other fixed charges to be considered. The most important categories of such additional fixed charges that we shall consider here are an interest equivalent on unrecorded pension obligations, principal repayment obligations such as sinking fund requirements, serial repayment provisions, and the principal repayment component of lease rentals. These items are not usually included as fixed charges, and the inclusion of some may be quite controversial. The inclusion of these fixed charges will not be illustrated here.

5. Interest equivalent on unrecorded pension obligations

Earlier in this chapter we concluded that an analyst may regard as unrecorded pension obligations the larger of unfunded vested pension liability (UVPL) or unfunded past service costs (UPSC). Since such unrecorded obligation is interest bearing, we can regard the interest on the unrecorded pension obligation as a fixed charge. While one could argue for use of the actuarial interest rate assumption, we are inclined to accept the suggestion[20] that an interest rate reflecting the cost of new debt capital be used. An approximation of that rate could also be the most recent interest rate incurred. Thus, if

---

[20] By Moody's Investor Service.

the unrecorded pension obligation is found to be $100 million and the appropriate interest rate is 9 percent, then the "interest equivalent" fixed charge is $9 million. It can be argued that the imputed interest number is an approximation of what *may* become an obligation which is, however, subordinated to debt requirements.

6. Principal repayment requirements

Principal repayment obligations are, from a cash-drain point of view, just as onerous as obligations to pay interest. In the case of rentals, the obligations to pay principal and interest must be met simultaneously.

A number of reasons have been advanced to indicate why the requirements for principal repayments are not given recognition in earnings-coverage ratio calculations:

1. The coverage of fixed-charges ratio is based on income. It is assumed that if the ratio is at a satisfactory level, it will be possible to refinance obligations as they become due or mature. Consequently, they may not have to be met from funds provided by earnings.
2. If the company has an acceptable debt to equity ratio it should be able to reborrow amounts equal to the debt repayments.
3. Another objection to the inclusion of sinking fund or other periodic principal repayment provisions in the calculation of the earnings-coverage ratio is that this may result in double counting, that is, the funds recovered by depreciation already provide for debt repayment. Thus, if earnings reflect a deduction for depreciation, then fixed charges should not include provisions for principal repayments.

    There is some merit to this argument if the debt was used to acquire depreciable fixed assets and if there is some correspondence between the pattern of depreciation charges and that of principal repayments. It must, moreover, be borne in mind that depreciation funds are recovered generally only out of profitable, or at least break-even, operations, and consequently this argument is valid only under an assumption of such operations.

    Our discussion of the definition of "earnings" to be included in the coverage-ratio calculations emphasized the importance of funds provided by operations as the measure of resources available to meet fixed charges. The use of this concept would, of course, eliminate the double-counting problem since nonfund-requiring charges such as depreciation would be added back to net income for the purpose of the coverage computations.

A more serious problem regarding the inclusion of debt repayment provisions among "fixed charges" arises from the fact that not all debt agreements provide for sinking fund payments or similar repayment obligations. Any arbitrary allocation of indebtedness over time would be an unrealistic theoretical exercise and would ignore the fact that to the extent that such payments are not required in earlier years, the immediate pressure on the cash resources of the enterprise is reduced. In the longer run, however, larger maturities as well as "balloon" payments will have to be met.

The most useful solution to this problem lies in a careful analysis and assessment of the yearly debt repayment requirements that will serve as the basis on which to judge the effect of these obligations on the long-term solvency of the enterprise. The assumption that debt can always be refinanced, rolled over, or otherwise paid off from current operations is not the most useful approach to the problem of risk evaluation. On the contrary, the existence of debt repayment obligations as well as the timing of their maturity must be recognized and included in an overall assessment of the long-term ability of the enterprise to meet its fixed obligations. The inclusion of sinking fund or other early repayment requirements in fixed charges is one way of recognizing the impact of such requirements on fund adequacy. Another method would, as a minimum, call for scheduling total debt repayment requirements over a period of 5 to 10 years into the future and relating these to aftertax funds expected to be available from operations.

7. Other fixed charges

While interest payments and debt repayment requirements are the fixed charges most directly related to the incurrence of debt, there is no logical justification to restrict the evaluation of long-term solvency only to these charges and commitments. Thus, a complete analysis of fixed charges that an enterprise is obliged to meet must include all long-term rental payment obligations[21] (not only the interest portion thereof) and particularly those rentals that must be met under any and all circumstances under noncancelable leases, otherwise known as "hell-and-high-water" leases.

The reason why short-term leases can be excluded from consideration as fixed charges is that they represent an obligation of limited duration, usually less than three years, and can consequently be discontinued in a period of severe financial stringency. Here, the analyst must, however, evaluate how essential the rented items are to the continuation of the enterprise as a going concern.

Other charges that are not directly related to debt but that may nevertheless be considered as long-term commitments of a fixed nature are long-term purchase contracts in excess of normal requirements not subject to cancellation and other similar obligations.

8. Guarantees to pay fixed charges

Guarantees to pay fixed charges of unconsolidated subsidiaries or of unaffiliated persons (such as suppliers) should result in additions to fixed charges if the requirement to honor the guarantee appears imminent.

---

[21] Capitalized long-term leases affect income by the interest charge implicit in them as well as by the amortization of the property right. Thus, to consider the "principal" component of such leases as fixed charges (after income was reduced by amortization of the property right) may amount to double counting.

RATIO OF EARNINGS TO FIXED CHARGES

In its 1982 revised regulations concerning the "Ratio of Earnings to Fixed Charges," the SEC's concept of computing this ratio moved so close to our own that we present it here as the standard conventional[22] way of computing the ratio:

The SEC's formula for computing the ratio is:

(Numerator)

(A) Pretax income from continuing operations *plus* (B) Interest expensed *plus* (C) Amortization of debt expense and discount or premium *plus* (D) Interest portion of operating rental expenses *plus* (E) Tax adjusted preferred stock dividend requirements of majority-owned subsidiaries *plus* (F) Amount of previously capitalized interest amortized during the period *minus* (G) Undistributed income of less than 50% owned persons (affiliates)

(Denominator)

(H) Total interest incurred *plus* (C) Amortization of debt expense and discount or premium *plus* (D) Interest portion of operating rental expenses *plus* (E) Tax adjusted preferred stock dividend requirements of majority-owned subsidiaries

The key letters above will serve for later reference to computations as well as for the summary amplifying notes below:

A   Income before discontinued operations, extraordinary items, and cumulative effects of accounting changes.

B   Interest incurred *less* interest capitalized.

C   Whether expensed or capitalized.

D   Since all financing leases are capitalized, the interest implicit in these is already included in interest expense—the interest portion of long-term operating leases is included on the theory that many long-term operating leases narrowly miss the criteria for a capital lease under *SFAS 13* but still have the characteristic of a financing transaction.

E   Excluding in all cases items eliminated in consolidation. The dividend has to be increased to pretax earnings that would be required to cover such dividend requirements, that is:

$$\frac{\text{Preferred stock dividend requirements}}{100 \text{ percent} - \text{Income tax rate*}}$$

* Based on relationship between applicable actual income tax provision to income *before* income taxes, extraordinary items, and cumulative effect of accounting changes.

---

[22] Still in some use but too simplistic to be considered here is the times interest earned ratio which considers only interest as a fixed charge to be covered, thus:

$$\frac{\text{Pretax income} + \text{Interest expense}}{\text{Interest expense}}$$

Exhibit 5–5

THE LEVERED CORPORATION

Abbreviated Income Statement

Net sales		$13,400,000
Undistributed income of less than 50%		
owned affiliates		600,000
		14,000,000
Cost of goods sold	$7,400,000	
Selling, general, and administrative expenses	1,900,000	
Depreciation (excluded from above costs) (3)	800,000	
Interest expense (1)—net	700,000	
Rental expense (2)	800,000	
Share of minority interests in		
consolidated income*	200,000	11,800,000
Income before taxes		2,200,000
Income taxes:		
Current	800,000	
Deferred	300,000	1,100,000
Income before extraordinary items		1,100,000
Gain on sale of investment in land (net of $67,000		
tax)		200,000
Net income		$ 1,300,000
Dividends:		
On common stock	200,000	
On preferred stock	400,000	600,000
Earnings retained for the year		$ 700,000

* These subsidiaries have fixed charges.

Selected notes to the financial statements:

1. The interest expense is composed of the following:

Interest incurred (except items below)	$740,000
Amortization of bond discount	60,000
Interest portion of capitalized leases	100,000
Interest capitalized	(200,000)
Interest expense	$700,000

2. Interest implicit in noncapitalized leases amounts to $300,000.
3. Depreciation includes amortization of previously capitalized interest of $80,000.

F   Applies to nonutility companies only. In most cases, disclosure of this amount is not made.

G   Minority interest in income of majority-owned subsidiaries that have fixed charges may be included in income.

H   Whether expensed or capitalized.

General

To reduce the complexity of the formula, two items (provisions) were left out:

1. In computing earnings, the *full* amount of losses of majority-owned subsidiaries should be considered.
2. Losses on investments in less than 50 percent owned companies accounted for by the equity method should not be included in earnings *unless* the company has guaranteed the debt of the affiliate.

If the ratio of earnings to fixed charges is less than one, the amount of insufficiency of earnings to cover the fixed charges should be given (rather than a ratio).

Illustration of earnings-coverage ratio calculations

Having discussed the various considerations that enter into the decision of what factors to include in the earnings-coverage ratio computation, we will address ourselves now to the question of how the ratio is computed. The computation of the various coverage ratios will be based on the illustration in Exhibit 5–5.

Using the data in Exhibit 5–5 and letter references to the above formula, we compute the ratio of earnings to fixed charges as follows (dollars in thousands):

$$\frac{\$2{,}200 \ (A) + \$700 \ (B \text{ and } C) + \$300 \ (D) + \$80 \ (F)}{\$840 \ (H) + \$60 \ (C) + \$300 \ (D)} = \underline{\underline{2.4}} \text{ times}$$

* The SEC permits the inclusion in income of the minority interest in the income of majority-owned subsidiaries that have fixed charges. This amount is added in order to reverse a similar deduction from income.

The ratio of earnings to fixed charges of Alfa, Inc. (see Appendix 2B), can be computed as follows (letter references are to the formula above—dollars in thousands):

$$\frac{\$25{,}368^{(1)} \ (A) + \$18{,}440^{(2)} \ (B) + \$19{,}767^{(3)} \ (D) + \$154^{(4)} \ (F)}{\$18{,}504^{(5)} \ (H) + \$19{,}767^{(3)} \ (D)} = \underline{\underline{1.67}} \text{ times}$$

[1] Item 8 .
[2] Item 5 — Item 6 .
[3] Interest component of *all* leases per Note 11 (item 99) — present value of leases (\$247,087) × .08 (average interest rate).
[4] Note 6 (item 82) discloses that income decreased in 19x6 because of interest capitalization. Based on this and other information given, we can reconstruct the effect on income of interest capitalization and derive the amount of amortization of previously capitalized interest:

	Dr. (Cr.)
Interest capitalized (given) item 6	\$ (64)
Amortization of previously capitalized interest	154 ←derived
	90
Income tax effect at 48%	(43)
Effect on net income (given)—item 82	\$ 47

[5] Item 5 .

At 1.67 times, Alfa's ratio of earnings to fixed charges is relatively low.

Ratio of earnings to fixed charges—expanded concept of fixed charges

If we adopt the point of view that failure to meet any fixed obligations can lead to trouble or to a chain of events leading to insolvency, then we want to establish how well such fixed obligations are covered by earnings. Thus, in addition to the fixed charges included in the computation in the preceding example based on Exhibit 5–5, the following must now be considered for inclusion:

Interest equivalent on unrecorded pension obligations. This represents, as discussed earlier in the chapter, interest that must be currently provided for by the enterprise. In the case of the Levered Corporation, the interest factor is 10 percent of a $400,000 unfunded vested pension liability, or $40,000.

Annual sinking fund requirements. The question of whether principal repayment requirements should be considered fixed charges has been discussed above. Their consideration as fixed charges is more valid when pre-depreciation earnings are used. See "Funds flow coverage of fixed charges" below.

PRO FORMA COMPUTATIONS OF COVERAGE RATIOS

In cases where fixed charges yet to be incurred are to be recognized in the computation of the coverage ratio, as, for example, interest costs under a prospective incurrence of debt, it is quite proper to estimate the offsetting benefits that will ensue from such future inflows of funds and to include these estimated benefits in the pro forma income. Benefits to be derived from a prospective loan can be measured in terms of interest savings obtainable from a planned refunding operation, income from short-term investments in which the proceeds may be invested, or similarly reasonable estimates of future benefits.

The SEC will usually insist on the presentation of a pro forma computation of the ratio of earnings to fixed charges that reflects changes to be effected under prospective financing plans when the effect of the refinancing changes the historical ratio by 10 percent or more.

FUNDS FLOW COVERAGE OF FIXED CHARGES

The discussion earlier in this chapter pointed out that net income is generally not a reliable measure of funds provided by operations that are available to meet fixed charges. The reason is, of course, that fixed charges are paid with cash or, from the longer-term point of view, with funds (working capital), while net income includes items of revenue that do not generate funds as well as expense items which do not require the current use of funds. Thus, a better measure of fixed-charges coverage may be obtained by using in the numerator funds obtained by operations rather than net income. This figure can be obtained from the SCFP.

Under this concept, the coverage ratio would be computed as follows:

$$\frac{\text{Funds provided by operations} + \text{Fixed charges}}{\text{Fixed charges}}$$

Using the data in Exhibit 5–5 we compute the coverage ratio as follows:

Funds provided by operations (pretax):

Income before extraordinary items		$1,100,000
Add-back—income taxes		1,100,000
Pretax income		2,200,000
Less: Nonfund generating income:		
Undistributed income of less than 50% owned affiliates		600,000
		1,600,000
Add: Expenses not requiring funds:		
Depreciation	$800,000	
Share of minority interests in consolidated income.....	200,000	
Amortization of bond discount	60,000	
Deferred income taxes (already added above)		1,060,000
Funds provided by operations (before taxes)		$2,660,000

The fixed charges to be added back to pretax funds provided by operations of

	$2,660,000
Interest expensed (less bond discount added back above)	$ 640,000
Interest portion of operating rental expense	300,000
Amount of previously capitalized interest amortized during period*	—
Total numerator	$3,600,000

* Assumed here to be included in depreciation (already added back).

Note that the numerator does not reflect a deduction of $600 (undistributed income of affiliates) because that figure, being a nonfund providing item, was already deducted at arriving at pretax funds provided by operations. Similarly, the "share of minority interests in consolidated income" has already been added back in arriving at the pretax funds provided by operations figure.

The fixed charges in the denominator are computed as follows:

Interest incurred	$ 900,000
Interest portion of operating rentals	300,000
	$1,200,000

Thus, the ratio of pretax funds provided by operations to fixed charges is:

$$\frac{\$3,600,000}{\$1,200,000} = \underline{\underline{3.0}}$$

Should the analyst wish to base the computation on "cash flow" or, more accurately, cash provided by operations, the "funds from operations" figure must be appropriately adjusted for changes in such operations related current items as accounts receivable, inventories, prepayments, accounts payable, and accruals.

As discussed earlier, the inclusion of principal repayment requirements, (tax adjusted) as fixed charges in this computation is justifiable because use of a pre-depreciation income figure here avoids the issue of double counting.

Other useful tests of funds flow relationships

A comprehensive study[23] found the ratio

$$\frac{\text{Working capital provided by operations}}{\text{Total debt and preferred stock}}$$

to be the best single predictor of financial failure. A deterioration in this ratio indicates that a firm is generating decreasing levels of funds from its operations in relation to the burden of debt it is carrying. This ratio is similar to the popular cash flow/debt ratio where "cash flow" is simply a crude measure of "funds from operations."

Net funds (or cash) flows as a percentage of capital expenditures relates funds provided by operations *after* dividends to needed capital plant and equipment replacements and additions. This is a measure of fund commitments to outlays that do not enter the fixed charges total but that may nevertheless be vital or important to the continuing operation of an enterprise.

STABILITY OF "FLOW OF FUNDS FROM OPERATIONS"

Since the relationship between the "flow of funds from operations" to the fixed charges of an enterprise is so important to an evaluation of long-term solvency, it is important to assess the stability of that flow. This is done by a careful evaluation of the elements that comprise the sources of funds from operations. For example, the depreciation add-back to net income is a more stable element than is net income itself because the recovery of the depreciation cost from selling prices precedes the earning of any net income, and has thus a higher degree of probability of happening. Even in very competitive industries selling prices must, in the long run, reflect the cost of plant and equipment used up in production.

---

[23] William H. Beaver, "Financial Ratios as Predictors of Failure," *Empirical Research in Accounting: Selected Studies 1966* (Chicago: The Institute of Professional Accounting, School of Business, University of Chicago, 1967), pp. 71–111.

EARNINGS COVERAGE OF PREFERRED DIVIDENDS

In the evaluation of preferred stock issues, it is often instructive to calculate the earnings coverage of preferred dividends, much in the same way the interest or fixed-charges coverage of debt issues is computed. The computation of the earnings coverage of preferred dividends must include as charges to be covered by earnings all fixed charges that take precedence over the payment of preferred dividends.[24] As is the case with all fixed-charges-coverage computations, the final ratio depends on a definition of "fixed charges."

Since preferred dividends are not tax deductible, aftertax income must be used to cover them. Consequently, the basic formula for computing preferred dividend coverage is:

$$\frac{\text{Income before tax} + \text{Fixed charges*}}{\text{Fixed charges*} + \text{Preferred dividends} \times \left(\dfrac{1}{1 - \text{Tax rate}}\right)}$$

* Which *are* tax deductible.

To the formula we used earlier (see page 179) to compute the ratio of earnings to fixed charges for The Levered Corporation based on data in Exhibit 5–5, we now add the tax-adjusted preferred dividend requirement in order to derive the preferred dividend coverage ratio as follows (dollars in thousands):

$$\frac{\begin{array}{c}\$2,200\ (A) + \$700\ (B\text{ and }C) + \$300\ (D) + \$80\ (F) \\ - \$600\ (G) + \$200*\end{array}}{\$840\ (H) + \$60\ (C) + \$300\ (D) + \$400\left(\dfrac{1}{1 - .50}\right)^{\dagger}} = \underline{\underline{1.44}}$$

* Minority interest in income of majority-owned subsidiaries (see prior discussion).
† Tax-adjusted preferred dividend requirement.

If there are two or more preferred issues outstanding, a by-class coverage ratio can be computed by omitting the dividend requirements of the junior issue but always including all prior fixed charges and preferred dividends.

EVALUATION OF EARNINGS-COVERAGE RATIOS

The earnings-coverage ratio test is a test of the ability of an enterprise to meet its fixed charges out of current earnings.[25] The orientation towards

---

[24] This is also the position of the SEC. Care must be exercised in comparing these coverage ratios because some analysts and financial services include only the preferred dividend requirements in the computation.

[25] W. B. Hickman, *Corporate Bond Quality and Investor Experience* (Princeton, N.J.: Princeton University Press, 1958), p. 11, found, for example, that bonds with poor earnings coverage had a probability of default 17 times greater than those with good coverage.

earnings is a logical one because the bondholder or other long-term creditor, while interested in asset coverage or what he can salvage in times of trouble, relies even more on the ability of the enterprise to stay out of trouble by meeting its obligations currently and as a going concern. Given the limited returns obtainable from debt instruments, an increase in the interest rate can rarely compensate the creditor for a serious risk of loss of principal. Thus, if the probability of the enterprise meeting its obligations as a going concern is not strong, then a creditor relationship can hardly be advantageous.

The coverage ratio is influenced by the level of earnings and by the level of fixed charges, which in turn depends importantly on the debt-to-equity relationship within the capitalization.

Importance of earnings variability

One very important factor in the evaluation of the coverage ratio is the pattern of behavior of cash flows over time, or the behavior of its surrogate—earnings. The more stable the earnings pattern of an enterprise or industry, the lower the relative earnings-coverage ratio that will be acceptable. Thus, a utility, which in times of economic downturn is likely to experience only a mild fall off in demand, can justify a lower earnings-coverage ratio than can a cyclical company such as a machinery manufacturer that may experience a sharp drop in sales in times of recession. Variability of earnings is, then, an important factor in the determination of the coverage standard. In addition, the durability and the trend of earnings are important factors that must be considered apart from their variability.[26]

Importance of method of computation and of underlying assumptions

The coverage standard will also depend on the method of computation of the coverage ratio. As we saw above, varying methods of computing the coverage ratio assume different definitions of "income" and of "fixed charges." It is reasonable to expect lower standards of coverage for the ratios that employ the most demanding and stringent definitions of these terms.

The SEC formula for computing the fixed-charges-coverage ratio that we have adopted here is based on income *before* discontinued operations, extraordinary items, and cumulative effects of accounting changes. While these exclusions impart a degree of stability to the earnings, they also remove from them important elements that must be considered as part of the operating experience of the entity. These elements should always be included in computing the *average* coverage ratio over a number of years.

---

[26] Most factors that will affect an entity's equity securities will also affect its bonds. For example, when Consolidated Edison Company passed its dividend in 1974, its bonds plunged along with its common stock which was the security directly affected. The market, aside from taking its cue from this action, may also have concluded that the company's ability to sell equity securities as well as its overall financing flexibility had been impaired.

The standards will also vary with the kind of earnings that are utilized in the coverage computation, that is, average earnings, the earnings of the poorest year, etc. Moreover, the quality of earnings is an important consideration (see Chapter 9).

It is not advisable to compute earnings-coverage ratios under methods that are not theoretically sound and whose only merit is that they are conservative. Thus, using aftertax income in the computation of the coverage ratio of fixed charges that are properly deductible for tax purposes is not logical and introduces conservatism in the wrong place. Any standard of coverage adequacy must, in the final analysis, be related to the willingness and ability of the lender to incur risk.

Appendix 5A includes references to standards of fixed-charges-coverage ratios used by rating agencies in determining the ratings of individual debt securities.

APPENDIX 5A

THE RATING OF DEBT OBLIGATIONS

Since the turn of the century, there has become established in the United States a comprehensive and sophisticated system for rating debt securities. Most ratings are performed by two highly regarded investment research firms, Moody's and Standard & Poor's (S&P).[1]

A bond credit rating is a composite expression of judgment about the credit worthiness of the bond issuer as well as the quality of the specific security being rated. A rating measure credit risk, that is, the probability of occurrence of developments adverse to the interests of the creditor.

This judgment of credit worthiness is expressed in a series of symbols that express degrees of credit risk. Thus, the top four rating grades of Standard & Poor's are:

AAA.   Bonds rated AAA are highest-grade obligations. They possess the ultimate degree of protection as to principal and interest. Marketwise they move with interest rates, and hence provide the maximum safety on all counts.

AA.   Bonds rated AA also qualify as high-grade obligations, and in the majority of instances differ from AAA issues only in small degree. Here, too, prices move with the long-term money market.

A.   Bonds rated A are regarded as upper medium grade. They have considerable investment strength but are not entirely free from adverse effects of changes in economic and trade conditions. Interest and principal

---

[1] In recent years, the ratings performed by Duff and Phelps have gained increasing acceptance in the marketplace. Many institutions also develop their own "in house" ratings.

are regarded as safe. They predominantly reflect money rates in their market behavior, but to some extent, also economic conditions.

BBB. The BBB, or medium-grade category is borderline between definitely sound obligations and those where the speculative element begins to predominate. These bonds have adequate asset coverage and normally are protected by satisfactory earnings. Their susceptibility to changing conditions, particularly to depressions, necessitates constant watching. Marketwise, the bonds are more responsive to business and trade conditions than to interest rates. This group is the lowest that qualifies for commercial bank investment.

The major reason why debt securities are widely rated while equity securities are not lies in the fact that there is a far greater uniformity of approach and homogeneity of analytical measures used in the evaluation of credit worthiness than there can be in the evaluation of the future market performance of equity securities. Thus, the wide agreement on what is being measured in credit risk analysis has resulted in a widespread acceptance of and reliance on published credit ratings.

The criteria that enter into the determination of a rating have never been precisely defined, and they involve both quantitative measures (e.g., ratio analysis) as well as qualitative factors such as market position and management quality. The major rating agencies refuse to be pinned down on what precise mix of factors enter into their rating process (which is a committee decision) because it is both art and science and also because to do so would cause endless arguments about the validity of the many judgmental factors that enter into a rating decision.

We can then see that in arriving at ratings these agencies must undertake analyses along the lines discussed throughout this book, the differences being mainly in the vast number of debt issues covered and the standardization of approaches which this entails. The following description of factors entering the rating process is based on published sources as well as on discussions with officials of the rating agencies.

THE RATING OF CORPORATE BONDS

In rating an industrial bond issue, the rating agency will focus on the issuing company's asset protection, financial resources, earning power, management, and the specific provisions of the debt security.

Also of great importance are size of firm, market share, industry position, susceptibility to cyclical influences,[2] and other broad economic factors.

Asset protection is concerned with measuring the degree to which a company's debt is covered by the value of its assets. One measure is net tangible

---

[2] There are, for example, no AAA rated companies in the steel or paper industries.

assets to long-term debt. At S&P, an industrial needs a ratio of 5 to 1 to get an AAA rating, a ratio of over 4 to 1 to qualify for an AA rating, 3 to 3.5 to 1 for an A, and about 2.5 to 1 for a BBB rating.

Understated assets, such as those of companies in the natural resource or real estate fields, are generally accorded recognition in the rating process.

The long-term debt as a percentage of total capitalization calls for a ratio of under 25 percent for an AAA, around 30 percent for a AA, 35 percent for an A, and about 40 percent for a BBB rating.

Other factors entering the consideration of asset protection include the determination of book value, the makeup of working capital, the quality and age of property, plant, and equipment as well as questions of off-balance sheet financing and unrecorded liabilities.

Financial resources encompass, in particular, such liquid resources as cash and other working capital items. Quality measures here include the collection period of receivables and inventory turnover. These are judged by means of industry standards. The use of debt, both short term and long term, as well as the mix between the two are also investigated.

Future earning power and the resulting cash generating ability is a factor of great importance in the rating of debt securities because the level and the quality of future earnings determine importantly an enterprise's ability to meet its obligations. Earning power is generally a more reliable source of security than is asset protection.

A prime measure of the degree of protection afforded by earning power is the fixed-charges-coverage ratio. To qualify for consideration for an AAA rating, an industrial company's earnings should cover its interest and rental charges after taxes above five to seven times; for an AA rating, above four times; for an A rating, over three times; and a BBB, over two times.

Another measure of debt service paying ability is cash flow (crudely net income plus depreciation) to total funded debt. It should be 65 percent or more for an AAA, 45 to 60 percent for an AA, 35 to 45 percent for an A, and 25 to 30 percent for a BBB rating.

Management abilities, philosophy, depth, and experience always loom importantly in any final rating judgment. Through interviews, field trips, and other analyses, the raters probe into the depth and breadth of management, as well as into its goals, the planning process, and strategies in such areas as research and development, product promotion, new product planning, and acquisitions.

The specific provisions of the debt security are usually spelled out in the bond indenture. What is analyzed here are the specific provisions in the indenture that are designed to protect the interests of bondholders under a variety of future conditions. Included in consideration here are, among others, conditions for issuance of future debt issues, specific security provisions such as mortgaging, sinking fund and redemption provisions, and restrictive covenants.

As can be seen, debt rating is a complex process involving quantitative as well as qualitative factors all of which culminate in the issuance of a single quality rating. The weights that may be assigned to each factor will vary among analysts, but the final conclusion will generally represent the composite judgment of several experienced raters.

THE RATING OF MUNICIPAL SECURITIES

Buyers of municipal bonds depend for their security of principal and interest on factors that are quite different from those that determine the quality of corporate debt. Hence, the processes of analysis differ.

Municipal securities, those issued by state and local governmental authorities, comprise a number of varieties. Many are general obligation bonds backed by the full faith and credit of the governmental unit that issues them. Others are special tax bonds that are limited in security to a particular tax that will be used to service and retire them. Then there are revenue bonds secured only by revenues of municipal enterprises. Other categories comprise housing authority bonds, tax anticipation notes, and so forth. Although the amount of information provided to buyers of municipal bonds is of very uneven quality, moves are afoot to correct this, primarily by way of legislation.

Raters require a great variety of information from issuers of municipal debt. In case of general obligation bonds, the basic security rests on the issuer's ability and willingness to repay the debt from general revenues under a variety of economic conditions.[3] The fundamental revenue source is the taxing power of the local municipality. Thus, the information they require includes current population and the trend and composition of population, the largest 10 taxpayers, the current market value of taxable properties, the gross indebtedness, and the net indebtedness (i.e., after deducting self-sustaining obligations, sinking fund, etc.), recent annual reports, budgets, and estimates of capital improvement and future borrowing programs, as well as an overall description of the area's economy.

While rating techniques have the same objectives as in the case of corporate bonds, the ratios used are adapted to the specific conditions that exist with respect to municipal debt obligations. Thus, debt as a percentage of market value of real estate is an important indicator: 10 percent is considered high while 3–5 percent is on the low side. Annual debt service of 10 percent of total revenue is considered comfortable while percentages in the high teens are considered as presenting a warning sign. Per capita debt of $400 or less is considered low while debt in the $900 to $1,000 area is considered

---

[3] The decision of New York State's highest court to overturn the New York City Moratorium on its notes strengthens the meaning of the concept of "full faith and credit." Said Chief Justice C. J. Breitel: "A pledge of the city's faith and credit is both a commitment to pay and a commitment of the city's revenue generating powers to produce the funds to pay . . . that is the way both words 'faith' and 'credit' are used and they are not tautological."

excessive and, hence, a negative factor. Tax delinquencies should generally not exceed 3–4 percent.

Other factors of interest include unfunded pension liabilities as well as the trend of indebtedness. A steady increase in indebtedness is usually a danger sign. As in all cases of debt rating, the factor of management, though largely intangible and subject to measurement only through ultimate results, is of critical importance.

LIMITATIONS OF THE RATING PROCESS

As valuable and essential as the rating process is to buyers of the thousands upon thousands of bond issues of every description, the limitations of this standardized procedure must also be understood. As is true in any phase of security analysis, the analyst who can, through superior analysis, improve on what is conventionally accepted stands to benefit accordingly. As was seen in Chapter 1, this is even more true in the case of debt securities than in the case of equity securities.

Bond ratings are very wide, and they consequently present opportunities for those who can identify these differences within a rating classification. Moreover, rating changes generally lag the market, and this presents additional opportunities to the analyst who with superior skill and alertness can identify important changes before they become generally recognized.

References

"The Rating Game." New York: The Twentieth Century Fund, 1974.

"Higher Stakes in the Bond-Rating Game." *Fortune,* April 1976.

H. C. Sherwood. *How Corporate and Municipal Debt Is Rated: An Inside Look at Standard & Poor's Rating System.* New York: John Wiley & Sons, 1976.

Corporate Bond Ratings: An Overview. New York: Standard & Poor's Corporation, 1978.

APPENDIX 5B

RATIOS AS PREDICTORS OF BUSINESS FAILURE

The most common use to which financial statement ratios are put is to use them as pointers in the direction of further investigation and analysis. Some investigation and experimentation has been undertaken to determine to what extent ratios can be used as predictors of failure. As such they could provide valuable additional tools in the analysis of long-term solvency.

The basic idea behind bankruptcy prediction models is that through observation of the trend and behavior of certain ratios of various firms before failure, those characteristics in ratios that predominate in failing firms can be identified and used for prediction purposes. The expectation is that signs of deterioration observed in ratio behavior can be detected early enough and clearly enough so that timely action can be taken to avoid substantial risk of default and failure.

Empirical studies

Among the earliest studies to focus on the behavior of ratios prior to the failure of firms were those of Winakor and Smith who studied a sample of 183 firms that experienced financial difficulties for as long as 10 years prior to 1931, the year when they failed.[1] Analyzing the 10-year trend of 21 ratios, they concluded that the ratio of net working capital to total assets was among the most accurate and reliable indicator of failure.

Fitzpatrick analyzed the three- to five-year trends of 13 ratios of 20 firms that had failed in the 1920–29 period.[2] By comparing them to the experience of a control group of 19 successful firms, he concluded that all of his ratios predicted failure to some extent. However, the best predictors were found to be the return on net worth and the net worth to total debt ratio.

Merwin studied the experience of a sample of 939 firms during the 1926–36 period.[3] Analyzing an unspecified number of ratios he found that three ratios were most sensitive in predicting "discontinuance" of a firm as early as four to five years before such discontinuance. The three ratios were the current ratio, net working capital to total assets, and net worth to total debt. They all exhibited declining trends before "discontinuance" and were at all times below estimated normal ratios.

Focusing on the experience of companies that experienced defaults on debt and bank credit difficulties, Hickman studied the experience of corporate bond issues during 1900–1943 and reached the conclusion that the times interest earned ratio and the net profit to sales ratio were useful predictors of bond issue defaults.[4]

In a study using more powerful statistical techniques than used in its predecessors, Beaver found that financial ratios proved useful in the prediction of bankruptcy and bond default at least five years prior to such failure. He determined that ratios could be used to distinguish correctly between failed

---

[1] Arthur Winakor and Raymond F. Smith, *Changes in Financial Structure of Unsuccessful Firms,* Bureau of Business Research (Urbana, Ill.: University of Illinois Press, 1935).

[2] Paul J. Fitzpatrick, *Symptoms of Industrial Failures* (Washington, D.C.: Catholic University of America Press, 1931); and Paul J. Fitzpatrick, *A Comparison of the Ratios of Successful Industrial Enterprises with Those of Failed Companies* (Washington, D.C.: The Accountants Publishing Co., 1932).

[3] Charles L. Merwin, *Financing Small Corporations: In Five Manufacturing Industries, 1926–36* (New York: National Bureau of Economic Research, 1942).

[4] W. Braddock Hickman, *Corporate Bond Quality and Investor Experience* (Princeton, N.J.: Princeton University Press, 1958), pp. 395–431.

and nonfailed firms to a much greater extent than would be possible by random prediction.[5]

Among his conclusions were that both in the short term and the long term, cash flow to total debt ratios were the best predictors, capital structure ratios ranked second, liquidity ratios third, while turnover ratios were the worst predictors.

In an investigation of the ability of ratios to predict bond rating changes and bond ratings of new issues, Horrigan found that the rating changes could be correctly predicted to a much greater extent by the use of ratios than would be possible through random prediction.[6]

Altman extended Beaver's univariate analysis to allow for multiple predictors of failure.[7] Altman used multiple discriminant analysis (MDA) that attempts to develop a linear function of a number of explanatory variables to classify or predict the value of a qualitative dependent variable; for example, bankrupt or nonbankrupt. Twenty-two financial ratios, based on data one period before bankruptcy, were examined, and Altman selected five of these to be included in his final discriminant function: working capital/total assets (liquidity), retained earnings/total assets (age of firm and cumulative profitability), earnings before interest and taxes/total assets (profitability), market value of equity/book value of debt (financial structure) and sales/total assets (capital turnover rate).

Altman was not able to use a cash flow variable, which Beaver found to be the most discriminating in his study since apart from other elements, Altman did not have depreciation figures.

Conclusions

The above research efforts, while pointing out the significant potential that ratios have as predictors of failure, nevertheless indicate that these tools and concepts are in an early stage of development.

The studies focused on experience with failed firms *after the fact*. While they presented evidence that firms that did not fail enjoyed stronger ratios than those that ultimately failed, the ability of ratios alone to predict failure has not been conclusively proved. Another important question yet to be resolved is whether the observation of certain types of behavior by certain ratios can be accepted as a better means of the analysis of long-term solvency than is the integrated use of the various tools described throughout this

---

[5] William H. Beaver, "Financial Ratios as Predictors of Failure," *Empirical Research in Accounting, Selected Studies, 1966*, Supplement to *Journal of Accounting Research 4*, pp. 71–127.

[6] James O. Horrigan, "The Determination of Long-Term Credit Standing with Financial Ratios," *Empirical Research in Accounting, Selected Studies, 1966*, Supplement to *Journal of Accounting Research 4*, pp. 44–62.

[7] Edward Altman, "Financial Ratios, Discriminant Analysis, and the Prediction of Corporate Bankruptcy," *Journal of Finance 22* (September 1968), pp. 589–609.

work. Further research may show that the use of ratios as predictors of failure will best complement and precede, rather than supplement, the rigorous financial analysis approaches suggested in this work. However, as screening,[8] monitoring, and attention-directing devices they hold considerable promise.

APPENDIX 5C

ILLUSTRATION OF THE COMPUTATION OF THE ANALYTICALLY ADJUSTED DEBT-TO-EQUITY RATIO

The conventional long-term debt to long-term debt and equity ratio is expressed as

$$\frac{LTD}{LTD + OE}$$

The formula that follows incorporates other analytical adjustments which can be made:

$$\frac{LTD + NFL + UPO\,(1 - TR) + LTDU}{LTD + NFL + UPO\,(1 - TR) + LTDU + OE + CDT + NDT + FIFOA + MSA - UPO\,(1 - TR)}$$

where:

LTD   = Long-term debt (including capitalized leases but excluding minority interests).

CDT   = Current deferred taxes—which are judged as unlikely to reverse in the foreseeable future.

NDT   = Noncurrent deferred taxes—which are judged as unlikely to reverse in the foreseeable future.

OE   = Owners' equity (including minority interests).

FIFOA = Excess of disclosed FIFO value of ending inventory over reported LIFO amount.

MSA   = Excess of market value of marketable securities over cost.

NFL   = Present value of noncapitalized financial leases.

UPO   = Present value of unrecognized pension obligations (the larger of unfunded vested benefits or unfunded prior service costs).

LTDU = Long-term debt of unconsolidated subsidiaries.

TR   = Marginal or statutory corporate tax rate.

---

[8] Banks have for years been using credit scoring for personal loans, which gives weight to credit worthiness characteristics such as income, employment, homeownership, etc. But for loans above $10,000–$25,000, banks no longer rely on the mass-production techniques of credit scoring.

This rationale behind these adjustments was discussed earlier in this chapter. The unrecognized pension obligation (UPO) adjustment merits further elaboration. Assuming a marginal tax rate of 48 percent, the analytical adjustment for a UPO of $100 is:

Retained Earnings ($100 × (1 − .48))	52
Deferred Taxes (future tax benefit on balance sheet)	48
Pension Obligation	100

Since the future tax benefit will be realized simultaneously with the payment of the UPO, it is proper to net the two and thus the analytical entry reduces to:

Retained Earnings (owners' equity)...........................	52
Pension Obligation	52

In the above formula we add UPO $(1 - TR)$ to debt in the numerator, add it to debt in the denominator, and reduce owners' equity by the same amount.

Using the 19x6 data of Alfa, Inc. (see Appendix 2B), we can now illustrate the adjustment of the conventional debt to debt + equity ratio (dollars in millions):

$$\text{Alfa's conventional ratio is } \frac{\$245^{(a)} + \$167^{(b)}}{\$245^{(a)} + \$167^{(b)} + \$331^{(c)}} = \underline{\underline{.55}}$$

Alfa's adjusted ratio is computed as follows:

$$\frac{\$245^{(a)} + \$167^{(b)} + \$22^{(d)} + \$32\,(1 - .48)^{(e)} + \$31^{(f)}}{\begin{array}{c}\$245^{(a)} + \$167^{(b)} + \$22^{(d)} + \$32(1 - .48)^{(e)} + \$31^{(f)} \\ + \$331^{(c)} + \$35^{(g)} + \$8^{(h)} - \$32(1 - .48)^{(e)}\end{array}} = \underline{\underline{.57}}$$

(a) LTD (item 38).

(b) Present value of long-term financing lease obligations (item 99)—these would normally be found recorded and in the balance sheet in accordance with *SFAS 13.* *

(c) Stockholders' equity (item 40) accepting the company's classification of "negative goodwill."

(d) Current deferred tax (item 34) considered here as debt.

(e) Present value of unfunded prior service pension costs (Note 14—item 105) times (1 − Tax rate).

(f) Long-term debt of nonconsolidated finance subsidiaries (Note 13—item 102).

(g) Noncurrent deferred taxes—considered here as equity.

(h) LIFO reserve (equivalent to difference between LIFO and FIFO)—per Note 5 (item 75)—added to equity.

* Thus leaving it for the analyst to decide which non-capitalized leases, or operating leases, should nevertheless be considered as long-term financing leases for purposes of analysis.

Two adjustments which are found in the model adjustment formula above were not made in Alfa's case. There were no marketable securities to adjust. Alfa discloses in Note 11 (item 99) "other" lease obligations with a present value of $80 million. The analyst has to make a judgment whether any of these should be capitalized as liabilities. In the above adjustment we omitted them on the assumption that they were all truly operating, rather than financing leases.

QUESTIONS

1. Generally speaking, what are the key elements in the evaluation of long-term solvency?
2. How should deferred income taxes be treated in the analysis of capital structure?
3. In the analysis of capital structure how should lease obligations that have not been capitalized be treated? Under what conditions should they be considered the equivalent of debt?
4. What is "off-balance sheet" financing? Name some examples.
5. What are liabilities for pensions? What factors should analysts assessing total pension obligations of the firm take into consideration?
6. When will information on unconsolidated subsidiaries be important to the analysis of long-term solvency?
7. How would you classify (i.e., equity or liability) the items that follow? State your assumptions and reasons.
    a. Minority interest in consolidated financial statement.
    b. General contingency reserve for indefinite purpose.
    c. Reserve for self-insurance.
    d. Guarantee for product performance on sale.
    e. Convertible debt.
    f. Preferred stock.
8. a. Why might the analyst need to adjust the book value of assets?
   b. Give three examples of the need for possible adjustments.
9. Why is the analysis of capital structure important?
10. What is meant by "financial leverage," and in what case(s) is such leverage most advantageous?
11. In the evaluation of long-term solvency why are long-term projections necessary in addition to a short-term analysis? What are some of the limitations of long-term projections?
12. What is the difference between common-size analysis and capital structure ratio analysis? Why is the latter useful?
13. The amount of equity capital shown on the balance sheets, which is based on historical cost, at times differs considerably from realizable market value. How should a financial analyst allow for this in the analysis of capital structure?
14. Why should the analyst compute the ratio of preferred stock to total stockholders' equity? How should preferred stock with mandatory redemption requirements be treated?
15. Why is the analysis of assets distribution necessary?
16. What does the earnings-coverage ratio measure and in what respects is it more useful than other tools of analysis?

17. For the purpose of earnings-coverage ratio computation, what are your criteria for inclusion of an item in "fixed charges"?

18. The company under analysis has a purchase commitment of raw materials under a noncancelable contract that is substantial in amount. Under what conditions would you include the purchase commitment in the computation of fixed charges?

19. Is net income generally a reliable measure of funds available to meet fixed charges? Why or why not?

20. What are some of the useful tests of funds flow relationships?

21. Company B is a wholly owned subsidiary of Company A. The latter is also Company B's principal customer. As potential lender to Company B, what particular facets of this relationship would concern you most? What safeguards, if any, would you require?

22. Comment on the statement: "Debt is a supplement to, not a substitute for, equity capital."

23. A company in need of additional equity capital decides to sell convertible debt thus postponing equity dilution and ultimately selling its shares at an effectively higher price. What are the advantages and disadvantages of such a course of action?

24. *a.* What is the basic function of restrictive covenants in long-term debt indentures (agreements)?
    b. What is the function of provisions regarding:
       (1) Maintenance of minimum working capital (or current ratio)?
       (2) Maintenance of minimum net worth?
       (3) Restrictions on the payment of dividends?
       (4) Ability of creditors to elect a majority of the board of directors of the debtor company in the event of default under the terms of the loan agreement?

25. What is your opinion on the use of ratios as predictors of failure? Your answer should recognize the empirical research that has been done recently in this area.

26. Dogwood Manufacturing, Inc., a successful and rapidly growing company, has always had a favorable difference between the rate of return on its assets and the interest rate paid on borrowed funds. Explain why the company should *not* increase its debt to the 90 percent level of total capitalization and thereby minimize any need for equity financing. (CFA)

27. Why are debt securities widely rated while equity securities are not?

28. On what aspects do the rating agencies focus in rating an industrial bond? Elaborate.

29. *a.* Municipal securities comprise a number of varieties. Discuss.
    b. What factors are considered in the rating of municipal securities?

30. Can the analyst improve on a rating judgment? Discuss.

6

Analysis of return on investment and of asset utilization

DIVERSE VIEWS OF PERFORMANCE

In this age of increasing social consciousness, there exist many views of what the basic objectives of business enterprises are or should be. There are those who will argue that the main objective of a business enterprise should be to make the maximum contribution to the welfare of society of which the enterprise is capable. That includes, aside from the profitable production of goods and services, consideration of such immeasurables as absence of environmental pollution and a contribution to the solution of social problems. Others, who adhere to the more traditional *laissez faire* school, maintain that the major objective of a business enterprise organized for profit is to increase the wealth of its owners and that this is possible only by delivering to society (consumers) that which it wants. Thus, the good of society will be served.

An extended discussion of these differing points of view on performance is beyond the purpose of this book. Since the analysis of financial statements is concerned with the application of analytical tools to that which can be measured, we shall concentrate here on those measures of performance that meet the objectives of financial analysis as outlined in Chapter 1. In that context, performance is the source of the rewards required to compensate investors and lenders for the risks that they are assuming.

CRITERIA OF PERFORMANCE EVALUATION

There are many criteria by which performance can be measured. Changes in sales, in profits, or in various measures of output are among the criteria frequently utilized.

No one of these measurements, standing by itself, is useful as a comprehensive measure of enterprise performance. The reasons for this are easy to grasp. Increases in sales are desirable only if they result in increased profits. The same is true of increases in volume of production. Increases in profits, on the other hand, must be related to the capital that is invested in order to attain these profits.

IMPORTANCE OF RETURN ON INVESTMENT (ROI)

The relationship between net income and the capital invested in the generation of that income is one of the most valid and most widely recognized measures of enterprise performance. In relating income to invested capital, the ROI measure allows the analyst to compare it to alternative uses of capital as well as to the return realized by enterprises subject to similar degrees of risk. The investment of capital can always yield some return. If capital is invested in government bonds, the return will be relatively low because of the small risk involved. Riskier investments require higher returns in order to make them worthwhile.[1] The ROI measure relates income (reward) to the size of the capital that was needed to generate it.

MAJOR OBJECTIVES IN THE USE OF ROI

Economic performance is the first and foremost purpose of business enterprise. It is, indeed, the reason for its existence. The effectiveness of operating performance determines the ability of the enterprise to survive financially, to attract suppliers of funds, and to reward them adequately. ROI is the prime measure of economic performance. The analyst uses it as a tool in three areas of great importance:

1. An indicator of managerial effectiveness.
2. A measure of an enterprise's ability to earn a satisfactory return on investment.
3. A method of projecting earnings.

An indicator of managerial effectiveness

The earning of an adequate or superior return on funds invested in an enterprise depends first and foremost on the resourcefulness, skill, ingenuity, and motivation of management. Thus, the longer-term ROI is of great interest and importance to the financial analyst because it offers a prime means of evaluating this indispensible criterion of business success: the quality of management.

---

[1] See Chapter 1 for an examination of the importance of the evaluation of risk and return in investing and lending decisions.

A measure of enterprise ability to earn a satisfactory ROI

While related to managerial effectiveness, this measure is a far more reliable indicator of long-term financial health than is any measure of current financial strength based only on balance sheet relationships. For this reason, ROI is of great importance and interest to longer-term creditors as well as to equity investors.

A method of projecting earnings

A third important function served by the ROI measure is that of a means of earnings projection. The advantage of this method of earnings projection is that it links the amount of earnings that it is estimated an enterprise will earn to the total invested capital. This adds discipline and realism to the projection process, which applies to the present and expected capital investment the return that is expected to be realized on it. The latter will usually be based on the historical and incremental rates of return actually earned by the enterprise and adjusted by projected changes, as well as on expected returns on new projects.

The rate of ROI method of earnings projection can be used by the analyst as either the primary method of earnings projection or as a supplementary check on estimates derived from other projection methods.

Internal decision and control tool

While our focus here is on the work of the external financial analyst, mention should be made of the very important role that ROI measures play in the individual investment decisions of an enterprise as well as in the planning, budgeting, coordination, evaluation, and control of business operations and results.

It is obvious that the final return achieved in any one period on the total investment of an enterprise is composed of the returns (and losses) realized by the various segments and divisions of which it is composed. In turn, these returns are made up of the results achieved by individual product lines, projects, and so forth.

The well-managed enterprise exercises rigorous control over the returns achieved by each of its "profit centers" and rewards its managers on the basis of such results. Moreover, in evaluating the advisability of new investments of funds in assets or projects, management will compute the estimated returns it expects to achieve from them and use these estimates as a basis for its decision.[2]

---

[2] Managements' emphasis on these techniques has recently been challenged. In their article "Managing Our Way to Economic Decline" in the *Harvard Business Review* of July–August 1980, Professors R. Hayes and W. Abernathy argue that this preoccupation with ROI and the related discounted cash flow measures has led to an emphasis on short-term profits at the expense of long-term risk taking based on improved technology.

BASIC ELEMENTS OF ROI

The basic concept of ROI is relatively simple to understand. However, care must be used in determining the elements entering its computation because there exist a variety of views, which reflect different objectives, of how these elements should be defined.

The basic formula for computing ROI is as follows:

$$\frac{\text{Income}}{\text{Investment}}$$

We shall now examine the various definitions of *investment* and of the related *income*.

Defining the investment base

There is no one generally accepted measure of capital investment on which the rate of return is computed. The different concepts of investment reflect different objectives. Since the term *return on investment (ROI)* covers a multitude of concepts of investment base and income, there is need for more specific terms to describe the actual investment base used.

Total assets. Return on total assets is perhaps the best measure of the *operating efficiency* of an enterprise. It measures the return obtained on *all* the assets entrusted to management. By removing from this computation the effect of the method used in financing the assets, the analyst can concentrate on the evaluation or projection of operating performance.

Modified asset bases. For a variety of reasons, some ROI computations are based not on total assets but rather on an adjusted amount.

One important category of adjustments relates to "unproductive" assets. In this category, assets omitted from the investment base include idle plant, facilities under construction, surplus plant, surplus inventories and surplus cash, intangible assets, and deferred charges. The basic idea behind these exclusions is not to hold management responsible for earning a return on assets that apparently do not earn a return. While this theory may have validity in the use of ROI as an internal management and control tool, it lacks merit when applied as a tool designed to evaluate management effectiveness on an overall basis. Management is entrusted with funds by owners and creditors, and it has discretion as to where it wants to invest them. There is no reason for management to hold on to assets that bring no return. If there are reasons for keeping funds invested in such assets, then there is no reason to exclude them from the investment base. If the long-run profitability of an enterprise is benefited by keeping funds invested in assets that have no return or a low return in the interim, then the longer-term ROI should reflect such benefits. In conclusion, it can be said that from the point of view of an enterprise evaluation by the external analyst, there is rarely any justification to omit assets from the investment base merely because they are not productively employed or do not earn a current return.

The exclusion of intangible assets from the investment base is often due to skepticism regarding their value or their contribution to the earning power of the enterprise. Under generally accepted accounting principles (GAAP), intangibles are carried at cost. However, if the cost exceeds their future utility, they must be written down or else the analyst will at least find an uncertainty exception regarding their carrying value included in the auditor's opinion. Arbitrary exclusion of intangible assets from the asset (investment) base must be justified on more substantial evidence than a mere lack of understanding of what these assets represent or an unsupported suspicion regarding their value.

Depreciable assets in the investment base. An important difference of opinion prevails with respect to the question of whether depreciable assets should be included in the investment base at original cost or at an amount net of the accumulated allowances for depreciation.

One of the most prominent advocates of the inclusion of fixed assets at gross amount in the investment base for purposes of computing the ROI is the management of E. I. du Pont de Nemours Company which pioneered the use of ROI as an internal management tool.

In a pamphlet describing the company's use of the ROI method in the appraisal of operating performance, this point of view is expressed as follows:

> *Calculation of return on investment.* Return on investment as presented in the chart series is based upon *gross* operating investment and earnings *net* of depreciation.
>
> Gross operating investment represents all the plant, tools, equipment and working capital made available to operating management for its use; no deduction is made for current or other liabilities or for the reserve for depreciation. Since plant facilities are maintained in virtually top productive order during their working life, the depreciation reserve being considered primarily to provide for obsolescence, it would be inappropriate to consider that operating management was responsible for earning a return on only the net operating investment. Furthermore, if depreciable assets were stated at net depreciated values, earnings in each succeeding period would be related to an ever-decreasing investment; even with stable earnings, Return on Investment would continually rise, so that comparative Return on Investment ratios would fail to reveal the extent of trend of management performance. Relating earnings to investment that is stable and uniformly compiled provides a sound basis for comparing the "profitability of assets employed" as between years and between investments.
>
> In the case of any commitment of capital—e.g., an investment in a security— it is the expectation that in addition to producing earnings while committed, the principal will eventually be recovered. Likewise, in the case of funds invested in a project, it is expected that in addition to the return earned while invested, the working capital will be recovered through liquidation at the end of the project's useful life and the plant investment will be recovered through deprecia-

tion accruals. Since earnings must allow for this recovery of plant investment, they are stated net of depreciation.[3]

It is not difficult to take issue with the above reasoning. It must, however, be borne in mind that the du Pont system is designed for use in the internal control of separate productive units as well as for the control of operating management. Our point of view here is, however, that of evaluating the operating performance of an enterprise taken as a whole. While by an enterprise operating at a profit, the recovery of capital out of sales and revenues (via depreciation) can be disregarded in the evaluation of a *single* division or segment, it cannot be disregarded for an enterprise taken as a whole because such recovery is reinvested somewhere within that enterprise even if it is not reinvested in the particular segment that gave rise to the depreciation and that is evaluated for internal purposes. Thus, for an enterprise taken as a whole, the "net of depreciation" asset base is a more valid measure of investment on which a return is computed. This is so for the reasons given above and also because the income that is usually related to the investment base is net of the depreciation expense.

The tendency of the rate of return to rise as assets are depreciated is offset by the retention of capital recovered by means of depreciation, on which capital a return must also be earned. Moreover, maintenance and repair costs rise as equipment gets older, thus tending to offset the reduction, if any, in the asset base.

Among other reasons advanced in support of the use of fixed assets at their gross amount is the argument that the higher amounts are designed to compensate for the effects of inflation on assets expressed in terms of historical cost. Price-level adjustments can validly be made only within the framework of a complete restatement of all elements of the financial statements. Crude "adjustments," as, for example, using the gross asset amount, are apt to be misleading and are generally worse than no adjustments at all.

Long-term liabilities plus equity capital.   The use of long-term liabilities plus equity capital as the investment base differs from the "total assets" base only in that current liabilities are excluded as suppliers of funds on which the return is computed. The focus here is on the two major suppliers of longer-term funds, that is, long-term creditors and equity shareholders.

Shareholders' equity.   The computation of return on shareholders' equity measures the return accruing to the owners' capital. As was seen in the discussion of financial leverage in Chapter 5, this return reflects the effect of the employment of debt capital on the owners' return. Since preferred stock, while in the equity category, is usually nevertheless entitled only to

---

[3] American Management Association, *Executive Committee Control Charts*, AMA Management Bulletin No. 6, 1960, p. 22.

a fixed return, it is also omitted from the calculation of the final return on equity computation.

Book versus market values in the investment base

Returns on asset calculations are most commonly based on book values appearing in the financial statements rather than on market or fair values that are, in most cases, analytically more significant and relevant. Also, quite often, a return is earned by enterprises on assets that either do not appear in the financial statements or are significantly understated therein. Examples of such assets are intangibles such as patents, trademarks, expensed research and development (R&D) costs, advertising and training costs, and so forth. Other excluded assets may include leaseholds and the value of natural resources discovered.

Recent developments have reinforced the trend toward current value accounting, and information on the current cost of assets of large corporations is already available. One alternative to the use of such data is to rely on the valuation that the market places on the equity securities of the enterprise in order to approximate fair values. Thus, we can substitute the market value of equity securities and debt for the book value of total assets in computing a proper investment base.

Difference between investor's cost and enterprise investment base

For purposes of computing the ROI, a distinction must be drawn between the investment base of an enterprise and that of an investor. The investor's investment base is, of course, the price he paid for his equity securities. Except for those cases in which he acquired such securities at book value, his investment base is going to differ from that of the company in which he has invested. In general, the focus in ROI computations is on the return realized by the enterprise rather than the return realized on the investment cost of any one shareholder.

Averaging the investment base

Regardless of the method used in arriving at the investment base, the return achieved over a period of time is always associated with the investment base that was, on average, actually available to the enterprise over that period of time. Thus, unless the investment base did not change significantly during the period, it will be necessary to average it.

The most common method of averaging for the external analyst is that of adding the investment base at the beginning of the year to that at the end of the year and dividing their total by two. Care must, however, be used in employing this method of averaging. Companies in some industries choose a "natural" rather than the calendar business year. Thus, for example, in retailing, the natural business year ends when inventories are at their lowest (e.g., January 31 after the holiday selling season) and when it is easiest to count them. In such case, averaging two year-ends may yield the *lowest* rather than the average amount of assets employed.

In such or similar cases, more accurate methods of averaging, where the data are available, are to average by month-end balances, that is, adding the month-end investment bases and dividing the total by 12, or to average on a quarterly basis.

Relating income to the investment base

In the computation of ROI, the definition of return (income) is dependent on the definition of the investment base.

If the investment base is defined as comprising total assets, then income *before* interest expense is used.[4] The exclusion of interest from income deductions is due to its being regarded as a payment for the use of money to the suppliers of debt capital in the same way that dividends are regarded as a reward to suppliers of equity capital. Before deductions for interest or dividends, income is used when it is related to total assets or to long-term debt plus equity capital (assuming most of the interest expense is on long-term obligations).

The income of a consolidated entity that includes a subsidiary that is partially owned by a minority interest usually reflects a deduction for the minority's share in that income. The consolidated balance sheet, however, includes all the assets of such a subsidiary, i.e., those belonging to the parent as well as those belonging to the minority. Because the investment in the denominator includes all the assets of the consolidated entity, the income (in the numerator) should include all the income (or loss), not just the parent's share. For this reason, the minority's share of earnings (or loss) must be added back to income in computing return on total assets. When the denominator is the equity capital only, the minority share in income (or loss) need not be added back if equity capital excludes minority interest.

When the return on the equity capital is computed, net income *after* deductions for interest and preferred dividends is used. If the preferred dividends are cumulative, they are deducted in arriving at the balance of earnings accruing to the common stock, whether these dividends were declared or not.

The final ROI must always reflect all applicable costs and expenses and that includes income taxes. Some computations of ROI nevertheless omit deductions of income taxes. One reason for this practice is the desire to isolate the effects of tax management from those of operating performance. Another reason is that changes in tax rates affect comparability over the years. Moreover, companies that have tax loss carry-forwards find that the deduction of taxes from income adds confusion and complications to the ROI computations.

---

[4] Interest expense means interest incurred less interest capitalized. In theory, the amount of previously capitalized interest currently amortized and included in expenses should also be added back to income.

It must, however, be borne in mind that income taxes reduce the final return and that they must be taken into consideration particularly when the return on shareholders' equity is computed.

ADJUSTING THE COMPONENTS OF THE ROI FORMULA

In computing any measure or ratio, the analyst uses the amounts in the financial statements only as starting points. As was seen in the discussion in Chapter 5 on the adjustment of the debt-to-equity ratios, some amounts need analytical adjustment and some amounts not found in the financial statements need to be included in the adjusted computation. Reference to the discussion in Chapter 5 will reveal that some of the items discussed therein, such as adjustment of inventory amounts, may affect the ROI computation while others, such as reclassification of deferred taxes, may not. Moreover, some adjustments, such as those relating to inventory amounts, affect both the numerator and the denominator of the formula, thus moderating the net effect on the ratio.

The computation of ROI under the various concepts of "investment base" discussed above will now be illustrated by means of the data contained in Exhibits 6–1 and 6–2. The computations are for the year 19x9 and based on figures rounded to the nearest million dollars.

Exhibit 6–1

AMERICAN COMPANY
Statement of Income
For Years Ended December 31, 19x8, and 19x9
(in thousands)

	19x8	19x9
Net sales	$1,636,298	$1,723,729
Costs and expenses	1,473,293	1,579,401
Operating income	163,005	144,328
Other income net	2,971	1,784
	165,976	146,112
Interest expense*	16,310	20,382
Income before tax	149,666	125,730
Provision for federal and other taxes on income	71,770	61,161
Net income	77,896	64,569
Less dividends:		
Preferred stock	2,908	2,908
Common stock	39,209	38,898
	42,117	41,806
Net income reinvested in the business	$ 35,779	$ 22,763

* In 19x9, interest on long-term debt was $19,695.

Exhibit 6–2

AMERICAN COMPANY
Statements of Financial Position
As at December 31, 19x8, and 19x9
(in thousands)

	19x8	19x9
Assets		
Current assets:		
Cash	$ 25,425	$ 25,580
Eurodollar time deposits and temporary cash		
investments	38,008	28,910
Accounts and notes receivable—net	163,870	176,911
Inventories	264,882	277,795
Total current assets	492,185	509,196
Investments in and receivables from nonconsolidated		
subsidiaries	33,728	41,652
Miscellaneous investments and receivables	5,931	6,997
Funds held by trustee for construction	6,110	
Land, buildings, equipment, and timberlands—net	773,361	790,774
Deferred charges to future operations	16,117	16,452
Goodwill and other intangible assets	6,550	6,550
Total assets..................................	$1,333,982	$1,371,621
Liabilities		
Current liabilities:		
Notes payable to banks—principally Eurodollar	$ 7,850	$ 13,734
Accounts payable and accrued expenses	128,258	144,999
Dividends payable	10,404	10,483
Federal and other taxes on income	24,370	13,256
Long-term indebtedness payable within one year	9,853	11,606
Total current liabilities	180,735	194,078
Long-term indebtedness	350,565	335,945
Deferred taxes on income	86,781	101,143
Total liabilities	618,081	631,166
Capital		
Preferred, 7% cumulative and noncallable, par		
value $25 per share; authorized 1,760,000 shares ..	41,538	41,538
Common, par value $12.50 per share; authorized		
30,000,000 shares	222,245	222,796
Capital in excess of par value.....................	19,208	20,448
Earnings reinvested in the business	436,752	459,515
Less: Common treasury stock	(3,842)	(3,842)
Total capital	715,901	740,455
Total liabilities and capital	$1,333,982	$1,371,621

Return on total assets

Applying the basic formula to the data of American Company for 19x9 we get:

$$\frac{\text{Net income} + \text{Interest expense} \times (1 - \text{Tax rate}) + \text{Minority interest in earnings}}{(\text{Beginning total assets} + \text{Ending total assets}) \div 2}$$

$$= \frac{\$65 + \$20\,(1 - .46) + 0*}{(\$1,334 + \$1,372) \div 2} = .056, \text{ or } 5.6 \text{ percent}$$

* No minority interest in this case.

The tax adjustment of the interest expense recognizes that interest is a tax-deductible expense and that if the interest cost is excluded, the related tax benefit must also be excluded from income. The *tax rate* we use is the *marginal* or corporate tax rate of 46 percent because the tax incidence with respect to any one item (such as interest expense) can be measured by the marginal tax rate. In computing the fixed-charges-coverage ratio (see Chapter 5), we use the *effective* tax rate because we have adopted the SEC's computation which requires its use.

The assets have been averaged by using the year-end figures for total assets. As discussed earlier, this method of computing the average may yield misleading results in some cases.

Return on modified asset bases. Since our discussion earlier in the chapter came to the conclusion that in normal circumstances most of the modifications in the amount of total assets are not logically warranted, no illustrations of such computation will be given.

Return on long-term liabilities plus equity capital

$$\frac{\begin{array}{c}\text{Net income} + \text{Interest expense*} \times (1 - \text{Tax rate}) \\ + \text{Minority interest in earnings}\end{array}}{\text{Average long-term liabilities} + \text{equity capital}}$$

Using the data in Exhibits 6–1 and 6–2 for 19x9:

$$\frac{\$65 + \$20*\,(1 - .46) + 0}{(\$437 + \$716 + \$437 + \$740) \div 2} = .065, \text{ or } 6.5 \text{ percent}$$

* On long-term debt ($19,695 rounded).

Decisions of how to classify items such as deferred taxes as between debt and equity will have to be made by the analyst using the considerations already discussed in Chapter 6. It should be noted that deferred taxes on income are included here among the long-term liabilities. In the computation of return on long-term liabilities and equity capital, the question of how to classify deferred taxes does not really present a problem because in this computation both debt and equity are aggregated anyway. The problem of classification becomes more real in computing the return on shareholders' equity.

In the examples that follow, we assume circumstances where deferred taxes are considered to be more in the nature of long-term liability than equity. In many cases, the classification decision can have a significant effect on the return computation.

Return on stockholders' equity. The basic computation of return on the equity excludes from the investment base all but the common stockholders' equity.

$$\frac{\text{Net income} - \text{Preferred dividends}}{\text{Average common stockholders' equity}}$$

Using data in Exhibits 6–1 and 6–2 for 19x9:

$$\frac{\$65 - \$3}{(\$674 + \$699) \div 2} = 9 \text{ percent}$$

The higher return on shareholders' equity as compared to the return on total assets reflects the positive workings of financial leverage.

Should it be desired, for whatever reason, to compute the return on total stockholders' equity, the investment base would include the preferred shareholders' equity, while net income would not reflect a deduction for preferred dividends. The formula[5] would then be:

$$\frac{\text{Net income}}{\text{Average total shareholders' equity (common and preferred)}}$$

Where convertible debt sells at a substantial premium above par and is clearly held by investors for its conversion feature, there is justification for treating it as the equivalent of equity capital. This is particularly true when the company can choose at any time to force conversion of the debt by calling it.

Analysis and interpretation of ROI

Earlier in the chapter we mentioned that ROI analysis is particularly useful to the analyst in the areas of evaluation of managerial effectiveness, enterprise profitability, and as an important tool of earnings projection.

The evaluation of ROI and the projection of earnings by means of ROI analysis are complex processes requiring thorough analysis. The reason for this is that the ROI computation usually includes components of considerable complexity.

---

[5] The return on common stockholders' equity may also be computed thus:

$$\frac{\text{Earnings per share}}{\text{Book value per share}}$$

But the results will often not be identical because the earnings per share computation includes adjustments for common stock equivalents.

Components of the ROI ratio.   If we focus first on return on total assets, we know that the primary formula for computing this return is:

$$\frac{\text{Net income} + \text{Interest} \times (1 - \text{Tax rate})^*}{\text{Average total assets}}$$

* Omitting the add-back of minority interest
in earnings in order to simplify the discussion does
not impair its validity.

For purposes of our discussion and analysis, let us look at this computation in a simplified form:

$$\frac{\text{Net income}}{\text{Total assets}}$$

Since sales are a most important yardstick in relation to which profitability is measured and are, as well, a major index of activity, we can recast the above formula as follows:

$$\frac{\text{Net income}}{\text{Sales}} \times \frac{\text{Sales}}{\text{Total assets}}$$

The relationship of net income to sales measures operating performance and profitability. The relationship of sales to total assets is a measure of asset utilization or turnover, a means of determining how effectively (in terms of sales generation) the assets are utilized. It can be readily seen that both factors, profitability as well as asset utilization, determine the return realized on a given investment in assets.

Profitability and asset utilization are, in turn, complex ratios that normally require thorough and detailed analysis before they can be used to reach conclusions regarding the reasons for changes in the return on total assets.

Exhibit 6–3 presents the major factors that influence the final return on total assets. In the next section, we shall be concerned with the interaction of profitability (net income/sales) and of asset utilization or turnover (sales/total assets) that in Exhibit 6–3 is regarded as the first level of analysis of the return on total assets. As can be seen from Exhibit 6–3, the many important and complex factors that, in turn, determine profitability and asset utilization represent a second level of analysis of the return on total assets. Chapters 7 and 8 will take up the analysis of results of operations, and Chapter 9 will deal with the evaluation and projection of earnings. The analysis of asset utilization will be discussed in subsequent sections of this chapter.

Relationship between profitability and asset turnover.   The relationship between return on total assets, profitability, and capital turnover (utilization) is illustrated in Exhibit 6–4, which indicates that when we multiply profitability (expressed as a percentage) by asset utilization (expressed as a turnover) we obtain the return on total assets (expressed as a percentage relationship).

Exhibit 6–3

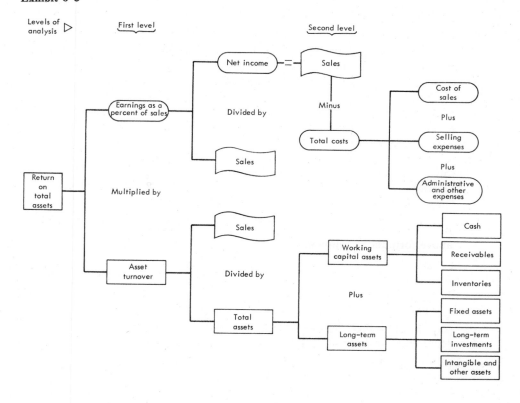

Exhibit 6–4: Analysis of return on total assets

		Company X	*Company Y*	*Company Z*
1.	Sales	$5,000,000	$10,000,000	$10,000,000
2.	Net income	500,000	500,000	100,000
3.	Total assets	5,000,000	5,000,000	1,000,000
4.	Profit as percent of sales $\left(\frac{2}{1}\right)$	10%	5%	1%
5.	Asset turnover $\left(\frac{1}{3}\right)$	1	2	10
	Return on total assets (4 × 5)	10%	10%	10%

Company X realizes its 10 percent return on total assets by means of a relatively high profit margin and a low turnover of assets. The opposite is true of Company Z, while Company Y achieves its 10 percent return by means of a profit margin half that of Company X and an asset turnover rate twice that of Company X. It is obvious from Exhibit 6–4 that there

are many combinations of profit margins and turnover rates that can yield
a return on assets of 10 percent.

In fact, as can be seen from Exhibit 6–5, there exists an infinite variety
of combinations of profit margin and asset turnover rates that yield a 10
percent return on assets. The chart in the exhibit graphically relates asset
turnover (vertical axis) to profitability (horizontal axis).

The curve, sloping from the upper left area of low profit margins and
high asset turnover rates, traces out the endless combinations of profitability
and asset turnover rates that yield a 10 percent return on total assets. The
data of Companies X and Y (from Exhibit 6–4) are represented by dots on
the graph, while the data of Company Z cannot be fitted on it since the
full curve has not been shown. The other lettered dots represent the profit-
turnover combination of other companies within a particular industry. This
clustering of the results of various companies around the 10 percent return
on assets slope is a useful way of comparing the returns of many enterprises
within an industry and the major two elements that comprise them.

The chart in Exhibit 6–5 is also useful in assessing the relative courses
of action open to different enterprises that want to improve their respective
returns on investments.

Companies B and C must, of course, restore profitability before the turnover
rate becomes a factor of importance. Assuming that all the companies represented in Exhibit 6–5 belong to the same industry and that there is an average
representative level of profitability and turnover in it, Company P will be

Exhibit 6–5

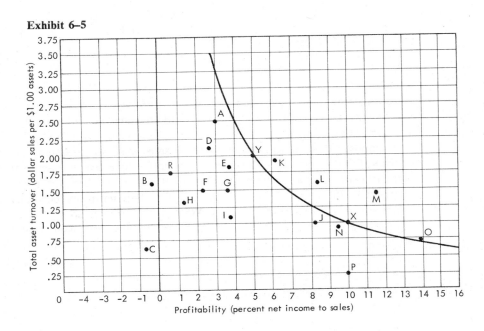

best advised to pay first and particular attention to improvement in its turnover ratio, while Company R should pay foremost attention to the improvement of its profit margin. Other companies, such as Company I, would best concentrate on both the turnover and the profit margin aspects of ROI improvement.

While the above analysis treats profitability and turnover as two independent variables, they are, in fact, interdependent. As will be seen from the discussion of break-even analysis in Chapter 8, when fixed expenses are substantial, a higher level of activity (turnover) will tend to increase the profit margin because within a certain range of activity, costs increase proportionally less than sales. In comparing two companies within an industry, the analyst, in evaluating the one having the lower asset turnover, will make allowance for the potential increase in profitability that can be associated with a projected increase in turnover that is based primarily on an expansion of sales.

Analysis of return on total assets can reveal the weaknesses as well as the potential strengths of an enterprise. Assume that two companies in the same industry have returns on total assets as follows:

		Company A	Company B
1.	Sales	$ 1,000,000	$20,000,000
2.	Net income	100,000	100,000
3.	Total assets	10,000,000	10,000,000
4.	Profitability $\left(\frac{2}{1}\right)$	10%	0.5%
5.	Turnover of assets $\left(\frac{1}{3}\right)$	.1 times	2 times
	Return on investment (4×5)	1%	1%

Both companies have poor returns on total assets. However, remedial action for them lies in different areas, and the analyst will concentrate on the evaluation of the feasibility of success of such improvement.

Company A has a 10 percent profit on sales that, let us assume, is about average for the industry. However, each dollar invested in assets supports only 10 cents in sales, whereas Company B gets $2 of sales for each dollar invested in its assets. The analyst's attention will naturally be focused on Company A's investment in assets. Why is its turnover so low? Are there excess assets that yield little or no return or are there idle assets that should be disposed of? Or, as often is the case, are the assets inefficiently or uneconomically utilized? Quite obviously, Company A can achieve more immediate and significant improvements by concentrating on improving turnover (by increasing sales, reducing investment, or both) than by striving to increase the profit margin beyond the industry average.

The opposite situation prevails with respect to Company B where attention should first be focused on the reasons for the low profit margin and to the improvement of it as the most likely avenue of success in increasing ROI. The reasons for low profitability can be many, including inefficient equipment and production methods, unprofitable product lines, excess capacity with attendant high fixed costs, excessive selling or administrative costs, etc.

The company with the low profitability may discover that changes in tastes and in technology have resulted in an increased investment in assets being needed to finance a dollar of sales. This means that in order to maintain its return on assets, the company must increase its profit margin or else production of the product is no longer worthwhile.

There is a tendency to regard a high profit margin as a sign of high earnings quality. This view was rebutted by W. M. Bennett who pointed out the importance of return on capital as the ultimate test of profitability.[6] He presented the following table comparing during a given year the similar profit margins of five companies with their respective returns on capital:

	Profit margin as percent of sales	Profit as percent of capital
Whirlpool	5.3	17.1
Corn Products	5.9	12.0
Goodyear	5.5	9.6
U.S. Plywood	5.5	8.0
Distillers Seagram	5.0	6.7

It is evident that in the case of these five companies, which have similar profit margins, the rate of capital turnover made the difference in the return on capital performance, and this must be taken into account by the analyst. Thus, a supermarket chain will be content with a net profit margin of 1 percent or less because it has a high rate of turnover due to a relatively low investment in assets and a high proportion of leased assets (such as stores and fixtures). Similarly, a discount store will accept a low profit margin in order to obtain a high rate of asset turnover (primarily of inventories). On the other hand, capital intensive industries such as steels, chemicals, and autos, which have heavy investments in assets and resulting low asset turnover rates, must achieve high net profit margins in order to offer investors a reasonable return on capital.

In most cases, the focus on single-year rates of return are apt to be misleading. The cyclical nature of many industries cause such swings in profitability

[6] William M. Bennett, "Capital Turnover vs. Profit Margins," *Financial Analysts Journal,* March–April 1966, pp. 88–95.

that some years' profits may appear exorbitant while others barely are sufficient to justify the related investment. Such enterprises can only be validly evaluated on the basis of average returns over a number of years covering a full economic cycle.

ANALYSIS OF ASSET UTILIZATION

As is graphically illustrated in Exhibit 6–3, the return on total assets depends on (1) getting the largest profit out of each dollar of sales and (2) obtaining the highest possible amount of sales per dollar of invested capital (net assets).

The intensity with which assets are utilized is measured by means of asset turnover ratios.[7] That utilization has as its ultimate measure the amount of sales generated since sales are in most enterprises the first and essential step to profits. In certain special cases, such as with enterprises in developmental stages, the meaning of turnover may have to be modified in recognition of the fact that most assets are committed to the development of future potential. Similarly, abnormal supply problems and strikes are conditions that will affect the state of capital utilization and, as such, will require separate evaluation and interpretation.

Evaluation of individual turnover ratios

Changes in the basic turnover ratio that enters the determination of the ROI calculation, that is,

$$\frac{\text{Sales}}{\text{Total assets}}$$

can be evaluated meaningfully only by an analysis of changes in the turnover rates of individual asset categories and groups that comprise the total assets.

Sales to cash. As was seen in the discussion in Chapter 3, cash and cash equivalents are held primarily for purposes of meeting the needs of day-to-day transactions as well as a liquidity reserve designed to prevent the shortages that may arise from an imbalance in cash inflows and outflows. In any type of business, there is a certain logical relationship between sales and cash level that must be maintained to support it.

Too high a rate of turnover may be due to a cash shortage that can

---

[7] P. F. Drucker in *Managing in Turbulent Times* (New York: Harper & Row, 1980) writes: "In the United States the General Electric Co., for example, does not owe its leadership position primarily to technological achievement. What sets it apart from Westinghouse, its closest competitor and the industry's number two, is above all productivity of capital. GE gets about twice as much work out of a dollar as Westinghouse does."

ultimately result in a liquidity crisis if the enterprise has no other ready sources of funds available to it.

Too low a rate of turnover may be due to the holding of idle and unnecessary cash balances. Cash accumulated for specific purposes or known contingencies may result in temporary decreases in the rate of turnover.

The basic trade-off here is between liquidity and the tying up of funds that yield no return or a very modest return.

Sales to receivables. Any organization that sells on credit will find that the level of its receivables is a function of sales. A relatively low rate of turnover here is, among other reasons, likely to be due to an overextension of credit, to an inability of customers to pay, or to a poor collection job.

A relatively high rate of turnover may indicate a strict credit extension policy or a reluctance or inability to extend credit. Determining the rate of turnover here is the trade-off between sales and the tying up of funds in receivables.

Sales to inventories. The maintenance of a given level of sales generally requires a given level of inventories. This relationship will vary from industry to industry depending on the variety of types, models, colors, sizes, and other classes of varieties of items that must be kept in order to attract and keep customers. The length of the production cycle as well as the type of item (e.g., luxury versus necessity; perishable versus durable) have a bearing on the rate of turnover.

A slow rate of turnover indicates the existence of problems such as overstocking, slow-moving or obsolete inventories, overestimating of sales, or a lack of balance in the inventory. Temporary problems such as strikes at important customers may also be responsible for such a condition.

A higher than normal rate of turnover may mean an underinvestment in inventory that can result in lack of proper customer service and in loss of sales.

In this case, the trade-off is between tying up funds in inventory, on one hand, and sacrificing customer service and sales, on the other.

Sales to fixed assets. While the relationship between property, plant, and equipment and sales is a logical one on a long-term basis, there are many short-term and temporary factors that may upset this relationship. Among these factors are conditions of excess capacity, inefficient or obsolete equipment, multishift operations, temporary changes in demand, and interruptions in the supply of raw materials and parts.

It must also be remembered that increases in plant capacity are not gradual but occur, instead, in lumps. This too can create temporary and medium-term changes in the turnover rates. Often, leased facilities and equipment, which do not appear on the balance sheet, will distort the relationship between sales and fixed assets.

The trade-off here is between investment in fixed assets with a correspondingly higher break-even point, on one hand, and efficiency, productive capacity, and sales potential, on the other.

Sales to other assets.   In this category, we find, among others, such assets as patents and deferred charges or other costs. While the direct relationship between these individual categories of assets and current sales levels may not be evident, no assets are held or should be held by an enterprise unless they contribute to sales or to the generation of income. In the case of deferred R&D costs, the investment may represent the potential of future sales. In the evaluation of rates of asset utilization, the analyst must allow for such factors.

Sales to short-term liabilities.   The relationship between sales and short-term trade liabilities is a predictable one. The amount of short-term credit that an enterprise is able to obtain from suppliers depends on its needs for goods and services, that is, on the level of activity (e.g., sales). Thus, the degree to which it can obtain short-term credit depends also importantly on the level of sales. This short-term credit is relatively cost-free and, in turn, reduces the investment of enterprise funds in working capital.

Use of averages

Whenever the level of a given asset category changes significantly during the period for which the turnover is computed, it is necessary to use averages of asset levels in the computation. The computation then becomes

$$\frac{\text{Sales}}{(\text{Asset at beginning of period} + \text{Asset at end of period}) \div 2}$$

To the extent that data is available and the variation in asset levels during the period dictates it, the average can be computed on a monthly or quarterly basis.

Other factors to be considered in return on asset evaluation

The evaluation of the return on assets involves many factors of great complexity. As will be seen from the discussion in Chapter 9, the inclusion of extraordinary gains and losses in single period and average net income must be evaluated. The effects of price-level changes on ROI calculations must also be taken into consideration by the financial analyst.

In analyzing the trend of return on assets over the years, the effect of acquisitions accounted for as poolings of interest must be isolated and their chance of recurrence evaluated. The effect of discontinued operations must be similarly evaluated.

The external analyst will not usually be able to obtain data on ROI by segments, product lines, or divisions of an enterprise. However, where his bargaining power or position allows him to obtain such data, they can make a significant contribution to the accuracy and reliability of his analysis.

A consistently high return on assets is the earmark of an effective management and can distinguish a growth company from one experiencing merely a cyclical or seasonal pickup in business.

An examination of the factors that comprise the return on assets will usually reveal the limitations to which their expansion is subject. Neither the profit margin nor the asset turnover rate can expand indefinitely. Thus, an expanding asset base via external financing and/or internal earnings retention will be necessary for further earnings growth.

Return on shareholders' equity

Up to now we have examined the factors affecting the return on total assets. However, of great interest to the owner group of an enterprise is the return on the stockholders' equity. The rate of return on total assets and that on the stockholders' equity differ because a portion of the capital with which the assets are financed is usually supplied by creditors who receive a fixed return on their capital or, in some cases, no return at all. Similarly, the preferred stock usually receives a fixed dividend. These fixed returns differ from the rate earned on the assets (funds) that they provide, and this accounts for the difference in returns on assets and those on stockholders' equity. This is the concept of financial leverage that was already discussed in Chapter 5.

ANALYSIS OF RETURN ON COMMON STOCKHOLDERS' EQUITY (ROCSE)

The ROCSE can be disaggregated into the following elements that facilitate its analysis:

$$\frac{\text{Net income} - \text{Preferred dividends}}{\text{Average common stockholders' equity}} = \frac{\text{Net income} - \text{Preferred dividends}}{\text{Sales}} \times \frac{\text{Sales}}{\text{Average total assets}} \times \frac{\text{Average total assets}}{\text{Average common stockholders' equity}}$$

Descriptively, we can express this formula as follows:

$$\frac{\text{Rate of return}}{\text{on CSE}} = \frac{\text{Net income margin}}{\text{after preferred}} \times \frac{\text{Assets turnover}}{\text{ratio}} \times \frac{\text{Common stockholders'}}{\text{leverage ratio}}$$
$$\text{dividends}$$

The net income margin represents the portion of the sales dollar that is left for the common shareholder after providing for all costs[8] and claims (e.g., those of the preferred shareholders). The asset turnover was discussed above. The common stockholders' leverage ratio measures the extent to which total assets are financed by common stockholders. The larger this ratio is the smaller the proportion of assets financed by common stockholders and the greater the extent of leverage. Leverage can also be measured by means of the financial leverage index as was illustrated in Chapter 5.

Using the data in Exhibits 6–1 and 6–2 of the American Company, we can compute the disaggregated ROCSE for 19x9 as follows (dollars in millions):

$$\frac{\$65 - \$3}{(\$674 + \$699) \div 2} = \frac{\$65 - \$3}{\$1,724} \times \frac{\$1,724}{(\$1,334 + \$1,372) \div 2} \times \frac{(\$1,334 + \$1,372) \div 2}{(\$674 + \$699) \div 2} \text{ or}$$

Rate of return on CSE		Net income margin after preferred dividends		Assets turnover ratio		Common stockholders' leverage ratio
9%	=	3.6%	×	1.27	×	1.97

Using the type of return on equity analysis that we have discussed above, here is how Tandy Corporation explained the growth in return on equity over a period of time:

June 30	Asset turnover	×	Return on sales	=	Return on assets	×	Financial leverage	=	Return on equity
1977	2.16	×	7.3%	=	15.7%	×	2.37	=	37.2%
1978	2.06	×	6.2	=	12.8	×	3.39	=	43.6
1979	2.09	×	6.9	=	14.3	×	3.35	=	47.9
1980	2.10	×	8.1	=	17.0	×	2.69	=	45.7
1981	2.06	×	10.0	=	20.6	×	1.93	=	39.7
1982	1.88	×	11.0	=	20.7	×	1.56	=	32.3

Equity growth rate

The equity growth rate by means of *earnings retention* can be calculated as follows:

$$\frac{\text{Net income* } - \text{ Dividend payout}}{\text{Average common shareholders' equity}} = \text{Percent increase in common equity}$$

* Minus preferred dividend requirements.

---

[8] A refinement can be introduced into this analysis by focusing first on the pretax profit margin and multiplying it by 1 — Marginal tax rate (referred to as tax retention rate) in order to arrive at the net income margin. This additional analysis focuses on the effect of tax management on the final return achieved by the CSE.

This is the growth rate due to the retention of earnings and assumes a constant dividend payout over time. It indicates the possibilities of earnings growth without resort to external financing. These increased funds, in turn, will earn the rate of return that the enterprise can obtain on its assets and thus contribute to growth in earnings.

For the American Company, the equity growth rate can be computed for 19x9 as follows:

$$\frac{\$65 - \$3 - \$39^*}{(\$674 + \$699) \div 2} = 3.4 \text{ percent}$$

* Common stock dividends.

Analysis of financial leverage effects

The effect that each noncommon equity capital source has on the return on the common equity can be analyzed in detail. Using the data of American Company that was included in Exhibits 6–1 and 6–2 earlier in this chapter, we can undertake such an analysis as follows:

An analysis of the American Company balance sheet as at December 31, 19x9[9] discloses the following major sources of funds (in thousands):

Current liabilities (exclusive of current portion of long-term debt)		$ 182,472
Long-term debt	$335,945	
Current portion	11,606	347,551
Deferred taxes		101,143
Preferred stock		41,538
Common stockholders' equity		698,917
Total investment or total assets		$1,371,621

The income statement for 19x9 includes (in thousands):

Income before taxes	$125,730
Income (and other) taxes	61,161
Net income	64,569
Preferred dividends	2,908
Income accruing to common shareholders	$ 61,661
Total interest expense	$ 20,382
Assumed interest on short-term notes (5%)	687
Balance of interest on long-term debt	$ 19,695

---

[9] A year-end based analysis (rather than one based on average for the year amounts) is used here in order to simplify the computations.

The return on total assets is computed as follows:

$$\frac{\text{Net income} + \text{Interest} \times (1 - \text{Tax rate})}{\text{Total assets (year-end)}}$$

$$= \frac{\$64,569 + \$20,382\,(1 - .46)}{\$1,371,621} = 5.51 \text{ percent}$$

The 5.51 percent return represents the average return on all assets employed by the company. To the extent that suppliers of capital other than the common stockholders get a lower reward than an average of 5.51 percent, the common equity benefits by the difference. The opposite is true when the suppliers of capital receive more than a 5.51 percent reward in 19x9.

Exhibit 6–6 presents an analysis showing the relative contribution and reward of each of the major suppliers of funds and their effect on the returns earned by the common stockholders.

Exhibit 6–6: **Analysis of composition of return on shareholders' equity (approximate computations in thousands of dollars)**

Category of fund supplier	Fund supplied	Earnings on fund supplied at rate of 5.51 percent	Payment to suppliers of funds	Accruing to (detracting from) return on common stock
Current liabilities	$ 182,472	$10,054	$ 371 [a]	$ 9,683
Long-term debt	347,551	19,150	10,635 [b]	8,515
Deferred taxes	101,143	5,573	none	5,573
Preferred stock	41,538	2,289	2,908 [c]	(619)
Earnings in excess of compensation to suppliers of funds				23,152
Add: Common stockholders' equity	698,917	38,510		38,510
Totals	$1,371,621	$75,576	$13,914	
Total income (return) on stockholders' equity				$61,662 [d]

[a] Interest cost of $687 less 46 percent tax.
[b] Interest cost of $19,695 less 46 percent tax.
[c] Preferred dividends—not tax deductible.
[d] Slight differences with statement figures are due to rounding.

As can be seen from Exhibit 6–6, the $9,683,000 accruing to the common equity from use of current liabilities is largely due to its being free of interest costs. The advantage of $8,515,000 accruing from the use of long-term debt is substantially due to the tax deductibility of interest. Since the preferred dividends are not tax deductible, the unimpressive return on total assets of 5.51 percent resulted in a disadvantage to the common equity of $619,000. The value of tax deferrals can be clearly seen in this case where the use of cost-free funds amounted to an annual advantage of $5,573,000.

We can now carry this analysis further (dollars in thousands):

The return on the common stockholder equity is as follows:

$$\frac{\text{Net income less preferred dividends}}{\text{Common stockholders' equity}} = \frac{\$61,661^*}{\$698,917} = 8.8 \text{ percent}$$

* Ties in (except for rounding difference) with total income accruing to common stockholders in Exhibit 6–6.

The net advantage that the common equity reaped from the working of financial leverage (Exhibit 6–6) is $23,152.

As a percentage of the common stockholders' equity, this advantage is computed as follows:

$$\frac{\substack{\text{Earnings in excess of compensation} \\ \text{to outside suppliers of funds}}}{\text{Common stockholders' equity}} = \frac{\$23,152}{\$698,917} = 3.3 \text{ percent}$$

The return on common stockholders' equity can now be viewed as being composed as follows:

Return on assets 5.51%
Leverage advantage accruing to common equity 3.30
Return on common equity 8.81%

QUESTIONS

1. Why is return on investment (ROI) one of the most valid measures of enterprise performance? How is this measure used by the financial analyst?

2. How is ROI used as an internal management tool?

3. Discuss the validity of excluding "nonproductive" assets from the asset base used in the computation of ROI. Under what circumstances is the exclusion of intangible assets from the asset base warranted?

4. Why is interest added back to net income when the ROI is computed on total assets?

5. Under what circumstances may it be proper to consider convertible debt as equity capital in the computation of ROI?

6. Why must the minority interest's share in net income be added back when ROI is computed on total assets?

7. Why must the net income figure used in the computation of ROI be adjusted to reflect the asset base (denominator) used in the computation?

8. What is the relationship between ROI and sales?

9. Company A acquired Company B because the latter had a record of profitability (net income to sales ratio) exceeding that of its industry. After the acquisition took place, a major stockholder complained that the acquisition resulted in a low ROI. Discuss the possible reasons for his complaint.

10. Company X's profitability is 2 percent of sales. Company Y has a turnover of assets of 12. Both companies have ROIs of 6 percent that are considered unsatisfactory by industry standards. What is the asset turnover of Company X and what is the profitability ratio of Company Y? What action would you advise to the managements of the respective companies?

11. What is the purpose of measuring the asset utilization of different asset categories?

12. What factors enter into the evaluation of the ROI measures?

13. How is the equity growth rate computed? What does it signify?

14. *a.* How do the rate of return on total assets and that on stockholders' equity differ?

    b. What are the components of the rate of return on common stockholders' equity and what do they represent?

15. *a.* What is *equity turnover* and how is it related to the rate of return on equity?

    b. "Growth in per share earnings generated from an increase in equity turnover probably cannot be expected to continue indefinitely." Do you agree or disagree? Explain briefly, bringing out in your answer the alternative causes of an increase in equity turnover. (CFA)

7

Analysis of results of operations—I

THE SIGNIFICANCE OF INCOME STATEMENT ANALYSIS

The income statement presents in summarized fashion the results of operations of an enterprise. These results, in turn, represent the major reason for the existence of a profit-seeking entity, and they are important determinants of its value and its solvency.

Some of the most important decisions in security analysis and credit evaluation are based on an evaluation of the income statements. To the security analyst, income is often the single most important determinant of security values, and hence the measurement and the projection of income are among his most important analytical objectives. Similarly, to the credit grantor, income and funds or cash provided by operations are the most natural as well as the most desirable source of interest and principal repayment. In almost all other aspects of financial analysis, the evaluation and projection of operating results assume great importance.

THE MAJOR OBJECTIVES OF INCOME ANALYSIS

In the evaluation of the income of an enterprise, the analyst is particularly interested in an answer to the following questions:

1. What is the relevant net income of the enterprise and what is its quality?
2. What elements in the income statement can be used and relied upon for purposes of earnings forecasting?
3. How stable are the major elements of income and expense and what is their trend?
4. What is the "earning power" of the enterprise?

These questions will be examined in this and in the two chapters that follow.

What is the relevant net income of the enterprise?

Based on the simple proposition that net income is the excess of revenues over costs and expenses during an accounting period, many people, including astute professional analysts, are exasperated at the difficulties they encounter in their search for the "true earnings" or the "real earnings" of an enterprise.

Why, they ask, should it be possible for so many different "acceptable" figures of "net income" to flow out of one set of circumstances? Given the economic events that the enterprise experienced during a given period, is there not only *one* "true" result, and is it not the function of accountancy to identify and measure such result?

Some readers, of course, will already know why the answer to the last question must be "no." In this chapter, dealing with the analysis of income, it is appropriate to summarize *why* this is so.

Net income is not a specific quantity. Net income is not a specific flow awaiting the perfection of a flawless meter with which it can be precisely measured. There are a number of reasons for this:

1. The determination of income is dependent on estimates regarding the outcome of future events. This peering into the future is basically a matter of judgment involving the assessment of probabilities based on facts and estimates.

While the judgment of skilled and experienced professionals, working on the basis of identical data and information, can be expected to fall within a narrow range, it will nevertheless *vary* within such a range. The estimates involve the allocation of revenues and costs as between the present and the future. Put another way, they involve the determination of the future utility and usefulness of many categories of unexpired costs and of assets as well as the estimation of future liabilities and obligations.

2. The accounting standards governing the determination and measurement of income at any given time are the result of the cumulative experience of the accounting profession, of regulatory agencies, of businessmen, and others. They reflect a momentary equilibrium that is based partly on knowledge and experience and partly on the compromise of widely differing interests and views on methods of measurement. There is always great variety in these views. While the accounting profession has moved to narrow the range of acceptable alternative measurement principles, alternatives nevertheless remain; and their complete elimination in the near future is unlikely.

3. Beyond the problem of honest differences in estimation and other judgments, as well as of the variety of alternative acceptable principles, is also the problem arising from the diverse ways in which the judgments and principles are applied.

Theoretically, the independent professional accountant should be concerned first and foremost with the fair presentation of the financial statements. He should make accounting a "neutral" science that gives expression and effect to economic events but does not itself affect the results presented. To this end, he should choose from among alternative principles those most applicable to the circumstances and should disclose all facts, favorable and adverse, that may affect the user's decision.

In fact, the accounting profession as a whole has not yet reached such a level of independence and detachment of judgment. It is subject to the powerful pressures on the part of managements who have, or at least feel that they have, a vital interest in the way in which results of operations are presented. The auditors are most vulnerable to pressures in those areas of accounting where widely differing alternatives are equally acceptable and where accounting theory is still unsettled. Thus, they may choose the lowest level of acceptable practice rather than that which is most appropriate and fair in the circumstances. Although relatively less frequent, cases of malpractice and collusion in outright deception by independent accountants nevertheless still surface from time to time.

The analyst cannot ignore these possibilities, and must be aware of them and be ever alert to them. It calls for constant vigilance in the analysis of audited data, particularly when there is reason to suspect a lack of independence and objectivity in the application of accounting principles.

In addition to the above reasons that are inherent in the accounting process, there exists another reason why there cannot be such a thing as an absolute measure of "real earnings." It is that financial statements are general-purpose presentations designed to serve the diverse needs of many users. Consequently, a single figure of "net income" cannot be relevant to all users, and that means that the analyst must use this figure and the additional information disclosed in the financial statements and elsewhere as a starting point and adjust it so as to arrive at a "net income" figure that meets his particular interests and objectives.

ILLUSTRATION 1.   To the buyer of an income-producing property, the depreciation expense figure that is based on the seller's cost is not relevant. In order to estimate the net income he can derive from such property, depreciation based on the expected purchase price of the property must be substituted.

ILLUSTRATION 2.   To the analyst who exercises independent judgment and uses knowledge of the company he is analyzing and the industry of which it is a part, the reported net income marks the start of his analysis. He adjusts the net income figure for changes in income and expense items that he judges to be warranted. These may include, for example, estimates of bad debts, of depreciation, and of research costs as well as the treatment of gains and losses that are labeled extraordinary. Comparisons with other companies may call for similar adjustments so that the data can be rendered comparable.

From the above discussion it should be clear that the determination of *a* figure of net income is from the point of view of the analyst secondary to the objective of being able to find in the income statement all the disclosures needed in order to arrive at an income figure that is relevant for the purpose at hand.

The questions regarding the quality of earnings, of what elements in the income statement can be relied on for forecasting purposes, of what the stability and the trend of the earning elements are, and finally, of what the "earning power" of the enterprise is, will all be considered in Chapter 9.

We shall now proceed to examine the specific tools that are useful in the analysis of the various components of the income statement.

ANALYSIS OF COMPONENTS OF THE INCOME STATEMENT

The analysis of the income statements of an enterprise can be conceived as being undertaken at two levels: (1) obtaining an understanding of the accounting standards used and of their implication and (2) using the appropriate tools of income statement analysis.

Accounting standards used and their implication

The analyst must have a thorough understanding of the standards of income, cost, and expense accounting and measurement employed by the enterprise. Moreover, since most assets, with the exception of cash and receivables actually collectible, represent costs deferred to the future, the analyst must have a good understanding of the standards of asset and liability measurements employed by the enterprise so that he can relate them to the income accounting of the enterprise as a means of checking the validity of that accounting. Finally, he must understand and assess the implications that the use of one accounting principle, as opposed to another, has on the measurement of the income of an enterprise and its comparison to that of other enterprises.

Tools of income statement analysis

The second level of analysis consists of applying the appropriate tools of analysis to the components of the income statement and the interpretation of the results shown by these analytical measures. The application of these tools is aimed at achieving the objectives of the analysis of results of operations mentioned earlier, such as the projection of income, the assessment of its stability and quality, and the estimation of earning power.

The remainder of this chapter will be devoted to an examination of these tools and to the interpretation of the results achieved through their use.

THE ANALYSIS OF SALES AND REVENUES

The analysis of sales and revenues is centered on answers to these basic questions:

1. What are the major sources of revenue?
2. How stable are these sources and what is their trend?
3. How is the earning of revenue determined and how is it measured?

Major sources of revenue

Knowledge of major sources of revenues (sales) is important in the analysis of the income statement particularly if the analysis is that of a multimarket enterprise. Each major market or product line may have its own separate and distinct growth pattern, profitability, and future potential.

The best way to analyze the composition of revenues is by means of a common-size statement that shows the percentage of each major class of revenue to the total. This information can also be portrayed graphically on an absolute dollar basis as shown in Exhibit 7–1.

Alfa, Inc. (see Appendix 2B), presents a five-year summary of segment revenues (item 106) and segment contribution as well as other data (item 107).

FINANCIAL REPORTING BY DIVERSIFIED ENTERPRISES

The user of the financial statements of diversified enterprises faces, in addition to the usual problems and pitfalls of financial analysis, the problem of sorting out and understanding the impact that the different individual segments of the business have on the sum total of reported results of operations and financial condition. The author of an important study in the reporting by diversified companies has defined a conglomerate company as follows:

> . . . one which is so managerially decentralized, so lacks operational integration, or has such diversified markets that it may experience rates of profitability, degrees of risk, and opportunities for growth which vary within the company to such an extent that an investor requires information about these variations in order to make informed decisions.[1]

Reasons for the need for data by significant enterprise segments

The above definition suggests some of the most significant reasons why financial analysts require as much information and detailed data as possible

---

[1] R. K. Mautz, "Identification of the Conglomerate Company," *Financial Executive,* July 1967, p. 26.

Exhibit 7–1:   Analysis of sales by product line over time

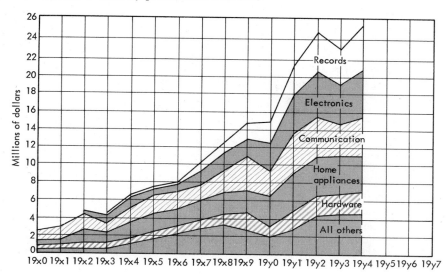

about the various segments of an enterprise. The analysis, evaluation, projection, and valuation of earnings require that these be broken down into
categories that share similar characteristics of variability, growth potential,
and risk. Similarly, the asset structure and the financing requirements of
various segments of an enterprise can vary significantly and thus require
separate analysis and evaluation. Thus, the credit grantor may be interested
in knowing which segments of an enterprise provide funds and which are
net users of funds.

The composition of an enterprise, the relative size and profitability of its
various segments, the ability of management to make profitable acquisitions,
and the overall performance of management represent additional important
information that the analyst seeks from its segmented data.[2] As will be seen
from the discussion in Chapter 9, among the best ways to construct an earnings
forecast is to build the projections, to the extent possible, segment by segment.

The evaluation of the growth potential of earnings requires that as much
information as possible be obtained about the different product lines or segments that make up the aggregate earnings. Rappaport and Lerner have
illustrated the use of a segmented earnings contribution matrix that may

---

[2] D. W. Collins in a study of 150 multisegment firms found that "SEC product-line revenue
and profit disclosures together with industry sales projections published in various government
sources provide significantly more accurate estimates of future total-entity sales and earnings
than do those procedures that rely totally on consolidated data." *Journal of Accounting Research,*
Spring 1976, pp. 163–77.

Table 7–1:   Earnings contribution and growth rates by industry segments

Industry	Earnings contributions (in thousands)	Growth rate of earnings contribution over the past three years
Leisure time:		
1. Camp equipment	$100	11%
2. Fishing equipment	50	2
3. Boats	72	15
4. Sporting goods	12	3
	234	
Agribusiness:		
1. Milk processing	85	2
2. Canning	72	8
3. Chicken farming	12	15
	169	
Education:		
1. Text publishing	40	3
2. Papers and supplies	17	6
	57	
Total	$460	

Table 7–2:   Segmented earnings contribution matrix

Industry	Growth rate (in percent) 0–5	5–10	10–15	Total
Leisure time	$ 62	$ 0	$172	$234
Agribusiness	85	72	12	169
Education	40	17	0	57
Total	$187	$89	$184	$460

prove useful in an assessment of earnings quality and growth potential, as well as in the valuation of aggregate earnings.[3] These are shown in Tables 7–1 and 7–2.

Disclosure of "line of business" data

The degree of informative disclosure about the results of operations and the asset base of segments of a business can vary widely. Full disclosure would call for providing detailed income statements, statements of financial position, and statements of changes in financial position (SCFPs) for each

---

[3] A. Rappaport and E. M. Lerner, *A Framework for Financial Reporting by Diversified Companies* (New York: National Association of Accountants, 1969), pp. 18–19.

significant segment. This is rarely found in practice because of the difficulty of obtaining such breakdowns internally, and also because of management's reluctance to divulge information that could harm the enterprise's competitive position. Short of the disclosure of complete financial statements by business segment, a great variety of partial detail has been suggested.

Income statement data

Revenues only. In most enterprises, this should not present great difficulties.

Gross profit. This involves complex problems of interdivisional transfer pricing as well as allocation of indirect overhead costs.

Contribution margin. Contribution margin reporting (see also Chapter 8) is based on assigning to each segment the revenues, costs, and expenses for which that segment is solely responsible. It is a very useful concept in management accounting, but for purposes of public reporting of segment data, it presents problems because there are no generally accepted methods of cost allocation and, consequently, they can vary significantly from company to company and even within one enterprise. Disclosure of allocation methods, while helpful, will not remove all the problems facing the user of such data.

Net income (after full cost allocation). The further down the income statement we report by segment, the more pervasive and the more complex the allocation procedures become. Reporting segment net income would require allocating all joint expenses to each specific business activity on some rational basis, even though they may not be directly related to any particular one.

Balance sheet data

A breakdown by segments of assets employed is needed in an assessment of the efficiency of operations by segment, in the evaluation of segmental management, as well as in the computation of divisional return on investment.

In most companies, only certain assets, such as, for example, plant and equipment, inventories, and certain intangibles, are identified directly with a specific segment. An allocation of all assets would have to be arbitrary since in many enterprises cash, temporary investments, and even receivables are centralized at the group or corporate headquarters level.

Research studies

Interest in the subject of reporting by diversified companies has sparked research efforts into the types of disclosures that are necessary and feasible and the problems related thereto.[4] The most extensive research effort was that undertaken by Professor R. K. Mautz,[5] and in 1974, the FASB published an extensive *Discussion Memorandum* on the subject.

Statement of Financial Accounting Standards 14

In 1976, the FASB issued *SFAS 14*, "Financial Reporting for Segments of a Business Enterprise." This *Statement* establishes requirements for disclosures to be made in company financial statements concerning information about operations in different industries, foreign operations, export sales, and major customers.

The *Statement* recognizes that evaluation of risk and return is the central element of investment and lending decisions. Since an enterprise operating in various industry segments or geographic areas may have different rates of profitability, degrees and types of risk, and opportunities for growth, disaggregated information will assist analysts in analyzing the uncertainties surrounding the timing and amount of expected cash flows—and hence the risks—related to an investment in or a loan to an enterprise that operates in different industries or areas of the world.

The *Statement* requires companies to report in their annual financial statements the revenues, operating profit (revenue less operating expenses), and identifiable assets of each significant industry segment of their operations. Certain other related disclosures are required. *SFAS 14* does not prescribe methods of accounting for transfer pricing or cost allocation. However, it does require that the methods in use be disclosed.

A segment is regarded as significant, therefore reportable, under the *Statement* if its sales, operating profit, or identifiable assets are 10 percent or more of the related combined amounts for all of a company's industry segments.[6] To ensure that the industry segments for which a company reports information represent a substantial portion of the company's overall operations, the *Statement* requires that the combined sales of all segments for

---

[4] See Morton Backer and Walter B. McFarland, *External Reporting for Segments of a Business* (New York: National Association of Accountants, 1968). Also see Robert T. Sprouse, "Diversified Views about Diversified Companies," *Journal of Accounting Research* 7, no. 1 (Spring 1969), pp. 137–59; and A. Rappaport and E. M. Lerner, *A Framework for Financial Reporting by Diversified Companies* (New York: National Association of Accountants, 1969).

[5] R. K. Mautz, *Financial Reporting by Diversified Companies* (New York: Financial Executives Research Foundation, 1968).

[6] Specifically, an industry segment is significant if in the latest period for which statements are presented:

1. Its revenue is 10 percent or more of the *combined* revenue of all industry segments; or
2. Its operating profit (loss) is 10 percent or more of the greater of *(a)* the combined operating profit of all segments that did not incur a loss, or *(b)* the combined operating loss of all segments that did incur a loss; or
3. Its identifiable assets are 10 percent or more of the combined identifiable assets of all industry segments.

which information is reported shall be at least 75 percent of the company's total sales. The *Statement* also suggests 10 as a practical limit to the number of industry segments for which a company reports information. If that limit is exceeded, it may be appropriate to combine certain segments into broader ones to meet the 75 percent test with a practical number of segments.

Under *SFAS 14,* if a company derives 10 percent or more of its revenue from sales to any single customer, that fact and the amount of revenue from each such customer also must be disclosed.

The *Statement* provides guidelines for determining a company's foreign operations and export sales and for grouping operations by geographic areas. Information similar to that required for industry segments also is required for a company's operations in different geographic areas of the world.

SEC reporting requirements

In 1969, the SEC took an early lead in requiring disclosure of sales and profit information by lines of business. Following promulgation of *SFAS 14,* the SEC, by means of *FRR* No. 1 Section 503, conformed SEC reporting requirements to those of the *Statement.* However, the SEC reporting requirements, incorporated in Regulation S-K, differ from *SFAS 14* in that it requires that segment revenue, operating profit, and asset information be presented for three years. Moreover, an additional narrative description is called for in Regulation S-K covering the registrant's business by reportable segments including information on competition, dependence on a few customers, principal products and services, backlog, sources and availability of raw materials, patents, research and development (R&D) costs, number of employees, and the seasonality of the business.

Implications for analysis

The increasing complexity of diversified business entities and the loss of identity that acquired companies suffer in the published financial statements of conglomerates have created serious problems for the financial analyst.

The disclosure requirements of *SFAS 14* as well as those of the SEC will increase the amount of segmental information available for analysis. However the analyst will have to be very careful in his assessment of the reliability of the data on which he bases his conclusions.

The more specific and detailed the information provided is, the more likely it is to be based on extensive allocations of costs and expenses. Allocation of common costs, as practiced for internal accounting purposes, are often based on such concepts as "equity," "reasonableness," and "acceptability to managers." These concepts have often little relevance to the objective of financial analysis.

Bases of allocating joint expenses are largely arbitrary and subject to differences of opinions as to their validity and precision. Some specific types of joint expenses that fall into this category are general and administrative expenses of central headquarters, R&D costs, certain selling costs, advertising, interest, pension costs, and federal and state income taxes.

There are, at present, no generally accepted principles of cost and expense allocation or any general agreement on the methods by which the costs of one segment should be transferred to another segment in the same enterprise. Moreover, the process of formulating such principles of reaching such agreement has barely begun. The analyst who uses segmented data must bear these limitations firmly in mind.

In *SFAS 14,* the Board has, in effect, recognized the above described limitations and realities. Consequently, the disclosure of profit contribution (revenue less only those operating expenses that are directly traceable to a segment), which was proposed in the exposure draft issued for public comment, was not required in the final *Statement.* Similarly, the Board concluded that revenue from intersegment sales or transfers shall be accounted for on whatever basis is used by the enterprise to price intersegment sales or transfers. No single basis was prescribed or proscribed.

Moreover, the Board concluded that certain items of revenue and expense either do not relate to segments or cannot always be allocated to segments on the basis of objective evidence, and consequently, there is no requirement in *SFAS 14* that net income be disclosed for reportable segments. The Board also noted in the *Statement* that "determination of an enterprise's industry segments must depend to a considerable extent on the judgment of the management of the enterprise."

The implication for analysts of this lack of firmer guidelines and definitions is that segmental disclosures are and must be treated as "soft" information that is subject to manipulation and preinterpretation by managements. Consequently, such data must be treated with a healthy degree of skepticism, and conclusions can be derived from them only through the exercise of great care as well as analytical skill.

STABILITY AND TREND OF REVENUES

The relative trend of sales of various product lines or revenues from services can best be measured by means of trend percentages as illustrated in Table 7–3.

Table 7–3:   **Trend percentage of sales by product line (19x1 = 100)**

	19x1	19x2	19x3	19x4	19x5
Product A	100	110	114	107	121
Product B	100	120	135	160	174
Product C	100	98	94	86	74
Service A	100	101	92	98	105

Sales indexes of various product lines can be correlated and compared to composite industry figures or to product sales trends of specific competitors.

Important considerations bearing on the quality and stability of the sales and revenues trend include:

1. The sensitivity of demand for the various products to general business conditions.
2. The ability of the enterprise to anticipate trends in demand by the introduction of new products and services as a means of furthering sales growth and as replacement of products for which demand is falling.
3. Degree of customer concentration (now required to be disclosed by *SFAS 14*), dependence on major customers, as well as demand stability of major customer groups.[7]
4. Degree of product concentration and dependence on a single industry.
5. Degree of dependence on relatively few star salesmen.
6. Degree of geographical diversification of markets.

MANAGEMENT'S DISCUSSION AND ANALYSIS OF FINANCIAL CONDITION AND RESULTS OF OPERATIONS

A significant new concept of disclosure from the analyst's point of view was instituted by the SEC in 1974 and further broadened in 1980 and is now codified in *FRR*, Section 501. The disclosures that are required are of an interpretative or explanatory nature that is necessary to enable investors to understand and evaluate significant period-to-period changes in the various items that report the enterprise's financial condition and results of operations.

Management's Discussion and Analysis of Financial Condition and Results of Operations (MDA) requirements, which were adopted as part of the SEC's new integrated disclosure system, now require three years of income statements and focus *in addition* to results of operations also on liquidity, capital resources, and the impact of inflation. These latter topics are discussed in Chapters 3, 4, and 5.

In the area of results of operations, MDA must cover revenue and expense components that are needed for understanding of results by the reader, major unusual or infrequent events that materially affect reported income from continuing operations, trends or uncertainties that have affected or are likely to affect results, and impending changes in cost/revenue relationships such as increases in materials or labor costs. MDA must also include a discussion of the extent to which material increases in revenues are attributable to increases in prices or to increases in volume or amount of goods or services

---

[7] *Statement on Auditing Standards (SAS) 6* (AICPA) requires disclosure of the economic dependency of a company on one or more parties with which it transacts a significant volume of business, such as a sole or major customer, supplier, franchisor, franchisee, distributor, borrower, or lender.

being sold or to the introduction of new products or services as well as a discussion of the impact of inflation and changing prices on the registrant's revenues and on income from continuing operations.

Overall, the SEC desires that MDA's emphasis be redirected from operations to financial results; that forward-looking information should, if possible, be included; and the discussion should focus on trends and implications that are not evident from an examination of the financial statements.[8]

IMPLICATIONS FOR ANALYSIS

In its instructions to the revised MDA requirements, the SEC states that the purpose of the discussion and analysis is to provide investors and others with information relevant to an assessment of the financial condition and results of operations of the registrant as determined by evaluating the amounts and the certainty of cash flows from operations and from outside sources.

Even more so than under the previous requirements, the instructions for preparation of MDA make it clear that managements have a great deal of discretion on how to communicate to the reader and what to stress in such communications. The aim is meaningful disclosure in narrative form by those in charge of operations who are really in a position to know and who can supply significant additional details not usually found in the financial statements. The results will depend on management's attitudes and objectives.

While analysts must be aware that much information included in MDA is likely to be "soft" in nature, it must be borne in mind that in reporting in accordance with SEC requirements, managements cannot risk being careless or deceptive in their statements in such financial filings.

On balance, the analyst will have here much information that is valuable, that provides added insights, and that cannot readily be obtained in other ways. Thus, without having to take them at face value, the analyst can nevertheless use these disclosures as valuable analytical supplements for both the information that they provide and the insights into the thinking and the attitude of managements which they afford.

METHODS OF REVENUE RECOGNITION AND MEASUREMENT

There are a variety of methods of revenue recognition and measurement that coexist in various industries. Some of these methods are more conservative

---

[8] In *FRR*, No. 1, Section 501, the SEC released the staff's assessment of disclosures contained in MDA in 1980 annual reports. Examples cited in the release cover areas such as impact on pretax income of closing unprofitable facilities; effect of LIFO inventory liquidation on pretax income; changes in revenues by segment; forward-looking information; cash flow from operations on a trend basis; available sources of liquidity; known or reasonably likely liquidity deficiencies; and impact of inflation on sales, cost of sales, assets, and liabilities.

than others. The analyst must understand the income recognition methods used by the enterprise and their implications as well as the methods used by companies with which the results of the enterprise under analysis are being compared. A foremost consideration is whether the revenue recognition method in use accurately reflects an entity's economic performance and earnings activities.

QUESTIONS

1. What are the major objectives of income analysis?
2. Why can "net income" not be a single specific quantity?
3. Two levels can be identified in the analysis of the income statement. Name them.
4. Why is knowledge of major sources of revenue (sales) of an enterprise important in the analysis of the income statement?
5. Why are information and detailed data about the segments of diversified enterprises important to financial analysts?
6. Disclosure of various types of information by "line of business" has been proposed. Comment on the value of such information and the feasibility of providing it in published financial statements.
7. What are the major provisions of *SFAS 14?*
8. To what limitations of public segmental data must the analyst be alert?
9. Which important considerations have a bearing on the quality and the stability of a sales and revenue trend?
10. How were the requirements for additional disclosures of an interpretive or explanatory nature in the form of Management's Discussion and Analysis of Financial Condition and Results of Operations (MDA) changed in 1980?
11. Cite some of the examples of the types of subjects that should be covered in the MDA.
12. What are the objectives of discussions required by the revised MDA?

Analysis of results of operations—II

This chapter continues the discussion of the analysis of results of operations begun in the preceding chapter.

ANALYSIS OF COST OF SALES

In most enterprises,[1] the cost of goods or services sold is, as a percentage of sales, the single most significant cost category. The many methods of determining cost of sales encompass a wide variety of alternatives. Moreover, there is, particularly in unregulated industries, no agreed-to uniform cost classification method that would result in a clear and generally accepted distinction among such basic cost and expense categories as cost of sales, administrative, general, sales, and financial expenses. This is particularly true in the classification of general and administrative expenses. Thus, in undertaking cost comparisons, the analyst must be ever alert to methods of classification and the effect they can have on the validity of comparisons within an enterprise or among enterprises.

GROSS PROFIT

The excess of sales over the cost of sales is the gross profit or gross margin. It is commonly expressed as a percentage:

Sales	$10,000,000	100%
Cost of sales	7,200,000	72
Gross profit	$ 2,800,000	28%

---

[1] Exceptions can be found, for example, in some land sales companies where selling and other costs may actually exceed the cost of land sold.

The gross profit percentage is a very important operating ratio. In the above example, the gross profit is $2,800,000, or 28 percent of sales. From this amount, all other costs and expenses must be recovered and any net income that is earned is the balance remaining after all expenses. Unless an enterprise has an adequate gross profit, it can be neither profitable nor does it have an adequate margin with which to finance such essential future-directed discretionary expenditures as research and development and advertising. Gross profit margins vary from industry to industry depending on such factors as competition, capital investment, the level of costs other than direct costs of sales that must be covered by the gross profit, and so forth.

Factors in the analysis of gross profit

In the analysis of gross profit, the analyst will pay particular attention to:

1. The factors that account for the variation in sales and costs of sales.
2. The relationship between sales and costs of sales and management's ability to control this relationship.

ANALYSIS OF CHANGES IN GROSS MARGIN[2]

A detailed analysis of changes in gross margin can usually be performed only by an internal analyst because it requires access to data such as the number of physical units sold, unit sales prices, as well as unit costs. Such data are usually not provided in published financial statements. Moreover, unless the enterprise sells a single product, this analysis requires detailed data by product line. The external analyst, unless he has special influence on the company analyzed, will usually not have access to the data required for the analysis of gross margin.

Despite the above limitations to which gross margin analysis is subject, it is instructive to examine its process so that the elements accounting for variations in gross margin can be more fully understood.

EXAMPLE OF ANALYSIS OF CHANGE IN GROSS MARGIN

Company A shows the following data for two years:

---

[2] In this discussion, the terms *gross profit* and *gross margin* are used interchangeably. Some writers reserve the term *gross margin* for situations where the cost of goods sold excludes overhead costs, that is, direct costing. This is not the intention here.

	Unit of measure	Year ended December 31		In- crease	De- crease
		19x1	*19x2*		
1. Net sales	Thousands of dollars	$657.6	$687.5	$29.9	
2. Cost of sales	Thousands of dollars	237.3	245.3	8.0	
3. Gross margin	Thousands of dollars	420.3	442.2	21.9	
4. Units of product sold	Thousands	215.6	231.5	15.9	
5. Selling price per unit (1 ÷ 4)	Dollars	$ 3.05	$ 2.97		$.08
6. Cost per unit (2 ÷ 4)	Dollars	1.10	1.06		.04

Based on the above data, Exhibit 8–1 presents an analysis of the changes in gross margin of $21,900 from 19x1 to 19x2.

Exhibit 8–1

COMPANY A
Statement Accounting for Variation in Gross Margin
Between Years 19x1 and 19x2 (in thousands)

I. *Analysis of variation in sales*
   1. Variation due to change in volume of products sold:
      Change in volume (15.9) × 19x1 unit selling price ($3.05) $48.5
   2. Variation due to change in selling price:
      Change in selling price (−$.08) × 19x1 sales
      volume (215.6) . . . .   −17.2
                                                                                                      31.3
   3. Variation due to combined change in sales volume
      (15.9) and unit sales price (−$.08) . . . .   − 1.3
      Increase in net sales 30.0*

II. *Analysis of variation in cost of sales*
   1. Variation due to change in volume of products sold:
      Change in volume (15.9) × 19x1 cost per unit ($1.10) 17.5
   2. Variation due to change in cost per unit sold:
      Change in cost per unit (−$.04) × 19x1
      sales volume (215.6) . . . .   − 8.6
                                                                                                      8.9
   3. Variation due to combined change in volume (15.9)
      and cost per unit (−$.04) . . . .   − .6
      Increase in cost of sales 8.3*
      Net variation in gross margin $21.7*

   * Differences are due to rounding.

This analysis is based on the principle of focusing on one element of change at a time. Thus, in Exhibit 8–1, the analysis of variation in sales involves the following steps:

Step 1: We focus on the year-to-year change in volume while *assuming* that the unit selling price remained unchanged at the former, 19x1, level. Since both the volume change (15.9) and the unit selling price ($3.05) are positive, the resulting product ($48.5) is positive.

Step 2. We focus next on the change in selling price that represents a year-to-year decrease (−$.08) and *assume* the volume (215.6) to be unchanged from the prior year level so as to single out the change due to price change. Algebraically, here the multiplication of a negative (price change) by a positive (volume) results in a negative product (−$17.2).

Step 3: We must now recognize that the *assumptions* used in steps 1 and 2 above, that is, that the volume remained unchanged while the unit price changed and vice versa, are temporary expedients used to single out major causes for change. To complete the computation, we must recognize that by making these assumptions we left out the *combined* change in volume and unit price. The change in volume of 15.9 represents an *increase* and, consequently, is *positive*. The unit selling price change represents a *decrease* (−$.08) and hence is *negative*. As a result, the product is negative (−$1.3).

Step 4: Adding up the—

Variation due to volume change	$48.5
Variation due to price change	−17.2
Combined change of volume and unit price	− 1.3
We account for the causes behind the sales increase	$30.0

The analysis of variation in the cost of sales follows the same principles.

Interpretation of changes in gross margin

The analysis of variation in gross margin is useful in identifying major causes of change in the gross margin. These changes can consist of one or a combination of the following factors:

1. Increase in sales volume.
2. Decrease in sales volume.
3. Increase in unit sales price.
4. Decrease in unit sales price.
5. Increase in cost per unit.
6. Decrease in cost per unit.

The presence of the "combined change of volume and unit sales price" and the "combined volume and unit cost" in the analysis presents no problem in interpretation since their amount is always minor in relation to the main causative factors of change.

The interpretation of the results of the analysis of gross margin involves the identification of the major factors responsible for change in the gross margin and an evaluation of the reasons for change in the factors. Such an analysis can also focus on the most feasible areas of improvement (i.e., volume, price, or cost) and the likelihood of realizing such improvements. For example, if it is determined that the major reasons for a decline in gross margin is a decline in unit sales prices and that it reflects a situation of overcapacity in the enterprise's industry with attendant price cutting, then the situation is a serious one because of the limited control management has on such a development. If, on the other hand, the deterioration in the gross margin is found to be due to increase in unit costs, then this may be a situation over which management can exercise a larger measure of control and, given its ability to do so, an improvement is a more likely possibility.

BREAK-EVEN ANALYSIS

The second level of cost analysis is importantly concerned with the relationship between sales and the cost of sales but goes beyond that segment of the income statement. This level encompasses break-even analysis and is concerned with the relationship of sales to most costs, including, but not limited to, the cost of sales.

Concepts underlying break-even analysis

The basic principle underlying break-even analysis is the behavior of costs. Some costs vary directly with sales while others remain essentially constant over a considerable range of sales. The first category of costs is classified as *variable* while the latter are known as *fixed* costs.

The distinction among costs according to their behavior can be best understood within the framework of an example. In order to focus first on the basic data involved and on the technique of break-even analysis, we shall examine it by means of a simple illustration:

An enterprising graduate student saw an opportunity to sell pocket calculators at a financial analysts' convention due to take place in his hometown. Upon inquiry, he learned that he would have to get a vendor's license from the convention organizing committee at a cost of $10 and that the rental of a room in which to sell would amount to $140. The cost of calculators was to be $3 each with the right to return any that were not sold. The student decided that $8 was the proper sales price per calculator and wondered whether the undertaking would be worthwhile. As a first step he decided to compute the number of calculators he would have to sell in order to break even.

Equation approach

We start from the elementary proposition that:

Sales = Variable cost + Fixed costs + Profit (or − Loss)

Since at break even there is neither gain nor loss, the equation is:

.Sales = Variable cost + Fixed costs

If we designate the number of calculators that must be sold to break even as X, we have

$$\$8X = \$3X + \$150$$

where:

Sales = Unit sales price ($8) × X
Variable costs = Variable cost per unit ($3) × X
Fixed costs = License fee ($10) + Rental ($140)

These costs are fixed because they will be incurred regardless of the number of calculators sold.

Solving the equation we get:

$$\$5X = \$150$$
$$X = \ \ 30 \text{ units or calculators}$$
$$\text{to be sold to break even}$$

In this example, the number of calculators to be sold is important information because the student needs to assess the likelihood of obtaining the size of demand that will make his venture profitable. This approach is, however, limited to a single product enterprise.

If, as is common in business, an enterprise sells a mix of goods, the unit sales break-even computation becomes impracticable and the focus is on dollar sales. This would be the situation if our student sold stationery and books in addition to calculators.

This more prevalent break-even computation can be illustrated with the data already given.

If we designate the dollar sales at break even as Y, we get:

$$Y = \text{Variable-cost percentage } Y + \text{Fixed costs}$$
$$= .375 Y + \$150$$
$$.625 Y = \$150$$
$$Y = \$240 \text{ (sales at break even)}$$

Exhibit 8–2:   Calculator illustration—break-even chart

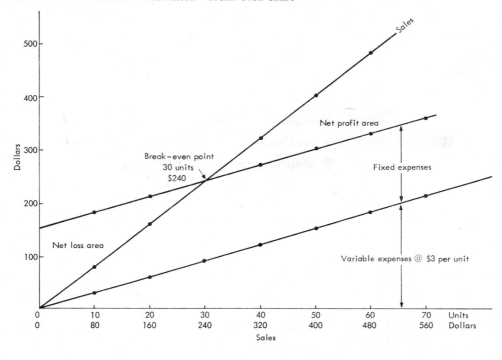

In this computation, the variable-cost percentage is the ratio of variable costs ($3) to sales price ($8). This means that each dollar of sales entails an incurrence of $.375 for variable costs, or 37.5 percent of the sales price.

Graphic presentation

Exhibit 8–2 portrays the results attained above in graphic form. A graph drawn to scale will yield a solution approximating in accuracy that obtained by the formula method. Moreover it portrays under one set of assumptions not only the break-even point but also a whole range of profitable operations above that point as well as the losses below it.

Contribution margin approach

Another technique of break-even analysis that can produce additional insights into the relationship of sales, costs, and profits is the contribution margin approach. It will be illustrated here by means of the foregoing pocket calculator example.

The contribution margin is what is left of the net sales price after deduction of the variable costs. It is from this margin that fixed costs must first be met and after that a profit earned.

Sales price per calculator $8
Variable costs per calculator 3
Unit contribution margin $5

Since each unit (calculator) sold contributes $5 to overhead and for profit, the break-even point in units is

$$\frac{\text{Fixed costs}}{\text{Unit contribution margin}} = \frac{\$150}{\$5} = 30 \text{ units}$$

Thus, after 30 units are sold, the fixed costs are covered and each additional unit sale yields a profit equal to the unit contribution margin, that is, $5.

If, as is more usual, the break-even point is to be expressed in dollars of sales, the formula involves use of the contribution margin ratio rather than the unit contribution margin. The contribution margin ratio is a percentage relationship computed as follows:

$$\frac{\text{Unit contribution margin}}{\text{Unit sales price}} = \frac{\$5}{\$8} = .625, \text{ or } 62.5 \text{ percent}$$

The calculator problem dollar break-even point can now be calculated as follows:

$$\frac{\text{Fixed costs}}{\text{Contribution margin ratio}} = \frac{\$150}{.625} = \$240$$

The contribution margin is an important tool in break-even analysis, and its significance will be the subject of further discussion later in this section.

Pocket calculator problem—additional considerations

The break-even technique illustrated above lends itself to a variety of assumptions and requirements. The following are additional illustrations, all using the original data of our example, unless changed assumptions are introduced:

ILLUSTRATION 1. Assume that our student decided that in order to make the venture worthwhile he requires a net profit of $400. How many calculators must be sold to achieve this objective?

$$\text{Sales} = (\text{Variable cost percent})(\text{sales}) + \text{Fixed costs} + \text{Profit}$$
$$S = .375S + \$150 + \$400$$
$$.625S = \$550$$
$$S = \$880$$
$$\frac{\$880}{\$8} = 110 \text{ units}$$

ILLUSTRATION 2. Assume that the financial analysts convention committee offered to provide the student with a room free of charge if he agreed to imprint on the calculators the Financial Analysts Society's seal. However, this would increase the cost of calculators from $3 to $4 per unit. Under the original assumptions, the break-even point was 30 calculators. What should it be if the student accepts the committee's proposal?

Here we have a reduction of fixed costs by $140 and an increase in variable costs of $1 per unit.

If X be the number of calculators sold at break-even point, then:

$$\text{Sales} = \text{Variable costs} + \text{Fixed costs}$$
$$\$8X = \$4X + \$10$$
$$\$4X = \$10$$
$$X = 2.5 \text{ calculators (rounded to 3)}$$

This proposal obviously involves a much lower break-even point and hence reduced risk. However, the lower contribution margin will at higher sales levels reduce total profitability. We can determine at what level of unit sales the original assumption of a $3 per unit variable cost and $150 fixed cost will equal the results of the $4 per unit variable cost and $10 fixed costs.

Let X be the number of units (calculators) sold, then:

$$\$4X + \$10 = \$3X + \$150$$
$$\$1X = \$140$$
$$X = 140 \text{ calculators}$$

Thus, if more than 140 calculators are sold, the alternative that includes the $3 variable cost will be more profitable.

Having examined the break-even analysis technique and some types of decisions for which it is useful, we will now turn to a discussion of the practical difficulties and the theoretical limitations to which this approach is subject.

Break-even technique—problem areas and limitations

The intelligent use of the break-even technique and the drawing of reasonably valid conclusions therefrom depend on a resolution of practical difficulties and on an understanding of the limitations to which the techniques are subject.

Fixed, variable, and semivariable costs. In the foregoing simple examples of break-even analysis, costs were clearly either fixed or variable. In the more complex reality found in practice, many costs are not so clearly separable into fixed and variable categories. That is, they either do not stay constant over a considerable change in sales volume or respond in exact proportion to change in sales.

We can illustrate this problem by reference to the costs of a food supermarket. As was discussed above, some costs will remain fixed within a certain range of sales. Rent, depreciation, certain forms of maintenance, utilities, and supervisory labor are examples of such fixed costs. The level of fixed costs can, of course, be increased by simple management decision unrelated to the level of sales; for example, the grocery manager's salary may be increased.

Other costs, such as the cost of merchandise, trading stamps, supplies, and certain labor will vary closely with sales. These costs are truly variable. Certain other costs may, however, contain both fixed and variable elements in them. Examples of such *semivariable* costs are repairs, some materials, indirect labor, fuel, utilities, payroll taxes, and rents that contain a minimum payment provision and are also related to the level of sales. Break-even analysis requires that the variable component of such expenses be separated from the fixed component. This is often a difficult task for the management accountant and an almost impossible task for the outside analyst to perform without the availability of considerable internal data.

Simplifying assumptions in break-even analysis.   The estimation of a variety of possible results by means of break-even calculations or charts requires the use of simplifying assumptions. In most cases, these simplifying assumptions do not destroy the validity of the conclusions reached. Nevertheless, in reaching such conclusions, the analyst must be fully aware of these assumptions and of their possible effect.

The following are some of the more important assumptions implicit in break-even computations:

1.   The factors comprising the model actually behave as assumed, that is:
     a.   That the costs have been reasonably subdivided into their fixed and variable components.
     b.   That variable costs fluctuate proportionally with volume.
     c.   That fixed costs remain fixed over the range relevant to the situation examined.
     d.   That unit selling prices will remain unchanged over the range encompassed by the analysis.
2.   In addition, there are certain operating and environmental assumptions that emphasize the static nature of any one break-even computation. It is assumed:
     a.   That the mix of sales will remain unchanged.
     b.   That efficiency of operations will remain constant.
     c.   That prices of costs factors will not change.
     d.   That the only factor affecting costs is volume.
     e.   That beginning and end-of-period inventory levels will remain substantially unchanged.
     f.   That there is no substantial change in the general price level during the period.

The formidable array of assumptions enumerated above points out the susceptibility of break-even computations to significant error. Not all the assumptions are, however, equally important, or, if not justified, will have an equal impact on the validity of conclusions. For example, the assumption that the selling price will not change with volume is contrary to economic theory and often is contrary to reality. Thus, the sales line is a curved rather than a linear function. However, the degree of error will depend on the actual degree of deviation from a strict linear relationship. Another basic assumption is that volume is *the* major, if not the only, factor affecting costs. We know, however, that strikes, political developments, legislation, and competition, to name a few other important factors, have a decided influence on costs. The analyst must, consequently, keep these simplifying assumptions firmly in mind and be aware of the dynamic factors that may require modifications in his conclusions.

Break-even analysis—uses and their implications

The break-even approach can be a useful tool of analysis if its limitations are recognized and its applications are kept in proper perspective.

The emphasis on the break-even, that is, zero profit, point is an unfortunate distortion of the objective of this type of analysis. Instead, the break-even situation represents but one point in a flexible set of projections of revenues and of the costs that will be associated with them under a given set of future conditions.

The managerial applications of break-even analysis are many. It is useful, among others, in price determination, expense control, and in the projection of profits. Along with standard cost systems it gives management a basis for pricing decisions under differing levels of activity. In conjunction with flexible budgets, it represents a powerful tool of expense control. The break-even chart is also a useful device with which to measure the impact of specific managerial decisions, such as plant expansion and new product introduction or of external influences, on the profitability of operations over various levels of activity.

To financial analysts, the function of profit projections is one of major importance. Moreover, the ability to estimate the impact of profitability of various economic conditions or managerial courses of action is also an extremely important one. Both of these are importantly aided by break-even analysis. The intelligent use of this technique and a thorough understanding of its operation are the factors that account for its importance to the external financial analyst.

Illustration of break-even technique application. Exhibit 8–3 presents the break-even chart of the Multi-Products Company at a given point in time. It is subject to the various assumptions that were discussed above including that relating to the ability to separate costs into their fixed and variable components.

Exhibit 8–3:   Multi-Products Company break-even-chart—all operations

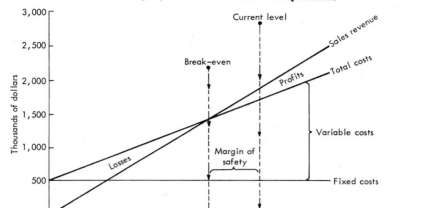

At break even, a very condensed income statement of Multi-Products Company will be as follows:

Sales		$1,387,000
Costs:		
Variable	$887,000	
Fixed..............	500,000	1,387,000
Net income		–0–

The variable-cost percentage is $887/$1,387, or about 64 percent. The contribution margin ratio is 36 percent (100 − Variable-cost percentage of 64). The variable-cost percentage means that on average, out of every dollar of sales 64 cents go to meet variable costs, that is, costs that would not be incurred if the sale did not occur. The contribution margin ratio is basically the complement of the variable-cost percentage.

Break-even point:
Sales	$1,387,000
Units	1,156,000
Average selling price per unit	$1.20

This indicates that each dollar of sales generates a contribution of 36 cents toward meeting fixed expenses and the earning of a profit beyond the break-even point. The contribution margin earned on sales of $1,387,000 is just sufficient to cover the $500,000 in fixed costs. Quite obviously, the lower the fixed costs, the less sales it would take to cover them and the lower the resulting break-even point. In the most unlikely event that the Multi-Products Company would have no fixed costs, that is, all costs varied directly with sales, the company would have no break-even point, that is, it would start making a profit on the very first dollar of sales.

The break-even chart reflects the sale of a given mix of products. Since each product has different cost patterns and profit margins, any significant change in the product mix will result in a change in the break-even point and consequently in a change in the relationship between revenues, costs, and results. Although Exhibit 8–3 shows the number of units on the sales (volume) axis, this figure and the average selling price per unit are of limited significance because they represent averages prevailing as a result of a given mix of products.

The importance of a relatively stable sales mix to the successful application of break-even analysis suggests that this technique cannot be usefully employed in cases where the product mix varies greatly over the short term. Nor, for that matter, can break-even analysis be usefully applied in cases where there are sharp and frequent fluctuations in sales prices or in costs of production, such as raw materials.

Exhibit 8–3 indicates that given the existing mix of products, the present level of fixed costs of $500,000 can be expected to prevail up to a sales level of approximately $2,400,000. This is the point at which 100 percent of theoretical capacity will be reached. The break-even point is at 60 percent of capacity, while the current level of sales is at about 75 percent of capacity. This means that when the 100 percent capacity level is reached, the fixed costs may have to undergo an upward revision. If Multi-Products is reluctant to expand its capacity and thus increase its fixed costs and break-even point, assuming that variable costs do not decrease, it may have to consider other alternatives such as:

1. Foregoing an increase in sales.
2. Increasing the number of shifts, which could increase variable costs significantly.
3. Subcontracting some of its work to outsiders, thus foregoing some of the profit of increased activity.

Exhibit 8–3 also presents to the analyst at a glance the company's present position relative to the break-even point. The current level of sales of $1,800,000 is about $413,000 above the break-even point. This is also known as the *safety margin,* that is, the margin that separates the company from a no-profit condition. This concept can be expanded to indicate on the chart at what point the company will earn a desired return on investment (ROI), at what point the common dividend may be in jeopardy, and at what point the preferred dividend may no longer be covered by current earnings.

It is obvious that the data revealed by a reliably constructed break-even chart or by the application of break-even computations are valuable in profit projection, in the assessment of operating risk, as well as in an evaluation of profit levels under various assumptions regarding future conditions and managerial policies.

Analytical implications of break-even analysis

From the above discussion of a specific situation, such as that illustrated in Exhibit 8–3, we will now turn to a more general review of conclusions that can be derived from break-even analysis.

The concept of operating leverage.   Leverage and fixed costs go together. As we have seen in Chapter 5, financial leverage is based on fixed costs of funds for a portion of the resources used by the enterprise. Thus, earnings above that fixed cost magnify the return on the residual funds and vice versa.

The fixed costs of a business enterprise, in the sense in which we have discussed them so far in this chapter, form the basis of the concept of operating leverage. Until an enterprise develops a volume of sales that is sufficient to cover its fixed costs, it will incur a loss. Once it has covered the fixed costs, further increments in volume will result in more than proportionate increases in profitability. The following will illustrate the nature of operating leverage:

Illustration of the working of operating leverage.   In a given enterprise, the cost structure is as follows:

$$\text{Fixed costs} = \$100,000$$
$$\text{Variable-cost percentage} = 60 \text{ percent}$$

The following tabulation presents the profit or loss at successively higher levels of sales and a comparison of relative percentage changes in sales volume and in profitability:

Sales	Variable costs	Fixed costs	Profit (loss)	Percentage increase over preceding step	
				Sales	Profit
$100,000	$ 60,000	$100,000	$(60,000)	—	—
200,000	120,000	100,000	(20,000)	100%	—
250,000	150,000	100,000	—	25	—
300,000	180,000	100,000	20,000	20	Infinite
360,000	216,000	100,000	44,000	20	120%
432,000	259,200	100,000	72,800	20	65%

The working of operating leverage is evident in the above tabulation. Starting at break even, the first 20 percent sales increase resulted in an infinite increase in profits because they started from a zero base. The next 20 percent increase in sales resulted in a 120 percent profit increase over the preceding level, while the sales increase that followed resulted in a 65 percent profit increase over the preceding level. The effects of leverage diminish as the sales increase above the break-even level because the bases to which increases in profits are compared get progressively larger.

Leverage, of course, works both ways. It will be noted that a drop in sales from $200,000 to $100,000, representing 50 percent decrease, resulted in a tripling of the loss.

One important conclusion from this to the analyst is that enterprises operating near their break-even point will have relatively larger percentage changes of profits or losses for a given change in volume. On the upside, the volatility will, of course, be desirable. On the downside, however, it can result in adverse results that are significantly worse than those indicated by changes in sales volume alone.

Another aspect is operating *potential,* sometimes erroneously referred to as leverage, which derives from a high level of sales accompanied by very low profit margins. The potential here, of course, is the room for improvements in profit margins. Even relatively slight improvements in profit margins, applied on a large sales level, can result in dramatic changes in profits. Thus, the popular reference to a semblance of leverage for what is really a potential for improvement.

Another aspect of the same *potential* occurs when the sales volume *per share* is large. Obviously an improvement in profitability will be translated into larger earnings per share improvements.

The significance of the variable-cost percentage

The volatility of profits is also dependent on the variable cost percentage. The low-cost enterprise will achieve higher profits for a given increment in volume once break-even operations are reached than will the high variable-cost enterprise.

ILLUSTRATION 3.   Company A has fixed costs of $70,000 and a variable cost equal to 30 percent of sales. Company B has fixed costs of $300,000 and variable costs equal to 70 percent of the sales. Assume that both companies have now reached sales of $1,000,000 and are, consequently, at break even. A $100,000 increment in sales will result in a profit of $70,000 for Company A and only in a profit of $30,000 for Company B. Company A has not only greater operating leverage but can, as a result, afford to incur greater risks in going after the extra $100,000 in sales than can Company B.

From the above example it is evident that the *level* of the break-even point is not the only criterion of risk assessment but that the analyst must also pay attention to the variable-cost ratio.

The significance of the fixed-cost level

Given a certain variable-cost percentage, the higher the fixed costs, the higher the break-even point of an enterprise. In the absence of change in other factors, a given percentage change in fixed costs will result in an equal percentage change in the break-even point. This can be illustrated as follows:

First break-even situation

Sales		$100,000
Variable expenses	$60,000	
Fixed costs	40,000	100,000
Profit		–0–

Second break-even situation—20 percent increase in fixed costs

Sales (increase of 20%)		$120,000
Variable expenses (60%)	$72,000	
Fixed costs ($40,000 + 20%)	48,000	120,000
		–0–

Thus, a fixed cost increase of 20 percent, with the variable-cost ratio remaining unchanged, resulted in a 20 percent increase in the break-even point.

An increase in the break-even point of an enterprise generally increases operational risk. It means that the enterprise is dependent on a higher volume of sales in order to break even. Looked at another way, it means that the enterprise is more vulnerable to economic downturns as compared to its situation with a lower break-even point. The substantial acquisition of the large capacity Boeing 747 aircraft by the airlines provides an example of the effects of high break-even points. While these large aircraft lowered the variable cost per passenger, they relied also on a projected increase in the number of passengers. When this failed to materialize, the airlines' profit margins deteriorated swiftly with many of them going into the red. There are other repercussions to high levels of fixed costs. Thus, for example, a higher break-even point may mean that the enterprise has less freedom of action in fields such as labor relations. A high level of fixed costs makes strikes more expensive and subjects the enterprise to added pressure to submit to higher wage demands.

Often, added fixed costs in the form of automatic machinery are incurred in order to save variable costs, such as labor, and to improve efficiency. That can be very profitable in times of reasonably good demand. In times of low demand, however, the higher level of fixed costs sets in motion the process of reverse operational leverage discussed above, with attendant rapidly shrinking profits or even growing losses. High fixed costs reduce an enterprise's ability to protect its profits in the face of shrinking sales volume.

Investments in fixed assets, particularly in sophisticated machinery, can bring about increases in fixed costs far beyond the cost of maintaining and replacing the equipment. The skills required to operate such equipment are quite specialized and require skilled personnel which the enterprise may be reluctant to dismiss for fear of not being able to replace them when business turns up again. This converts what should be variable costs into de facto fixed costs.

While fixed costs are incurred in order to increase capacity or to decrease variable costs, it is often advisable to cut fixed costs in order to reduce the risks associated with a high break-even point. Thus, a company may reduce fixed costs by switching from a salaried sales force to one compensated by commissions based on sales. It can avoid added fixed costs by adding work shifts, buying ready-made parts, subcontracting work, or discontinuing the least profitable product lines.

In evaluating profit performance, past and future, of an enterprise, the analyst must always keep in mind the effect that the level of fixed costs can have on operating results under a variety of business conditions. Moreover, in projecting future results, the analyst must bear in mind that any given level of fixed costs is valid only up to the limits of practical capacity within a range of product mixes. Beyond such a point, a profit projection must take into consideration not only the increased levels of fixed costs required but also the financial resources that an expansion will require as well as the cost and sources of the funds that will be needed.

The importance of the contribution margin

The analyst must be alert to the absolute size of an enterprise's contribution margin because operating leverage is importantly dependent on it. He must, moreover, be aware of the factors that can change this margin, that is, changes in variable costs as well as changes in selling prices.

While we have focused on the individual factors that affect costs, revenues, and profitability, in practice, changes result from a combination of factors. Projected increases in sales volume will increase profits only if costs, both fixed and variable, are controlled and kept within projected limits. Break-even analysis assumes that efficiency remains constant. However, experience teaches us that cost controls are more lax in times of prosperity than they are in times of recession. Thus, the analyst cannot assume constant efficiency any more than he can assume a constant product mix. The latter is also an important variable that must be watched by the analyst. Questions of why an enterprise realized lower profits on a higher volume of sales can often be explained, at least in part, by reference to changes in sales mix.

In spite of its important limitations, the break-even approach is an important tool of analysis to the financial analyst.

Its ability to aid the external analyst in performance evaluation and in profit projection makes its use worthwhile to him in spite of the laborious work that it often entails and the fragmentary and scarce amounts of information on which, of necessity, it must be based.

ADDITIONAL CONSIDERATIONS IN THE ANALYSIS
OF COST OF SALES

Gross margin analysis focuses on changes in costs, prices, and volume. Break-even analysis, in turn, focuses on the behavior of costs in relation to sales volume and on management's ability to control costs in the face of rising and falling revenues. The effectiveness of these and other methods of cost analysis depends on the degree of data availability as well as on an understanding of the accounting principles that have been applied.

The ability of the analyst to make the rough approximations that are necessary to separate costs into fixed and variable components depends on the amount of detail available. Disclosure of major cost components such as materials, labor, and various overhead cost categories can be helpful. The more detailed the breakdowns of expense categories, the more likely is the analyst to be able to construct meaningful break-even estimates.

In the evaluation of the cost of sales and the gross margin, and particularly in its comparison with those of other enterprises, the analyst must pay close attention to distortions that may arise from the utilization of a variety of accounting principles. While this is true of all items of cost, attention must be directed particularly to inventories and to depreciation accounting. These two areas merit special attention which are usually substantial in amount but also because of the proliferation of alternative principles that may be employed in accounting for them.

DEPRECIATION

Depreciation is an important cost element particularly in manufacturing and service enterprises. It is mostly fixed in nature because it is computed on the basis of elapsed time. However, if its computation is based on production activity, the result is a variable cost.

Because depreciation is computed in most cases on the basis of time elapsed, the ratio of depreciation expense to income is not a particularly meaningful or instructive relationship. In the evaluation of depreciation expense, the ratio of depreciation to gross plant and equipment is more meaningful. The ratio is computed as follows:

$$\frac{\text{Depreciation expense}}{\text{Assets subject to depreciation}}$$

This ratio can, of course, be computed by major categories of assets. The basic purpose is to enable the analyst to detect changes in the composite rate of depreciation used by an enterprise as a means of evaluating its adequacy and of detecting attempts at income smoothing.

AMORTIZATION OF SPECIAL TOOLS AND SIMILAR COSTS

The importance of the cost of special tools, dies, jigs, patterns, and molds varies from industry to industry. It is of considerable importance, for example, in the auto industry where special tool costs are associated with frequent style and design changes. The rate of amortization of such costs can have an important effect on reported income and is important to the analyst in an assessment of that income as well as in its comparison with that of other entities within an industry. The ratios that can be used to analyze changes in the deferral and amortization policies of such costs are varied and focus on their relationship to sales and other classes of assets.

The yearly expenditure for special tools can be related to and expressed as a percentage of (1) sales and (2) net property and equipment.

The yearly amortization of special tools can be related to (1) sales, (2) unamortized special tools, and (3) net property and equipment.

A comparison of the yearly trend in these relationships can be very helpful in an analysis of the consistency of income reporting of a single enterprise. The comparison can be extended further to an evaluation of the earnings of two or more enterprises within the same industry. This approach is indicative of the type of analysis which various elements of cost lend themselves to.

MAINTENANCE AND REPAIRS COSTS

Maintenance and repairs costs vary in significance with the amount invested in plant and equipment as well as with the level of productive activity. They have an effect on the cost of goods sold as well as on other elements of cost. Since maintenance and repairs contain elements of both fixed and variable costs, they cannot vary directly with sales. Thus, the ratio of repairs and maintenance costs to sales, while instructive to compare from year to year or among enterprises, must be interpreted with care. To the extent that the analyst can determine the fixed and the variable portions of maintenance and repairs costs, his interpretation of their relationship to periodic sales will be more valid.

Repairs and maintenance are, to a significant extent, discretionary costs. That is, the level of expense can, within limits, be regulated by management for a variety of reasons including those aimed at the improvement of reported income or at the preservation of liquid resources. Certain types of repairs cannot, of course, be postponed without resulting breakdowns in productive equipment. But many types of preventive repairs and particularly maintenance can be postponed or skimped on with results whose effects lie mainly in the future. Thus, the level of repairs and maintenance costs both in relation to sales and to plant and equipment is of interest to the analyst. It has, of course, a bearing on the quality of income, a subject that we shall consider in the next chapter.

The level of repairs and maintenance costs is also important in the evaluation of depreciation expense. Useful lives of assets are estimated by the use of many assumptions including those relating to the upkeep and maintenance of the assets. If, for instance, there is a deterioration in the usual or assumed level of repairs and maintenance, the useful life of the asset will, in all probability, be shortened. That may, in turn, require an upward revision in the depreciation expense or else income will be overstated.

OTHER COSTS AND EXPENSES—GENERAL

Most, although not all, cost and expense items found in the income statement have some identifiable or measurable relationship to sales or revenues. This is so because sales are the major measure of activity in an enterprise except in instances when production and sales are significantly out of phase.

Two analytical tools whose usefulness is based, in part, on the relationship that exists between sales and most costs and expenses should be noted here:

1. The *common-size income statement* expresses each cost and expense item in terms of its percentage relationship to net sales. This relationship of costs and expenses to sales can then be traced over a number of periods or compared with the experience of other enterprises in the same industry. Appendix 2B of Chapter 2 contained an illustration of a common-size income statement covering a number of years.

2. The *index number analysis of the income statement* expresses each item in the income statement in terms of an index number related to a base year. In this manner, relative changes of income statement items over time can be traced and their significance assessed. Expense item changes can thus be compared to changes in sales and to changes in related expense items. Moreover, by use of common-size balance sheets, percentage changes in income statement items can be related to changes in assets and liabilities. For example, a given change in sales would normally justify a commensurate change in inventories and in accounts receivable. Appendix 2B of Chapter 2 contained an illustration of an index number analysis.

Selling expenses

The analysis of selling costs has two main objectives:

1. The evaluation over time of the relationship between sales and the costs needed to bring them about.
2. An evaluation of the trend and the productivity of future-directed selling costs.

The importance of selling costs in relation to sales varies from industry to industry and from enterprise to enterprise. In some enterprises, selling costs take the form of commissions and are, consequently, highly variable in nature, while in others, they contain important elements of fixed costs.

After allowing for the fixed and variable components of the selling expenses, the best way to analyze them is to relate them to sales. The more detailed the breakdown of the selling expense components is—the more meaningful and penetrating can such analysis be. Exhibit 8–4 presents an example of such an analysis.

Analysis of Exhibit 8–4 indicates that for the entire period selling costs have been rising faster than sales and that in 19x3 they took 5.6 percent more of the sales dollar than they did in 19x0. In this period, salesmen's salaries increased by 1.0 percent of sales, advertising by 3.6 percent of sales, and branch expenses by 2.2 percent of sales. The drop in delivery expense may possibly be accounted for by the offsetting increase in freight costs.

A careful analysis should be made of advertising costs in order to determine to what extent the increase is due to the promotion of new products or the development of new territories that will benefit the future.

Exhibit 8–4

TRYON CORPORATION
Comparative Statement of Selling Expenses
(in thousands)

	19x3		19x2		19x1		19x0	
Sales	$1,269		$935		$833		$791	
Trend percentage		160.0%		118.0%		105.0%		100.0%
Selling expenses (percent are of sales):								
Advertising . .	$ 84	6.6	$ 34	3.6	28	3.4	24	3.0
District branch expenses* . .	80	6.3	41	4.4	38	4.6	32	4.1
Delivery expense (own trucks)	20	1.6	15	1.6	19	2.3	22	2.8
Freight-out . .	21	1.7	9	1.0	11	1.3	8	1.0
Salesmen's salary expense . . .	111	8.7	76	8.1	68	8.1	61	7.7
Salesmen's travel expense . . .	35	2.8	20	2.1	18	2.2	26	3.3
Miscellaneous selling expense	9	.7	9	1.0	8	.9	7	.9
Total . . .	$ 360	28.4%	$204	21.8%	$190	22.8%	$180	22.8%

* Includes rent, regional advertising, etc.

When selling expenses as a percentage of sales show an increase, it is instructive to focus on the selling expense increase that accompanies a given increase in sales. It can be expected that beyond a certain level, greater sales resistance is encountered in effecting additional sales. That sales resistance or the development of more remote territories may involve additional cost. Thus, it is important to know what the percentage of selling expense to sales is or to new sales as opposed to old ones. This may have, of course, implications on the projection of future profitability. If an enterprise can make additional sales only by increasing selling expenses, its profitability may suffer. Offsetting factors, such as those related to break-even operations or to economies of scale, must also be considered.

BAD DEBT EXPENSES

These expenses are often regarded as a cost of marketing. Since the size of the expense is importantly tied to the size of "allowance for doubtful accounts," it is best evaluated in terms of the relationship between that allowance and gross accounts receivable. The following analysis[3] of the allowance for doubtful accounts of Mattel, Inc., is an example of such an evaluation:

	Fiscal 1982—quarter ending		
	Aug. 1, 1981	May 2, 1981	Jan. 31, 1981
Allowance for doubtful accounts (in thousands)	$ 13,500	$ 15,600	$ 19,200
Gross receivables (in thousands)	343,319	223,585	179,791
Allowance as percent of gross receivables	3.93%	6.98%	10.68%

	Fiscal 1981—quarter ending		
	Aug. 2, 1980	May 3, 1980	Feb. 2, 1980
Allowance for doubtful accounts (in thousands)	$ 16,600	$ 15,000	$ 12,200
Gross receivables (in thousands)	331,295	215,660	172,427
Allowance as percent of gross receivables	5.01%	6.96%	7.07%

It is noteworthy that there was a significant decline in Mattel's allowance for doubtful accounts in relation to gross receivables in the fiscal 1982 quarters

---

[3] Source "Quality of Earnings Report, November 20, 1981," issued by Reporting Research Corporation, Englewood Cliffs, N.J.

as compared to similar quarters in the preceding year. The reasons can be varied including improvement in the collectibility of receivables or inadequate provisions that result in understated bad debt expense. This analysis certainly calls for further investigation by the analyst.

Future directed marketing costs

Certain categories of sales promotion costs, particularly advertising, result in benefits that extend beyond the period in which they were incurred. The measurement of such benefits is difficult if not impossible, but it is a reasonable assumption that there is a relationship between the level of expenditures for advertising and promotion and the sales level, present and future.

Since expenditures for advertising and other forms of promotion are discretionary in nature, the analyst must carefully follow the year-to-year trend in these expenditures. Not only does the level of such expenditures have a bearing on future sales estimates, but it also indicates whether management is attempting to "manage" reported earnings. The effect of discretionary costs on the "quality" of earnings reported will be the subject of further discussion in the chapter that follows.

GENERAL, ADMINISTRATION, FINANCIAL, AND OTHER EXPENSES

Most costs in this category tend to be fixed in nature. This is largely true of administrative costs because such costs include significant amounts of salaries and occupancy expenditures. However, there may be some "creep" or tendency for increases in this category, and this is particularly true in prosperous times. Thus, in analyzing this category of expense, the analyst should pay attention to both the trend of administrative costs as well as to the percentage of total sales that they consume.

Financial costs

Financial costs are, except for interest on short-term indebtedness, fixed in nature. Moreover, unless replaced by equity capital, most borrowed funds are usually refinanced. This is because of the long-term nature of most interest-bearing obligations. Included in these costs are the amortization of bond premium and discount as well as of debt issue expenses. A good check on an enterprise's cost of borrowed money as well as credit standing is the calculation of the average effective interest rate paid. This rate is computed as follows:

$$\frac{\text{Total interest cost}}{\text{Average total indebtedness subject to interest}}$$

Alfa, Inc.'s (see Appendix 2B) average interest rate on long-term debt can be computed for 19x6 as follows:

$$\frac{\$14,883^{(a)}}{(\$244,954 + \$194,690 + \$7,328 + \$8,701)^{(b)} \div 2} = \underline{\underline{6.5}} \text{ percent}$$

(a) Long-term debt interest expense (item $\boxed{81}$).
(b) Beginning + Ending balances of long-term debt (item $\boxed{38}$) + Beginning and ending current portion of long-term debt (note 8—item $\boxed{94}$) ÷ 2.

The average effective interest rate paid can be compared over the years or compared to that of other enterprises. It is also significant in that it sheds light on the credit standing of the enterprise.

A measure of sensitivity to interest changes is obtained by determining the portion of debt that is tied to the prime rate. In periods of rising interest rates, a significant amount of debt tied to the prime rate exposes an enterprise to sharply escalating interest costs. Conversely, falling interest rates are a beneficial factor to such an enterprise.

"Other" expenses

"Other" expenses are, of course, a nondescript category. The total amount in this category should normally be rather immaterial in relation to other costs. Otherwise, it can obscure substantial costs that, if revealed, may provide significant information about the enterprise's current and future operations. Nonrecurring elements may also be included in the "other expense" category, and this may add to the significance of this category to the analyst.

The analyst must also be alert to the tendency to offset "other" expenses against "other" income. Here too the major problem is one of concealment of important information and data. Here it is important that details of the major items comprising the offset amount be given.

OTHER INCOME

Miscellaneous income items that are small in amount are usually of no significance to the analyst. However, since "other income" may include returns from various investments, it may contain information about new ventures and data regarding investments that is not available elsewhere. Such investments may, of course, have future implications, positive or negative, that exceed by far in significance the amounts of current income that are involved.

INCOME TAXES

Income taxes represent basically a sharing of profits between an enterprise and the governmental authority by which they are imposed. Since most enterprises with which this book is concerned are organized in corporate form, we shall focus primarily on corporate income taxes.

Income taxes are almost always significant in amount and normally can amount to about half of a corporation's income before taxes. For this reason, the analyst must pay careful attention to the impact that income taxes have on net income.

Except for a lower rate on a first modest amount of income (e.g., $100,000), corporate income is normally taxed at the rate of about 50 percent (presently 46 percent). Differences in the timing of recognition of income or expense items as between taxable income and book income should not influence the effective tax rate because of the practice of interperiod income tax allocation that aims to match the tax expense with the book income regardless of when the tax is paid.

The relationship between the tax accrual and the pretax income, otherwise known as the effective tax rate or tax ratio, will, however, be influenced by permanent tax differences.[4]

The effective tax rate or tax ratio is computed as follows:

$$\frac{\text{Income tax expense for period}}{\text{Income before income taxes}}$$

For Alfa, Inc. (see Appendix 2B), the effective tax rate is:

$$\frac{\$7,600 \ (\text{item } \boxed{9})}{\$25,368 \ (\text{item } \boxed{8})} = 30 \text{ percent}$$

For purposes of evaluation of the level of earnings, the trend of earnings, as well as for net income projection, the analyst must know the reasons why the tax ratio deviates from the normal or the expected. Income taxes are such an important element of cost that even relatively small changes in the effective tax rate can explain important changes in net income. Moreover, without an understanding of the factors that cause changes in the effective tax rate of a company, the analyst is missing an important ingredient necessary in the forecasting of future net income.

Financial Reporting Release (FRR) No. 1 Section 204 contains rules in which the SEC expanded significantly the required analytical disclosures concerning current and deferred income taxes.

The analysis of these and other aspects of income tax disclosures are important to the analyst and will be discussed and illustrated in the section that follows.

---

[4] This term includes differences due to state and local taxes, foreign tax rate differentials, and investment tax credits.

ANALYSIS OF INCOME TAX DISCLOSURES

Objectives of the analysis

The analysis of income tax disclosures may be undertaken with specific or specialized objectives in mind. However, the more general objectives of such an analysis are:

- To understand the tax accounting of the enterprise and its impact on income, on related assets and liabilities, as well as on the sources and uses of funds or cash.
- To judge the adequacy of the enterprise's tax disclosure.
- To provide a basis for assessing the effect of taxes on future income and funds flows.
- To provide a basis for informed queries to be put to management in order to clear up questions arising during the analysis.
- To identify unusual gains or losses not otherwise disclosed but whose tax effect is highlighted.

Analytical steps and techniques

A.   Establish a T-account for each tax-related account in the balance sheet and income statement.

   A current tax liability and/or a current receivable for overpayment or tax refunds will almost always be found. In addition, there will be one or two deferred tax accounts (one current and one noncurrent) in the balance sheet.

   Care must be taken to identify the income taxes (current and possibly deferred) that relate to each separate section of the income statement: (1) continuing operations, (2) discontinued operations, (3) extraordinary items, and (4) cumulative effect of change(s) in accounting principles.

   The analyst should be aware that information on income tax effects can be found in parenthetical notes to financial statement items, in sections containing management discussion, and in footnotes in general and particularly in those relating to income taxes.

B.   A good next step is to attempt to reconstruct as best as is possible the summary entry by means of which the tax expense for the period was booked. It is easier to do this if the entry is divided into the current and the deferred portions of the tax expense.

C.   After the opening and closing balances of all tax-related balance sheet T-accounts have been posted the tax expense entries and the relevant tax-related accounts and data should be used to aid in as complete a reconstruction of these accounts as is possible.

   The changes in the deferred tax accounts on the balance sheet should generally agree with the deferred tax expense for the period as shown in the income statement or in related footnotes. Nonfund adjustments to net income and other information in the statement of changes in financial position (SCFP) often can provide added insights. If all attempts at reconciliation fail, it is possible that a deferred tax account is buried or combined under some other caption in the balance sheet, or that the company made some undisclosed entries for purposes of correcting errors or for other reasons. In such a situation, the analyst can only identify the needed balancing amount and label it as such, realizing that the correctness of any conclusions regarding balancing (plugged) amounts in the reconciliation is subject to the validity of assumptions that have been made. The Taxes Currently Payable account should be credited, and the related income statement tax expense will consist of various debits and credits to items in the four income statement categories mentioned above as applicable. In case of a loss there may instead be a debit to a "Tax Refund Receivable account."

D. The accounting for the investment tax credit (ITC) requires care. If the company uses the *flow-through method,* the ITC should be debited to Current Taxes Payable and credited to Income Tax Expense. In this case, the "current" income tax expense is also the amount payable. If the *deferral method* is used, the reconstruction involves debiting this year's amortization of the ITC to the Deferred ITC account with a credit to Tax Expense. The actual amount of the ITC earned (realized) in the current year is debited to Current Taxes Payable and credited to Deferred ITC account.

E. After using knowledge of tax accounting and all the disclosures in the financial statements, as well as the assumptions required in the situation, the tax T-accounts should be fully reconstructed. At this point, the amount of taxes paid during the year is arrived at as a "plug" to the current Taxes Payable account.

It should be noted that the quality of the analysis will depend on the quality of disclosure found in the financial statements. A lack of good disclosure will require more analytical ingenuity such as the combining of certain accounts (such as current tax receivable and payable accounts). The analyst must also be aware that the acquisition or disposition of businesses during a period will result in related additions or deductions to balance sheet tax accounts.

Illustration of income tax analysis of Alfa, Inc.

Let us first analyze the changes in Alfa's 19x5 and 19x6 income tax accounts. The *first* step is to draw a T-account for each tax-related balance sheet account and one for each income tax expense and tax effect account in the 19x5 and 19x6 income statements. (All number references are to Alfa's financial statements in Appendix 2B.)

Income Tax Payable—Current

		21,670	*(a)*	(19x5) BB
		32,135	*(d)*	
Plug paid	44,967			
		8,838	*(a)*	(19x6) BB
		1,678	*(k)*	
Plug paid	7,868			
		2,648	*(t)*	EB

Deferred Tax (current liability)

		38,820	*(b)*	(19x5) BB
(e)	19,665			
		19,155	*(b)*	(19x6) BB
		2,401	*(i)*	
		21,556	*(g)*	

Deferred Tax (noncurrent liability)

		31,676	*(c)*	(19x5) BB
		207	*(e)*	
		31,883	*(c)*	(19x6) BB
		3,521	*(i)*	
		35,404	*(h)*	EB

Tax Expense*

19x5	*(d)*	52,458	19,458	*(e)*	
EB		33,000			
19x6	*(i)*	5,922			
	(k)	1,678			
EB		7,600			

* In certain cases, the analysis process can be simplified by subdividing the Tax Expense account into (1) Tax Expenses—Current, (2) Tax Expenses—Deferred (current portion) and (3) Tax Expenses—Deferred (noncurrent portion).

Tax Effect of Discontinued Operations

	1,083	(d)
	1,083	Total 19x5

Tax Effect of Cumulative Effect of Accounting Change

	19,240	(d)
	19,240	Total 19x5

The *second* step is to enter the beginning balance (BB) and the ending balance (EB) of each balance sheet account. Note that since we are, for purposes of illustration, analyzing *two* years, the EB of 19x5 coincides with the BB of 19x6. Letter references in the notes that follow refer to various entries in the T-accounts.

(a) Since we do not have the 19x4 balance sheet, we do not have the BB of this account. We can, however, derive it by using the 19x5 EB of $8,838 (income taxes—including deferred $27,993 less $19,155 deferred portion—see item 34). To the $8,838 EB of 19x5, we *add the change in* currently payable taxes for 19x5 of $12,832 located in the funds statement (see item 67) to get the 19x5 BB of $21,670.

(b) Using a similar approach to the one in *(a)* above, we can derive the 19x5 BB of the Deferred Tax (current) account: 19x5 EB $19,155 (item 34) plus the change in 19x5 deferred taxes (current) account of $19,665 (item 68) equals 19x5 BB of $38,820.

(c) The 19x5 BB of this account can be derived only after the 19x5 activity has been posted. The 19x5 EB of this account is given as $31,883 (item 36).

The *third* step is to enter the activity during 19x5 based on all available information in the financial statements and notes.

(d) The current tax expense entry can be reconstructed as follows:

			Source—Alfa item
Tax Expense (current)	52,458		92
Tax Effect of Discontinued Operations		1,083*	13
Tax Effect Cumulative Accounting Change		19,240	15
Taxes Payable—Current		32,135	Plug

* $2,083 − $1,000 (source is Note 3)

This is accomplished by making sure that all tax expense (or credit) items are identified in the income statement.

(e) The deferred tax entry can be reconstructed as follows:

Deferred Taxes (current)	19,665		68	*
— Tax Expense		19,458	93	
Deferred Taxes (noncurrent)		207	43	*

* In this case all amounts are fully corroborated in the financial statements. Sometimes one unknown amount may have to be derived in order to balance the entry.

Note that the Deferred Taxes (noncurrent) can *usually* be found in the "add-back" section of the funds statement. In this case, the entry is also validated by the fact that the changes in the tax expense of $33,000 (Alfa 9). Deferred Taxes—Current, and Deferred Taxes—Noncurrent accounts are now fully explained.

We can now *plug* the amount of taxes paid in 19x5 ($44,967) with a debit to the Taxes Payable account.

The analytical process can now be repeated for 19x6. This is somewhat simpler because of the absence of "below the line" tax items in the income statement. We have the beginning balances 19x6 already in place (from the 19x5 analysis), and we enter the ending balances as follows:

(f) $24,204 − $21,556 = $2,648 34 .

(g) Deferred taxes given in balance sheet, $21,556 34 .

(h) 36 .

Now we reconstruct the deferred tax portion of the 19x6 tax expense:

				Source
(i) Tax Expense—Deferred	5,922			93
Deferred Taxes (current)		2,401		68
Deferred Taxes (noncurrent)		3,521		43

This entry is further corroborated by the fact that it explains fully the changes in the deferred tax balance sheet accounts.

Next, we post the current tax expense:

(k) Tax Expense—Current	1,678		92
Taxes Payable		1,678	Derived

With this entry we have fully explained all changes in the tax accounts of Alfa for 19x5 and 19x6. The plugged figure of $7,868 in the Income Taxes Payable account represents taxes paid in 19x6.

In some instances, the analysis may not go as smoothly, in which case certain accounts may have to be combined or certain amounts may have to be plugged if the amounts are significant. Such cases provide the basis for informed questions to management concerning unexplained tax entries.

Explaining the tax rate

At another level of analysis, we can explain how Alfa with a pretax income of \$25,368 in 19x6 could report only \$828 (items 89 — 90) of current federal income tax.

		Source	
Expected federal income tax at 48% = \$25,368 × .48 = ...		8	\$12,176
Less 48% of State tax = \$1,540 × .48*		88	739
Computed federal tax at statutory rate of 48% (per Note 7)		83	11,437
Less permanent differences:			
For income taxable at capital gains rate	\$ 782	84	
For other items, net	284	86	1,066
Subtotal			10,371
Less deferred tax:			
Total (per Note 7)	5,922	83	
Current portion = \$1,540 − \$850)	690	88 − 91	
Deferred federal tax			5,232
Reported current federal tax (before investment tax credit)		89	5,139
Less investment tax credit		90	4,311
Current federal income tax			\$ 828

* The pretax income of \$25,368 *excludes* the state tax of \$1,540 which is, however, tax deductible. Thus, the related tax benefit reduces the total federal tax.

Focus on pretax earnings

While the focus on net income and on earnings per share requires a thorough analysis of changes in the effective tax rate, it must be borne in mind that many analysts attach great importance to pretax earnings. This is due to the greater importance that is assigned to pretax operating results, which require management skills of a higher order, as compared with changes due to variations in the effective tax rate over which, it is assumed, management has comparatively more limited control.

THE OPERATING RATIO

The operating ratio is yet another intermediate measure in the analysis of the income statement. It measures the relationship between all operating costs and net sales and is computed as follows:

$$\frac{\text{Cost of goods sold} + \text{Other operating expenses}}{\text{Net sales}}$$

The ratio is designed to enable a comparison within an enterprise or with enterprises of the proportion of the sales dollar absorbed by all operating

Exhibit 8–5

ALFA, INC.
Statement Accounting for Variations in Net Income
For the Year Ended December 31, 19x6

			Percentage increase (decrease)
Items tending to increase net income:			
Increase in gross margin on sales:			
Increase in net sales:			
Net sales, 19x6	$1,251,088		
Net sales, 19x5	1,133,817	$117,271	10.3
Deduct: Increase in cost of goods sold:			
Cost of goods sold, 19x6	840,043		
Cost of goods sold, 19x5	730,280	109,763	15.0
Net increase in gross margin:			
Gross margin, 19x6	411,045		
Gross margin, 19x5	403,537	7,508	1.9
Decrease in income taxes:			
Income taxes, 19x6	7,600		
Income taxes, 19x5	33,000	25,400	(77.0)
Decrease in loss from discontinued operations:			
Loss, 19x6	–0–		
Loss, 19x5	1,000	1,000	(100.0)
Decrease in negative cumulative effect, net:			
Effect, 19x6	–0–		
Effect, 19x5	17,407	17,407	(100.0)
Total of items tending to increase income		$51,315	
Items tending to decrease net income:			
Increase in selling, administrative, and general expenses (SAG):			
SAG, 19x6	343,023		
SAG, 19x5	296,893	46,130	15.5
Increase in depreciation and amortization (DA):			
DA, 19x6	24,214		
DA, 19x5	21,158	3,056	14.4
Increase in interest expensed:			
Interest expensed, 19x6	18,440		
Interest expensed, 19x5	16,319	2,121	13.0
Decrease in "equity on income" (19x5 − 19x6 = $2,329 − $1,371)		958	41.0
Total of items tending to decrease net income		52,265	
Net decrease in net income:			
Net income, 19x6	19,139		
Net income, 19x5	20,089	$ (950)	(4.7)

costs. Only other income and expense items as well as income taxes are excluded from the computation of this ratio.

In effect, this ratio represents but an intermediate step in the common-size analysis of the income statement. It is, in and of itself, not of great analytical significance because it is a composite of many factors that require separate analysis. These factors comprise the analysis of gross margin and of other major expense categories discussed earlier. Thus, the operating ratio cannot be properly interpreted without a thorough analysis of the reasons accounting for variations in gross margin and for changes in selling, general, administrative, and other costs.

NET INCOME RATIO

The net income ratio is the relationship between net income and total revenues and is computed as follows:

$$\frac{\text{Net income}}{\text{Total revenues}}$$

It represents the percentage of total revenue brought down to net income. In addition to its usefulness as an index of profitability, the net profit ratio represents, as was seen in Chapter 6, a main component of the computation of the return on investment (ROI).

Statement accounting for variation in net income

In the analysis of year-to-year changes in net income, it is useful to separate the elements that contributed to an increase in net income from those that contributed to a decrease. A statement that does this and also indicates the percentage increase or decrease in these factors is the "statement accounting for variations in net income." Exhibit 8–5 presents such a statement for Alfa, Inc., based on its income statements included in Appendix 2B.

QUESTIONS

1. What are the most important elements in the analysis of gross profit?
2. What is the basic principle underlying break-even analysis? What are fixed costs? Variable costs? Semivariable costs?
3. Certain assumptions that underlie break-even computations are often referred to as simplifying assumptions. Name as many of these as you can.
4. In break-even computation, what is the *variable-cost percentage?* What is its relationship to the *contribution margin ratio?*
5. What alternatives to an increase in fixed costs can an enterprise consider when it approaches 100 percent of theoretical capacity?

6. What is operating leverage? Why do leverage and fixed costs go together? What are the analytical implications of operating leverage?

7. Of what analytical significance are *(a)* the break-even point and *(b)* the variable-cost ratio?

8. What is a useful measure of the adequacy of current provisions for depreciation?

9. To what factors can maintenance and repairs costs be meaningfully related?

10. What are the main objectives of an analysis of selling expenses?

11. How can bad debt expense be evaluated most meaningfully? To what can a decline in the allowance to doubtful accounts be attributed?

12. *a.* What is the tax ratio and how is it computed?
    b. What are the objectives of an analysis of income tax disclosures?

The evaluation and projection of earnings

OBJECTIVES OF EARNINGS EVALUATION

In the preceding chapters, we examined the steps that have to be taken and the understanding that must be brought to bear on the analysis of the operating performance of an enterprise. This chapter will examine the additional considerations involved in the achievement of the major objectives of income statement analysis:

The evaluation of the quality of earnings.

Evaluation of the earnings level and trend.

The forecasting of earnings.

The estimation of earning power.

Monitoring performance and results.

EVALUATION OF THE QUALITY OF EARNINGS

The discussions throughout this book have pointed out that much of the accounting process of income determination involves a high degree of estimation. It is also important to remember that the income of an enterprise, as measured by the accounting process, is not a specific amount but can vary depending on the assumptions used and the various principles applied. Complicating these measurements still further is the fact that numerous accounting periods can receive benefits from a single cash outlay and that it may take a number of periods before a transaction results in the collection of all amounts due. For that reason, creditors, in particular, are greatly interested in the cash equivalent of reported earnings.

This distinction between accrual income and the related cash flows has led some of those uninitiated in the income determination process to doubt the validity of all accounting measurements. This, however, is an extreme and unwarranted position because, as any student of accounting should know, the concept of income is the result of a series of complex assumptions and conventions, and exists only as the creation and the approximation of this system of measurement. This system is always subject to reexamination and is, despite its shortcomings, still the most widely accepted method of income determination.

In examining the level of reported income of an enterprise, the analyst must determine the effect of the various assumptions and accounting principles used on that reported income. Beyond that he must be aware of the "accounting risk" as well as the "audit risk" to which these determinations are subject.

Over the years, and especially since the enactment of the Securities Acts of 1933 and 1934, and with improvement in the audit function in this country, the incidence of outright fraud and deliberate misrepresentation in financial statements has diminished markedly. But they have not been completely eliminated and probably never will. Nor can the analyst ever rule out the possibility of spectacular failures in the audit function. While each major audit failure tends to contribute to the improvement of regulation and of auditing, they have not prevented the recurrence of such failures as the security holders of McKesson & Robbins, of Seaboard Commercial Corporation, of H. L. Green, of Miami Window, of Yale Express, of BarChris Construction Company, of Continental Vending Company, of Mill Factors Corporation, of W. T. Grant, and of Equity Funding Company, well know.

The analyst must always assess the vulnerability to failure and to irregularities of the company under analysis and the character and the propensities of its management, as a means of establishing the degree of risk that it will prove to be the exception of the general rule. (The audit process is discussed in the appendix.)

The evaluation of the earnings level and of the earnings trend is intimately tied in with the evaluation of management. The evaluation of the management group cannot be separated from the results that they have actually achieved. Whatever other factors may have to be considered, results over a period of time are the acid test of management's ability, and that ability is perhaps the most important intangible (i.e., unquantifiable) factor in the prediction of future results. The analyst must be alert to changes in the management group and must assess its depth, stability, and possible dependence on the talents of one or a few individuals.

The analyst must also realize that not only is it impossible to arrive at a single figure of "net income" but that identical earnings figures may possess different degrees of "quality."

The concept of earnings quality

The concept of earnings quality arose out of a need to provide a basis of comparison among the earnings of different entities as well as from the need to recognize such differences in "quality" for valuation purposes. There is almost no general agreement on definitions of or on assumptions underlying this concept. The elements that comprise the "quality of earnings" can be classified as follows:

a. One type of factor that affects the quality of earnings is the accounting and computational discretion of management and that of the attesting accountants in choosing from among accepted alternative accounting principles. These choices can be liberal, that is, they can assume the most optimistic view of the future, or they can be conservative. Generally, the quality of conservatively determined earnings is higher because they are less likely to prove overstated in the light of future developments than those determined in a "liberal" fashion. They also minimize the possibility of earnings overstatement and avoid retrospective changes. LIFO inventory accounting in rising markets and accelerated depreciation methods are examples of conservative accounting methods. On the other hand, unwarranted or excessive conservatism, while contributing to the temporary "quality" of earnings, actually results in a lack of reporting integrity over the long run and cannot be considered as a desirable factor. Quite apart from the impact that these accounting choices have on the financial statements, they also hold important clues to management's propensities and attitudes.

b. The second type of factor affecting the quality of earnings is related to the degree to which adequate provision has been made for the maintenance of assets and for the maintenance and enhancement of present and future earning power. In most enterprises, there exists considerable managerial discretion over the size of income streams, and particularly over the reported amounts of costs and expenses. Discretionary types of expenses, such as repairs and maintenance, advertising, and research and development (R&D) costs can be varied for the sole purpose of managing the level of reported net income (or loss) rather than for legitimate operating or business reasons. Here, too, the analyst's task is to identify the results of management practices and to judge its motivations.

c. The third major factor affecting the quality of earnings is not primarily a result of discretionary actions of managements, although skillful management can modify its effects. It is the effect of cyclical and other economic forces on earnings, on the stability of their sources, and particularly on their variability. Variability of earnings is generally an undesirable characteristic, and, consequently, the higher the variability the lower the quality of these earnings.

The fairly broad tolerances within which generally accepted accounting principles (GAAP) can be applied have been discussed throughout this book. A consideration of other aspects that affect earnings quality follows.

Evaluation of discretionary and future-directed costs.   Discretionary costs are outlays that managements can vary to some extent from period to period in order to conserve resources and/or to influence reported income. For this reason, they deserve the special attention of analysts who are particularly interested in knowing whether the level of expenses is in keeping with past trends and with present and future requirements.

   Maintenance and repairs. As was already discussed in the preceding chapter, management has considerable leeway in performing maintenance work and some discretion with respect to repairs. The analyst can relate these costs to the level of activity because they do logically vary with it. Two ratios are particularly useful in comparing the repair and maintenance levels from year to year:

$$\frac{\text{Repairs and maintenance}}{\text{Sales}}$$

   This ratio relates the costs of repairs and maintenance to this most available measure of activity. In the absence of sharp inventory changes, sales are a good indicator of activity. If year-to-year inventory levels change appreciably, an adjustment may be needed whereby ending inventories at approximate selling prices are added to sales, and beginning inventories, similarly adjusted, are deducted from them.

ILLUSTRATION 1. For the years 1976, 1977, 1978, 1979, and 1980, General Electric had maintenance and repairs expenses that amounted, as a percentage of sales, to 3.41 percent, 3.42 percent, 3.42 percent, 3.45 percent, and 3.14 percent, respectively. The significant decline in repair and maintenance costs as a percent of sales in 1980 deserved further analysis.

   The other ratio is:

$$\frac{\text{Repairs and maintenance}}{\substack{\text{Property, plant, and equipment (exclusive of land)} \\ \text{net of accumulated depreciation}}}$$

   It measures repair and maintenance costs in relation to the assets for which these costs are incurred. Depending on the amount of information available to the analyst, the ratio of repair and maintenance costs to specific categories of assets can be developed. It should be noted that substandard repairs and maintenance on assets may require revisions in the assumptions of useful lives for depreciation purposes.

   The absolute trend in repair and maintenance costs from year to year can be expressed in terms of index numbers and compared to those of related accounts. The basic purpose of all these measurements is to determine whether the repair and maintenance programs of the enterprise have been kept at normal and necessary levels or whether they have been changed in a way that affects the quality of income and its projection into the future.

   Advertising. Since a significant portion of advertising outlays has effects beyond the period in which it is incurred, the relationship between advertising outlays and short-term results is a tenuous one. This also means that managements can, in certain cases, cut advertising costs with no commensurate immediate effects on sales, although it can be assumed that over the longer term sales will suffer. Here again, year-to-year variations in the level of advertising expenses must be examined by the analyst with the objective of assessing their impact on future sales and consequently on the quality of reported earnings.

There are a number of ways of assessing the trend in advertising outlays. One is to convert them into trend percentages using a "normal" year as a base. These trend percentages can then be compared to the trend of sales and of gross and net profits. An alternative measure would be the ratio of

$$\frac{\text{Advertising expenses}}{\text{Sales}}$$

which, when compared over the years, would also indicate shifts in management policy.

ILLUSTRATION 2. During 1978, 1979, and 1980, Ford Motor Company's percentages of advertising costs to sales were .8 percent, 1.0 percent, and 1.6 percent respectively. In this case, far from reducing earnings quality, these costs were intended to stem declining sales and profits as well as a significant loss in 1980.

The ratio of

$$\frac{\text{Advertising}}{\text{Total selling costs}}$$

must also be examined so as to detect shifts to and from advertising to other methods of sales promotion.

An analysis of advertising to sales ratios over several years will reveal the degree of dependence of an enterprise on this promotional strategy. Comparison of this ratio with that of other companies in the industry will reveal the degree of market acceptance of products and the relative promotional efforts needed to secure it.

Research and development costs. The significance and the potential value of R&D costs are among the most difficult elements of the financial statements to analyze and interpret. Yet they are important, not only because of their relative size but even more so because of their significance for the projection of future results.

R&D costs have gained an aura of glowing potential in security analysis far beyond that warranted by actual experience. Mentioned most frequently are some of the undeniably spectacular and successful commercial applications of industrial research in the post–World War II era in such fields as chemistry, electronics, photography, and biology. Not mentioned are the vast sums spent for endeavors labeled *research* which are expensed or written off while benefits from these fall far short of the original costs.

The analyst must pay careful attention to R&D costs and to the absence of such costs. In many enterprises, they represent substantial costs, much of them fixed in nature, and they can represent the key to future success or failure. We must first draw a careful distinction between what can be quantified in this area and, consequently, analyzed in the sense in which we consider analysis in this book, and what cannot be quantified and must, consequently, be evaluated in qualitative terms.

In the area of R&D costs, the qualitative element looms large and important. The definition of what constitutes "research" is subject to wide-ranging interpretations as well as to outright distortion. The label *research* is placed on activities ranging from those of a first-class scientific organization engaged in sophisticated pure and applied research down to superficial and routine product-and-market-testing activities.

Among the many factors to be considered in the evaluation of the quality of the research effort are the caliber of the research staff and organization, the eminence of its leadership, as well as the commercial results of their research efforts. This qualitative evaluation must accompany any other kinds of analysis. Finally, a distinction must be drawn between government or outsider sponsored research and company directed research that is most closely identified with its own objectives. From the foregoing discussion it is clear that research cannot be evaluated on the basis of the amounts spent alone. Research outlays represent an expense or an investment depending on how they are applied. Far from guaranteeing results, they represent highly speculative ventures that depend on the application of extraordinary scientific as well as managerial skills for their success. Thus, spending on research cannot guarantee results and should not be equated with them.

Having considered the all-important qualitative factors on which an evaluation of R&D outlays depends, the analyst should attempt to determine as best he can how much of the current R&D outlays that have been expensed have future utility and potential.

From the point of view of the analyst, the "future potential" of R&D costs is a most important consideration. Research cost productivity can be measured by relating R&D outlays to:

1. Sales growth.
2. New product introductions.
3. Acquisition of plant and equipment (to exploit the results of research).
4. Profitability.

Another important aspect of R&D outlays is their discretionary nature. It is true that those enterprises that have established R&D departments impart a fixed nature to a segment of these costs. Nevertheless, they can be increased or curtailed at the discretion of managements, often with no immediate adverse effects on sales. Thus, from the point of view of assessing the quality of reported income, the analyst must evaluate year-to-year changes in R&D

outlays. This he can do by means of trend percentage analysis as well as by years of analysis of ratios such as the ratio of

$$\frac{\text{R\&D outlays}}{\text{Sales}}$$

A careful comparison of outlays for R&D over the years will indicate to the analyst whether the effort is a sustained one or one that varies with the ups and downs of operating results. Moreover, "one shot" research efforts lack the predictability or quality of a sustained, well-organized longer-term research program.

Other future-directed costs.   In addition to advertising and R&D, there are other types of future-directed outlays. An example of such outlays are the costs of training operating, sales, and managerial talent. Although these outlays for the development of human resources are usually expensed in the year in which they are incurred, they may have future utility, and the analyst may want to recognize this in his evaluation of current earnings and of future prospects.

Balance sheet analysis as a check on the validity and quality of reported earnings

The amounts at which the assets and liabilities of an enterprise are stated hold important clues to an assessment of both the validity as well as the quality of its earnings. Thus, the analysis of the balance sheet is an important complement to the other approaches of income analysis discussed in this chapter, and elsewhere in this book.

Importance of carrying amounts of assets.   The importance that we attach to the amounts at which assets are carried on the balance sheet is due to the fact that, with few exceptions such as cash, some investments, and land, the cost of most assets enters ultimately the cost stream of the income statement. Thus, we can state the following as a general proposition: Whenever assets are overstated, the cumulative income[1] is overstated because it has been relieved of charges needed to bring such assets down to realizable values.

It would appear that the converse of this proposition should also hold true; that is, that to the extent to which assets are understated, cumulative income is also understated. Two accounting conventions qualify this statement importantly. One is the convention of conservatism which calls for the recognition of gains only as they are actually realized. Although there has been some movement away from a strict interpretation of this convention, in general most assets are carried at original cost even though their current market or realizable value is far in excess of that cost.

---

[1] The effect on any one period cannot be the subject of generalization.

The other qualifying convention is that governing the accounting for business combinations. The pooling of interests concept allows an acquiring company to carry forward the old book values of the assets of the acquired company even though such values may be far less than current market values or the consideration given for them. Thus, the financial analyst must be aware of the fact that such an accounting will allow the recording of profits, when the values of such understated assets are realized, which represents nothing more than the surfacing of such hitherto understated assets. Since such profits have, in effect, previously been bought and paid for, they cannot be considered as representing either the earning power of the enterprise or an index of the operating performance of the enterprise's management.

Importance of provisions and liabilities. Continuing our analysis of the effect of balance sheet amounts on the measurement of income, we can enunciate the further proposition that an understatement of provisions and liabilities will result in an overstatement of cumulative income because the latter is relieved of charges required to bring the provision or the liabilities up to their proper amounts. Thus, for example, an understatement of the provision for taxes, for product warranties, or for pensions means that cumulative income is overstated.

Conversely, an overprovision for present and future liabilities or losses results in the understatement of income or in the overstatement of losses. Provisions for future costs and losses that are excessive in amount in effect represent attempts to shift the burden of costs and expenses from future income statements to that of the present.

Bearing in mind the general propositions regarding the effect on income of the amounts at which assets and liabilities are carried in the balance sheet, the critical analysis and evaluation of such amounts represent an important check on the validity of reported income.

Balance sheet analysis and the quality of earnings. There is, however, a further dimension to this kind of analysis in that it also has a bearing on an evaluation of the quality of earnings. This approach is based on the fact that various degrees of risk attach to the probability of the future realization of different types of assets.

Thus, for example, the future realization of accounts receivable has generally a higher degree of probability than has the realization of, say, inventory or unrecovered tools and dies costs. Moreover, the future realization of inventory costs can, generally, be predicted with greater certainty than can the future realization of goodwill or of deferred start-up costs. The analysis of the assets carried in the balance sheet by risk class or risk category holds clues to and is an important measure of the quality of reported income. Stated another way, if the income determination process results in the deferral of outlays and costs which carry a high degree of risk that they may not prove realizable in the future, then that income is of a lower quality than income that does not involve the recording of such high-risk assets.

Effect of valuation of specific assets on the validity and quality of reported income. In order to illustrate the importance of balance sheet analysis to an evaluation of reported income, let us now examine the effect of the valuation of specific assets on the validity and quality of that income.

Accounts receivable. The validity of the sales figure depends on the proper valuation of the accounts receivable that result from it. This valuation must recognize the risk of default in payment as well as the time value of money. On the latter score, *APB Opinion 21* provides that if the receivable does not arise from transactions with customers or suppliers in the normal course of business under terms not exceeding a year, then, except for some other stated exceptions, it must be valued using the interest rate applicable to similar debt instruments. Thus, if the receivable bears an interest rate of 8 percent while similar receivables would, at the time, be expected to bear an interest rate of 12 percent, both the receivable and the sale from which it arose would be restated at the lower discounted amount.

The relative level of accounts receivable and its relationship to sales can hold clues to income quality. If an increase in accounts receivable represents merely a shifting of inventory from the company to its customers because of aggressive sales promotion or costly incentives, then these sales accomplish nothing more than "borrowing from the future" and thus reduce earnings quality.

Inventories. Overstated inventories lead to overstated profits. Overstatements can occur due to errors in quantities, errors in costing and pricing, or errors in the valuation of work in process. The more technical the product and the more dependent the valuation is on internally developed cost records, the more vulnerable are the cost estimates to error and misstatement. The basic problem here arises when costs that should have been written off to expense are retained in the inventory accounts.

An understatement of inventories results from a charge-off to income of costs that possess future utility and that should be inventoried. Such an understatement of inventories results in the understatement of current income and the overstatement of future income.

Deferred charges. Deferred charges such as deferred tooling or start-up and preoperating costs must be scrutinized carefully because their value depends, perhaps more than that of other assets, on estimates of future probabilities and developments. Experience has shown that often such estimates have proven overoptimistic or that they did not contain sufficient provisions for future contingencies. Thus, the risk of failure to attain expectations is relatively higher here than in the case of other assets.

The effect of external factors on the quality of earnings. The concept of earnings quality is so broad that it encompasses many additional factors that, in the eyes of analysts, can make earnings more reliable or more desirable.

The effect of changing price levels on the measurement of earnings is a factor here. In times of rising price levels, the inclusion of "inventory profits" or the understatement of expenses such as depreciation lowers in effect the reliability of earnings and hence their quality.

The quality of foreign earnings is affected by factors such as difficulties and uncertainties regarding the repatriation of funds, currency fluctuations, the political and social climate as well as local customs and regulation. With regard to the latter, the inability to dismiss personnel in some countries in effect converts labor costs into fixed costs.

Regulation provides another example of external factors that can affect earnings quality. The "regulatory environment" of a public utility affects the "quality" of its earnings. Thus, an unsympathetic or even hostile regulatory environment that causes serious lags in the obtaining of rate relief will detract from earnings quality because of uncertainty about the adequacy of future revenues.

The stability and reliability of earnings sources affect earnings quality. Defense related revenues can be regarded as nonrecurring in time of war and affected by political uncertainties in peacetime.

Finally, some analysts regard complexity of operations and difficulties in their analysis (e.g., of conglomerates) as negative factors.

EVALUATION OF THE EARNINGS LEVEL AND TREND

The analyst will concentrate on identifying those elements in the income and cost streams that exhibit stability, proven relationships, and predictability, and will separate them from those elements that are random, erratic, or nonrecurring and that, consequently, do not possess the elements of stability required for a reasonably reliable forecast or for inclusion in an "earning power" computation.

The analyst must be on his guard against the well-known tendency of managements to practice income smoothing, thus trying to give to the income and expense streams a semblance of stability that in reality they do not possess. This is usually done in the name of "removing distortions" from the results of operations, whereas what is really achieved is the masking of the natural and cyclical irregularities that are part of the reality of the enterprise's experience and with which reality it is the analyst's primary task to come to grips.

Factors affecting the level of earnings

We have, so far, discussed the *qualitative* factors that may cause the analyst either to adjust the earnings number of a given period (generally, a year) or to adjust the valuation (e.g., the price-earnings multiple) accorded such earnings.

The next step in the determination of the *level* of earnings of a given period is to recast the published income statements in such a way that the stable, normal, and continuing elements in the income statement are separated and distinguished from random, erratic, unusual or nonrecurring elements that require separate analytical treatment or consideration. Moreover, such recasting also aims at identifying those elements included in the income statement of a given period that should more properly be included in the operating results of one or more prior periods.

The analytical, recasting, and adjustment of income statements

The income statement along with all other financial statements and data contained in management's report represent the logical starting point of the analysis. It is clear that reported income is but the *starting point* of analysis and that from the point of view of the intelligent analyst, the most desirable income statement is the one containing a maximum of meaningful disclosure rather than one containing built-in interpretations that channel him to specific conclusions.

Over the years, notable shifts have occurred in the thinking of the accounting profession regarding the function of the income statement. An early position was that items of gain or loss should be included or excluded from income on the basis of the accountant's interpretation of what "normal operations" are. This position has resulted in much controversy and criticism to the point where the profession has adopted the "clean surplus" approach of including *all*[2] items of gain and loss in the income of the period in which they occur and, with few exceptions, such as corrections of errors, has also taken a position against the restatement of prior period results.

Major sources of information. As a consequence, the analyst will find data needed for the analysis of the results of operations and for their recasting and adjustment in:

1. The income statement which is generally subdivided into the following:

    Income from continuing operations.
    Income from discontinued operations (which includes gain or loss from disposal).
    Extraordinary gains and losses.
    Cumulative effect of changes in accounting principles.

2. The other financial statements and the footnotes thereto.

---

[2] It should be noted that a departure from this position occurred in *SFAS 52* where, with few exceptions, gains and losses on the translation of foreign currency financial statements of subsidiaries bypass income and are accumulated in a separate stockholders' equity account. To a more limited extent, *SFAS 12* also represented such a departure.

3. Management's comments found throughout its published report.
4. "Management's Discussion and Analysis of Financial Condition and Results of Operations" as required by the SEC's 1980 revised disclosure system (see also Chapter 7).

The analyst may also find "unusual" items segregated within the income statement (generally on a pretax basis), but their disclosure is optional. Such disclosure may not include items that the analyst may regard as significant, noteworthy, or unusual; and, consequently, the analyst will consult all the above-mentioned sources as well as management, if possible, in order to obtain the needed facts. These will include facts that affect the comparability and the interpretation of income statements, such as product-mix changes, production innovations, strikes, and raw material shortages that may or may not be included in management's mandatory discussion and analysis of the results of operations.

The recasting and adjusting procedure

Once the analyst has secured as much information as it is possible to obtain, the income statements of a number of years (generally at least five) should be recast and adjusted in such a way as to facilitate their further analysis to evaluate the trend of earnings as well as to aid in determining the average earning power of the enterprise for the period. While this procedure can be accomplished in one statement, it is simpler and clearer to subdivide it into two distinct steps: (1) recasting and (2) adjusting.

The recasting process. The recasting process aims at a rearranging of the items within the income statement in such a way so as to provide the most meaningful detail and the most relevant format needed by the analyst. At this stage, the individual items in the income statement may be rearranged, subdivided, or tax effected, but the total must reconcile to the net income of each period as reported.

The analytical reclassification of items *within* a period will help in the evaluation of the earnings level. Thus, discretionary and other noteworthy expenses should be segregated. The same applies to net items such as equity in income or loss of unconsolidated subsidiaries or associated companies, which are usually shown net of tax. Items shown in the pretax category must be removed *together* with their tax effect if they are to be shown below normal "income from continuing operations."

Expanded tax disclosure enables the financial analyst to segregate factors that reduce taxes as well as those that increase them, thus enabling an analysis of the degree to which these factors are of a recurring nature. All material permanent differences and credits, such as the investment tax credit, should be included. The analytical procedure involves computing taxes at the statutory rate (currently 46 percent) and deducting tax benefits such as arising

Exhibit 9–1

ALFA, INC.
Analytically Recast Income Statements for 19x2–19x6
(in thousands)

	Item reference no.	19x6	19x5	19x4	19x3	19x2
Revenues (a)	[1]	$1,251,020	$1,134,104	$1,145,362	$881,368	$695,900
Costs and expenses:						
Cost of sales (b)	[2]	820,441	712,650	677,665	561,228	435,088
Selling, general, and administrative expenses (c)	[3]	325,575	280,946	271,606	228,029	186,742
Depreciation and amortization (d)	[4]	24,214	21,158	25,157	17,781	12,598
Maintenance and repairs (b)	[77]	19,602	17,630	13,412	8,120	6,770
Advertising (c)	[78]	16,006	14,055	12,413	9,611	8,668
Research and development costs (c)	[79]	1,442	1,892	1,291	1,317	1,261
Net deferral (amortization) of pre-opening expense and initial losses of new department stores and hotels (d)	[80]			(3,149)	(808)	1,800
Interest expense	[5]	18,504	16,319	25,054	18,859	11,092
Interest capitalized	[6]	(64)	—	(3,267)	(1,287)	(463)
Total costs and expenses	[7]	1,225,720	1,064,650	1,020,182	842,850	663,556
Income before taxes		25,300	69,454	125,180	38,518	32,344
Taxes at 48% (before items marked (e) below)		12,144	33,338	60,086	18,489	15,525
Income from continuing operations		13,156	36,116	65,094	20,029	16,819
Benefit for income taxable at capital gains rate (e)	[84]	782	818	1,610	3,115	2,670
Investment tax credit (e)	[90]	4,311	2,734	1,618	1,483	1,898
State income taxes (e)	[88]	(1,540)	(6,300)	(11,290)	(1,390)	(1,319)
Tax benefit equal to 48% of state income taxes above* (e)		740	3,024	5,419	666	632

Other tax adjustments—net [e]	86	284	(76)	(1,352)	508	334
Equity in earnings or (loss) of unconsolidated subsidiaries [a]†		35	(149)	1,001	(505)	(490)
Net income of nonconsolidated finance subsidiaries‡	11	1,371	2,329	2,068	3,609	3,095
Income (loss) from discontinued operations	13	—	(1,000)	(7,325)	(957)	657
Cumulative effect on prior years of accounting changes	15	—	(17,407)	—	—	—
Net income as reported	16	$ 19,139	$ 20,089	$ 56,843	$ 26,558	$ 24,296

* Note 7 shows the computed federal tax at statutory rate net of tax benefit on state income tax expense—for example, the $11,437 (item 83) federal tax at statutory rate for 19x6 is computed as follows: 48 percent of $25,368 (pretax income as per income statement) = $12,177 − $740 (48 percent of $1,540 state income tax expense) = $11,437.

† Net of tax of 48 percent (this rate may or may not be applicable). In 19x6, 52 percent of $68 = $35, and in 19x5, 52 percent of $287 loss or $149—see note (a) below. Note, however, that a good case can also be made for the assumption that the equity in earnings of other unconsolidated subsidiaries is stated after tax (e.g., $68 in 19x6) and consequently revenues include the pretax amount, i.e., 68 ÷ .52 or 131.

‡ Note that these are shown net of income taxes in the income statement.

(a) Equity in earnings of unconsolidated subsidiaries (item 44) consists of net income of nonconsolidated finance subsidiaries (item 11) shown separately net of tax *and* equity in income or loss of other nonconsolidated domestic subsidiaries (see also Note 5) which is assumed to be included in revenues (item 1). In 19x6, for example, the latter was derived by deducting $1,371 (item 11) from $1,439 (item 44) to get $68 as equity in income of other nonconsolidated domestic subsidiaries, which figure is deducted from revenues (item 1) and included, net of tax, in the lower part of the recast statement so as to be highlighted separately. A similar process of derivation for 19x5 determined that the equity in *loss* of other nonconsolidated subsidiaries was $287 ($2,329 − $2,042). Analysis revealed that no dividends were received from unconsolidated subsidiaries in 19x6 and none were assumed to have been received in preceding years.

(b) Maintenance and repairs (item 77) was deducted from cost of sales so that it can be shown separately for analytical purposes.

(c) Selling, general, and administrative expenses were reduced by advertising (item 78) and research and development costs (item 79) which are highlighted separately.

(d) Net deferral (amortization) of pre-opening expense and initial losses of new department stores and hotels (see Note 6) excluded from normal depreciation and amortization on continuing operations and shown separately.

(e) All items marked (e) below income from continuing operations modify the federal tax, at the statutory 48 percent rate, on pretax income from continuing operations and are shown separately for analytical purposes (they are disclosed in Note 7).

Other comments:

Per Note 2, Alfa's net income for 19x4 was reduced by $7,634 because of changes to preferable accounting methods in two areas: a switch to LIFO in the Lamb-Weston Division (reducing income by $6,112) and a switch from deferral to current expensing of preoperating expenses of new department stores and hotels (reducing income by $1,522). The specific income statement categories affected by these changes are not disclosed.

from investment tax credits, capital gains rates, tax-free income, or lower foreign tax rates, and adding factors such as additional foreign taxes, nontax-deductible expenses, and state and local taxes (net of federal tax benefit). Immaterial items may be considered in one lump sum labeled "other."

Analytically recast income statements will contain as much detail as is needed for analysis and are supplemented by explanatory footnotes. Exhibit 9–1 presents the analytically recast income statements of Alfa, Inc., which are annotated with key numbers for ease of reference to the financial statements of Alfa found in Appendix 2B.

The adjustment process

Based on data developed in the recast income statements as well as on other available information, certain items of income or loss are to be assigned by the analyst to the period to which they most properly belong.

The reassignment of extraordinary items or unusual items (net of tax) to other years must be done with care. Thus, the income tax benefit of the carry-forward of operating losses should generally be moved to the year in which the loss occurred. The costs or benefits from the settlement of a lawsuit may relate to one or more preceding years. The gain or loss on disposal of discontinued operations will usually relate to the results of operations over a number of years.

If possible, all years under analysis should be placed on a comparable basis when a change in accounting principle or accounting estimate occurs. If, as is usually the case, the *new* accounting principle is the desirable one, prior years should, if possible, be restated to the new method, or a notation made regarding a lack of comparability in certain respects. This procedure will result in a redistribution of the "cumulative effect of change in accounting principle" to affected prior years. Changes in estimates can be accounted for only prospectively and GAAP prohibit prior year restatements except in specified cases. The analyst's ability to place all years on a comparable basis will depend on availability of information.

Before the trend in earnings can be evaluated it is necessary to obtain the best approximation possible of the adjusted earnings *level* of each year. All items in the income statement must be considered, and none can be excluded or "dropped by the wayside." Thus, if it is decided that an item in the income statement does not properly belong in the year in which it appears, it may be either:

1. Shifted (net of tax) to the result of another year or a number of other years, or
2. If it cannot be identified with another specific year or years, it should be included in the *average* earnings of the period under analysis. While the averaging process helps in the determination of average earning power, it is not helpful in the determination of earnings trend.

It must be realized that moving an item of gain or loss to another year or recording one's inability to assign an item to the proper year does not remedy the fact that the results of some prior year(s) have been misstated. For example, a damage award in one year for patent infringement means that prior years had suffered from lost sales or similar damage.

Exhibit 9–2 presents the analytically adjusted income statements of Alfa, Inc.

Determining the trend of income over the years

Having determined the size of a company's basic earnings as well as the factors that require adjustment before those earnings can be used as a basis for forecasts, the analyst will next determine the variability of these earnings, that is, changes in their size over the business cycle and over the longer term.

Evaluation of earnings variability.   Earnings that fluctuate up and down with the business cycle are less desirable than earnings that display a larger degree of stability over such a cycle. The basic reason for this is that fluctuating earnings cause fluctuations in market prices. Earnings that display a steady growth trend are of the most desirable type. In the evaluation of earnings, the intelligent analyst realizes the limitations to which the earnings figure of any one year is subject. Therefore, depending on his specific purposes, he will consider the following earnings figures as improvements over the single-year figure:

1. *Average earnings* over periods, such as 5 to 10 years, smooth out erratic and even extraordinary factors as well as cyclical influences, thus presenting a better and more reliable measure of "earning power" of an enterprise.
2. *Minimum earnings* are useful in decisions, such as those bearing on credit extension, which are particularly sensitive to risk factors. They indicate the worst that could happen during a complete business cycle, based on recent experience.

The importance of earnings trends.   In addition to the use of single, average, or minimum earnings figures, the analyst must be alert to earnings trends. These are best evaluated by means of trend statements such as those presented on page 83. The relevant earnings numbers to be included in the trend analysis will be derived from adjusted income statements as exemplified in Exhibit 8–2. The earnings trend contains important clues to the nature of the enterprise (i.e., cyclical, growth, defensive) and the quality of its management.

Distortions of trends.   Analysts must be alert to accounting distortions that affect trends. Among the most important are changes in accounting principles and the effect of business combinations, particularly purchases. These must be adjusted for.

Exhibit 9–2

ALFA, INC.
Analytically Adjusted Income Statements for 19x2–19x6
(in thousands) (Dr.) Cr. [a]

	Total	19x6	19x5	19x4	19x3	19x2
Net income as reported	$146,925	$19,139	$20,089	$56,843	$26,558	$24,296
Assignment of cumulative effect of accounting change to prior years (Dr.) Cr. [b]			17,407	(15,367)	(2,040)	
Anticipated losses on phaseout of Wilhelm Foods Division [c]			1,083	884		
Losses expected in liquidation of mobile home parks, etc. [c]				1,853		
Gains from sale of food processing plant [d]					(2,100)	
Gains from sale of surplus property [e]					(1,824)	(1,573)
Adjusted net income for individual years [f]		$19,139	$38,579	$44,213	$20,594	$22,723
Total net income for period [g]	$146,925					
Average earnings for period [g]	$ 29,385					

[a] The Dr. and Cr. framework is very useful in keeping track of the direction of adjustments. Here we start with net income figures that are all credits. Since a debit adjustment will reduce the amount of net income, it is convenient to show the debit adjustments in parenthesis. For example, the gain from sale of food processing plant of $2,100 is removed from net income of 19x3 by a debit adjustment.

(b) This adjustment is based on information obtained from pro forma amounts (item 20) which shows net income after giving *retroactive* effect to accounting changes:

	19x5	19x4	19x3
Pro forma net income 20	$37,496	$ 41,476	$ 24,518
Net income as reported 16	20,089	56,843	26,558
Difference	$17,407	$(15,367)	$ (2,040)

Thus, of the cumulative change of $17,407 made in 19x5, $15,367 belonged to 19x4 and $2,040 to 19x3.

(c) Note 3 (item 73) contains information on various discontinued operations. Gains and losses on disposition of discontinued operations usually relate to operating performance over a number of years, but rarely does the analyst have enough information to assign these to specific periods. Thus, while we remove these losses from the results of the year in which they occurred, we cannot assign them to other specific periods. We distinguish gains or losses on *disposition* from the *operating* losses of discontinued divisions before and during the phaseout period, which while significant for purposes of estimating future results are not removed from the year in which they occur for purposes of trend analysis. The figures given in Alfa's income statement (item 13) aggregate both kinds of losses.

Since the provisions for anticipated losses of Wilhelm Foods are stated before tax, we convert them to an aftertax basis by multiplying them by (1 − Tax rate). Thus, in 19x5, $2,083 × .52 = $1,083; in 19x4, $1,700 × .52 = $884. Information on losses on mobile parks is provided net of tax. This, as well as the other two adjustments discussed in notes *(d)* and *(e)* below, while modifying the results of individual years for trend evaluation purposes are incorporated for purposes of computing average earnings for the five-year period which must include *all* gains and losses experienced by the enterprise.

(d) and *(e)* These gains reported in Note 3 are removed from (debited to) the net income of the respective years.

(f) Because adjustments *(c)*, *(d)*, and *(e)* have been made to individual years only, the adjusted net income figures, which are used for trend analysis, do not add up to the total income for the period. Analysts must also consider the effect of business acquisitions on earning trends. Acquisitions accounted for as poolings of interest are restated while those accounted for as purchases include results from date of acquisition.

(g) The average earnings for the period include all items of gain or loss incurred during the period, and except for most unusual circumstances, they represent the average earnings power experienced by the enterprise during this period.

Some of the most common and most pervasive manipulative practices in accounting are designed to affect the presentation of earnings trends. These manipulations are based on the assumptions, generally true, that the trend of income is more important than its absolute size; that retroactive revisions of income already reported in prior periods have little, if any, market effect on security prices;[3] and that once a company has incurred a loss, the size of the loss is not as significant as the fact that the loss has been incurred.

These assumptions and the propensities of some managements to use accounting as a means of improving the appearance of the earnings trend has led to techniques that can be broadly described as income smoothing.

Income smoothing and income distortion

A number of requirements must be met by the income-smoothing process so as to distinguish it from outright falsehoods and distortions.

The income-smoothing process is a rather sophisticated and insidious device. It does not rely on outright or patent falsehoods and distortions but rather uses the wide leeway existing in alternatively acceptable accounting principles and their interpretation in order to achieve its ends. Thus, income smoothing is performed within the framework of GAAP. It is a matter of form rather than one of substance. Consequently, it does not involve a real transaction (e.g., postponing an actual sale to another accounting period in order to shift revenue) but only a redistribution of credits or charges among periods. The general objective is to moderate income variability over the years by shifting income from good years to bad years, by shifting future income to the present (in most cases presently reported earnings are more valuable than those reported at some future date), or vice versa. Similarly, income variability can be moderated or modified by the shifting of costs, expenses, or losses from one period to another.

Income smoothing may take many forms. Hereunder are listed some forms of smoothing to which the analyst should be particularly alert:

1. Changing accounting methods or assumptions with the objective of improving or modifying reported results. For example, to offset the effect on earnings of slumping sales and of other difficulties, Chrysler Corporation revised upwards the assumed rate of return on its pension portfolio, thus increasing income significantly. Similarly, in 1980, Union Carbide improved results by switching to a number of more liberal accounting alternatives.

2. Misstatements, by various methods, of inventories as a means of redistributing income among the years. The Londontown Manufacturing Com-

---

[3] This was recognized by *APB Opinion 20* and later *SFAS 16,* which, with but two exceptions, forbid the retroactive restatement of prior year financial statements.

pany case provides a classic example of such practices.[4] Some of these practices are outside the framework allowed by GAAP.

3. The offsetting of extraordinary credits by identical or nearly identical extraordinary charges as a means of removing an unusual or sudden injection of income that may interfere with the display of a growing earnings trend.

4. The provision of reserves for future costs and losses as a means of increasing the adverse results of what is already a poor year and utilizing such reserves to relieve future years of charges against income that would otherwise be properly chargeable against it. (Abuses in this area have been curtailed by *SFAS 5*.)

5. The substantial write-downs of operating assets (such as plant and equipment) or of intangibles (such as goodwill) in times of economic slowdown when operating results are already poor. The reason usually given for such write-downs is that carrying the properties at book value cannot be economically justified. (For example, Cudahy Packing Company has effected such a write-down of plant but had to reverse it in a subsequent year.) Particularly unwarranted is the practice of writing down operating assets to the point at which a target return on investment (which management thinks it *should* earn) is realized.

6. Timing the inclusion of revenues and costs in periodic income in such a way as to influence the overall trend of income (or loss) over the years. (Examples are the timing of sales or other disposition of property, incurring and expensing of discretionary costs such as R&D, advertising, maintenance, etc.) This category, unlike most others, entails more than accounting choice in that it may involve the timing of actual business transactions. Thus, in recent years, Franklin Mint inflated sales and income by accelerating shipments to customers ahead of a schedule called for by customer subscription terms and booking these as sales immediately.

Income smoothing and income distortion—some implications for analysis

There are powerful factors and incentives at work that motivate companies and their employees to engage in income smoothing.

Companies in financial difficulties may be motivated to engage in such practices for what they see and justify as their battle for survival. Successful companies will go to great lengths to uphold a hard-earned and well-rewarded image of earnings growth by smoothing those earnings artificially. Moreover, compensation plans or other incentives based on earnings will motivate man-

---

[4] Details can be found in an SEC decision issued October 31, 1963 (41 SEC 676–688).

agements to accelerate the recognition of income by anticipating revenues or deferring expenses.

THE H. J. HEINZ COMPANY CASE.   The recent case of H. J. Heinz Company has shown that even second-tier divisional executives, motivated by self-interest in meeting earnings targets and in smoothing earnings, can without the knowledge of top management engage in income manipulation. In this case, "hidden reserves" were created during 1971 to 1978 by prepaying for services not yet received, such as advertising, and by the improper recording of sales.

THE J. W. T. GROUP, INC., CASE.   This case, first brought to light in 1982, did not seem to involve a desire for personal gain but is rather a case of falsifying records in order to make the syndication department look good by meeting its goals.

The department purchased programming from independent producers and bartered the programs to television stations in return for future commercial time that was in turn used to build "time banks" for sale to agency clients. The accounting deception involved the creation of fictitious time banks, fictitious clients, and fictitious revenues over a period of four years. So successful was the computerized deception that for a time, management invested additional capital in the division lured by the substantial, if fictitious, returns it appeared to earn.

Analysts must appreciate the great variety of incentives and objectives that lead managements and, at times, second-tier management without the knowledge of top management, to engage in practices ranging from smoothing to the outright falsification of income.

The smoothing of earnings is often achieved by first understating reported earnings. Thus, in the 1970s, Firestone Tire and Rubber Company engaged in the practice of hiding income in secret accounts for the purpose of drawing on these during leaner years.

Some serious academicians have suggested that smoothing is justified if it can help a company report earnings closer to its true "earning power" level. Such is not the function of financial reporting. As we have repeatedly seen in this book, the analyst will be best served by a full disclosure of periodic results and the components that comprise them. It is up to the analyst to average, smooth, or otherwise adjust reported earnings in accordance with specific analytical purposes.

The accounting profession has earnestly tried to promulgate rules that discourage practices such as the smoothing of earnings. However, given the above mentioned powerful propensities of companies and of their owners and employees to engage in such practices, analysts must realize that where there is a will to smooth or even distort earnings, ways to do so are available and will be found. Consequently, particularly in the case of companies where incentives to smooth are likely to be present, analysts should analyze and scrutinize accounting practices in order to satisfy themselves to the extent possible, regarding the integrity of the income reporting process.

Extraordinary gains and losses

The evaluation of current earnings levels, the determination of earnings trends as well as the projection of future earnings rely importantly on the separation of the stable elements of income and expense from those that are random, nonrecurring, and erratic in nature.

Stability and sustainability are important characteristics that enter significantly into the determination of earning power. Moreover, in making earnings projections, the forecaster relies also on repetitiveness of occurrence. Thus, in order to separate the relatively stable elements of income and expense of an enterprise from those that are random or erratic in nature, it is important, as a first step, to identify those gains and losses that are nonrecurring and unusual as well as those that are truly extraordinary.

This separation is a first step that is mostly preparatory in nature. Following it is a process of judgment and analysis that aims at determining how such nonrecurring, unusual, or truly extraordinary items should be treated in the evaluation of present income, and of management performance as well as in the projection of future results.

Significance of accounting treatment and presentation. The value of any accounting treatment and presentation is largely dependent on its usefulness to those who make decisions on the basis of financial statements. Unfortunately, particularly in the area of the accounting for, and the presentation of, extraordinary gains and losses, the usefulness of this accounting has been impaired because of the great importance attached to it by those who report the results of operations and who are judged by them.

The accounting for, and the presentation of, extraordinary gains and losses has always been subject to controversy. Whatever the merits of the theoretical debate surrounding this issue, the fact remains that one of the basic reasons for the controversial nature of this topic is reporting management's great interest in it. Managements are almost always concerned with the amount of net results of the enterprise as well as with the manner in which these periodic results are reported. This concern is reinforced by a widespread belief that most investors and traders accept the reported net income figures, as well as the modifying explanations that accompany them, as true indexes of performance. Thus, extraordinary gains and losses often become the means by which managements attempt to modify the reported operating results and the means by which they try to explain these results. Quite often these explanations are subjective and are designed to achieve the impact and impression desired by management.

The accounting profession has tacitly, if not openly, recognized the role that the foregoing considerations play in the actual practice of reporting extraordinary gains and losses. The profession's most recent pronouncement on this subject has at least ensured a fuller measure of disclosure of extraordinary gains and losses and their inclusion in the income statement. This represents an improvement over prior pronouncements that, in an attempt to arrive at a "true" index of operating performance, sanctioned the exclusion of certain extraordinary gains and losses from the income statement.

Analysis and evaluation.   The basic objectives in the identification and evaluation of extraordinary items by the analyst are:

1. To determine whether a particular item is to be considered "extraordinary" for purposes of analysis, that is, whether it is so unusual, nonoperating, and nonrecurring in nature that it requires special adjustment in the evaluation of current earnings levels and of future earning possibilities.
2. To decide what form the adjustment for items that are considered as "extraordinary" in nature should take.

Determining whether an item of gain or loss is extraordinary.   The infirmities and shortcomings of present practice as well as the considerations which motivate it, lead to the inescapable conclusion that the analyst must arrive at his own evaluation of whether a gain or loss should be considered as extraordinary, and if so, how to adjust for it.

In arriving at this decision, it is useful to subdivide items, commonly classified as unusual or extraordinary, into three basic categories:

a.   Nonrecurring operating gains or losses.   By "operating" we usually identify items connected with the normal and usual operations of the business. The concept of normal operations is more widely used than understood and is far from clear and well defined. Thus, in a company operating a machine shop, operating expenses would be considered as those associated with the work of the machine shop. The proceeds from a sale above cost of marketable securities held by the company as an investment of excess cash would be considered a nonoperating gain. So would the gain (or loss) on the sale of a lathe, even if it were disposed of in order to make room for one that would increase the productivity of the shop.

The concept of recurrence is one of frequency. There are no predetermined generally accepted boundaries separating the recurring event from the nonrecurring. An event (which in this context embraces a gain or loss) occurring once a year can be definitely classified as "recurring." An event, the occurrence of which is unpredictable and which in the past has either not occurred or occurred very infrequently, may be classified as nonrecurring. On the other hand, an event that occurs infrequently but whose occurrence is predictable raises some question as to its designation. An example of the latter would be the relining of blast furnaces. They last for many years; while their replacement is infrequent, the need for it is predictable. Some companies provide for their replacement by means of a reserve. Casualties do not, however, accrue in similar fashion.

Nonrecurring operating gains or losses are, then, gains or losses connected with or related to operations that recur infrequently and/or unpredictably.

In considering how to treat nonrecurring, operating gains and losses, the analyst would do best to recognize the fact of inherent abnormality and the lack of a recurring annual pattern in business and treat them as belonging to the results of the period in which they are reported.

We must also address ourselves to the question of what should be considered as "normal operations." Thus, it is a bakery's purpose to bake bread, rolls, and cakes, but it is presumably outside its normal purpose to buy and sell marketable securities for gain or loss, or even to sell baking machinery that is to be replaced for the purpose of more efficient baking.

This narrow interpretation of the objectives of a business has undergone considerable revision in modern financial theory. Thus, rather than the "baking bread" or any other specific objective, the main objective and task of management is viewed as that of increasing the capital of the owners, or expressed differently, the enhancing of the value of the common stock. This, according to modern financial theory, can be accomplished by means of the judicious combination of an optimal financing plan and any mix of operations opportunities that may be available to achieve the desired purpose.

The analyst should not be bound by the accountant's concept of "normal operations," and thus he can usefully treat a much wider range of gains and losses as being derived from "operations." This approach reinforces our conclusion that from the point of view of analysis, most nonrecurring, *operating* gains and losses should be considered part of the operating results of the year in which they occur.

This approach is offered as a general guideline rather than as a mechanical rule. After examination of all attendant circumstances, the analyst may conclude that some such items require separation from the results of a single year. The relative size of an item could conceivably be a factor requiring such treatment. In this case, the best approach is to emphasize *average earnings* experience over, say, five years rather than the result of a single year. This approach of emphasizing average earnings becomes almost imperative in the case of enterprises that have widely fluctuating amounts of nonrecurring and other extraordinary items included in their results. After all, a single year is too short and too arbitrary a period on the basis of which to evaluate the earnings power of an enterprise or the prospects for future results. Moreover, we are all familiar with enterprises that defer expenses and postpone losses and come up periodically with a loss year that cancels out much of the income reported in preceding years.

   b. Recurring nonoperating gains or losses. This category includes items of a nonoperating nature that recur with some frequency. An example would be the recurring amortization of a "bargain purchase credit." Other possible examples are interest income and the rental received from employees who rent company-owned houses.

While items in this category may be classified as unusual in published financial statements, the narrow definition of *nonoperating* which they involve as well as their recurrent nature are good reasons why they should not be excluded from current results by the analyst. They are, after all, mostly the result of the conscious employment of capital by the enterprise, and their recurrence requires inclusion of these gains or losses in estimates designed to project future results.

    c. Nonrecurring nonoperating gains or losses. Of the three categories, this one possesses the greatest degree of "abnormality." Not only are the events here nonrepetitive and unpredictable, but they do not fall within the sphere of normal operations. In most cases, these events are extraneous, unintended, and unplanned. However, they can rarely be said to be totally unexpected. Business is ever subject to the risk of sudden adverse events and to random shocks, be they natural or man-made. In the same manner, business transactions are also subject to unexpected windfalls. One good example in this category is the loss from damage done by the crash of an aircraft on a plant not located in the vicinity of an airport. Other, but less clear-cut, examples in this category may also include:

1.   Substantial uninsured casualty losses that are not within the categories of risk to which the enterprise can reasonably be deemed to be subject.
2.   The expropriation by a foreign government of an entire operation owned by the enterprise.
3.   The seizure or destruction of property as a result of an act of war, insurrection, or civil disorders, in areas where this is totally unexpected.

    It can be seen readily that while the above occurrences are, in most cases, of a nonrecurring nature, their relation to the operations of a business varies. All are occurrences in the regular course of business. Even the assets destroyed by acts of God were acquired for operating purposes and thus were subject to all possible risks.

    Of the three categories, the third comes closest to meeting the criterion of being "extraordinary." Nevertheless, truly unique events are very rare. What looks at the time as unique may in the light of experience turn out to be the symptom of new sets of circumstances that affect and may continue to affect the earning power as well as the degree of risk to which an enterprise is subject.

    The analyst must bear in mind such possibilities, but barring evidence to the contrary, items in this category can be regarded as extraordinary in nature and thus can be omitted from the results of operations of a *single* year. They are, nevertheless, part of the longer-term record of results of the enterprise. Thus, they enter the computation of *average earnings,* and the propensity of the enterprise to incur such gains or losses must be considered in the projection of future average earnings.

    The foregoing discussion has tried to point out that the intelligent classification of extraordinary items provides a workable solution to their treatment by the analyst. There are, however, other aspects of the evaluation of extraordinary items that must be considered here. One is the effect of extraordinary items on the resources of an enterprise; the other is their effect on the evaluation of management performance.

Effect of extraordinary items on enterprise resources. Every extraordinary gain or loss has a dual aspect. In addition to recording a gain (whether extraordinary or not), a business records an increase in resources. Similarly, a loss results in a reduction of resources. Since return on investment (ROI) measures the relationship of net income to resources, the incurrence of extraordinary gains and losses will affect this important measure of profitability. The more material the extraordinary item, the more significant that influence will be. In other words, if earnings and events are to be used to make estimates about the future, then extraordinary items convey something more than past performance. Thus, if an extraordinary loss results in the destruction of capital on which a certain return is expected, that return may be lost to the future. Conversely, an extraordinary gain will result in an addition of resources on which a future return can be expected.

This means that in projecting profitability and return on investment, the analyst must take into account the effect of recorded "extraordinary" items as well as the likelihood of the occurrence of future events that may cause extraordinary items.

Effect on evaluation of management. One implication frequently associated with the reporting of extraordinary gains and losses is that they have not resulted from a "normal" or "planned" activity of management and that, consequently, they should not be used in the evaluation of management performance. The analyst should seriously question such a conclusion.

What is "normal activity" in relation to management's deliberate actions? Whether we talk about the purchase or sale of securities, of other assets not used in operations, or of divisions and subsidiaries that definitely relate to operations, we talk about actions deliberately taken by management with specific purposes in mind. Such actions require, if anything, more consideration or deliberation than do ordinary everyday operating decisions because they are most often unusual in nature and involve substantial amounts of money. They are true tests of management ability. The results of such activities always qualify or enhance the results of "normal" operations, thus yielding the final net results.

Similarly, management must be aware of the risk of natural or manmade disasters or impediments in the course of business. The decision to engage in foreign operations is made with the knowledge of the special risks that this involves and the decision to insure or not is a normal operating decision. Nothing can really be termed completely unexpected or unforeseeable. Management does not engage, or is at least not supposed to engage, in any activity unconsciously; hence, whatever it does is clearly within the expected activity of a business. Every type of enterprise is subject to specific risks that are inherent in it, and managements do not enter such ventures blindly.

When it comes to the assessment of results that count and results that build or destroy value, the distinction of what is normal and what is not fades almost into insignificance. Management's beliefs about the quality of its decisions are nearly always related to the normalcy, or lack thereof, of surrounding circumstances. This can be clearly seen in the management report section of many annual reports. Of course, management has to take more time to explain failure or shortcomings than to explain success. Success hardly needs an explanation, unless it involves circumstances not likely to be repeated. Failure often evokes long explanations, and more often than not, unusual or unforeseeable circumstances are blamed for it. If only normal conditions had prevailed, everything would have been much better. But in a competitive economy, normal conditions hardly ever prevail for any length of time. Management is paid to anticipate and expect the unusual. No alibis are permitted. Explanations are never a substitute for performance.

THE FORECASTING OF EARNINGS

A major objective of income analysis is the forecasting of income. From an analytical point of view, the evaluation of the level of earnings is closely related to their forecast. This is so because a valid forecast of earnings involves an analysis of each major component of income and a considered estimate of its probable future size. Thus, some of the considerations discussed above are also applicable to earnings forcasting.

Forecasting must be differentiated from extrapolation. The latter is based on an assumption of the continuation of an existing trend and involves, more or less, a mechanical extension of that trend into the uncharted territory of the future.

Forecasting, on the other hand, is based on a careful analysis of as many individual components of income and expense as is possible and a considered estimate of their future size taking into consideration interrelationships among the components as well as probable future conditions. Thus, forecasting requires as much detail as is possible to obtain. In addition, the "stability" of the individual components must be assessed in terms of the likelihood of their future recurrence. This lends particular importance to the analysis of nonrecurring factors and of extraordinary items. Some of the mechanics of earnings forecasting were considered in Chapter 4 as part of the process of projecting short-term fund flows.

A financial or earnings projection differs from a forecast in that the assumptions used may not necessarily be the most probable, but rather the assumptions represent a conditon that the projection desires to test.

Forecasting requires the use of an earnings record covering a number of periods. Repeated or recurring performance can be forecast with a better degree of confidence than can random events.

Forecasting also requires use of enterprise data by product line or segment wherever different segments of an enterprise are subject to different degrees of risk, possess different degrees of profitability, or have differing growth potentials.

For example, the following tabulation of divisional earnings results indicates the degree to which the results of a component of an enterprise can be masked by the aggregate results:

	Earnings in millions			
	19x1	*19x2*	*19x3*	*19x4*
Segment A	$1,800	$1,700	$1,500	$1,200
Segment B.................	600	800	1,100	1,400
Total net income	$2,400	$2,500	$2,600	$2,600

Judgment on the earnings potential of the enterprise depends, of course, importantly on the relative importance of, as well as the future prospects of, segment B. The subject of product line reporting is discussed in Chapter 7.

Can earnings be forecast?

Statistical studies by Little,[5] and Little and Rayner[6] in England, and by Brealey[7] in the United States documented the apparent random behavior of reported earnings. Since these studies showed that earnings growth occurs in an almost purely random fashion, the implication was drawn that earnings changes cannot be accurately forecasted. Here again we have the problem of deriving from the behavior of large aggregates conclusions about what can or cannot be done in individual cases. Operationally, such generalized conclusions are of very limited practical use.

Serious forecasting is not done by the naive extrapolation of past growth trends of earnings. It is done by a painstaking analysis of the *components* of earnings, the revenues, and the expenses, as well as of all factors that are known or are expected to alter these in the period of the forecast. No knowledgeable forecaster would work only with the earnings figure that is merely a net residual. Thus, it was reported[8] that Days Inns, a motel chain, had been including forecasts in its annual reports for years and that their accuracy was satisfactory to many users, including bankers. Nor is it hard to envisage highly accurate forecasts in such businesses as apartment buildings or hospitals. It is equally easy to find business categories where forecasting would be very difficult and unreliable.

---

[5] I. M. D. Little, "Higgledy Piggledy Growth" (Oxford, England: Oxford University Institute of Statistics, 1962).

[6] I. M. D. Little, "Higgledy Piggledy Growth Again" (Oxford, England: Basil Blackwell, 1966).

[7] Richard A. Brealey, *Introduction to Risk and Return from Commerce Stocks* (Boston: MIT Press, 1969), chap. 8.

[8] *Forbes,* October 26, 1981, p. 189.

A paper[9] that undertook a comprehensive review of the research on earnings forecasts concluded: "We feel that both the properties of earnings forecasts and the question of their value continues to be a fertile area of research." It is equally clear that those seriously interested in the earnings forecasting function will find the study of specific tools and conditions to be of considerably more value than the statistical study of large aggregates.

SEC disclosure requirments—aid to forecasting

The "Management's Discussion and Analysis of Financial Condition and Results of Operations" disclosure requirements of the SEC (see Chapter 7) contain a wealth of information on management's views and attitudes as well as on factors that can influence enterprise operating performance. Consequently, the analyst may find much information in these analyses to aid in the forecasting process. Moreover, while not requiring it, the SEC encourages the inclusion in these discussions of forward-looking information.

Elements in earnings forecasts

Granted that the decision maker is interested primarily in future prospects, his approach to assessing them must be based primarily on the present as well as on the past. While expected future changes in conditions must be given recognition, the experience of the present and the past form the base to which such adjustments are applied. In doing this, the analyst relies on the degree of continuity and perseverance of momentum that is the common experience of the enterprise and the industry of which it is part. Random shocks and sudden changes are always possible, but they can rarely be foreseen with any degree of accuracy.

The importance to the analyst of the underlying continuity of business affairs should not be overemphasized. One should not confuse the basis for the projection of future results, which the past record represents, with the forecast which is the end product. As a final objective, the analyst is interested in a projection of net income. Net income is the result of the offset of two big streams: (1) total revenues and (2) total costs.

Considering that net income represents most frequently but a relatively small portion of either stream, one can see how a relatively minor change in either of these large streams can cause a very significant change in net income.

A significant check on the reasonableness of an earnings projection is to test it against the return on invested capital which is implicit in the forecast. If the result is at variance with returns realized in the past, the underlying

---

[9] A. R. Abdel-Khalik and R. B. Thompson, "Research on Earnings Forecasts: The State of the Art," *The Accounting Journal,* Winter 1977–78.

assumptions must be thoroughly examined so that the reasons for such deviations can be pinpointed.

In terms of the framework examined in Chapter 6, the ROI depends on earnings that are a product of *management* and of *assets* that require funds for their acquisition.

1. Management. It is well known that it takes resourceful management to "breathe life" into assets by employing them profitably and causing their optimum utilization. The assumption of stability of relationships and trends implies that there has been no major change in the skill, the depth, and the continuity of the management group or a radical change in the type of business in which their skill has been proven by a record of successful performance.

2. Assets. The second essential ingredient to profitable operations is funds or resources with which the assets essential to the successful conduct of business are acquired. No management, no matter how ingenious, can expand operations and have an enterprise grow without an adequate asset base. Thus, continuity of success and the extrapolation of growth must be based on an investigation of the sources of additional funds that the enterprise will need and the effect of the method of financing on net income and earnings per share.

The financial condition of the enterprise, as was seen in Chapters 3 and 5, can have a bearing on the results of operations. A lack of liquidity may inhibit an otherwise skillful management, and a precarious or too risky capital structure may lead to limitations by others on its freedom of action.

The above factors, as well as other economic, industry, and competitive factors, must be taken into account by the analyst when forecasting the earnings of an enterprise. Ideally, in forecasting earnings, the analyst should add a lot of knowledge about the future to some knowledge of the past. Realistically the analyst must settle for a lot of knowledge about the past and present and only a limited knowledge of the future.

In evaluating earnings trends, the analyst relies also on such indicators of future conditions as capital expenditures, order backlogs, as well as demand trends in individual product lines.

It is important to realize that no degree of sophistication in the techniques used in earnings forecasting can eliminate the inevitable uncertainty to which all forecasts are subject. Even the best and most soundly based projections retain a significant probability of proving widely off the mark because of events and circumstances that cannot be foreseen.

The most effective means by which the analyst and decision maker can counter this irreducible uncertainty is to keep close and constant watch over how closely actual results conform to his forecasts. This requires a constant monitoring of results and the adjustment and updating of projections in the light of such results. The monitoring of earnings is considered later in this chapter.

Publication of financial forecasts

Recent years have witnessed intensified interest in publication by companies of forecasts of earnings and other financial data. The publication of forecasts in Britain in certain specialized situations as well as a belief that forecasts would be useful to investors were major factors behind this interest. This type of forecasting by insiders (i.e., management) is to be distinguished from forecasts made by financial analysts that are based on all the information that they can obtain.

In early 1977, an advisory committee to the SEC recommended that the agency design procedures to encourage companies to make forecasts of their economic performance. Following this, the SEC deleted in its regulations a reference to predictions of "earnings" as possibly misleading in certain situations. Thus the Commission will no longer object to disclosure in filings with it of projections that are made in good faith and have a reasonable basis, provided that they are presented in appropriate form and are accompanied by information adequate for investors to make their own judgments. In 1978 the SEC issued "Guides for Disclosure of Projections of Future Economic Performance."

Following this up, in 1979 the SEC issued a rule intended to encourage companies to make public their financial forecasts by protecting them from lawsuits in case their predictions did not come true, these "safe harbor" rules against fraud charges will protect companies as long as their projections have a "reasonable basis" and are made in good faith.

The interest in financial forecasts has resulted in a formal consideration of some of the issues by the AICPA which in 1975 issued two statements on the subject.[10]

These statements recommend, among others, that financial forecasts should be presented in a historical financial statement format and that they include regularly a comparison of the previous forecast with attained results.

Both statements recognize the primary importance that assumptions play in the reliability and creditability of a financial forecast. Consequently, those assumptions that management thinks most crucial or significant to the forecast—or are key factors upon which the financial results of the enterprise depends—should be disclosed to provide the greatest benefit to users of forecasts. There ordinarily should be some indication of the basis or rationale for these assumptions.

In 1980, the Financial Forecasts and Projections Task Force of the AICPA issued a *Guide for a Review of a Financial Forecast.* This publication set forth the scope as well as the procedures to be followed by an accountant in reviewing a financial forecast and the method of reporting on such a review.

---

[10] "Guidelines for Systems for the Preparation of Financial Forecasts" and "Presentation and Disclosure of Financial Forecasts," AICPA, 1975. (Auditing implications are also being considered.)

Speagle, Clark, and Elgers have categorized assumptions underlying forecasted financial statements as (1) "ongoing assumptions relating to the forecast methodology, company operating characteristics, and so on; (2) standard assumptions bearing upon the continuity in accounting policy, company management, supply sources, etc.; and (3) transitory assumptions covering events in a particular year such as recapitalizations, labor settlements, new product introductions, facilities expansion, etc."[11]

The validity of any forecasted financial data depends to a high degree on the assumptions, both implicit and explicit, upon which the forecasting technique is based. The financial analyst who uses a management forecast as input to his own projections should pay first and primary attention to the assumptions on which it is based.

THE CONCEPT OF EARNINGS POWER

The best possible estimate of the *average* earnings of an enterprise, which can be expected to be sustained and be repeated with some degree of regularity over a *span of future years,* is referred to as its earning power. Except in specialized cases, earning power is universally recognized as the single most important factor in the valuation of an enterprise. Most valuation approaches entail in one form or another the capitalization of earning power by a factor or multiplier that takes into account the cost of capital as well as future expected risks and rewards.

The importance of "earning power" is such that most analyses of the income and related financial statements have as one of their ultimate objectives the determination of its amount. Earning power is a concept of financial analysis, not of accounting. It focuses on stable and recurring elements and thus aims to arrive at the best possible estimate of repeatable average earnings over a span of future years. Accounting, as we have seen, can supply much of the essential information for the computation of earning power. However, the process is one involving knowledge, judgment, experience, and a time horizon, as well as a specialized investing or lending point of view, such as is described in Chapter 1.

Investors and lenders look ultimately to future cash flows as sources of rewards and safety. Accrual accounting, which underlies income determination, aims to relate sacrifices and benefits to the periods in which they occur. In spite of known shortcomings, this framework represents the most reliable and relevant indicator of longer-term future probabilities of *average* cash inflows and outflows presently known.

While in its objectives, valuation is *future* oriented, we must recognize that the only sound and realistic basis for estimating future conditions and

---

[11] R. E. Speagle, J. J. Clark, and P. Elgers, *Publishing Financial Forecasts: Benefits, Alternatives, Risk* (Laventhol Krekstein Horwath & Horwath, 1974).

probabilities is the actual track record of the enterprise's achievement in the most recent past. Not only does such an earning record over a representative span of years, usually encompassing an entire business cycle, represent what has in fact been achieved as the actual operating experience of the enterprise, but it also represents the operating model on the basis of which we can give effect to assumptions about future conditions that we expect to differ from those prevailing in the past.

In this context, it must be realized that valuation, whether it is performed for purposes of investment, taxation, or the adjudication of disputes as to value, is of such importance to the parties at interest that estimates, if they are made, must be most soundly based. Thus, any departure from actual experience must be most carefully verified and justified. Our ability to pierce the veil of the future is limited indeed. As Bennian[12] stated it:

> It is impossible to make an economic forecast in which full confidence can be placed. No matter what refinements of techniques are employed, there still remain at least some exogenous variables. It is thus not even possible to say with certainty how likely our forecast is to be right. We must be brash enough to label a forecast as "most probable," but this implies an ability on our part to pin an approximate probability co-efficient on a forecast: 1.0 if it is virtual certainty, 0.0 if it is next to an impossibility, or some other co-efficient between these extremes. But, again, since we have no precise way of measuring the probability of our exogenous variables behaving as we assume them to do, there is no assurance that the estimated probability co-efficient for our forecast is anything like 100 percent correct.

It is for this reason that the courts and others have been reluctant, except in the most persuasive of circumstances, to substitute guesses about the future for the experience of the past, and, for this reason, *average* past earnings enter very importantly into the determination of earning power.

Earning power time horizon

It can be readily recognized that one year represents too short and too arbitrary a time period for purposes of income measurement and evaluation. Because of the length of time required to assess the ultimate workout and the results of many investments and outlays, because of the ups and downs of the business cycle, and because of the presence of numerous nonrecurring and extraordinary factors, the earning power of an enterprise is best measured by means of average earnings realized over a number of years. Thus, while gains and losses may be unusual or extraordinary with respect to any one period, they are, nevertheless, still part of the enterprise's longer-term operating experience.

---

[12] Edward G. Bennian, "Capital Budgeting and Game Theory," *Harvard Business Review,* November–December 1956, pp. 115–23.

The period of time over which an earnings average should be calculated will vary with the industry of which the enterprise is part and with other special circumstances. However, in general, a from 5- to 10-year earnings average will smooth out many of the distortions and the irregularities that impair the significance of a single year's results. A five-year earnings average will, in most cases, be adequate to retain an emphasis on recent experience while avoiding the inclusion of years that may no longer be representative or relevant.

Our discussion of the analysis of the income statement has shown that the analysis must focus on the level of income for each year as well as on the *trend* of earnings over time. Trend is an important factor in valuation.

If the earnings are subject to a sustainable trend, the averaging process may have to be weighted so as to accord more weight to most recent earnings. Thus, in a five-year average computation, the last year may be given a weight of 5/15, the preceding year a weight of 4/15, and the first year a weight of 1/15.

The more representative the most recent enterprise experience and the nature of its operations are of what can be expected in the future, the more valid the averaging process is. Conversely, if there have been significant recent changes in the nature of the enterprise's operations, the averaging period may have to be shortened and/or greater emphasis may have to be placed on estimation of future conditions.

Adjustment of reported earnings per share

In our discussion of the adjustment of earnings, we concluded that in determining the earning power of an enterprise, no item of income and expense should be completely excluded. Since every item of income or expense is part of the enterprise's operating experience, the question is only to what year items should be assigned or into what period of time they should be included when an average of earnings is computed.

For purposes of analysis or comparison, analysts may, however, wish to focus on an adjusted level of earnings for a short period, for example, for two years. This can be done by adding to, or removing from, reported earnings per share selected items of income or expense that were included therein. If this is to be done on a per share basis, every item must be adjusted for tax effect (by using the enterprise's effective tax rate unless the tax rate is otherwise specified) and must be divided by the number of shares that are used in the basic computation of earnings per share.

The following example of such suggested analytical adjustments is based on a tabulation prepared by "The Quality of Earnings Report"[13] concerning the reported earnings of A. H. Robins Company.

---

[13] Published by Reporting Research Corporation, Englewood Cliffs, N.J., and dated April 15, 1981.

Per share earnings impact

Item	1980	1979
Effective tax rate change	+.02	
Settlement of Hartz litigation	+.07	+.57
Change to straight-line depreciation	+.02	
Reserves for losses on Iranian assets	+.02	−.15
Loss on sale of divisions	−.19	
Change to LIFO	−.07	
Litigation settlements and expense	−.09	−.12
Foreign exchange translation	−.03	−.04
Above trend R&D expenditures	−.11	
Higher percent allowance for doubtful accounts	−.02	
± Per share earnings impact	−$ .38	+$ .26
Per share earnings as reported	*$1.01*	*$1.71*
Add back negative (−) impact to 1980	.38	
Subtract positive (+) impact from 1979		(.26)
Adjusted earnings per share	*$1.39*	*$1.45*

(+) Positive.
(−) Negative.

In the above tabulation, items that increased earnings are listed as positive (+) and items that diminished earnings are listed as negative (−). Thus, in order to remove them from reported earnings, positive items are deducted while negative items are added back. The validity of each adjustment is, of course, a matter for the analyst's judgment.

MONITORING PERFORMANCE AND RESULTS

The judgments of what the proper financial forecast of an enterprise is or what its earning power is, are based on estimates that hinge on future developments that can never be fully foreseen. Consequently, the best course of action is to monitor performance closely and frequently and to compare it with earlier estimates and assumptions. In this way, one can constantly revise one's estimates and judgments and incorporate the unfolding reality into earlier judgments and conclusions. One of the best ways of monitoring performance is to follow interim reports closely.

Interim financial statements

The need to follow closely the results achieved by an enterprise requires frequent updatings of such results. Interim financial statements, most frequently issued on a quarterly basis, are designed to fill this need. They are used by decision makers as means of updating current results as well as in the prediction of future results.

If, as we have seen, a year is a relatively short period of time in which to account for results of operations, then trying to confine the measurement of results to a three-month period involves all the more problems and imperfections. For this and other reasons the reporting of interim earnings is subject to serious limitations and distortions. The intelligent use of reported interim results requires that we have a full understanding of these possible problem areas and limitations. The following is a review of some of the basic causes of these problems and limitations, as well as their effect on the determination of reported interim results.

Year-end adjustments. The determination of the results of operations for a year requires a great many estimates, as well as procedures, such as accruals and the determination of inventory quantities and carrying values. These procedures can be complex, time-consuming, and costly. Examples of procedures requiring a great deal of data collection and estimation include estimation of the percentage of completion of contracts, determination of cost of work in process, the allocation of under- or overabsorbed overhead for the period, and the estimation of year-end inventory levels under the LIFO method. The complex, time-consuming, and expensive nature of these procedures can mean that they are performed much more crudely during interim periods and are often based on records that are less complete than are their year-end counterparts. The result inevitably is a less accurate process of income determination which, in turn, may require year-end adjustments that can modify substantially the interim results already reported.

Seasonality. Many enterprises experience at least some degree of seasonality in their activities. Sales may be unevenly distributed over the year, and so it may be with production and other activities. This tends to distort comparisons among the quarterly results of a single year. It also presents problems in the allocation of many budgeted costs, such as advertising, R&D, and repairs and maintenance. If expenses vary with sales, they should be accrued on the basis of expected sales for the full year. Obviously, the preparer of yearly financial statements has the benefit of hindsight that the preparer of interim statements does not. There are also problems with the allocation of fixed costs among quarters.

ILLUSTRATION 3.   A study of the affairs of Mattel, Inc., reveals how company executives came up with targeted earnings quarter by quarter in fiscal years ending January 31, 1971, and 1972 using misleading or blatantly false methods to increase recorded sales or to decrease recorded expenses to reach targets. Mattel used an accounting practice known as *annualization* to match incurred expenses against sales on a year-to-year basis and these were juggled to achieve preselected results.

ILLUSTRATION 4.   The tenuous nature of quarterly gross profit estimates is exemplified
by this note by Bristol Products, Inc.: "Results of Fourth Quarter, 1974—As indicated
in Note 1, the Company's interim financial statements for 1974 reflected results
of operations using estimated gross profit percentages for its wholesale divisions.
Physical inventories of these divisions at December 31, 1974, disclosed that the
interim gross profit estimates and resultant net income were understated. If fourth
quarter 1974 results were computed using the annual gross profit percentages
determined for the wholesale divisions, fourth quarter net income would have
amounted to approximately $114,000 or $.10 per share. This compares with fourth
quarter net income of $228,645 or $.24 per share computed by substracting interim
results reported for the first three quarters of 1974 from results for the year."

ILLUSTRATION 5.   The following is an example of adjustments that can result from seasonal
variations: "Because of a seasonal production cycle, and in accordance with practices followed by the Company in reporting interim financial statements prior to
19x4, $435,000 of unabsorbed factory overhead has been deferred at July 4,
19x5. Due to uncertainties as to production and sales in 19x4, $487,000 of such
unabsorbed overhead was expensed during the first 6 months of 19x4."

APB Opinion 28

In its *Opinion 28,* the APB concluded that interim reports should be
prepared in accordance with GAAP used in the preparation of the latest
financial statements. Adopting mostly the point of view that a quarterly
report is an integral part of a full year rather than a discrete period, it
calls for the accrual of revenues and for the spreading of certain costs among
the quarters of a year. For example, it sanctions the accrual of such year-
end adjustments as inventory shrinkages, quantity discounts, and uncollectible
accounts; but it prohibits the accrual of advertising costs on the ground
that benefits of such costs cannot be anticipated. Losses cannot, generally,
be deferred beyond the interim period in which they occur. LIFO inventory
liquidations should be considered on an annual basis. Only permanent declines
in inventory values are to be recorded on an interim basis. Moreover, the
Opinion calls for the inclusion of extraordinary items in the interim period
in which they occur.[14] Income taxes should be accrued on the basis of the
effective tax rate expected to apply to the full year.

SEC interim reporting requirements

The SEC took a relatively early and strong interest in interim reporting
and as a result brought about very significant improvements in reporting

---

[14] *SFAS 3* specifies that "if a cumulative effect type accounting change is made in other
than the first interim period of an enterprise's fiscal year, no cumulative effect of the change
shall be included in net income of the period of change. Instead, financial information for the
pre-change interim periods of the fiscal year in which the change is made shall be restated by
applying the newly adopted accounting principle to those pre-change interim periods."

and disclosure in this area. In 1972, it required quarterly reports (on Form 10-Q) and reports on current developments (Form 8-K), disclosure of separate fourth quarter results and details of year-end adjustments.

In 1975, the SEC issued requirements (now in codification of *FRR*, Sections 301, 303, and 304) that served to expand substantially the content and the utility of interim reports filed with the Commission. The principal requirements include:

> Comparative quarterly and year-to-date abbreviated income statement data—this information may be labeled *unaudited* and must also be included in annual reports to shareholders. (Small companies are exempted).
>
> Year-to-date statements of changes in financial position.
>
> Comparative balance sheets.
>
> Increased pro forma information on business combinations accounted for as purchases.
>
> Conformity with the principles of accounting measurement as set forth in professional pronouncements on interim financial reports. Increased disclosure of accounting changes with a letter from the registrant's independent public accountant stating whether or not he judges the changes to be preferable.
>
> Management's narrative analysis of the results of operations, explaining the reasons for material changes in the amount of revenue and expense items from one quarter to the next. (See discussion in Chapter 7).
>
> Indications as to whether a Form 8-K was filed during the quarter—reporting either unusual charges or credits to income or a change of auditors.
>
> Signature of the registrant's chief financial officer or chief accounting officer.

In promulgating these expanded disclosure requirements, the Commission indicated that it believed that these disclosures will assist investors in understanding the pattern of corporate activities throughout a fiscal period. It maintained that presentation of such quarterly data will supply information about the trend of business operations over segments of time which are sufficiently short to reflect business turning points.

Implications for analysis

While there have been some notable recent improvements in the reporting of interim results, the analyst must remain constantly aware that accuracy of estimation and the objectivity of determinations are and remain problem areas that are inherent in the measurement of results of very short periods. Moreover, the limited association of auditors with interim data, while lending some unspecified degree of assurance, cannot be equated to the degree of assurance that is associated with fully audited financial statements. SEC insistence that the professional pronouncements on interim statements (such as *APB Opinion 28*) be adhered to should offer analysts some additional comfort. However, not all principles promulgated by the APB on the subject of interim financial statements result in presentations useful to the analyst. For example, the inclusion of extraordinary items in the results of the quarter in which they occur will require careful adjustment to render them meaningful for purposes of analysis.

While the normalization of expenses is a reasonable intraperiod accounting procedure, the analyst must be aware of the fact that there are no rigorous standards or rules governing its implementation and that it is consequently, subject to possible abuse. The shifting of costs between periods is generally easier than the shifting of sales; and, therefore, a close analysis of sales may yield a more realistic clue to a company's true state of affairs for an interim period.

Since the price of the common stock influences the computation of earnings per share, the analyst should in his evaluation of per share results be alert to the separation of these market effects from those related to the operating fundamentals of an enterprise.

Some problems of seasonality in interim results of operations can be overcome by considering in the analysis not merely the results of a single quarter, but also the year-to-date cumulative results which incorporate the results of the latest available quarter. This is the most effective way of monitoring the results of an enterprise and bringing to bear on its analysis the latest data on operations that are available.

QUESTIONS

1. Distinguish between income and cash flow. Why should there be a distinction between the two?
2. *a.* What is meant by *quality of earnings?* Why do analysts assess it?
    b. On what major elements does the quality of earnings depend?
3. *a.* What are discretionary costs?
    b. Of what significance are discretionary costs to an analysis of the quality of earnings?
4. *a.* Why is the evaluation of R&D costs important in the analysis and projection of income?
    b. What are some of the precautions required in analyzing R&D expenses?
5. *a.* What is the relationship between the carrying amounts of various assets and the earnings reported?
    b. What is the relationship between the amounts at which liabilities, including provisions, are carried and the earnings reported?
6. In what way is balance sheet analysis a check on the validity as well as the quality of earnings?

7. Comment on the effect which the "risk category" of an asset has on the quality of reported earnings.
8. Explain briefly the relationship between the quality of earnings and the following balance sheet items:
    a. Accounts receivable.
    b. Inventories.
    c. Deferred charges.
9. What is the effect of external factors on the quality of earnings?
10. What is the objective of recasting the income statement?
11. Where will the analyst find data needed for the analysis of the results of operations and for their recasting and adjustment?
12. What is the aim of the recasting process and how is the recasting accomplished?
13. Describe the income statement adjustment process.
14. What is income smoothing? How can it be distinguished from outright false-hoods?
15. Name and explain three forms of income smoothing.
16. *a.* What factors and incentives motivate companies to engage in income smoothing?
    b. What are the implications for analysis?
17. Why are managements so greatly interested in the reporting of extraordinary gains and losses?
18. What are the basic objectives of the analyst in the identification and the evaluation of extraordinary items?
19. *a.* Into what categories can items which are described as unusual or extraordinary in the financial statements be usefully subdivided for purposes of analysis?
    b. Give examples of each such category.
    c. How should the analyst treat items in each category? Is such a treatment indicated under all circumstances? Explain.
20. What are the effects of extraordinary items on—
    a. Enterprise resources?
    b. The evaluation of managements?
21. Comment on the following statement:
    "Extraordinary gains or losses have not resulted from a 'normal' or 'planned' activity of management and, consequently, they should not be used in the evaluation of managerial performance."
    Do you agree?
22. What is the difference between forecasting and extrapolation of earnings?
23. How can SEC disclosure requirements aid in forecasting?
24. What are the categories of assumptions underlying forecasted financial statements? Give examples of each category. What is the importance of these assumptions to the financial analyst?
25. What is earning power? Why is it important?
26. *a.* What are interim financial statements used for?
    b. What accounting problems which are peculiar to interim statements must the analyst be aware of?

27. Interim financial reporting can be subject to serious limitations and distortions. Discuss some of the reasons for this.

28. What are the major disclosure requirements by the SEC with regard to interim reports? What are the objectives behind them?

29. What implications do interim reports hold for the financial analyst?

10

Comprehensive analysis of financial statements

THE METHODOLOGY OF FINANCIAL STATEMENT ANALYSIS

The marshalling, arrangement, and presentation of data for purposes of financial statement analysis can be standardized to some extent in the interest of consistency and organizational efficiency. However, the actual process of analysis must be left to the judgment of the analyst so that he or she may allow for the great diversity of situations and circumstances that are likely to be encountered in practice, and thus give full reign to his or her own initiative, originality, and ingenuity. Nevertheless, there are some useful generalizations and guidelines that may be stated as to a general approach to the task of financial statement analysis.

To begin with, financial statement analysis is oriented towards the achievement of definite objectives. In order that the analysis best accomplish these objectives, the first step is to define them carefully. The thinking and clarification leading up to such a definition of objectives is a very important part of the analytical process, for it ensures a clear understanding of objectives, that is, of what is pertinent and relevant and what is not, and thus also leads to avoidance of unnecessary work. This clarification of objectives is indispensable to an *effective* as well as to an *efficient* analysis; *effective,* in that, given the specifications, it focuses on the most important and most relevant elements of the financial statements; *efficient,* in that it leads to an analysis with maximum economy of time and effort.

ILLUSTRATION 1. The bank loan officer, dealing with a request for a short-term loan to finance inventory, may define his objective as assessing the intention and the ability of the borrower to repay the loan on time. Thus, the analyst can concentrate on what is needed to achieve this objective and need not, for instance, address himself to industry conditions that can affect the borrowing entity only over the longer term.

311

Once the objective of the analysis has been defined, the next step is the formulation of specific questions the answers to which are needed in the achievement of such objectives.

ILLUSTRATION 2.   The loan officer in Illustration 1 now needs to define the critical criteria that will affect his decision. For instance, the question of the borrower's *willingness* to repay the short-term loan bears on his character; and financial statement analysis can reveal only the history of past loans granted it. Thus, tools other than financial statement analysis will have to be employed to get complete information on the borrower's character.

Among the other questions on which the loan officer will need information are the following:

1.   What is the enterprise's short-term liquidity?
2.   What will its sources and uses of cash be during the duration of the loan agreement?

Financial statement analysis can go far towards providing answers to such questions.

Having defined the objective and having translated it into specific questions and criteria that must be resolved, the analyst is ready for the third step in the analysis process. This is to decide which tools and techniques of analysis are the most appropriate, effective, and efficient ones to use in working on the particular decision problem at hand.

ILLUSTRATION 3.   Following the sequence developed in Illustrations 1 and 2, the loan officer will now decide which financial statement analysis tools are the most appropriate to use in this case. He may choose one or more of the following:

1.   Short-term liquidity ratios.
2.   Inventory turnover measures.
3.   Cash flow projections.
4.   Analyses of changes in financial position.

These analyses will have to include estimates and projections of future conditions toward which most, if not all, financial analysis is oriented.

The fourth and final step in analysis is the interpretation of the data and measures assembled as a basis for decision and action. This is the most critical and difficult of the steps, and the one requiring the application of a great deal of judgment, skill, and effort. Interpretation is a process of investigation and evaluation, and of envisaging the reality that lies behind the figures examined. There is, of course, no mechanical substitute for this process of judgment. However, the proper definition of the problem and of the critical questions that must be answered, as well as the skillful selection of the most appropriate tools of analysis available in the circumstances, will go a long way towards a meaningful interpretation of the results of analysis.

ILLUSTRATION 4. Following the sequence of the first three examples above, the collection, by the loan officer, of the data described in Illustration 3 is, of course, not the end result of his analysis. These data must be integrated, evaluated, and interpreted for the purposes of reaching the basic decision of whether to make the loan and, if so, in what amount.

By way of analogy, the weather forecasting function provides an example of the difference between the availability of analytical data and its successful interpretation. Thus, the average listener to weather information does not know how to interpret barometric pressure, relative humidity, or wind velocity. What one needs to know is the weather forecast that results from an interpretation of these data.

The intelligent analyst and interpreter of financial statement data must always bear in mind that a financial statement is at best an abstraction of an underlying reality. Further mathematical manipulation of financial data can result in second, third, and even further levels of abstractions; and the analyst must always keep in mind the business reality behind the figures. No map of the Rocky Mountains can fully convey the grandeur of the terrain. One has to see them in order to appreciate them because maps, like financial statements, are, at best abstractions. That is why security analysts must, at some point, leave the financial statements and visit the companies that they analyze in order to get a full understanding of the phenomena revealed by their analysis. This is particularly true because the static reality portrayed by the abstractions found in the financial statements cannot remain stable for very long. Reality is ever changing.

A recognition of the inherent limitations of financial data is needed for intelligent analysis. This does not detract from their importance because financial statements and data are the only means by which the financial realities of an enterprise can be reduced to a common denominator that is quantified and that can be mathematically manipulated and projected in a rational and disciplined way.

SIGNIFICANCE OF THE "BUILDING BLOCK" APPROACH TO FINANCIAL ANALYSIS

The six major building blocks of financial analysis that we have examined in this text are:

1. Short-term liquidity.
2. Funds flow.
3. Capital structure and long-term solvency.
4. Return on investment (ROI)
5. Asset utilization.
6. Operating performance.

The building block approach to financial statement analysis involves:

1. The determination of the major objectives that a particular financial analysis is to achieve.
2. Arriving at a judgment about which of the six major areas of analysis (i.e., our "building blocks") must be evaluated with what degree of emphasis and in what order of priority.

For example, the security analyst, in the evaluation of the investment merit of a particular issue of equity securities, may attach primary importance to the earning capacity and potential of the enterprise. Thus, the first building block of the analysis will be the evaluation of *operating performance* and the next, perhaps, *return on investment (ROI)*. A thorough analysis will, of course, require that attention be paid to the other four major areas of analysis, although with perhaps lesser degrees of emphasis, that is, depth. This attention to the other major areas of analysis is necessary in order to detect possible problem areas, that is, areas of potential risk. Thus, further analysis may reveal a liquidity problem arising from a "thin" working capital condition, or it may reveal a situation of inadequate capital funds that may stifle growth and flexibility. It is conceivable that these problem areas may reveal themselves to be so important as to overshadow the question of earning power, thus leading to a change in the relative emphasis that the analyst will accord to the main areas of his particular analysis.

While the subdivision of the analysis into six distinct aspects of a company's financial condition and performance is a useful approach, it must be borne in mind that these areas of analysis are highly interrelated. For example, the operating performance of an enterprise can be affected by the lack of adequate capital funds or by problems of short-term liquidity. Similarly, a credit evaluation cannot stop at the point where a satisfactory short-term liquidity position has been determined because existing or incipient problems in the "operating performance" area may result in serious drains of funds due to losses. Such drains can quickly reverse the satisfactory liquidity position that may prevail at a given point in time.

At the start of his analysis, the analyst will tentatively determine the relative importance of the areas that he will examine and the order in which they will be examined. This order of emphasis and priority may subsequently change in the light of his findings and as the analysis progresses.

THE EARMARKS OF GOOD FINANCIAL ANALYSIS

As we have noted, the foundation of any good analysis is a thorough understanding of the objectives to be achieved and the uses to which it is going to be put. Such understanding leads to economy of effort as well as to a useful and most relevant focus on the points that need to be clarified and the estimates and projections that are required.

In practice, rarely can all the facts surrounding a particular analysis be obtained, so that most analyses are undertaken on the basis of incomplete and inadequate facts and data. The process of financial analysis is basically one of reducing the areas of uncertainty—which can, however, never be completely eliminated.

A written analysis and report is not only a significant medium of communication to the reader but it also serves importantly to organize the thinking of the analyst as well as to allow him or her to check the flow and the logic of the presentation. The process of writing reinforces our thinking and vice versa. As we revise our words, we also refine our thoughts—and improvements in style lead, in turn, to the sharpening and improvement in the thinking process itself.

A good analysis separates clearly for the reader the interpretations and conclusions of the analysis from the facts and data upon which they are based. This not only separates fact from opinion and estimate but also enables the reader to follow the rationale of the analyst's conclusions and allows him to modify them as his judgment dictates. To this end, the analysis should contain distinct sections devoted to:

1. General background material on the enterprise analyzed, the industry of which it is a part, and the economic environment in which it operates.
2. Financial and other data used in the analysis as well as ratios, trends, and other analytical measures that have been developed from them.
3. Assumptions as to the general economic environment and as to other conditions on which estimates and projections are based.
4. A listing of positive and negative factors, quantitative and qualitative, by important areas of analysis.
5. Projections, estimates, interpretations, and conclusions based on the aforementioned data. (Some analyses list only the positive and negative factors developed by the analysis and leave further interpretations to the reader.)

A good analysis should start with a brief "Summary and Conclusion" section as well as a table of contents to help the busy reader decide how much of the report he wants to read and on which parts of it to concentrate.

The writer of an analytical report must guard against the all-too-common tendency to include irrelevant matter. For example, the reader need not know the century-old details of the humble beginnings of the enterprise under analysis nor should he be taken on a "journey" along all the fruitless byways and missteps that the analyst inevitably encountered in his process of ferreting out and separating the important from the insignificant. Irrelevant bulk or "roughage" can only serve to confuse and distract the reader of a report.

Ambiguities and equivocations that are employed to avoid responsibility or to hedge conclusions do not belong in a good analytical report. Finally, the writers of such reports must recognize that we are all judged on the basis of small details. Consequently, the presence of mistakes in grammar or of obvious errors of fact in a report can plant doubt in the reader's mind as to the competence of the author and the validity of the analysis.

SPECIAL INDUSTRY OR ENVIRONMENTAL CHARACTERISTICS

In this book, the analysis of the various segments of financial statements was treated from the point of view of the ordinary commercial or industrial enterprise. The financial analyst must, however, recognize that there are industries with distinct accounting treatments that arise either from their specialized nature or from the special conditions, such as governmental regulation, to which they are subject. The analysis of the financial statements of such enterprise requires a thorough understanding of the accounting peculiarities to which they are subject, and the analyst must, accordingly, prepare himself for his task by the study and the understanding of the specialized areas of accounting that affect his particular analysis.

Thus, for example, the analysis of a company in the oil and gas industry requires a thorough knowledge of such accounting concepts peculiar to that industry such as the determination of "cost centers," prediscovery costs, discovery costs, and the disposition of capitalized costs. There are particular problems in the treatment of exploratory, development, and other expenditures as well as in amortization and depletion practices.

Life insurance accounting, to cite another example, also requires specialized knowledge that arises from the peculiarities of this industry and from the regulation to which it is subject. There are special problems in the area of recognition of premium revenues, the accounting for acquisition costs of new business, and the determination of policy reserves.

Public utility regulation has resulted in specialized accounting concepts and problems of which even utility analyst must be aware. There are tax allocation problems resulting in differences among companies that "normalize" taxes versus those which "flow" them through. Then there are problems related to the adequacy of provisions for depreciation, and problems concerning the utility's "rate base" and the method by which it is computed.

SFAS 71 "Accounting for the Effects of Certain Types of Regulation," gives guidance for public utilities and certain other rate-regulated companies, and generally endorses the principal accounting practices that those entities currently follow. It holds that if the rate-setting process for a regulated enterprise gives assurance that incurred costs will be eventually recovered, they should be deferred until the corresponding revenues are recognized. Conversely, if rates are set to cover future costs, current receipts should be recorded as liabilities until the associated costs are incurred.

The Statement upholds the industry practice of capitalizing interest costs of financing construction based on the amounts used for rate-setting purposes, which could include an imputed interest cost on equity funds. Changes from current industry practice include a requirement to capitalize leases if *SFAS*

13 tests are met, and a prohibition against prior period adjustments for refunds to customers.

The Statement applies primarily to public utilities that provide services or products subject to rate-setting by independent, third-party regulators. The rates must be set to recover the utility's specific costs, and be chargeable to and collectible from customers, not the regulator itself.

As in any field of endeavor, specialized areas of inquiry require that specialized knowledge be brought to bear upon them. Financial analysis is, of course, no exception.

ILLUSTRATION OF A COMPREHENSIVE ANALYSIS OF FINANCIAL STATEMENTS—MARINE SUPPLY CORPORATION

The following analysis of the financial statements and other data of the Marine Supply Corporation will serve as an illustration of this process.

Introduction

The Marine Supply Corporation, a leader in the outboard motor industry, was incorporated some 40 years ago. While outboard motor engines and related marine products still account for the bulk of the company's sales, other products are gaining in importance and growing at a rate much faster than the primary products (see Exhibit 10–1, sales breakdown).

Snow vehicle production was launched in fiscal year 19x4. Its growth rate looks dramatic because it starts from extremely low base. Outboard motors can be regarded as the primary base of the company's growth, and outboard engines contribute an even larger portion of corporate profits.

Exhibit 10–1

MARINE SUPPLY CORPORATION
Sales Breakdown
(in millions)

Product	19x5 Sales	19x5 Percent	19y0 Sales	19y0 Percent	Sales increase 19x5– y0 percent	Annual growth rates* percent
Marine products	$135.0	74.5	$217.3	71.0	+ 61	10
Lawn care equipment . .	16.2	9.0	30.5	10.0	+ 88	13
Vehicles	14.1	7.8	19.6	6.4	+ 39	7
Chain saws	9.4	5.2	9.5	3.1	+ 1	0
Snow vehicles	5.1	2.8	23.4	7.7	+359	36
Miscellaneous	.9	.7	4.2	1.8	+367	36
Total	$180.7	100.0	$304.5	100.0	+ 69	11.2

* Five-year period, compounded annually.

While most of Marine Supply Corporation's products have some commercial applications, they are sold primarily for recreation or leisure-time purposes. Being generally big-ticket items, the company's sales are greatly subject to swings in consumer buying cycles.

The use of outboard motors and the majority of the company's other products is largely confined to the warmer months of late spring, summer, and early fall. This means peak retail demand for these items is seasonal; dealer buying tends to be concentrated in this period as well. As a result, the first quarter of the company's fiscal year (ending December) frequently produces a nominal deficit while the June quarter generates 40 percent or more of annual profits.

Marine Supply is one of the world's largest manufacturers of outboard motors; its twin lines command something more than one half the U.S.-Canadian market (by far the most important), and the company estimates a similar proportion overseas. Competition in the industry is keen but is generally centered on performance (racing) results rather than price. Marine Supply's principal advantages are:

1. A highly efficient sales-distribution-repair network (currently about 8,000 dealers) in North America.
2. Exceptional brand loyalty.
3. Almost total domination of the lower horsepower ranges where the vast majority of engines are still sold.

Marine Supply's position in golf carts is also dominant, but its degree of domination is less pronounced. While an important factor in snow vehicles, lawn care, and chain saws, these are highly fragmented markets with many competitors. Still, the company's marketing strategy is the same as in outboards: build a quality product with a strong dealer organization, use intensive advertising, and maintain a premium price structure. This approach has been successful in lawn mowers where Lawn King is a strong competitor despite tremendous product similarity among all brands. In snow vehicles—a comparatively new product to which Marine Supply was a comparative late comer— the company has not yet been totally successful in building its market share.

Financial statements

The financial statements of Marine Supply Corporation are presented in Exhibits 10–2, 10–3, and 10–4 below.

The auditor's opinion on the financial statements has been unqualified for the past six years.

Additional information

Marine Supply has a good, if very cyclical, historic operating performance record. In 19w4, for example, sales were only $73 million as against $304.5

Exhibit 10–2

MARINE SUPPLY CORPORATION
Balance Sheets
As of September 30 for Years 19x5–19y0
(in millions)

	19x5	19x6	19x7	19x8	19x9	19y0
Assets						
Current assets:						
Cash and equivalents	$ 15.00	$ 24.30	$ 12.10	$ 17.40	$ 19.50	$ 17.48
Receivables	22.50	24.50	31.40	35.40	46.50	53.70
Inventories	49.50	57.60	64.70	78.90	100.80	97.32
Other current assets	—	.00	.00	.10	.00	.00
Total current assets	87.00	106.40	108.20	131.80	166.80	168.50
Gross plant	85.20	88.60	98.70	114.70	129.70	137.90
Accumulated depreciation	(45.20)	(48.70)	(52.50)	(56.10)	(60.80)	(65.88)
Net plant	40.00	39.90	46.20	58.60	68.90	72.02
Intangibles and other assets ...	7.00	6.40	10.70	11.90	12.70	15.45
Total assets	$134.00	$152.70	$165.10	$202.30	$248.40	$255.97
Liabilities and Capital						
Current liabilities:						
Accounts payable	$ 1.10	$ 1.10	$ 7.00	$ 15.20	$ 24.60	$ 24.53
Other current liabilities	15.80	24.90	23.50	26.90	35.00	36.75
Total current liabilities....	16.90	26.00	30.50	42.10	59.60	61.28
Long-term debt	14.50	13.50	12.40	28.70	45.70	46.04
Deferred taxes and investment						
credits	1.94	2.19	2.57	4.58	5.38	7.14
Other liabilities	2.39	2.57	2.03	1.52	2.57	1.05
Total liabilities	35.73	44.26	47.50	76.90	113.25	115.51
Net worth..................	98.27	108.44	117.60	125.40	135.15	140.46
Total liabilities and						
capital	$134.00	$152.70	$165.10	$202.30	$248.40	$255.97

Exhibit 10–3

MARINE SUPPLY CORPORATION
Income Statements
For Years Ending September 30
(in millions)

	19x5	19x6	19x7	19x8	19x9	19y0
Net sales	$180.70	$212.50	$233.40	$280.20	$327.10	$304.48
Other income	—	—	—	—	—	.19
Total revenue	180.70	212.50	233.40	280.20	327.10	304.67
Cost of goods sold*						
(excluding depreciation)	113.35	130.95	145.03	180.16	209.52	190.58
Depreciation	4.28	4.26	4.40	4.75	5.59	6.25
Gross profit	63.07	77.29	83.97	95.29	111.99	107.84
Selling, general, and adminis-						
trative expense	41.98	47.04	54.04	61.99	71.44	72.99
Operating income	21.09	30.25	29.93	33.30	40.55	34.85
Interest expense..........	.70	1.05	1.23	2.10	4.73	6.60
Other expenses	.62	.54	.62	1.05	1.54	—
Income before tax	19.77	28.66	28.08	30.15	34.28	28.25
Income taxes:						
Deferred	.47	.26	.38	.37	.80	1.75
Current	8.66	12.73	12.47	14.12	16.40	13.11
Net income	10.64	15.67	15.23	15.66	17.08	13.39
Common dividends	5.13	6.35	6.37	7.98	8.06	8.08
Retained earnings	$ 5.51	$ 9.32	$ 8.86	$ 7.68	$ 9.02	$ 5.31
* Includes:						
R&D costs	11.8	11.2	13.4	12.1	12.4	12.8
Maintenance and repairs .	10.3	10.4	11.6	12.4	12.7	11.5

million in 19y0, more than 300 percent increase. Over the same span net income grew from $5.5 million to $13.4 million, an increase of 144 percent. The slower gain in net income, reflecting sharply reduced operating margins due largely to Federal Trade Commission action in the mid 19w0s, has meant erosion of the company's ROI from an exceptional 25 percent (on net worth) in the 19w4–w6 period to just over 11 percent for the last three years.

Exhibit 10–5, 15-year growth rates—annually compounded, compares various growth rates, first using single years, then a 3-year span.

Note that with the exception of sales per share, the growth rates are still higher for the single-year comparisons. This is attributable to the very low 19w4 base and the tremendous gains from 19w4 through 19w6—a three-year span in which sales, net income, dividends, and book value each increased from 75 percent to 133 percent.

Exhibit 10–6, five-year growth rates—annually compounded indicates the most recent five-year performance, first on a single-year basis, then using three-year "smoothed" base. On either basis, the company's record looks better in recent years than over the long pull.

Exhibit 10-4

MARINE SUPPLY CORPORATION
Statement of Changes in Financial Position
For Years Ending September 30
(in thousands)

	19x5	19x6	19x7	19x8	19x9	19y0	Total Percent	Total Amount
Sources:								
From operations:								
Net earnings	$10,642	$15,666	$15,375	$15,662	$17,078	$13,390	46.5	$ 87,813
Depreciation	4,284	4,264	4,448	4,747	5,587	6,254	15.7	29,584
Amortization of tooling	—	3,360	2,755	4,595	6,484	6,637	12.6	23,831
Other—principally provision for deferred income taxes	755	527	493	372	800	1,753	2.5	4,700
Total from operations	15,681	23,817	23,071	25,376	29,949	28,034	77.3	145,928
Proceeds from sale of:								
Long-term borrowings	—	—	—	17,030	18,202	1,391	19.4	36,623
Plant and equipment (net)	174	662	326	146	347	112	.9	1,767
Common stock	52	859	294	317	732	—	1.2	2,254
Other items, net	—	—	45	1,808	413	—	1.2	2,266
	15,907	25,338	23,736	44,677	49,643	29,537	100.0	188,838
Applications:								
Additions to plant and equipment	2,964	4,739	11,177	16,639	16,109	9,461	32.3	61,089
Tooling expenditures	—	2,565	7,635	6,430	6,825	7,398	16.3	30,853
Long-term debt maturing currently	1,136	1,073	1,126	1,035	1,142	1,073	3.6	6,585
Dividends paid	5,128	6,351	6,369	7,981	8,060	8,080	22.2	41,969
Other items, net	408	355	—	1,199	—	3,526	2.9	5,488
Total applications	9,636	15,083	26,307	33,284	32,136	29,538	77.3	145,984
Working capital increase (decrease)	$ 6,271	$10,255	$(2,571)	$11,393	17,507	$ (1)	22.7	$ 42.854

Exhibit 10–5

MARINE SUPPLY CORPORATION
Fifteen-Year Growth Rates
(annually compounded)

Per share	19w4–y0	19w4–w6 to 19x8–y0
Sales	8.0%	8.0%
Net income	4.6	3.3
Dividends	10.0	7.4
Book value	11.0	7.4

Exhibit 10–6

MARINE SUPPLY CORPORATION
Five-Year Growth Rates
(annually compounded)

Per share	19x5–y0	19x5–x7 to 19x8–y0
Sales	10.5%	7.4%
Net income	4.2	1.9
Dividends	9.0	6.0
Book value	7.0	6.9

Two noteworthy points should be made about this record:

1. The gains represent almost solely internal growth. Acquisitions have been few, their relative size quite small, and their profit contributions have often been negative.
2. No adjustments need be made for dilution. The company has no convertible securities outstanding; stock options are also insignificant.

Exhibits 10–7 through 10–10 are based on the financial statements of Marine Supply Corporation.

While the economy in general was slow in 19y0, 19x8 and 19x9 were good years for boat sales; and responses at boat shows across the country were strong in those years. Compared to automobiles, revolutionary model changes are rare in the boating industry.

The company's contract with the union expired at the end of 19y0, and the company was not sure during 19y0 whether it could avoid a strike.

After careful analysis, we conclude that about one half of deferred taxes and investment credits account balances will be reversed in the future; however, the possibility of reversal in the foreseeable future for the remaining one half is very remote. "Other liabilities" represent various debts having the characteristic of long-term debt. "Other current liabilities" represent amounts owing to various banks under revolving credit agreement.

The company is nearing its production capacity limits, necessitating new

Exhibit 10–7

MARINE SUPPLY CORPORATION
Common-Size Balance Sheets

	19x5	19x6	19x7	19x8	19x9	19y0
Assets						
Cash assets:						
Cash and equivalents	11%	16%	7%	9%	8%	7%
Receivables	17	16	19	17	18	21
Inventories	37	38	39	39	41	38
Total current assets	65	70	65	65	67	66
Land, plant, and equipment, net	30	26	28	29	28	28
Intangibles and other assets	5	4	7	6	5	6
Total assets	100%	100%	100%	100%	100%	100%
Liabilities and Equity						
Current liabilities	13%	17%	18%	21%	24%	24%
Long-term debt	11	9	8	14	18	18
Deferred taxes and investment credits	1	1	2	2	2	3
Other liabilities	2	2	1	1	1	—
Total liabilities	27	29	29	38	45	45
Net worth	73	71	71	62	55	55
Total liabilities and equity	100%	100%	100%	100%	100%	100%

Exhibit 10–8

MARINE SUPPLY CORPORATION
Common-Size Income Statements

Item	19x5	19x6	19x7	19x8	19x9	19y0	Industry composite 19y0
Net sales	100.0%	100.0%	100.0%	100%	100.0	100.0%	100.0%
Cost of goods sold* (excluding depreciation)	62.7	61.6	62.1	64.3	64.1	62.6	64.6
Depreciation	2.4	2.0	1.9	1.7	1.7	2.0	2.8
Gross profit	34.9	36.4	36.0	34.0	34.2	35.4	32.6
Selling, general, and administrative expenses	23.2	22.2	23.2	22.1	21.8	24.0	21.0
Operating income	11.7	14.2	12.8	11.9	12.4	11.4	11.6
Interest expense	.4	.5	.5	.8	1.4	2.2	0.8
Other interest (expense)	(.3)	(.2)	(.3)	(.4)	(.5)	.1	0.2
Net income before tax	11.0	13.5	12.0	10.7	10.5	9.3	11.0
Deferred taxes	.3	.1	.2	.1	.3	.6	.3
Income taxes	4.8	6.0	5.3	5.0	5.0	4.3	4.9
Net income	5.9	7.4	6.5	5.6	5.2	4.4	5.8
*Including:							
R&D costs	6.5	5.2	5.7	4.3	3.8	4.2	5.4
Maintenance and repairs	5.7	4.9	5.0	4.4	3.9	3.9	6.2

Exhibit 10–9

MARINE SUPPLY CORPORATION
Trend Index of Selected Accounts
(19x5 = 100)

Account	19x6	19x7	19x8	19x9	19y0
Cash	162	81	116	130	117
Accounts receivable	109	140	157	207	239
Inventory	116	131	159	204	197
Total current assets	122	124	151	192	194
Total current liabilities	154	180	249	353	363
Working capital	115	111	128	153	153
Fixed assets	100	116	147	172	180
Other assets	94	157	175	187	227
Long-term debt	93	86	198	315	318
Total liabilities	124	133	215	317	323
Equity capital	110	120	128	138	143
Net sales	118	129	155	181	169
Cost of goods sold	116	128	159	185	168
Gross profit	123	133	151	178	171
Selling, general, and administrative expenses	112	132	148	170	174
Interest expense	150	176	300	676	945
Total expenses	114	128	155	182	172
Operating income	143	142	158	192	165
Profit before taxes	145	142	153	173	143
Net income	147	143	147	161	126

Exhibit 10–10

MARINE SUPPLY CORPORATION
Selected per Share Results

Item	19x5	19x6	19x7	19x8	19x9	19y0
Sales	$22.90	$26.71	$29.28	$34.85	$40.48	$37.68
Net income	1.35	1.97	1.91	1.95	2.11	1.66
Dividends	.65	.80	.80	1.00	1.00	1.00
Book value	12.43	13.63	14.76	15.60	16.73	17.38

construction. For example, in 19x8 and 19x9, the company was forced to utilize some aging facilities on a multishift basis.

The period 19x5–y0 has been by far the most prosperous in Marine Supply's history. Sales and earnings have each reached peak levels, although the last six years have not been as profitable as mid 19w0s.

Based on the foregoing data and information, we are to analyze the financial statements of Marine Supply Corporation with the following alternative points of view (objectives) in mind:

1. That of a bank to extend to the company a short-term loan of $15 million.

2. That of an insurance company to whom the company wants to sell privately $30 million of 25-year bonds.

3. That of an investor considering a substantial investment in the company.

These diverse and broad points of view require that we analyze all major aspects of the company's financial condition and results of operations, that is:

1. Short-term liquidity.
2. Funds flow.
3. Capital structure and long-term solvency.
4. Return on investment (ROI).
5. Asset utilization.
6. Operating performance.

The following assumptions will be used in the projection of operating results and of fund flows for 19y1:

It is expected that the annual growth rate by product line will continue except that snow vehicles and miscellaneous are expected to grow at a rate of 29 percent and 30 percent, respectively. Improvements in production facilities will lower the cost of goods (exclusive of depreciation) to 60 percent of sales. The composite depreciation rate (depreciation expense as a percent of ending net plant) is expected to be 10 percent. Amortization of tooling costs included in cost of goods sold will be 10 percent higher than in 19y0. Selling expenses, which amount to one fourth of the selling, general, and administrative group of expenses, are expected to go up by 10 percent in 19y1. The other three fourths of this category will remain unchanged. Taxes will average 53 percent of income before taxes, and the amount of deferred taxes will amount to the same proportion of the total tax accrual as in 19y0. Dividend payout is expected to amount to 50 percent of net income.

In order to retire $15 million in revolving credit notes (shown under current liabilities) and to finance a major plant expansion and modernization program just starting, the company expects to sell at par, early in 19y1, $30 million in 30-year, 7 percent sinking fund bonds. That will leave $20 million in revolving credit notes outstanding. Interest expenses in 19y1 are estimated at $5,810,000. The maturities and sinking fund requirements of long-term debt are as follows:

	(In millions)
19y1	$ 1.0
19y2	2.3
19y3	4.4
19y4	8.6
19y5	12.2

R&D outlays are expected to amount to $3 million in 19y1, and outlays for tooling are planned at $13 million.

The company plans to spend $30 million in 19y1 on plant and equipment. Sales of equipment are expected to bring in $200,000 after tax. The chain-saw division which has a book value of $5 million is expected to be disposed of for $2 million, net of tax.

The problem of obtaining a meaningful and valid standard of external comparison for this analysis has been a difficult one. Two major sources of such data are industry statistics, such as those compiled by Robert Morris Associates, Standard & Poor's, or Dun & Bradstreet, or comparative data derived from companies of similar size and in similar lines of business. In this case, comparative data was developed from the published reports of companies in lines of business similar to those of Marine Supply Company.

Analysis of short-term liquidity

Exhibit 10–11 presents some important liquidity measures of Marine Supply Corporation over the last six years. Both the current ratio and the acid-test ratio have been declining over this period. However, they are still at sound levels in 19y0 on an absolute basis and also when compared to industry averages. The downward trend in these measures must be interpreted in the light of management's possible policy and intent. It is quite conceivable, particularly in view of the lower levels of the comparable industry ratios, that the current position in earlier years was unnecessarily strong and represented a wasteful tying up of resources that did not earn an acceptable return for the company. A glance at the common-size analysis in Exhibit 10–7 reveals the changes that have occurred in the composition of working capital elements over the past six years; the proportion of cash and cash equivalents among the current assets has dropped by almost half even though the absolute amount of cash and equivalents has not diminished on average. There has been a significant increase in current liabilities; they now represent almost a quarter of the funds invested in the enterprise, whereas in 19x5 they represented 13 percent of the total. This is confirmed in the trend index analysis (Exhibit 10–9) that shows that since 19x5 current liabilities have increased 3.63 times while cash increased 1.17 times, receivables 2.39 times, and inventories only 1.97 times. That the increase in current liabilities was out of proportion to that of sales is seen by the fact that during the same period sales increased only 1.69 times. That means that Marine Supply Corporation was somehow able to secure short-term credit from suppliers and banks at a rate twice as fast as that warranted by growth in sales. This, in turn, is importantly responsible for the steady decline in the current and the acid-test ratios.

A more serious problem area is the quality of the two important elements of current assets: accounts receivable and inventories. The accounts receivable turnover has undergone constant decline over the past six years, reaching a low point of 5.67 in 19y0. In that year, it compared unfavorably as to 8.2 turnover in the industry. The alternative measure of "days' sales in accounts receivable" presents a similar picture with an increasing number of "days'

Exhibit 10–11

MARINE SUPPLY CORPORATION
Short-Term Liquidity Analysis

Units		19x5	19x6	19x7	19x8	19x9	19y0	Industry composite 19y0
Ratio	Current ratio	5.15	4.09	3.55	3.13	2.80	2.75	2.40
Ratio	Acid-test ratio	2.22	1.88	1.43	1.26	1.11	1.16	.90
Times	Accounts receivable turnover	8.03	8.67	7.43	7.92	7.03	5.67	8.20
Times	Inventory turnover	2.29	2.27	2.24	2.28	2.08	1.96	2.30
Days	Days sales in receivables	44.80	41.50	48.50	45.5	51.20	63.50	43.90
Days	Days to sell inventory	157.20	158.60	160.70	157.9	173.10	183.70	156.50
Days	Conversion period	202.00	200.10	209.20	203.4	224.30	247.20	200.40
%	Cash to current assets	17.24	22.84	11.18	13.20	11.69	10.37	9.80
%	Cash to current liabilities	88.76	93.46	39.67	41.33	32.72	28.52	29.60
$(MM)	Working capital	70.10	80.40	77.70	89.70	107.20	107.22	—
#	Liquidity index	127	118	139	134	150	163	—

sales" tied up in receivables. The 19y0 figure of 63.5 days compares to an industry experience of 44.0 days. It also compares unfavorably to the company's most common terms of sales of net 30 days. Thus, it is possible that the collectibility and the liquidity of accounts receivable have deteriorated.

Inventory turnover has also decreased over the past six years, although the deterioration has not been as marked as has been the case with receivables. A number of factors could account for this, including a larger number and variety of outboard motors, lawn mowers, and snow vehicles models that must be stocked, the larger variety of spare parts that these require, as well as a possible accumulation of raw materials in anticipation of a strike at suppliers. It is also possible that Marine Supply Corporation overestimated sales for 19y0, while sales dropped 7 percent from the 19x9 level, inventories dropped by only 3 percent, thus contributing to the turnover slowdown. The 19y0 turnover of Marine Supply Corporation of 1.96 compares unfavorably with the 2.3 industry average. In 19y0, it took 183.7 days to sell the average inventory compared to an industry average of 156.2 days. The comparable figure for the company in 19x5 was 157.2 days.

The deterioration in the liquidity of the principal operating assets of the current asset group, accounts receivable, and inventories is also seen in the period of days it takes to convert inventories into cash. It grew from 202 days in 19x5 to 247.2 days in 19y0 and compares to an industry average of only 200.2 days in the latter year.

The liquidity index at 163 in 19y0 up from 127 in 19x5 also corroborates the deterioration in the liquidity of the current assets that we have already determined in the analysis of individual components of working capital.

It is conceivable that further analysis and inquiry from management will reveal that the slowdown in the turnover of accounts receivable and inventories does not affect their ultimate realization even if that would take a longer time. In that case, the repercussions of such a slowdown lie in the area of liquidity and funds flow as well as in the area of asset utilization which will be examined later in this analysis.

Cash from operations

The amount of cash generated from operations is another important aspect of liquidity. Marine Supply generated cash from operations as follows (in millions):

	19x6	19x7	19x8	19x9	19y0	Total
Cash from operations	$22.8	$13.6	$18.8	$14.4	$26.0*	$95.6

* Cash from operations was computed, for example, for 19y0 as follows: working capital from operations (28.0) plus increase in current liabilities (1.7) plus decrease in inventories (3.5) less increase in accounts receivable (7.2). "Other current liabilities" are assumed to relate to operations.

While operations provided significant amounts of cash each year, it should be noted that the amounts of cash provided by operations were lower *each* year compared to the amounts of working capital provided by operations, the disparity being over $15 million in 19x9. Over the five-year span, cash from operations was lower than working capital from operations by about $35 million. The reasons for this disparity were significant increases in accounts receivable ($31.2 million) and inventories ($47.8 million) partially offset by increases in liabilities. A continuation of these trends suggests the need for a more permanent financing of working capital needs.

Analysis of funds flow

This analysis has two main objectives:

1. To supplement the static measures used to assess short-term liquidity by means of a short-term funds flow forecast.
2. To analyze the statement of changes in financial position (SCFP) in order to assess its implications on the longer-term flow of funds (i.e., long-term solvency).

Our first step will be to build a funds flow forecast for Marine Supply Corporation in 19y1. Since sources of funds from operations are an important element of funds and a projection of earnings will be necessary anyway, we start with such a projection for 19y1, using the data and the supplementary information provided (see Exhibit 10–12).

Having established the estimated net income for 19y1, we can now proceed, using the data and the additional information we now have, to construct an estimated statements of sources and uses of working capital (funds) for 19y1.

Exhibit 10–13 projects an increase in working capital of about $16 million. If this forecast proves reasonably accurate, the current ratio should improve to about 3:1. As is true of all forecasts, their reliability depends on the validity of the assumptions on which they are based.

The assumption that Marine Supply Corporation can sell $30 million in 7 percent sinking fund bonds appears reasonable in the light of the company's present capital structure. Its failure to do so would require either the abandonment or deferral of expansion and modernization plans or it will result in a deterioration of the current ratio to about 2.5.

The projected net income of $16.6 million for 19y1 appears reasonable because it is based on the assumption of a continuation of present sales trends and a reduction in the growth rate of two product line categories. However, it is more vulnerable on the expense side. The increase in the gross margin is predicated on increases in productivity that are envisaged but which are yet to be realized. Moreover, any program of expansion and modernization is subject to the risk of delays, misjudgments, and short falls that may delay, postpone, or completely undermine the realization of improvements and economies. On the other hand, the increases in fixed costs that such a program entails are a reality with which the enterprise must live for a long time.

Any degree of failure to realize savings and improvements will also affect the short-term flow of funds. Thus, for example, continuing the assumption

Exhibit 10–12

MARINE SUPPLY CORPORATION
Projected Income Statement for 19y1
(in millions)

	19y0 sales level	Incre- ment factor	19y1 esti- mated amount	Total	Percent
Net sales:					
Marine products	$217.3 ×	1.10	$239.03		
Lawn care equipment	30.5 ×	1.13	34.47		
Vehicles	19.6 ×	1.07	20.97		
Snow vehicles	23.4 ×	1.29	30.19		
Miscellaneous	4.2 ×	1.30	5.46	$330.12	100.0
Cost of goods sold (exclusive of depreciation)			198.07		60.0
Depreciation (a)			8.70		2.6
				206.77	62.6
Gross profit				123.35	37.4
Selling, general, and administrative expenses:					
General and administrative (b) . . .			54.74		
Selling (c)			20.08		
Amortization of deferred start-up costs			1.00	75.82	23.0
				47.53	14.4
Interest expenses				5.81	1.8
Income before taxes				41.72	12.6
Income taxes:					
Current			19.24		
Deferred (d)			2.88	22.12	6.7
				19.60	5.9
Loss on disposal of chain-saw division (net of tax)				3.00	.9
Net income				$ 16.60	5.0

(a) Beginning net plant plus half of 19y1 additions times 10 percent: (72.2 + 15.0) × 10%. It is assumed that the plant additions were in use, on average, half of the year.

(b) Three fourths of 72.99 (last year selling, general, and administrative).

(c) Selling expenses at 10 percent above the 19y0 level (72.99 − 54.74) × 1.10.

(d) Deferred taxes at 13 percent of the total provision for the year which amounts to 53 percent of pretax income.

Exhibit 10–13

MARINE SUPPLY CORPORATION
Projected Statement of Sources and Uses of Funds for 19y1
(in millions)

Sources of funds:

From operations:

Net income	$16.60	
Add: Items not requiring current funds:		
Depreciation	8.70	
Amortization of tooling costs	7.30	
Deferred income taxes	2.88	
Amortization of start-up costs	1.00	
Loss on sale of chain-saw division	3.00	
Total from operations.........................		$39.48
Proceeds from sale of 7% sinking fund bonds		30.00
Sale of chain-saw division		2.00
Sale of equipment		0.20
Total sources		71.68

Uses of funds:

Additions to plant and equipment	30.00	
Outlays for tooling	13.00	
Outlays for R&D	3.00	
Long-term debt maturities	1.00	
Dividends declared	8.30	
Total uses		55.30
Increase in working capital		$16.38

that 50 percent of the net income will be distributed as dividends, a 5 percent increase in cost of goods sold (exclusive of depreciation) will lower the inflow of funds as follows:

	In millions (approximately)
Increase in cost of goods sold (exclusive of depreciation)—5% of $198 million	$9.90
Less: Tax effect at 53%	5.25
	4.65
Less: Dividend reduction (50%)	2.32
	2.33
Less: Deferred taxes (13% of 5.25)	.68
Reduction in funds available from operations	$1.65

A similar computation can, of course, be made for any other change in assumptions. The likelihood of any of the above assumptions materializing and the probability attached to them is, ultimately, a matter of judgment.

The longer-range funds flow picture is subject to a great many uncertainties. Examination of the company's historical pattern of fund flows over the 19x5 to 19y0 period (see Exhibit 10–4) is revealing. Funds from operations provided 77 percent of all funds inflows while long-term borrowing provided most of the rest. Such borrowing occurred mostly in 19x8 and 19x9. Equity financing was negligible.

Additions to plant and equipment used about 32 percent of all funds available. These outlays were, however, twice as high as the provision for depreciation. With the company bumping against the ceiling of its practical capacity in many lines, this trend is likely to continue. Already in 19y1, capital expenditures are planned at three times the 19y0 level and long-term debt will be incurred to finance this as well as the working capital needs of an expanding business. As will be discussed further under "capital structure," there is, of course, a limit to the company's debt capacity, and equity financing will be required. This may explain the company's relatively generous dividend policy over the recent years.

In spite of relatively heavy long-term borrowing in 19x8 and 19x9, long-term debt maturities and sinking fund requirements are low. These will, however, increase sharply from $1 million in 19y1 to $12 million in 19y5. The proposed $30 million bond issue in 19y1 will undoubtedly add to these maturities.

The longer-term fund flow outlook of Marine Supply Corporation is one of increasing demand for funds due to accelerating outlays for plant equipment and tooling as well as sharply rising debt service outlays. While funds from operations have been significant and are growing, they will have to continue to do so to meet increasing demands. Since funds from operations represented 77 percent of all sources of funds in the past six years, the company's fund flow is particularly vulnerable to any reduction in net income. Working capital needs will also increase along with the expected increase in sales volume.

It should be borne in mind that focusing on *net* working capital does not tell the whole story of Marine Supply Corporation's borrowing. Included in current liabilities are $35 million in revolving credit notes. The company may well want to convert this short-term interest sensitive debt into a longer-term type of obligation. A beginning towards this goal is expected to be made in 19y1. That too will require using up some of the company's shrinking capacity to finance by means of long-term debt.

Analysis of capital structure and long-term solvency

Having just examined the funds aspect of Marine Supply Corporation's long-term solvency, we now turn to an examination of its capital structure and the risk inherent in it. The change in the company's capital structure can be gauged by means of a number of measurements and comparisons.

Looking at Exhibit 10–7, we see that the contribution of equity capital to the total funds invested in the enterprise has shrunk from 73 percent in 19x5 to 55 percent in 19y0. With the expected issuance of $30 million of additional bonds, this proportion can be expected to dip below 50 percent. The long-term debt portion of the total funds invested in the enterprise increased from 11 percent in 19x5 to 18 percent in 19y0 and is headed considerably higher in 19y1.

In Exhibit 10–9, we can see the relative change in debt, equity, and other related elements in the financial statements. On a basis of 19x5 = 100, long-term debt rose to 318 while equity capital increased only to 143. In the same period, net sales rose only to 169, net income to 126, while interest costs soared to 945. Quite clearly the company decided to finance its needs by means of debt, both short and long term. Reasons for this could be an unwillingness to dilute the equity or a desire to incur monetary liabilities in times of inflation. Whatever the reason, the leverage and hence the risk in the capital structure increased substantially. This is particularly true because Marine Supply Corporation is in a relatively cyclical industry and relies on a share of the consumer's discretionary dollar.

The capital structure and long-term solvency ratios in Exhibit 10–14 bear

Exhibit 10–14

MARINE SUPPLY CORPORATION
Capital Structure and Long-Term Solvency Ratios

	19x5	19x6	19x7	19x8	19x9	19y0	19y0 industry composite
Equity to total	99.24*	109.54	118.89	127.69	137.84	144.03	
debt	34.76	43.16	46.21	74.61	110.56	111.94	
	= 2.86	= 2.54	= 2.57	= 1.71	= 1.25	= 1.29	1.4
Equity to long-	99.24	109.54	118.89	127.69	137.84	144.03	
term debt	17.86*	17.16	15.71	32.51	50.96	50.66	
	= 5.56	= 6.38	= 7.57	= 3.93	= 2.70	= 2.84	3.1
Total debt to total capital ...	.259	.283	.280	.369	.445	.437	N.A.
Equity to net fixed assets	2.48	2.75	2.57	2.18	2.00	2.00	2.2
Ratio of earnings to fixed charges	29.24	28.30	23.83	15.36	8.25	5.28	8.6

Computed as following:

One half of deferred income taxes	.97
Net worth shown	98.27
Adjusted net worth	99.24
Total liabilities shown	35.73
Less: One half of deferred income taxes	.97
Adjusted total liabilities	34.76
Less: Total current liabilities	16.90
Adjusted long-term debt	17.86

out these conclusions. Equity to total debt stands at 1.29 in 19y0 compared to 2.86 in 19x5, and compares to an industry composite of 1.4. Similarly, equity to long-term debt stands at 2.84 in 19y0 compared to an industry composite of 3.1. Debt as a percentage of total capital has been increasing steadily from about 26 percent in 19x5 to almost 44 percent in 19y0—a significant increase in leverage.

The trend in the ratio of earnings to fixed charges bears out the deterioration in the margin of safety for creditors. This ratio plummeted from 29.24 in 19x5 to 5.28 in 19y0 and compares with an industry composite of 8.6. The income projections as well as the borrowing plans for 19y1 would result in an improved earnings to fixed charges ratio of 8.2 as a consequence of the refinancing of high-interest short-term debt and also because the 7 percent bonds will be outstanding for only part of the year. This improvement in the ratio may, however, prove to be only temporary in nature given the longer-term trend we observe here.

As we saw from the longer-term funds flow analysis, the company is now entering a period of increasing capital investment needs and of increasingly heavy debt service schedules. It does this at a time when its debt is high in relation to its equity capital and when shrinking ratios of earnings to fixed charges exert downward pressure on its credit rating. Moreover, the increasing fixed charges that stem from recent substantial additions to plant and equipment make operating results more vulnerable to cyclical downturn with the result that sources of funds from operations are similarly vulnerable.

Analysis of return on investment

The return that the company realizes on total assets, Exhibit 10–15, has been on the decline in recent years, having declined from 10.6 percent in 19x6 (which was the best year in this respect) to 6.4 percent in 19y0. Even if we regard 19x6 as an unusually good year, the decline from the prior year return levels is quite significant. In comparison with an industry return on total assets in 19y0 of 9.3 percent, the company's 6.4 percent return is also significantly worse. This negative trend over the past six years is reason for concern and requires further investigation. The two major elements which make up the return on total assets, that is, net profit margin and asset turnover, will be examined later in this analysis.

In comparison with the return on total assets, the decline in the return on equity has not been quite as significant. This is mainly due to the relatively advantageous use of short-term and long-term credit. The financial leverage index (Exhibit 10–15) that in 19y0 stands at 1.33 is practically unchanged from its 19x5 level. It must be noted, however, that the company cannot expand its debt much more from the present level since over the past six years debt has expanded very significantly. Thus, in the immediate future an adequate return on equity will be dependent primarily on improvements

Exhibit 10–15

MARINE SUPPLY CORPORATION
Return on Investment Ratios

	19x5	19x6	19x7	19x8	19x9	19y0	19y0 industry composite
Return on total assets	8.2% (1)	10.6%	9.6%	8.3%	7.8%	6.4%	9.3%
Return on equity capital	10.8% (2)	14.5%	13.0%	12.5%	12.6%	9.5%	12.8%
Return on long-term liabilities and equity	9.4% (3)	12.8%	11.8%	10.5%	10.3%	8.5%	10.6%
Financial leverage index	1.32 (4)	1.37	1.23	1.27	1.32	1.33	1.38
Equity growth rate .	5.6 (5)	8.6	7.5	6.1	6.7	3.88	—

Notes:

1. $\dfrac{\text{Net income} + \text{Interest expense} \times (1 - \text{Tax rate})}{\text{Total assets}} = \dfrac{10.64 + .7(1 - .46)}{134}$

2. $\dfrac{\text{Net income}}{\text{Net worth}} = \dfrac{10.64}{98.27}$

3. $\dfrac{\text{Net income} + \text{Interest expense} \times (1 - \text{Tax rate})}{\text{Long-term liabilities} + \text{Equity}} = \dfrac{11.018}{134.0 - 16.90}$

4. $\dfrac{\text{Return on equity capital}}{\text{Return on total assets}} = \dfrac{10.8}{8.2}$

5. $\dfrac{\text{Net income} - \text{Payout}}{\text{Common shareholders' equity}} = \dfrac{\text{Amount retained}}{\text{Common shareholders' equity}} = \dfrac{5.51}{98.27}$

in profitability and in asset utilization. Because of the significant increase in debt in recent years, growth in leverage cannot be expected to benefit that return in the future to the extent it did in these past years. As can be seen from Exhibit 10–15, the equity growth rate from earnings retention has shrunk in 19y0 to 3.8 percent from over 6 percent in the two years before that and from 8.6 percent in 19x6. This is largely due to the maintenance of a generous dividend policy in the face of shrinking earnings. This shrinkage in the internal equity growth rate comes at a time when the company is increasingly in need of additional equity capital. Conceivably, however, a liberal dividend record can facilitate the future raising of equity capital.

Analysis of asset utilization

Exhibit 10–16 indicates that in most categories the asset utilization ratios have been declining over the past six years. The sales to total assets ratio is down to 1.2 in 19y0 from the 1.4 level in 19x8 and compares to an industry average 1.5 times. The impact of this change can be assessed as follows:

Exhibit 10–16

MARINE SUPPLY CORPORATION
Asset Utilization Ratios

	19x5	19x6	19x7	19x8	19x9	19y0	19y0 industry composite
Sales to cash and equivalents	12.0	8.7	19.3	16.1	16.8	17.4	9.1
Sales to receivables	8.0	8.7	7.4	7.9	7.0	5.7	10.6
Sales to inventories	3.7	3.7	3.6	3.6	3.2	3.1	4.1
Sales to working capital	2.6	2.6	3.0	3.1	3.1	2.8	4.0
Sales to fixed assets	4.5	5.3	5.1	4.8	4.7	4.2	6.4
Sales to other assets	25.8	33.2	21.8	23.4	25.8	19.7	22.3
Sales to total assets	1.3	1.4	1.4	1.4	1.3	1.2	1.5
Sales to short-term liabilities	10.7	8.2	7.7	6.7	5.5	5.0	—

Given the company's net income to sales ratio in 19y0 of 4.4 percent and a net of tax interest expense of about 1.1 percent (Exhibit 10–8) a total asset turnover of 1.4 (the 19x8 rate) would have yielded a return on total assets of 7.7 percent [(4.4 + 1.1) × 1.4] rather than the 6.4 percent return actually realized in 19y0. At a rate of turnover of 1.5 (industry average), the present profit rate would yield a ROI of about 8.2 percent [(4.4 + 1.1) × 1.5].

The asset categories where the turnover rate has dropped most sharply over the six years are "other assets" and "receivables." Only cash showed an increase in turnover (utilization). Judging by the fact that there were significant fixed asset additions in 19x8 and 19x9 (see Exhibit 10–9), the drop in the fixed asset turnover rate was moderate. It must be borne in mind that it takes time before fixed asset additions become sufficiently productive to generate an expected volume of sales. In addition, certain types of fixed asset outlays represent improvements in production facilities which lead to efficiencies and savings rather than to expansion of productive capacity. Such outlays, consequently, do not lead to greater sales but rather to savings in variable costs and result in improvements in profit margins. Exhibit 10–8 indicates that while profit margins are below the 19x6–x7 levels, they have been in an improving trend in the last three years. The drop over the six-year span in the turnover of the "other assets" group reflects growth in deferred charges, particularly tooling.

Analysis of operating performance

Exhibit 10–8 presents common-size income statements of the company for the six years, 19x5–y0.

The gross profit of Marine Supply Corporation has held within a relatively narrow range over the last six years. In 19y0, at 35.3 percent, the gross profit margin is higher than in the preceding two years but is below the levels reached in 19x6 and 19x7. It does compare favorably to the industry gross margin of 32.6 percent. However, the R&D costs as well as the repair and maintenance costs included in the cost of goods sold figure are lower, as a percentage of sales than the industry composite. This aspect of the quality of earnings will be further discussed below.

In 19y0, the percentage relationship between depreciation expense and sales was 2.1 percent up from 1.7 percent the year before. The disparity between this percentage and the industry composite of 2.8 percent is noteworthy because it may affect the quality of Marine Supply Corporation's earnings. It would appear that an inadequate amount of depreciation is recorded by Marine Supply Corporation. Before a definite judgment can be made, additional information would be required. The company is now approaching the limit of practical capacity in many of its product lines. Competitors may have more reserve capacity available and that may express itself in a relatively higher composite depreciation rate. It is also possible that Marine Supply Corporation's equipment is, on average, of an older vintage, and hence lower cost, than the equipment of its competitors. On the other hand, a lower composite depreciation rate than necessary is a factor that lowers the quality of the company's earnings.

We have two more measures available to judge the size of the yearly depreciation charge:

	19x5	19x6	19x7	19x8	19x9	19y0
Accumulated depreciation as a percentage of gross plant	53	55	53	49	47	48
Annual depreciation expense as a percentage of gross plant	5.0	4.8	4.4	4.2	4.3	4.5

The decline in the percentage of accumulated depreciation in relation to gross plant most likely reflects the substantial additions of new equipment in recent years. The decline of depreciation expense as a percentage of gross plant is, however, indicative of a less conservative depreciation policy in the more recent years.

Selling, general, and administrative expenses as a percentage of sales have, generally, been on the rise. In 19y0, they stood at 24 percent which compares to an industry composite figure of only 21 percent. Thus, by the time we reach operating income, the advantage that the company held over the industry because of larger gross margin has now been neutralized. Operating income for Marine Supply Corporation represents 11.4 percent of sales, and that compares with 11.6 percent for the industry. Further inquiries should be made to determine whether the selling expense component or the general and administrative part are responsible for the increase in this category.

Interest expenses have shown by far the steepest increase over the past six years. On the basis of 19x5 = 100, they have grown to 945 (almost tenfold) by 19y0 (Exhibit 10–9). This is due, of course, primarily to the sharp expansion of debt. Moreover, the short-term revolving debt is interest sensitive and thus introduces a measure of uncertainty in the forecasting of future interest charges.

Two other aspects of the quality of Marine Supply Corporation's earnings should be noted.

R&D costs as a percentage of sales have been in a declining trend having reached 4.2 percent in 19y0 down from 6.5 percent in 19x5 (Exhibit 10–3). This raises a question about the effect on future sales and profits of the decline in the R&D cost outlays in relation to sales. Similarly, the percentage of sales devoted to repairs and maintenance has declined from 5.7 percent in 19x5 to 3.8 percent in 19y0, a matter of concern particularly in the light of the fact that Marine Supply Corporation's facilities are, on average, older now than in 19x5. In the latter year, the percentage of repair and maintenance expense in relation to gross plant was 12.1 percent. In 19y0, that relationship dropped to 8.3 percent. This *prima facie* evidence of a deterioration in the quality of Marine Supply Corporation's earnings merits further investigation.

The total effective tax rate of Marine Supply Corporation in 19y0 is 52 percent which compares to the industry composite effective rate of 47 percent. The net income to sales of Marine Supply Corporation is 4.4 percent for 19y0, significantly below the industry composite of 5.8 percent for that year. However, since 19y0 was a year of labor trouble for the company, the percentages of net income to sales prevailing in the prior years, which are closer to the industry average, may be taken as more representative of the company's earning power.

Exhibit 10–17 analyzes the change occurring in net income between the 19x5–x7 period and the 19x8–y0 period. Sales increased by 46 percent, but due largely to greater increases in the cost of goods sold (49 percent) and interest expenses (353 percent) the increase in net income was held to only 11 percent.

Summary and conclusions

This analysis has examined all facets of Marine Supply Corporation's record of results of operations and financial position and has estimated the projected results and fund flows for one year. An analysis such as this is an indispensable step in arriving at a decision on the three questions posed. Nevertheless, essential as the data and information developed by this analysis

Exhibit 10–17

MARINE SUPPLY CORPORATION
Statement Accounting for Variations in Net Income
Three-Year Period 19x5–19x7 (average) Compared to
Three-Year Period 19x8–19y0 (average)
(in millions)

Items tending to increase net income:			
Increase in net sales:			
Net sales, 19x8–y0	$303.93		
Net sales, 19x5–x7	208.87	$95.06	46%
Deduct increase in cost of goods sold:			
Cost of goods sold, 19x8–y0	193.42		
Cost of goods sold, 19x5–x7	129.78	63.64	49
Net increase in gross margin		$31.42	
Items tending to decrease in net income:			
Increase in depreciation:			
Depreciation, 19x8–y0	5.53		
Depreciation, 19x5–x7	4.31	1.22	28
Increase in selling, general, and administrative expenses:			
SGA, 19x8–y0	68.81		
SGA, 19x5–x7	47.69	21.12	44
Increase in interest expense:			
Interest expense, 19x8–y0	4.48		
Interest expense, 19x5–x7	.99	3.49	353
Increase in other income and expense:			
Other income and expense, 19x8–y0	.80		
Other income and expense, 19x5–x7	.59	.21	36
Net increase in expenses		26.04	
Net increase in profit before taxes ..		5.38	21
Increase in income taxes:			
Income taxes, 19x8–y0	15.52		
Income taxes, 19x5–x7	11.66	3.86	33
Net increase in net income		1.52	11

are, it is not sufficient in most cases to arrive at a final conclusion. This is so because qualitative and other factors can have an important bearing on the final conclusion. Only when all the factors, those developed by the analysis as well as the others, have been assembled can a decision be reached by the application of judgment.

For example, the *bank* that is asked to extend short-term credit must take into consideration the character of the management, past loan experience, as well as the ongoing relationship with the loan applicant.

In addition to the foregoing intangibles, the long-term lender will focus on such matters as security arrangements and provisions that safeguard the solvency of the recipient of the loan.

The *equity investor* is, of course, interested in earning power and in earnings per share, but many considerations and judgments must be joined with these data before an investment decision is made. Thus, for instance, what earnings are, and what they are likely to be, is the product of financial analysis. At what price-earnings ratio they should be capitalized is a question for investment judgment. Similarly, the risk inherent in an enterprise, the volatility of its earnings, and the breadth and quality of the market for its securities are factors which must also be considered. They determine whether an investment fits into the investor's portfolio and whether it is compatible with his investment objectives.

Since the ultimate conclusions regarding problems, such as the lending and investing decision that we consider in this case, are based on more than the data and facts brought out by financial analysis alone, it follows that the most useful way to present the results of financial analysis is to summarize them by listing the most relevant and salient points which were developed by the analysis and which the decision maker should consider. This we shall do in this case.

The following are the main points that have been developed by our analysis of Marine Supply Corporation.

Short-term liquidity.   The current ratio is in a downtrend but still stands at a relatively sound level. The downtrend may, in part, represent a correction of former excessive levels in the ratio.

The current assets are, as a whole, less liquid than in former years. The slower turnover in accounts receivable indicates a possible deterioration in collectibility. The decline in inventory turnover may be due to diversity of product line rather than to unsalable or obsolete items in stock.

Current liabilities have risen sharply in recent years, and they now represent one fourth of all funds available to the enterprise.

The decline in liquidity is evidenced by a rise in the liquidity index.

Fund projections for 19y1 indicate a projected increase in working capital of $16 million by the end of that year. This assumes, however, the successful sale of $30 million in bonds and that expense projections which incorporate benefits of efficiencies will be realized. There is a moderate amount of risk that these projections may not be realized.

Capital structure and long-term solvency.   In 19y0, equity capital represented 55 percent of total funds invested in the enterprise down from 73 percent in 19x5. In recent years (see Exhibit 10–9), long-term debt increased drastically (3.18 times), out of proportion to such measures as growth in sales (1.69 times) or in equity (1.43 times).

The reduction of equity capital relative to debt and all funds invested in the company is not a favorable development in view of the fact that Marine Supply Corporation is in a cyclical industry. The company may be nearing the limit of its debt capacity.

The ratio of earnings to fixed charges is down to 5.28 in 19y0 (from 29.24 to 19x5). If a portion of rentals would be included as fixed charges, the coverage ratio would drop lower still. Next year, assuming the $30 million in long-term bonds are sold, this ratio is slated to improve to 8.2 times.

Over the last six years 77 percent of all funds inflows were funds generated by operations. Thus, a very substantial source of funds is vulnerable to changes in operating results. Over the longer term, demand for funds is expected to increase significantly. Long-term debt maturities are slated to increase sharply even excluding those from the $30 million bond issue that is expected to be sold in 19y1. There will be a growing need of funds for plant and equipment. Provisions for depreciation were consistently below fixed-asset additions in recent years.

Return on investment and asset utilization. The ROI is in a declining trend. In 19y0, the return on total assets was 6.4 percent compared with an industry composite of 9.3 percent. The return on equity capital was 9.5 percent in 19y0, making the disparity with the industry composite of 12.8 percent somewhat less marked.

The decline in return on total assets is due to the twin effects of declining asset utilization rates as well as a decline in profitability per dollar of sales. The effect of increasing leverage has slowed the decline of return on equity in comparison with the return on total assets.

Operating performance. The company's gross profit percentage has held relatively steady over the past six years. Other costs have neutralized Marine Supply Corporation's higher gross margin compared to the industry. Interest expenses have risen sharply over recent years. Both R&D expenses and repair and maintenance outlays have declined as a percentage of sales in recent years.

The significant decline in net income as a percentage of sales to 4.4 percent in 19y0 (industry composite 5.8 percent) is due to the particularly adverse labor and economic conditions of that year. In prior years, the company's net as a percentage of sales compared more favorably to industry experience.

Projected income for 19y1, based on the assumptions stated in the analysis, is $16.6 million after a loss of $3 million on disposal of the chain-saw division. On a per share basis, the net income per share is expected to be $2.06 per share compared to earnings per share in 19y0 of $1.66 and in 19x9 of $2.11. In 19y0, income per share before the loss on the chain-saw division is projected at $2.43.

USES OF FINANCIAL STATEMENT ANALYSIS

The foregoing analysis of the financial statements of Marine Supply Corporation consists of two major parts: (1) the detailed analysis and (2) the summary and conclusions. As was mentioned earlier, in a formal analytical report the summary and conclusions section may precede the detailed analysis so that the reader is presented with material in the order of its importance to him.

The *bank* loan officer who has to decide on the short-term loan application by the company will normally give primary attention to short-term liquidity analysis and to the funds flow projection and secondarily to capital structure and operating results.

The investment committee of the *insurance company* may, in taking a longer-term point of view, pay attention first to capital structure and long-term solvency and then to operating performance, ROI, asset utilization, and short-term liquidity, and in that order of emphasis.

The *potential investor* in Marine Supply Corporation's shares will, of course, be interested in all the aspects of our analysis. His emphasis may, however, be different again and take the following order of priority: results of operations, ROI, capital structure, and long-term solvency and short-term liquidity.

An adequate financial statement analysis will, as the Marine Supply Corporation analysis illustrates, contain in addition to the analysis of the data, enough information and detail so as to allow the decision maker to follow the rationale behind the analyst's conclusions as well as to allow him to expand it into areas not covered by the analysis.

QUESTIONS

1. What kind of processes should normally precede an analysis of financial statements?

2. What are the analytical implications of the fact that financial statements are, at best, an abstraction of underlying reality?

3. Name the six major "building blocks" of financial analysis. What does the "building block" approach involve?

4. What are some of the earmarks of a good analysis? Into what distinct sections should a well-organized analysis be divided?

5. What additional knowledge and analytical skills must an analyst bring to bear upon the analysis of enterprises in specialized or regulated industries?

Appendix: The auditor's opinion— meaning and significance

An entity's financial statements are the representations of its management. Management bears a primary responsibility for the fairness of presentation and the degree of informative disclosure in the financial statements it issues to interested parties, such as present and potential owners, creditors, and others. It has, however, become generally accepted that there is a need for an independent check on management's financial reporting.

The profession that serves society's need in this respect by performing the attest function is the public accounting profession. It may be readily observed that the more developed a country's economy and the more diverse, free, and mobile its capital and money markets, the stronger and the more important its public accounting profession is likely to be. Surely, the United States' experience supports this conclusion, for the public accounting profession here is perhaps the world's largest and most vital.

Some states recognize and license "Public Accountants" and "Licensed Accountants," and the requirements for practice under these titles vary from strict to feeble. However, there is another title that has the most consistent significance—that of "Certified Public Accountant." It can be acquired only by those who have passed the CPA examination, a rigorous series of tests that are uniform in all states and that are graded centrally under the auspices of the American Institute of Certified Public Accountants (AICPA). While no profession can ensure uniformity of quality among its members, the successful completion of these examinations does ensure that the candidate has demonstrated a sufficiently acceptable knowledge of accounting and auditing principles and practices.

Since the CPAs represent by far the most important segment of public accounting practice in the United States, our consideration of the auditor's opinion will be confined to that issued by the CPA and governed by the various pronouncements issued by their professional association, the AICPA.

In spite of the many real and imagined shortcomings of the auditor's work, and, and, as this book illustrates, there are many of both varieties, the auditor's function is of critical importance to the financial analyst. While improvements are needed in many areas of the auditor's work, his attestation to the fair presentation of the financial statements greatly increases their reliability to the analyst as well as the degree and quality of disclosure provided in them.

As in many areas of endeavor, so in the analysis of financial statements, partial or incomplete knowledge can be more damaging than a complete lack of it. This truth applies to the analyst's understanding and knowledge of the auditor's work and the significance of his opinion.

WHAT THE ANALYST NEEDS TO KNOW

In relying on the auditor's opinion, which covers the financial statements subject to review, the analyst must—

1. Learn as much as he can about the auditor upon whom he is relying.
2. Understand fully what the auditor's opinion means and the message it is designed to convey to the user.
3. Appreciate the limitations to which the opinion is subject, as well as the implications that such limitations hold for the analysis of financial statements covered by the opinion.

Knowing the auditor

The possession by the auditor of the CPA certificate does assure the analyst of a reasonable qualification for practice as an auditor. However, as is the case in other professions, differences in ability, competence, and qualifications can be considerable.

The relationship between the auditor and those who rely on his opinion differs markedly from that existing in other professional relationships. While the auditor has both an obligation and a concurrent responsibility to users of his opinion, he is in most cases neither appointed nor compensated by them. He must look mostly to management for both recommendation for his appointment and the determination of his fee. When management's desires with respect to financial reporting are in conflict with the best interests of the outside users of financial statements, the auditor's integrity and independence are put to a stern test. Thus, one criterion of the auditor's reliability is his reputation for integrity and independence in the community at large and among respected members of the financial community. Whatever else the auditor must have, and his qualifications and skill must be considerable, without these attributes nothing else counts for very much. The reputation of an auditor for competence and for knowledge of his work can be established in a variety of ways. The auditor's professional credentials, including the length, breadth, and quality of his experience, are one element, his membership and standing in state and national accounting associations another, and his participation in professional organizations yet another factor to be assessed by the analyst. An auditing firm's activities and past performance are usually well known in the community in which it operates.

Finally, the analyst, from his own experience is often able to form a judgment about the auditor's reputation for quality work. Since there exists considerable leeway in adherence to audit standards and in the application of accounting principles, an audit firm's "track record" of actual level of performances in these critical areas provides a firsthand guide to its reliability and integrity. The analyst would do well to note instances in which a CPA firm has accepted the least desirable acceptable accounting principle among the available alternatives, has equivocated unnecessarily in its opinion, or was found wanting in its application of auditing procedures.

Good sources of information on the capabilities of an audit firm include local bankers, investment bankers, and attorneys.

What the auditor's opinion means

The auditor's opinion is the culmination of a lengthy and complicated process of auditing and investigation. It is here, and only here, that the auditor reports on the nature of his work and on the degree of responsibility he assumes. While his influence may be indirectly felt throughout the financial statements by the presentation, description, and footnote disclosure that he may have suggested or insisted upon, the opinion, and the opinion alone, remains his exclusive domain. Thus, the opinion and the references to the financial statements which it contains should always be carefully read. To ignore the auditor's opinion, or to assume that it does not mean what it says, or that it means more than it says, is foolhardy and unwarranted.

The auditor's responsibility to outsiders whom he does not know and who rely on his representations is considerable, and his exposure to liability arising therefrom is growing. Thus, the obligations that the standards of his profession impose on him, while extensive, are at the same time defined and limited. Consequently, no analyst is justified in assuming that the association of the auditor's name with the financial statements goes beyond what the auditor's opinion says, or is a form of insurance on which the analyst can rely to bail him out of bad decisions.

What exactly does the auditor's opinion say? The best starting point for us is an examination of an auditor's "clean opinion," that is, an opinion that is not qualified in any way. This will give us an idea of the greatest degree of responsibility the auditor is willing to assume. The "clean opinion," which covers two annual examinations, reads as follows:

> To the Shareowners and Board of Directors
> (Name of Company)
>   We have examined the balance sheet of (name of company) as of (date), and the related statements of income and retained earnings, and the statement

of changes in financial position for the year then ended. Our examination was made in accordance with generally accepted auditing standards, and accordingly included such tests of the accounting records and such other auditing procedures as we considered necessary in the circumstances. We previously examined and reported upon the financial statement of the Company for the year ended (date).

In our opinion, the aforementioned financial statements present fairly the financial position of (name of company) at (date) and (date), and the results of its operations and the changes in its financial position for the years then ended, in conformity with generally accepted accounting principles applied on a consistent basis.

(Name of accountants)

(City and date)

THE AUDITOR'S REPORT

The auditor's report is divided into two distinct parts: (1) the scope of the audit and (2) the auditor's opinion.

The scope of the audit

The scope paragraph of the auditor's report sets forth the financial statements examined, the period of time that they cover, and the scope of the audit to which they and the underlying records have been subjected.

The standard terminology refers to an examination made in accordance with "generally accepted auditing standards." This is "shorthand" for a very comprehensive meaning that is elaborated upon in the profession's literature and particularly in *Statements on Auditing Standards* and subsequent codifications. These auditing standards are broad generalizations classified under three headings: (1) general standards (2) standards of fieldwork, and (3) standards of reporting.

General standards define the personal qualities required of the independent CPA. They are:

- a. The examination is to be performed by a person or persons having adequate technical training and proficiency as an auditor.
- b. In all matters relating to the assignment an independence in mental attitude is to be maintained by the auditor or auditors.
- c. Due professional care is to be exercised in the performance of the examination and the preparation of the report.

Standards of fieldwork embrace the actual execution of the audit and cover the planning of the work, the evaluation of the client's system of internal control, and the quality and sufficiency of the audit evidence obtained. *SAS 1* enumerates them as follows:

1. The work is to be adequately planned and assistants, if any, are to be properly supervised.

2. There is to be a proper study and evaluation of the existing internal control as a basis for reliance thereon and for the determination of the resultant extent of the tests to which auditing procedures are to be restricted.
3. Sufficient competent evidential matter is to be obtained through inspection, observation, inquiries and confirmations to afford a reasonable basis for an opinion regarding the financial statements under examination.

Reporting standards govern the preparation and presentation of the auditor's report. They are intended to ensure that the auditor's position is clearly and unequivocally stated and that the degree of responsibility he assumes is made clear to the reader. These standards are four in number:

1. The report shall state whether the financial statements are presented in accordance with generally accepted accounting principles.
2. The report shall state whether such principles have been consistently observed in the current period in relation to the preceding period.
3. Informative disclosures in the financial statements are to be regarded as reasonably adequate unless otherwise stated in the report.
4. The report shall either contain an expression of opinion regarding the financial statements, taken as a whole, or an assertion to the effect that an opinion cannot be expressed. When an overall opinion cannot be expressed, the reasons therefore should be stated. In all cases where an auditor's name is associated with financial statements, the report should contain a clear-cut indication of the character of the auditor's examination, if any, and the degree of responsibility he is taking.

Audit standards are the yardsticks by which the quality of audit procedures are measured.

Auditing procedures. The second phrase of the scope section states that the examination "included such tests of the accounting records and such other auditing procedures" as were considered necessary in the circumstances.

This statement encompasses the wide sweep of auditing theory brought to bear on the particular examination, as well as the professional discretion the auditor uses in the performance of his work.

The subject of auditing is, of course, a discipline in itself requiring for successful mastery a period of study and practical application. Thus, while we obviously cannot go with any degree of detail into what constitutes the process of auditing, it behooves all who use its end product to have a basic understanding of the process by which the auditor obtains assurance about the fair presentation of the financial statements as to which he expresses an opinion.

A basic objective of the financial audit is the detection of errors and irregularities, intentional or unintentional, which if undetected would materially affect the fairness of presentation of financial summarizations or their conformity with GAAP.

To be economically feasible and justifiable, auditing can aim only at a reasonable level of assurance in this respect about the data under review.

This means that under a testing system, assurance can never be complete, and that the final audit conclusions are subject to this inherent probability of error.

Briefly stated, the auditor's basic approach is as follows: to gain assurance about financial summarizations the auditor must examine the accounting system of which they are a final product. If the system of internal control is well conceived, properly maintained, and implemented, it is assumed that it should result in valid financial records and summarizations.

Thus, the need for and the extent of the testing of the records is dependent on the degree of proper operation of the system of internal control.

The importance of internal control. The importance of the review of the system of internal control in the total audit framework can be gauged from a reading of the scope paragraph of the original standard opinion (used from about 1939 to 1948) which read in part as follows:

> have reviewed the system of internal control and the accounting procedures of the company, and, without making a detailed audit of the transactions, have examined or tested accounting records of the company and other supporting evidence by methods, and to the extent we deemed appropriate.

Even though these specific words have been deleted from the form of the present opinion, the phrase still accurately describes the auditor's work.

After ascertaining, by means of investigation and inquiry, what management's plan and design for a system of internal control is, if any, the auditor proceeds to test the system in order to ascertain whether it is in existence and is, in fact, being implemented as intended. This testing is called compliance testing.

If after application of compliance testing, the system of internal control is found to be well conceived and in proper operation, the amount of testing to which income statement items or individual assets and liabilities will be subjected can be significantly restricted. The latter type of testing, which may be called substantive testing, will have to be increased significantly if compliance testing reveals the system of internal control to be deficient or not operational.

This method of checking out the system and then performing additional sample tests on the basis of its evaluation does, of course, leave room for a great deal of professional discretion, for "corner-cutting," and for a variety of qualities of judgment. Hence, it is subject to the risk of failure. Moreover, since the usual audit is based on a system of selective testing, it cannot be relied on to disclose defalcations, although their discovery may result.

From the above discussion it should be clear that reliance on an audit must be based on an understanding of the nature of the audit process and the limitations to which it is subject.

The opinion section

The first paragraph of the auditor's report, which we discussed above, deals with the scope of his examination and the limitations or restrictions, if any, to which it was subject. The second paragraph (in practice the order of these paragraphs may be reversed) sets forth the auditor's opinion on:

1. The fairness of presentation of the financial statements.
2. Their conformity with GAAP.
3. The consistent application of these principles in the financial statements.

"Fair presentation"

One of the great debates among auditors and between auditors and society in general, particularly the courts, concerns the meaning of the phrase "present fairly" which is found in the auditor's report. Most auditors maintain that financial statements are fairly presented when they conform to GAAP and that "fairness" is meaningful only in this context.

Yet, clearly, in quite a number of cases reaching the courts in recent years, financial statements that, according to expert testimony were prepared in accordance with GAAP, were nevertheless found to be misleading in an overall sense. This became particularly apparent in the landmark Continental Vending case where the lack of disclosure of certain highly dubious transactions was defended as not being, at that time, required by GAAP. In refusing to instruct the jury that conformity with GAAP was a complete defense to the charge of fraud, the trial judge maintained that the critical question was whether Continental's financial statements, taken as a whole, "fairly presented" its financial picture. He found that while conformity with GAAP might be very persuasive evidence of an auditor's good faith, it was not necessarily conclusive evidence of it.

The auditors, in an attempt to respond to a clear divergence between their and society's views of what is meant by "present fairly," issued a statement on the matter in 1975. While still maintaining that "fairness" must be applied within the framework of GAAP, they stated that "fair presentation" also requires that—

a. The accounting principles selected and applied must have general acceptance.[1]
b. The accounting principles must be appropriate in the circumstances.
c. The financial statements must be "informative of matters that may affect their use, understanding, and interpretation."
d. The information must be presented and summarized "in a reasonable manner, that is, neither too detailed nor too condensed."

---

[1] *SAS 43* (1982) details the hierarchy of sources of established accounting principles.

   e. The financial statements must reflect "the underlying events and transactions" in a way that states the results within "a range of acceptable limits that are reasonable and practicable."

As part of the accounting profession's periodic attempts at self-examination and assessment, especially in the face of congressional and public scrutiny and criticism, an AICPA appointed Commission on Auditor's Responsibilities issued its "Report, Conclusions, and Recommendations" in 1978. Only some of the commission's recommendations may ultimately be adopted in modified form.

Modification of the opinion

The standard short-form report presented earlier in the chapter contained a "clean opinion;" that is, the auditor had no qualifications to record as to any of the three criteria enumerated above. Any modifications of substance in the language of the auditor's opinion paragraph is, technically speaking, considered to be a qualification, a disclaimer, or an adverse opinion. Not all modifications are, of course, of equal significance to the user. Some deviations in language are explanatory in character reflecting matters that the auditor wishes to emphasize and may not affect the auditor's opinion significantly. References to the work of other auditors is not regarded as a qualification but rather an indication of divided responsibility for the financial statements. Other explanatory comments may not carry over to affect the auditor's opinion and, at times, one may wonder why mention of them is necessary. On the other hand, certain qualifications or disclaimers are so significant as to cast doubt on the reliability of the financial statements or their usefulness for decision-making purposes.

Let us then examine the major categories of the auditor's qualifications and disclaimers, the occasions on which they are properly used, and the significance which they hold to the user of financial statements.

CIRCUMSTANCES GIVING RISE TO QUALIFICATIONS, DISCLAIMERS, OR ADVERSE OPINIONS

There are four main categories of conditions that require qualifications, an adverse opinion, or a disclaimer of opinion:

1. Limitations in the scope of the auditor's examination affected by *(a)* conditions that preclude the application of auditing procedures considered necessary in the circumstances or *(b)* restrictions imposed by the client.
2. The financial statements do not present fairly the financial position and/or results of operations because *(a)* they fail to conform with GAAP or *(b)* they do not contain adequate disclosure.
3. There exist uncertainties about the future resolution of material matters,

the effect of which cannot presently be estimated or the outcome of which cannot reasonably be determined.

4. A change in comparability affects the consistency of presentation.

Before we consider the variety of conditions that call for qualified opinions, let us examine the major types of qualifications that the auditor may express.

QUALIFICATIONS—"EXCEPT FOR" AND "SUBJECT TO"

These qualifications express an opinion on the financial statements except for repercussions stemming from conditions that must be disclosed. They may arise from limitations in the scope of the audit which, because of circumstances beyond the auditor's control or because of restrictions imposed by the audited company, result in a failure to obtain reasonably objective and verifiable evidence in support of events which have taken place. They may arise from a lack of conformity of the financial statements to GAAP. When they arise because there are uncertainties about future events that cannot be resolved or the effect of which cannot be estimated or reasonably provided for at the time the opinion is rendered, the words *subject to* are substituted for *except for.*

An uncertainty, such as one due to operating losses or serious financial weakness that calls into question the fundamental assumption that an entity can continue to operate as a going concern, calls for a "subject to" qualification. In cases of pervasive uncertainty that cannot be adequately measured, an auditor may, but is not required to, issue a disclaimer of opinion rather than a "subject to" opinion.

ADVERSE OPINIONS

An adverse opinion should be rendered in cases when the financial statements are not prepared in accordance with GAAP, and this has a significant effect on the fair presentation of those statements. An adverse opinion results generally from a situation in which the auditor has been unable to convince his client to amend the financial statements so that they reflect the auditor's estimate about the outcome of future events or so that they otherwise adhere to GAAP. The issuance of an adverse opinion must always be accompanied by a statement of the reasons for such an opinion.

DISCLAIMER OF OPINION

A disclaimer of opinion is a statement of inability to express an opinion. It must be rendered when, for whatever reason, insufficient competent evidential matter is available to the auditor to enable him to form an opinion on the financial statements. It can arise from limitations in the scope of the audit as well as from the existence of uncertainties the ultimate impact of which cannot be estimated. Material departures from GAAP do not justify a disclaimer of opinion.

Adverse opinions versus disclaimers of opinion

The difference between adverse opinions and disclaimers of opinion can be best understood in terms of the difference that exists between exceptions that affect the quality of the financial statements, on one hand, and those that express uncertainties affecting the auditor's opinion, on the other. Thus, a situation that may call for an "except for" opinion may at some point result in such a degree of pervasive or material disagreements with management that it will require an adverse opinion. Similarly, pervasive and/or material uncertainties may, at some point, result in the conversion of a "subject to" opinion into a disclaimer of opinion.

THE FORM OF THE REPORT

Whenever the auditor expresses a qualified opinion, he must disclose in a middle paragraph, or in a footnote that is referred to in that paragraph, the substantive reasons for the qualification. The explanatory paragraph should disclose the principal effects of the subject matter of the qualification on financial position, results of operations, and changes in financial position, if reasonably determinable. The paragraph should also make it clear whether the qualification results because of a difference of opinion between the auditor and the client or whether it results because of an uncertainty not subject to present resolution.

All qualifications must be referred to in the opinion paragraph, and a qualification due to scope or lack of sufficient evidential matter must be also referred to in the scope paragraph. Thus, a mere explanatory statement should not be referred to in either the scope or the opinion paragraphs.

Having covered the various types of opinions an auditor can express, let us now turn to the various conditions that call for qualifications in such opinions.

LIMITATIONS IN THE SCOPE OF THE AUDIT

A limitation in the scope of the auditor's examination, that is, an inability to perform certain audit steps that he considers necessary, will, if material, result in a qualification or disclaimer of his opinion.

Some limitations in the scope of the auditor's examination arise from an inability to perform certain audit steps because of conditions beyond the auditor's and the client's control, for example, an inability to observe the opening inventory where the audit appointment was not made until the close of the year. Other limitations may result from a client-imposed restriction on the auditor's work. Whatever the reason for an incomplete examination, the auditor must report the inadequacy of the examination and the conclusions that flow from such an inadequacy.

The accounting profession has given special status to procedures with respect to observation of inventories and the confirmation of accounts receivable. If these steps cannot be reasonably or practically performed, the auditor must, in order to issue an unqualified opinion, satisfy himself about the inventories and accounts receivable by alternative means. He must, however, no longer indicate such an omission of regular procedures in his opinion.

FAILURE OF FINANCIAL STATEMENTS TO CONFORM TO GENERALLY ACCEPTED ACCOUNTING PRINCIPLES

The auditor brings to bear his expertise in the application of auditing techniques and procedures to satisfy himself about the existence, ownership, and validity of presentation of the assets, the liabilities, and net worth as well as the statement of results. As an expert accountant, the auditor judges the fairness of presentation of financial statements and their conformity with GAAP. The latter is one of the most important functions of the auditor's opinion.

Fair presentation is, to an important extent, dependent on the degree of informative disclosure provided. Adherence to GAAP, which is another prerequisite of fairness of presentation, depends on the employment, in the financial statements, of principles having authoritative support. *Opinions* of the APB and *Statements* of the FASB enjoy, by definition, authoritative support. If the accountant concurs in a company's use of an accounting principle which differs from that approved by an authoritative body but which he believes enjoys the support of other authoritative sources, he need not qualify his opinion, but he must disclose that the principle used differs from those approved by such authoritative body. This, of course, puts the onus on the auditor in justifying the departure from a principle which enjoys authoritative approval.

If, because of lack of adequate disclosure or the use of accounting principles that do not enjoy authoritative support, the auditor concludes that the financial statements are not fairly presented, he must qualify his opinion or render an adverse opinion. The decision of whether to make his opinion an "except-for" type, which is a qualified opinion, or to render an adverse opinion, which states that the "financial statements do not present fairly . . ." hinges on the materiality of the effect of such a deficiency on the financial statements taken as a whole. The concept of materiality in accounting and auditing is, however, very vague and remains so far undefined.

It is obvious that a qualification due to a lack of disclosure or a lack of adherence to GAAP is the result of the auditor's inability to persuade his client to modify the financial statements. Thus, an "except for" type of opinion is not proper, and an adverse opinion is called for together with a full description of the shortcomings in the financial statements as well as their total impact thereon.

The following are pertinent excerpts from an opinion qualified because of lack of adherence to GAAP:

> As explained in Note A, the 19x3 financial statements include interest expense that has not been capitalized as required by *SFAS 34*.
>
> In our opinion, except that in 19x3 interest expense has not been capitalized as described in the preceding paragraph . . .

FINANCIAL STATEMENTS SUBJECT TO UNRESOLVED KNOWN UNCERTAINTIES

Whenever uncertainties about the future exist that cannot be resolved, or whose effect cannot be estimated or reasonably provided for at the time of the issuance of the auditor's opinion, a qualified opinion or a disclaimer of opinion may be indicated. Such uncertainties may relate to lawsuits, tax matters, or other contingencies, the outcome of which is dependent upon decisions of parties other than management. Or the uncertainties may relate to the recovery of the investment in certain assets through future operations, or through their disposition.

The practical effect of an uncertainty qualification is to state the auditor's inability to assess the impact of the contingency, or the likelihood of its occurrence, and to pass on to the reader the burden of its evaluation.

One variety of qualification relates to the question of whether the going-concern assumption in accounting is justified. This question arises when a company is incurring continued operating losses, deficits in the stockholder's equity, working capital insufficiencies, or defaults under loan agreements. In such cases, the auditor expresses his doubt about the propriety of applying practices implicit in the going-concern concept such as the valuation of fixed assets at cost.

The following are examples of pertinent portions of auditor reports relating to uncertainties:

> As discussed in Note 4, because of the uncertainty of mining plans it may be necessary at some indeterminate future date to write off a significant amount of net book investment in the Company's Questa mine and mill.
>
> In our opinion, subject to the realization of the Company's investment in Questa property referred to above.
>
> *   *   *   *   *
>
> The accompanying financial statements of the Company have been prepared on the basis of a going concern, although the ability of the Company to continue

as a going concern is dependent upon future earnings. In this connection, it should be noted that in the period from commencement of operations through June 30, 19x8, the Company accumulated a net loss of $150,340.

Except for the appropriateness of the going-concern concept and for the ability of the Company to realize its unamortized programming development costs through future profitable operations, in our opinion the accompanying financial statements present fairly.

EXCEPTIONS AS TO CONSISTENCY

The second standard of reporting requires that the auditor's report state whether the principles of accounting employed "have been consistently observed in the current period in relation to the preceding period."

The basic objective of the consistency standard is to assure the reader that comparability of financial statements as between periods has not been materially affected by changes in the accounting principles employed or in the method of their application. Thus, if a change has been made affecting the comparability of the financial statements, a statement of the nature of the changes and their effect on the financial statements is required.

There are three types of changes that must be considered here:

1. Changes in accounting principles employed; for example, a change in the method of depreciation.
2. Changes required by altered conditions; for example, a change in the estimated useful life of an asset.
3. Changed conditions unrelated to accounting that nevertheless have an effect on comparability; for example, the acquisition or disposition of a subsidiary.

Changes of type 1 involve the consistency standard and must be dealt with in the auditor's opinion. Changes of type 2 and 3 affect comparability, and while not requiring comment in the auditor's report, they do require footnote disclosure.

SPECIAL REPORTS

In certain cases the standard short-form report of the auditor is not appropriate because of special circumstances or because of the limited scope of the examination that the auditor is requested to undertake. It is particularly important that the analyst read such reports carefully so that he is not misled into believing that the auditor is assuming here his ordinary measure of responsibility. The following are some types of special reports that the reader may encounter:

1. Reports by companies on a cash or incomplete basis of accounting.
2. Reports by nonprofit organizations.
3. Reports prepared for limited purposes. Such reports usually deal with certain aspects of the financial statements (such as computations of royalties, rentals, profit-sharing arrangements, or compliance with provisions of bond indentures, etc.).

In *FRR* No. 1, Section 304 the SEC has called for the auditor's "association" with published interim reports based on performance of a limited review.

REPORTS ON "COMPILED" AND "REVIEWED" FINANCIAL STATEMENTS

In 1979, the AICPA made available to "nonpublic entities" compilation and review services that, while falling short of a full audit, provide the reader with lower defined levels of assurance.

Compiled financial statements are accompanied by a report that indicates that a compilation has been performed and that such a service is limited to presenting, in financial statement format, information that is the representation of management or owners. The report should also state that the financial statements have not been audited or reviewed; thus no opinion or any other form of assurance is expressed on them. No reference is made to any other procedures performed before or during the compilation engagement.

Reviewed financial statements are accompanied by a report that indicates that a review was performed in accordance with AICPA standards. The report describes a review engagement, states that the information in the financial statements is the representation of management (or owners), and disclaims an opinion on the financial statements taken as a whole. The report should state that: "The accountant is not aware of any material modifications that should be made to the financial statements in order for them to be in conformity with generally accepted accounting principles, other than those modifications, if any, indicated in his report." No reference is made to any other procedures performed before or during the review engagement.

THE SEC'S IMPORTANT ROLE

The SEC has in recent years moved particularly forcefully to monitor auditor performance as well as to strengthen the hands of auditors in their dealings with managements.

Disciplinary proceedings against auditors were expanded to include requirements for improvements in internal administration procedures, professional education, and a review of a firm's procedures by outside professionals.

SEC *FRR* No. 1, Section 603, in moving to strengthen the auditor's position, requires increased disclosure of the relationship between auditors and their clients, particularly in cases where changes in auditors take place. Disclosure must include details of past disagreements, including those resolved to the satisfaction of the replaced auditor, as well as footnote disclosure of the effects on the financial statements of methods of accounting advocated by a former auditor but not followed by the client.

IMPLICATIONS FOR ANALYSIS

Auditing as a function and the auditor's opinion as an instrument of assurance are widely misunderstood. The responsibility for this lack of communication cannot be all laid at the auditor's door, for the profession has published a number of pamphlets in which it has endeavored to explain its function. Nor should the readers of financial statements bear the full responsibility for this state of affairs, because the accounting profession's message in this area is often couched in technical and cautious language and requires a great deal of effort and background information for a full understanding.

A useful discussion of the implications of the current state of auditing to the user of audited financial statements may be presented in two parts:

1. Implications stemming from the nature of the audit process.
2. Implications arising from the professional standards which govern the auditor's opinion.

Implications inherent in the audit process

Auditing is based on a sampling approach to the data under audit. Statistical sampling uses a rigorous approach to this process, which lends itself to a quantification of conclusions. Nevertheless, many audit tests are based on "judgmental samples" of the data, that is, samples selected by the auditor's intuition, judgment, and evaluation of many factors. Often the size of the sample is necessarily limited by the economics of the accounting practice.[2]

The reader must realize that the auditor does not aim at, nor can he ever achieve, complete certainty. Even a review of every single transaction—a process that would be economically unjustifiable—would not achieve a complete assurance.

Auditing is a developing art. Even its very basic theoretical underpinnings are far from fully understood or resolved. There is, for instance, no clear

---

[2] This and other "inherent limitations of the auditing process," are emphasized in an SAS issued in 1977 on "The Independent Auditor's Responsibility for the Detection of Errors and Irregularities." The *Statement* declares that the auditor's examination is subject to the inherent risk that material errors or irregularities, if they exist, will not be detected.

relationship between the auditor's evaluation of the effectiveness of the system of internal controls, which is a major factor on which the auditor relies, and the extent of audit testing and the nature of audit procedures employed. If we add to that the fact that the qualities of judgment among auditors do vary greatly, we should not be surprised to find that the history of auditing contains many examples of spectacular failure. On the other hand, as is the case with the risk of accidental death in commercial aviation, the percentage of failure to the total number of audits performed is very small indeed. Thus, while the user of audited financial statements can, in general, be reassured about the overall results of the audit function, he must remember that there is substantial risk in reliance on its results in specific cases. Such risks are due to many factors, including the auditor's inability to detect fraud at the highest level and the application of proper audit tests to such an end (McKesson and Robbins case through the Cenco, Inc., case and all the way to the Equity Funding case), the auditor's inability to grasp the extent of a deteriorating situation (the Yale Express case), the auditor's conception of the range of his responsibilities to probe and disclose (the Continental Vending and National Student Marketing cases), and the quality of the audit (Bar Chris Construction, U.S. Financial, Whittaker Corporation, Mattel, and McCormick Company, cases).

Thus, while the audit function may generally justify the reliance that financial analysts place on audited financial statements, such a reliance cannot be a blind one. The analyst must be aware that the entire audit process is a probabilistic one subject to many risks. Even its flawless application may not necessarily result in complete assurance, and most certainly cannot ensure that the auditor has elicited all the facts, especially if there is high-level management collusion to withhold such facts from him. Finally, the heavy dependence of the auditing process on judgment will, of necessity, result in a wide range of quality of performance.

An insight into what can be missed, and why, in the internal and external audit of a large corporation can be obtained from a reading of the *Report of the Special Review Committee of the Board of Directors of Gulf Oil Corporation* (the McCloy report—December 1975). In searching for reasons why Gulf's internal financial controls, its internal auditors, and its external auditors failed to detect or curb the expenditure of large amounts of corporate funds through "off the books" bank accounts for unlawful purposes the review committee concluded that internal control committees chose not to control; that the corporate comptroller did not exercise the control powers vested in him, that the internal auditing department (reporting to the comptroller rather than to an audit committee of the board) lacked in independence and stature, and that while it is clear that the external auditors had some knowledge of certain unusual transactions, the extent of their knowledge could not be determined.

To provide the reader with insights into how wrong things can go in the "audit" of a major corporation, let us focus on the landmark Equity

Funding case.[3] This case includes expected elements such as human greed and shortcomings, the resulting fraud and deception and audit failure. It also includes the highly unusual in that never before have public accountants been charged with knowing complicity in a fraud extending over many years.

THE EQUITY FUNDING CASE.   The Equity Funding Corporation of America (EFCA) was an organization which sold mutual fund shares and used these as security against which the investor could borrow moneys for the payment of life insurance premiums on his or her behalf (the "funding" concept). From its inception as a public company in 1964, the major holders of its stock were obsessed with a desire to keep aloft the market price of its stock by fraudulently inflating reported earnings. As the fraud progressed and grew, vanity, pride, and the fear of being discovered provided added incentives to keep the fraud going.

An amazing aspect of this case is the relatively crude and unsophisticated design and execution of the fraud which relied on fictitious manual accounting entries lacking any real support.

In its early stages, the fraud consisted of recording nonexistent commission income with the charge (debit) going to a greatly inflated "Funding Loans Receivable" asset, supposedly representing borrowings by customers for life insurance premiums, etc. Over the years, $85 million in such bogus income was recorded. As is true with most frauds, the fictitious entries involved do not, of course, create cash. Thus, to provide cash and at the same time keep the mushrooming "Funding Loans Receivable" in check, the conspirators borrowed money (on the basis of glowing earning results), and instead of booking the corresponding liabilities, credited the Funding Loans Receivable account. Other complicated shams involved foreign subsidiaries.

As the cash-hungry fraud monster grew, the expanding circle of fraud participants, now including senior as well as lower-management levels, had to invent new cash raising schemes. This led to the involvement of Equity Funding Life Insurance Company (EFLIC), a unit involved in reinsurance, i.e., in the sale to others of insurance risks in force. Starting with intermediate, less crass and ambitious steps, there ultimately evolved a practice of creating totally fictitious products (insurance policies) that were sold to unsuspecting reinsurers who provided significant cash inflows. The process involved the "creation" of all needed documentation and related fictitious records. But, it also created the need for EFLIC to remit increasing amounts of cash to these reinsurers representing the premium payments which the company presumably collected from the fictitious policyholders. This created monumental documentation problems as well as severe cash flow problems (in 1972 reaching $1.7 million in cash flow deficit). These ever-growing fictions and problems that fed on themselves created a "house of cards" that would have collapsed of its own weight even without the whistle blowing of a disgruntled dismissed employee in early 1973.

The sheer size of the deception as well as its duration should give pause to any analyst. From 1964 through 1972, at least $143 million in fictitious pretax

---

[3] Most of the public documents as well as commentaries on this case are contained in L. J. Seidler, F. Andrews, and M. J. Epstein, *The Equity Funding Papers: The Anatomy of a Fraud* (New York: Wiley, 1977).

income was reported in EFCA's financial statements. During the same period, the net income reported by the company amounted to about $76 million. Thus, this company whose reported success captured the imagination of Wall Street, in fact never earned a dime.

The bankruptcy proceedings and investigation which started in 1973 also revealed that:

> Latecomers to the fraud benefited from and were motivated by prestigious and well-paying positions. This in turn led to a climate of dishonesty which included theft, expense account padding, and other manifestations of a breakdown of restraint and morality.

> The small audit firm performed its audit during 1961–70 with such manifest incompetence that it could only be explained by a knowledge of the fraud. A larger successor audit firm that purchased the practice of the smaller firm changed practically nothing in the sloppy and uncoordinated audit approach.

> The "big 8" audit firm of EFLIC failed to review internal controls and based its audit conclusions almost solely on internal records, thus omitting the crucial audit steps of independent outside verification.

> The auditors had to settle for about $39 million in damages.

Rigorous financial analysis should have revealed the propensities of the defrauders if not the specific elements of the fraud. Thus, a comparison of quarterly reports in 1971 would have revealed that derived fourth-quarter income was inflated while the related expenses were understated in relation to the revenue amounts. The EFCA fraud holds many important lessons about the dynamics of a fraudulent process as well as the weak points that it can reveal to a trained and inquisitive eye.

In relying on audited financial statements, the analyst must be ever aware of the risks of failure inherent in an audit; he must pay attention to the identity of the auditors and to what their record has been; and armed with a knowledge of what auditors do and how they do it, he must himself assess the areas of possible vulnerability in the financial statements. This brings us to the concept of audit risk.

Audit risk and its implications

The concept of accounting risk is concerned with the degree of realism and conservatism of accounting presentations. Audit risk, while related, is of a different dimension and represents, as a study of some of the above-mentioned cases will reveal, an equally clear and present danger to lenders and investors who rely on audited financial statements.

It is impossible for the analyst to substitute completely his judgment for that of the auditor. However, armed with an understanding of the audit process and its limitations, he can, through identification of special areas of vulnerability, make a better assessment of the degree of audit risk present in a given situation. The following are circumstances that can point to such areas of vulnerability:

Glamour industry and company with need for continuing earnings growth to justify high market price or to facilitate acquisitions.

Company in difficult financial condition requiring credit urgently and frequently.

Company with high market visibility issuing frequent progress reports and earnings estimates.

Managements dominated mostly by one or a few strong-willed individuals or consisting mostly of financial people including CPAs.

Management compensation or stock options importantly dependent on reported earnings.

Managements that have displayed a propensity for earnings maximization and manipulation by various means.

Indications of personal financial difficulties by members of the senior management team.

Deterioration in operating performance.

Deterioration in liquidity or long-term solvency.

A capital structure far too complex for company's operations or site.

Problem industry displaying weaknesses, in such areas as receivable collection, inventories, contract cost overruns, dependence on few products, and so forth.

Dealings with insiders or related parties, stockholder lawsuits, frequent turnover of key officers, legal counsel, or auditors.[4]

Audit conducted by a firm that has, for whatever reason, experienced a higher than normal incidence of audit failures.

While none of the above situations can be relied on to indicate situations of higher audit risk, they have been shown by experience to have appeared in a sufficient number of problem cases to warrant the analyst's close attention.

Implications stemming from the standards that govern the auditor's opinion

In relying on the auditor's opinion, the analyst must be aware of the limitations to which the audit process is subject, and this was the subject of the preceding discussion. Moreover, he must understand what the auditor's opinion means and particularly what the auditor himself thinks he conveys to the reader by means of his opinion.

Let us first consider the unqualified opinion or the so-called "clean" opinion. The auditor maintains that he expresses an opinion on *management's* statements. He is very insistent on this point and attaches considerable impor-

---

[4] The SEC in *FRR* No. 1, Section 603, required increased disclosure of relationships between registrants and their independent public accountants, including disputes, particularly in cases where changes in accountants occur.

tance to it. It means that normally he did not prepare the financial statements nor did he choose the accounting principles embodied in them. Instead, he reviews the financial statements presented to him by management and ascertains that they are in agreement with the books and records that he audited. He also determines that generally acceptable principles of accounting have been employed in the preparation of the financial statements, but that does not mean that they are the *best* principles that could have been used. It is a well-known fact that management will often rely on the auditor, as an expert in accounting, to help them pick the principle that, while still acceptable, will come nearest to meeting their reporting objectives. Finally, the auditor will determine that the minimum standards of disclosure have been met so that all matters essential to a fair presentation of the financial statements are included in them.

One might well ask what difference it makes whether the auditor prepared the statements or not so long as he expresses an unqualified opinion on them. The accounting profession has never clearly explained what the implications of this really are to the user of the financial statements. However, a number of such possible implications should be borne in mind by the analyst:

1. The auditor's knowledge about the financial statements is not as strong as that of the preparer who was in more intimate contact with all the factors which gave rise to the transactions. He knows only what he can discern on the basis of a sampling process and may not know all that he should know.

2. Since many items in the financial statements are not capable of exact measurement, he merely reviews such measurements for reasonableness. His are not the original determinations, and unless he can successfully prove otherwise (as for example in the case of estimates of useful lives of property), management's determination will prevail. Thus, the auditor's opinion contains no reference to "present exactly" or "present correctly" but rather states that the statements "present fairly."

3. While the auditor may be consulted on the use of accounting principles, he, as auditor rather than as preparer of such statements, does not select the principles to be used. Moreover, he cannot insist on the use of the *best* available principle any more than he is likely to *insist* on a degree of disclosure above the minimum considered as acceptable at the time.

4. The limitations to which the auditor's ability to audit are subject have never been spelled out by the accounting profession. Knowledgeable auditors do, of course, know about them; but there seems to be a tacit agreement, of doubtful value to the profession, not to discuss them. For example, is the auditor really equipped to audit the value of complex technical work in progress? Can he competently evaluate the adequacy of insurance reserves? Can he second-guess the client's estimate of the percentage of completion of a large contract? While such questions are rarely raised in public, let alone answered, they cannot be unequivocally answered in the affirmative.

5. While the preparer must, under the rules of double-entry bookkeeping, account for all items, large or small, the auditor is held to less exacting standards of accuracy in his work. Thus, the error tolerances are wider. He leans on the doctrine of materiality that in its basic concept simply means that the auditor need not concern himself, in either the auditing or the reporting phases of his work, with trivial or unimportant matters. What is important or significant is, of course, a matter of judgment, and so far the profession has neither defined the concept nor set limits or established criteria to govern the overall application of the concept of materiality. This has given it an unwarranted degree of reporting latitude.[5]

Of course, auditors even as a profession, in contra-distinction to a business, must pay attention to the economics of their function and to the limits of the responsibilities they can assume. Thus, whether the foregoing limitations on the auditor's function and responsibility are justified or not, the analyst must recognize them as standards applied by auditors and evaluate his reliance on audited financial statements with a full understanding of them.

The auditor's reference to "generally accepted accounting principles" in his opinion should be well understood by the user of the financial statements. Such reference means that the auditor is satisfied that such principles, or standards, have authoritative support and that they have been applied "in all material respects." Aside from understanding the operation of the concept of materiality, here the analyst must understand that the definition of what constitutes "generally accepted accounting principles" is often vague and subject to significant latitude in interpretation and application. For example, a *SAS* issued in 1975 states that "when criteria for selection among alternative accounting principles have not been established to relate accounting methods to circumstances (e.g., as in case of inventory and depreciation methods) the auditor may conclude that more than one accounting principle is appropriate in the circumstances."

Similarly indeterminate are present-day standards relating to disclosure. While minimum standards are increasingly established in professional and SEC pronouncements, accountants have not always adhered to them. The degree to which the lack of disclosure impairs the fair presentation of the financial statements remains subject to the auditor's judgment and discretion, and there are no definite standards that indicate at what point lack of disclosure is material enough to impair fairness of presentation thus requiring a qualification in the auditor's report.

When the auditor qualifies his opinion, the analyst is faced with an additional problem of interpretation, that is, what is the meaning and intent of

---

[5] See Leopold A. Bernstein, "The Concept of Materiality," *The Accounting Review,* January 1967; and Sam M. Woolsey, "Approach to Solving the Materiality Problem," *Journal of Accountancy,* March 1973. As of now the FASB has published a *Discussion Memorandum* on the subject and held public hearings on it.

the qualification and what effect should such qualifications have on his reliance on the financial statements? The usefulness of the qualification to the analyst depends, of course, on its clarity, its lack of equivocation, and on the degree to which supplementary information and data enable an assessment of its effect.

An additional dimension of confusion and difficulty of interpretation is introduced when the auditor includes explanatory information in his report, merely for emphasis, without a statement of conclusions or of a qualification. The analyst may in such situations be left wondering why the matter was emphasized in this way and whether the auditor is attempting to express an unstated qualification or reservation.

ILLUSTRATION 1.   The U and I Incorporated auditor report contains the following explanatory middle paragraph:

> As discussed in Note B to the consolidated financial statements, in February 1979 the Company discontinued its sugar processing operations and is in the process of selling or otherwise disposing of the related assets.

In light of a full footnote explanation of the matter, the analyst is left wondering why the auditors chose to emphasize this particular matter.

Qualification, disclaimers, and adverse opinions

As discussed in an earlier part of this chapter, generally when an auditor is not satisfied with the fairness of presentation of items in the financial statements, he issues an "except-for" type of qualification, and when there are uncertainties that he cannot resolve, he issues a "subject to" qualification. At some point, the size and importance of items under qualification must result in *adverse opinions* or *disclaimers of opinion,* respectively. Where is this point? At what stage is a specific qualification no longer meaningful and an overall disclaimer of opinion necessary? Here again, the analyst won't find any guidelines by turning to the auditor's own professional pronouncements or literature. The boundaries are left entirely to the realm of judgment without the existence of even the broadest of criteria or guidelines.

ILLUSTRATION 2.   Callahan Mining Corporation indicated in Note 5 of its 1980 annual report that at December 31, 1980, capitalized expenditures for exploration projects aggregated $4,612,000, the recovery of which is subject to the success of the project which cannot be forecast at this time.

The auditor report stated:

> As described in Note 5 to the consolidated financial statements, the recovery of the Company's investment in the Caladay Project, which is carried at cost, is subject to the success of the project and cannot be forecast at this time.

It was left to the reader to judge the significance of these disclosures.

Uncertainty qualifications.   When the auditor cannot assess the proper carrying amount of an asset or determine the extent of a possible liability or find other uncertainties or contingencies that cannot be determined or measured, he will issue a "subject to" opinion describing such uncertainties. The analyst using financial statements that contain such a qualification is, quite bluntly, faced with a situation where the auditor has passed on to him the uncertainty described and, consequently, the task of evaluating its possible impact. The analyst should recognize the situation for what it really is and not assume that he is dealing with a mere formality designed only for the auditor's self-protection. Moreover, the auditor's efforts to estimate future uncertainties cannot normally be expected to exceed those of management itself. As a *SAS* issued in 1974 put it, "The auditor's function in forming an opinion on financial statements does not include estimating the outcome of future events if management is unable to do so."

In those cases where the "subject to" opinion is given because of uncertainties that cannot be resolved, it is hard to blame the auditor for shifting the burden of evaluation on to the reader. At the same time, it must be remembered that as between the reader and the auditor, the latter, due to his firsthand knowledge of the company's affairs, is far better equipped to evaluate the nature of the contingencies as well as the probabilities of their occurrence. Thus, the analyst is entitled to expect, but will unfortunately not always get, a full explanation of all factors surrounding the uncertainty.

Lest the absence of an uncertainty qualification in the auditor's report lull the analyst into a false sense of security, it must be borne in mind that there are many contingencies and uncertainties that do not call for a qualification but that may nevertheless have very significant impact on the company's financial condition or results of operations. Examples of such contingencies or possibilities are:

1.   Obsolescence of a major product line.
2.   Loss of a significant customer.
3.   Overextension of a business in terms of management capabilities.
4.   Difficulty of getting large and complex production units on stream on time.

These matters must, however, be discussed by management in the SEC mandated "Management's Discussion and Analysis of Financial Condition and Results of Operations" (see Chapter 7).

From the above discussion it should be obvious that the analyst must read with great care the auditor's opinion as well as the supplementary information to which it refers. The analyst can place reliance on the auditor, but regardless of the latter's standing and reputation, the analyst must maintain an independent and open-minded attitude.

QUESTIONS

1. In relying on an auditor's opinion what should the financial analyst know about the auditor and his work?

2. What are "generally accepted auditing standards"?

3. What are auditing procedures? What are some of the basic objectives of a financial audit?

4. What does the opinion section of the auditor's report usually cover?

5. The auditors, in an attempt to respond to a clear divergence between their and the society's views of what is meant by "fair presentation," issued a statement on the matter in 1975. What are the major points of that statement?

6. Which are the three major categories of conditions that require the auditor to render qualifications, disclaimers, or adverse opinions?

7. What is an "except-for" type of audit report qualification?

8. What is a (a) disclaimer of opinion and (b) an adverse opinion? When are these properly rendered?

9. What is the practical effect of an uncertainty qualification in an auditor's report?

10. What types of changes may result in a consistency qualification in the auditor's report?

11. Give two examples of auditor reports that, while falling short of a full audit, provide the reader with lower-defined levels of assurance.

12. What are the major disclosures required by SEC's *FRR* No. 1, Section 603 on the relationship between auditors and clients?

13. What are some of the implications to financial analysis which stem from the audit process itself?

14. The auditor does not prepare the financial statements on which he expresses an opinion but instead he samples the data and examines them in order to render a professional opinion on them. List some of the possible implications of this to those who rely on the financial statements.

15. What does the auditor's reference to "generally accepted accounting principles" mean to the analyst of financial statements?

16. Of what significance are "uncertainty qualifications" to the financial analyst? What type of contingencies may not even be considered by the auditor in his report?

17. What are some of the circumstances which can point to areas of higher audit risk?

Index

A

Abdel-Khalik, A. R., 298 n
Abernathy, W., 198 n
Accelerated depreciation, 14
Accountant's work flow, 23
Accounting; *see also* Generally accepted accounting principles (GAAP)
  annualization, 305–6
  changing methods and assumptions, 288
  effect of changes on security prices, 14
  profession, 344–45
  treatment of extraordinary gains and losses, 291–92
"Accounting for the Effects of Certain Types of Regulation," 316
Accounting changes, 63–64
Accounting policies, 62–63
Accounting principles
  analytical review, 45–48
  assumptions and standards, 45–48
  in capital structure analysis, 148–53
  convertible debt, 153
  deferred taxes, 149–50
  long-term leases, 150
  minority interests, 152–53
  off-balance sheet financing, 150–51
  preferred stock, 153
  provisions/reserves/contingent liabilities, 152
  unconsolidated subsidiaries, 152
  unfunded vested pension liabilities, 151
Accounting Principles Board (APB) *Opinions,* 354
  Opinion 18, 96
  Opinion 20, 288 n
  Opinion 21, 278
  Opinion 28, 306, 308
Accounting risk, in income reporting, 271
Accounting standards, income statements, 225
Accounts payable, 89

Accounts receivable
  aging schedule, 100
  average turnover ratio, 97–101
  collection period, 98–99
  as current assets, 88
  ending gross receivable, 99
  evaluation of average turnover ratios, 99–101
  inclusion of notes receivable, 98
  measures of liquidity, 97
  sales figure, 98
  size in relation to sales, 93
Acid-test ratio, 113
Acquisition analysts, 19
Add-back fixed charges, 171
Adverse opinion, 365–66
  by auditors, 352
  compared to disclaimers of opinion, 353
Advertising costs, 273–74
Aggregate investor behavior, 14
AICPA; *see* American Institute of Certified Public Accountants
Almanac of Business and Industrial Financial Ratios, 49
Altman, Edward, 191
American Institute of Certified Public Accountants (AICPA), 344
  Commission of Auditor's Responsibilities, 351
  computation and review services, 357
  Financial Forecasts and Projections Task Force, 300
  Guide for a Review of a Financial Forecast, 300
  time-sharing program library, 44
American Management Association, 201 n
American Meat Institute, 50
Andrews, F., 360 n
Annualization, 305–6; *see also* Seasonality of sales
APB; *see* Accounting Principles Board
Archibald, T., 14 n

369

Asset bases
  modified, 199–200
  return on modified, 206
Asset protection, 186–87
Asset utilization, 42
  analysis of, 213–16
  evaluation of individual turnover ratios, 213–15
  factors, 215–16
  Marine Supply Company, 336–37
  return on shareholders' equity, 216
  use of averages of asset levels, 215
Assets
  accounts receivable, 278
  adjustments of book value, 153–54
  coverage, 168
  bankers' views of, 4
  current; see Current assets
  deferred charges, 278
  depreciable, 200–201
  financing of, 167–68
  intangible, 154, 200, 202
  measures of distribution, 167–69
  return on total, 199, 206
  role in earnings forecasts, 299
  turnover and profitability, 208–13
  unproductive, 199
  write-downs of, 289
  working; see Working assets
Audit risk, in income statements, 271
Auditing
  general standards, 347
  implications of process, 358–61
  improvements in, 271
  objectives, 19
  standards of fieldwork, 347–48
  standards of reporting, 348
Auditing process, 348–49
  detection of fraud, 359
  risk and implications, 361–62
Auditor(s)
  conformity with generally accepted accounting
    principles, 354–55
  implications from standards, 362–65
  objectives in financial analysis, 19–20
  problem of unresolved known uncertainties,
    355–56
  qualifications and competence, 345–46
  special reports, 356–57
  value of opinion, 346–47
  work on financial statement analysis, 344–66
Auditor's report
  adverse opinions, 352, 365–66
  on compiled and reviewed financial statements,
    357
  conformity with generally accepted accounting
    principles, 350
  disclaimers of opinion, 352–53, 365–66
  exceptions as to consistency, 356
  fairness of presentation, 350–51

Auditor's report—Cont.
  form of, 353
  implications for analysis, 358
  internal control, 349
  limitations in scope, 353–54
  modification of the opinion, 351
  opinion section, 350
  procedures, 348–49
  qualifications of findings, 351–52, 365–66
  scope of audit, 347–49
  SEC requirements, 357–58
  special, 356–57
  uncertainty qualifications, 366
Average earnings, 285
Average effective interest rate paid, 258–59

                                    B

Babson, David L., 16–17
Backer, Morton, 230 n
Bad debt expenses, 257–58
Balance sheet analysis
  accounts receivable, 278
  carrying amounts of assets, 276–77
  effect of valuation of assets on quality of re-
    ported income, 278
  provisions and liabilities, 277
  and quality of earnings, 277–78
Balance sheet data, 229
Ball, R., 13 n
Bankruptcy
  empirical studies, 190–91
  Equity Funding case, 361
  multiple discriminant analysis, 191
  ratios as predictors of, 189–92
Banks
  credit scoring, 192 n
  views of assets, 4
Bar Chris Construction case, 359
Beaver, William H., 11 n, 13 n, 182 n, 190–91
Bennett, William M., 212
Bennian, Edward G., 302
Bernstein, Leopold A., 20, 364 n
Beta index theory, 10, 16
Bond credit ratings, 185–89
  asset protection, 186–87
  limitations, 189
  municipal securities, 188–89
Bonds
  convertible, 2
  interest on, 171–72
  valuation tables, 6–7
  value calculation, 6
Borrowing capacity, 115
Break-even analysis, 42, 240–53
  analytical implications, 249–50
  concepts underlying, 240–41
  contribution margin, 252
  contribution margin approach, 242–44
  equation approach, 241–42
  for financial analysts, 246

Break-even analysis—*Cont.*
 fixed-cost level, 251–52
 fixed/variable/semivariable costs, 244–45
 managerial implications, 246
 operating leverage concept, 249–50
 safety margin, 248
 simplifying assumptions, 245–46
 technique application, 246–49
 variable-cost percentage, 250
 uses and implications, 246–49
Brealey, Richard A., 297
Breitel, C. J., 188 n
Bristol Products, Inc., 306
Brown, P., 13 n
Building block approach, 313–14
Business activities and transactions, reconstruction of, 23–25
Business enterprise, adverse views of, 196
Business loans; *see* Credit grantors
Business risk, 11

C

Capital, cost of, 155
Capital asset, return components, 13
Capital assets pricing model, 16
 theory of investment, 12–13
Capital structure, 42
 accounting principles, 148–53
 adjusted ratio of debt to equity, 166
 adjustments to book value of assets, 153–54
 common-size statements, 161–62
 composition of, 147–48
 convertible debt, 153
 deferred taxes, 149–50
 earning power, 169
 effect on long-term solvency, 160
 equity and debt, 154–56
 fixed assets equity capital, 168
 intangible assets, 154, 200, 202
 interpretation of measures, 167
 inventories, 153–54
 long-term leases, 150
 long-term projections, 160–61
 Marine Supply Company, 333–35, 341–42
 marketable securities, 154
 measures of assets distribution, 167–69
 measures of earnings coverage, 169–76
 minority interests, 152–53
 net tangible assets as a percentage of long-term debt, 168
 preferred stock, 153, 166
 provisions/reserves/contingent liabilities, 152
 reasons for employment of debt, 156–60
 significance, 154–56
 unconsolidated subsidiaries, 152
 unfunded past or prior service costs, 151
 unfunded vested pension liabilities, 151
Capital structure ratios, 162–66
 equity capital at market value, 164–65
 long-term debt/equity capital

Capital structure ratios—*Cont.*
 short-term debt, 164
 total debt to total capital, 162–63
 total debt to total equity capital, 163
Capitalized interest, 172
Capitalized long-term leases, 176 n
CAPM; *see* Capital assets pricing model
Cash
 as asset, 87
 conversion into investments, 123
 purpose of holding, 92–93
Cash from operations, 320–30
Cash equivalents
 as assets, 87
 purpose of holding, 92–93
Cash flow; *see also* Funds flow
 limitation of concept, 124
 overview of patterns, 121–24
 related measures, 114–15
Cash forecasts, 42
Cash ratios
 definition, 96
 evaluation, 96–97
Casualty losses, 294
Certified public account(s) (CPA), 46, 344–45
 standards, 347–48
Chambers, R. J., 14 n
Changes in financial position, 42; *see also* Statements of changes in financial position
Chottiner, S., 6
Chrysler Corporation, 288
Clark, J. J., 301
Coleman, Delbert, 17
Collins, D. W., 227 n
Common-size financial statements analysis, 31–34
 current assets, 111
 in current ratio, 107, 111–12
 income statement, 33, 255
 intercompany comparisons, 33–34
Common-size income statements
 cost and expense items, 255
Common-size statements of capital structure, 161–62
Common stock
 approaches to valuation, 5–7
 data for valuation, 7–9
 efficient market hypothesis, 13–18
 investment theory, 9–18
 present value theory, 5
 price-earnings ratio, 6
 valuation, 4–5
 valuation tables, 6–7
Comparison process, 26
Comparative financial statements
 creation of, 28–30
 trend, 28–30
 year-to-year change, 30
COMPUSTAT, 44
Computer-assisted financial analysis, 42–45
 credit extension, 44

Computer-assisted financial analysis—*Cont.*
  data storage/retrieval/computational ability, 43–44
  limitations, 43
  screening large masses of data, 44
  security analysis, 44–45
  sensitivity analysis, 44–45
  specialized financial analysis, 44–45
Conditional sales, 2
Conglomerate(s)
  definition, 226
  financial reporting on, 226–32
  pooling of interests concept, 277
  segmented earnings contribution matrix, 227–28
Consolidated Edison Company, 184 n
Continental Vending case, 359
Contingent liabilities, 152
Contribution margin
  approach to break-even analysis, 242–44, 252
  reporting, 229
Convertible bonds, 2
Convertible debt, 153
Corporate bond rating, 186–88
Cost of sales
  amortization of tools, 254
  analysis, 236
  break-even analysis, 240–53
  changes in gross margin, 237–40
  common-size income statement, 255
  depreciation, 253
  and gross profit, 236–37
  index number analysis, 255
  maintenance and repair costs, 254–55, 273
Cost analysis, 236–68
Costs
  advertising, 273–74
  bad debt expenses, 257–58
  of capital, 155
  discretionary; *see* Discretionary costs
  financial, 258–59
  fixed, 251–52, 258–59
  fixed and variable, 240–41, 244–45
  future directed, 272
  future directed marketing, 258
  income taxes, 259–66
  maintenance and repair, 254–55, 273
  other expenses, 259
  research and development (R & D), 274–76
  selling expenses, 255–57
  of tools, 254
Cottle, S., 5, 165 n, 173 n
Coverage ratio; *see* Earnings coverage ratio *and* Fixed charges
CPA; *see* Certified public accountant(s)
Credit
  liberal extension of, 101
  long-term, 2
  offsetting, 289

Credit—*Cont.*
  short-term, 2
  sources, 2
Credit analysis, 3–4
Credit extension, computer assisted analysis, 44
Credit grantors
  compared to equity investors, 3
  fixed rewards, 2–3
  objectives in financial analysis, 2–4
  risk-reward ratio, 3
Credit scoring, by banks, 192 n
Credit worthiness, 185–89
Cudahy Packing Company, 289
Current assets
  accounts receivable, 88, 97–101
  common-size analysis, 111
  convertibility to cash, 87
  definition, 86
  equity investments, 87
  inventories, 88, 101–5
  liquidity index, 112
  and operating cycle, 87
  prepaid expenses, 89
  types, 87
  ways of measuring, 86–105
Current liabilities, 89–90
  days purchases in accounts receivable ratio, 107
  level, 93–94
  nature of, 106–7
  ways of measuring, 106–7
Current ratio
  common-size analysis of current assets, 111
  evaluation of cash ratios, 96–97
  implications and limitation, 94–95
  importance of sales, 111
  interpretation, 107–12
  interpretation of changes over time, 108
  limitations, 92–94
  liquidity index, 112
  manipulation, 108–9
  measures of accounts receivable liquidity, 97
  measures that supplement, 96–97
  net trade cycle, 110
  reasons for use, 91–92
  tool of analysis, 95–96
  trend analysis, 107
  use of "rule of thumb" standards, 109
  uses, 94–95
  valid working capital standards, 111
Customers, interest in financial analysis, 20

D

Data
  basic, 27
  retrieval, 43–44
  screening large masses, 44
  uses of external, 26–27
Data bases, 43
Days Inns, 297
Days sales in accounts receivable, 98–99

Days purchases in accounts receivable ratio, 107
Days to sell inventory, 103
Debt
  advantages of financial leverage, 156–59
  effect of financial leverage, 159–60
  long- and short-term, 155
  rating of obligations, 184–85
  reasons for employment of, 156–60
  relation to equity capital, 4
  repayment requirements, 175–76
  tax deductibility of interest, 158
Debt hierarchy, 147 n
Debt-to-equity ratio, 35
  computation, 192–93
  Marine Supply Company, 334–35
  relationship, 155–56
  screening device, 167, 169
Debt instrument; see Bonds
Deferred charges as assets, 278
Deferred income tax credit account, 262, 265
Deferred income taxes, 149–50
Deferred tax accounting, 90
Delay rentals, 173
Depreciation, 253
Direct measurements, 26
Disclaimers of opinion by auditors, 352–53, 365–66
  compared to adverse opinions, 353
Discount Merchandiser, 50
Discretionary costs, 272–73
  research and development, 275–76
Discussion Memorandum, 230
Dividend payout ratio, 40
Dividend yield, 40
Dividends
  claims of equity investors, 4
  from current earnings, 4–5
Dodd, D. L., 165 n, 173
Donaldson, Gordon, 141
Drucker, Peter F., 213 n
Dun and Bradstreet, Inc., 48, 100

E

E. I. du Pont de Nemours Company, 200–201
Earning power, 169
  adjustment of reported earnings per share, 303–4
  concept, 301–2
  future, 187
  time horizon, 302–3
Earnings; see also Income
  adjustment of income statements, 280–85
  annualization, 305–6
  average, 285
  determining trend over the years, 285–88
  distortion of trends, 285–88
  effect of extraordinary items, 295
  evaluation of level and trend, 279–96
  evaluation of quality, 270–79
  evaluation of variability, 285

Earnings—Cont.
  extraordinary gains and losses, 281–86
  factors affecting level of, 279–80
  growth ratios, 5
  income smoothing or distortion, 288–90
  importance in stock evaluation, 5
  importance of trends, 285–88
  measures of coverage, 169–76
  to meet fixed charges, 169–71
  minimum, 285
  objectives of evaluation, 270
  payout ratios, 5
  projected, 8, 198
  ratio of fixed charges to, 177–80
  seasonality, 305–6
  source of dividends, 4–5
Earnings-coverage ratio
  evaluation, 183–85
  fixed charges to be included, 171–73
  impact of income taxes, 171
  level of income, 171
  of preferred dividends, 183
  pro forma computations, 180
Earnings forecasting, 296–301
  elements of, 298–99
  publications of, 300–301
  role of assets, 299
  role of management, 299
  SEC requirements, 298
Earnings quality
  balance sheet analysis, 276
  changing price levels, 279
  concept, 271–76
  external factors, 278–79
  factors affecting, 272–76
  foreign income, 279
  regulation, 279
  stability of sources, 279
Earnings retention, 217–18
Earnings variability, 184
Earnings yield, 40
Economic risk, 11
Effective tax rate, 260
Efficient market hypothesis (EMH)
  aggregate behavior evaluation, 14
  definition, 13–14
  implications for financial analysis, 14–18
  semistrong form, 13
  strong form, 13
  weak form, 13
Electric utilities, 94 n
Elgers, P., 301
EMH; see Efficient market hypothesis
Ending gross receivable, 99
Epstein, M. J., 360 n
Equation approach to break-even analysis, 241–42
Equity
  in capital structure, 154–55
  shareholders', 201–2

Equity capital, 201
  at market value, 164–65
  relation to debt, 4
  return on, 206–7
Equity Funding case, 359–60
Equity growth rate, 217–18
Equity interest, 4
Equity investments as current assets, 87
Equity investors
  common stock valuation, 4–9
  compared to lenders, 3
  dividend claims, 4
  objectives in financial analysis, 4–9
Expropriation of business, 294
Extraordinary gains and losses
  accounting treatment, 291–92
  analysis and evaluation, 292–96
  casualty losses, 294
  determination of, 292–94
  effect on evaluation of management, 295–96
  expropriation, 294
  extraordinary items, 295
  income determination, 291
  nonrecurring nonoperating, 294
  nonrecurring operating, 292–93
  recurring nonoperating, 293–94
  seizure or destruction of property, 294

F

Fair Lanes, 94 n
Fama, E. F., 13 n
FASB; see Financial Accounting Standards Board
Federal government, source of information on ratios, 49–50
Federal Trade Commission, 49, 320
FIFO; see First-in, first-out inventory method
Financial Accounting Standards Board (FASB), 172
  Discussion Memorandum, 230
  Statements, 354
Financial analyst, 345–46
Financial costs, 258–59; *see also* Costs *and* Fixed charges
Financial flexibility concept, 115
Financial forecasting; *see also* Earnings forecasting
  of funds flow, 121–24
  statements of changes in financial position, 132–44
Financial Forecasts and Projections Task Force of the AICPA, 300
Financial leverage
  advantages, 158–59
  definition, 156–58
  effects, 218–20
  index, 159–60
  measuring effect, 159–60
Financial mobility, 141
Financial resources, 187
Financial risk, 11

Financial reporting by diversified enterprises, 226–32
"Financial Reporting for Segments of a Business Enterprise," 230–32
Financial Reporting Releases; see Securities and Exchange Commission
Financial statements
  comparative; see Comparative financial statements
  failure to conform to accounting principles, 354–55
  unresolved known uncertainties, 355–56
Financial statements analysis
  accounting principles, 45–48
  approaches to, 1–2
  asset utilization, 213–16
  auditor's work, 344–66
  basic approaches, 22–23
  break-even analysis, 240–53
  building block approach, 313–14
  building blocks, 42
  capital structure, 146–94
  common-size financial statements, 32–34
  common stock valuation, 4–9
  comparative financial statements, 28–30
  comparison process, 26
  computer-assisted, 42–45
  costs of operations, 236–68
  and customers, 20
  data conversion, 1
  defining objectives, 311–12
  definition, 1
  detailed or summary, 342–43
  diagnostic tool, 1
  direct measurements, 26
  dividend payout ratio, 40
  dividend yield, 40
  earnings valuation, 270–308
  earnings yield, 40
  efficient market hypothesis, 14–18
  Equity Funding case, 359–61
  forecasting tool, 1
  foundation, 314–16
  funds flow adequacy ratio, 143–44
  funds flow analysis, 121–24
  funds reinvestment ratio, 144
  income statements, 222–35
  index number trend series, 30–31
  indirect evidence, 26
  individual enterprises, 16
  and Internal Revenue Service, 20
  investment theory, 18
  and labor unions, 20
  and lawyers, 20
  life insurance companies, 316
  long-term solvency, 146–94
  management evaluation, 1
  Marine Supply Company, 317–43
  market measures, 40
  methodology, 311–13

Financial statements analysis—*Cont.*
  new information evaluation, 15
  objectives of
    acquisition analysts, 19
    auditors, 19–20
    credit grantors, 2–4
    equity investors, 4–9
    management, 18–19
    merger analysts, 19
  occupancy-capacity analysis, 42
  oil and gas industry, 316
  predictive functions, 26
  price-earnings ratio, 40
  principal tools, 28–40
  public utilities, 316–17
  rate analysis, 34–40
  ratio change, 18
  reconstruction of business activities and transac-
    tions, 23–25
  and regulatory agencies, 20
  return on investment, 192–213
  return on stockholders' equity, 216–20
  screening tool, 1
  sections of, 315
  short-term cash forecasts, 124–32
  short-term liquidity, 85–119
  sources of information, 27
  sources of information on ratios, 48–50
  special industry or environmental characteris-
    tics, 316–17
  specialized tools, 41–42
  statements of changes in financial position, 25–
    27, 132–44
  structured, 32–44
  techniques used by lenders, 3–4
  testing understanding of tools, 40–42
  total information set, 28
  trend analysis, 18; *see also* Trend analysis
  uses, 26–27, 342–43
Finney, A. H., 112
Firestone Tire and Rubber Company, 290
First-in, first-out inventory method, 102, 153
Fitzpatrick, Paul J., 190
Fixed assets equity capital, 168
Fixed charges
  add-back of, 171
  annual sinking fund requirements, 180
  capitalized interest, 172
  earnings to meet, 169–71
  funds flow coverage, 180–82
  guarantees to pay, 176
  income tax adjustment, 174
  income taxes, 171
  interest equivalent on unrecorded pension obli-
    gations, 174–75, 180
  interest implicit in lease obligations, 173
  interest incurred, 171–72
  long-term rental payments, 176
  minority interests, 170–71
  preferred dividends, 170

Fixed charges—*Cont.*
  preferred stock dividend requirements, 173
  principal repayment requirements, 175–76
  ratio of earnings to, 177–80
  treatment of extraordinary gains and losses, 170
Fixed-cost level, 251–52
Fixed costs, 240–41
Franklin Mint, 289
Fraud
  detection, 359
  Equity Funding case, 359–61
Funds flow, 42; *see also* Earnings
  adequacy ratio, 143–44
  coverage of fixed charges, 180–82
  long- and short-term projections, 160–61
  long-term cash forecasts, 130–32
  net as percentage of capital expenditure, 182
  from operations, 182
  ratios, 113–14
  short-term cash forecasts, 124–30
  source in sales, 123–24
  statements of changes in financial position, 132–
    44
Funds flow analysis
  financial mobility, 141
  Marine Supply Company, 330–33
  sales estimates, 125
Funds flow patterns, 121–24
Funds reinvestment ratio, 144
Funds statements; *see* Statements of changes in
  financial position
Future-directed costs, 272
Future directed marketing costs, 258
Future earnings power, 187

                              G

GAAP; *see* Generally accepted accounting principles
Gains and losses; *see* Extraordinary gains and
  losses
Generally   accepted   accounting   principles
  (GAAP), 19, 23, 27, 47, 148, 200, 272, 284,
  288–89, 306, 348, 350, 352
  failure to conform to, 354–55
General standards of auditing, 347
Gordon-Shapiro formula for stock valuation, 5–6
Graham, B., 5, 165 n, 173
W. T. Grant Company failure, 35
Gross margin
  changes in, 237–40
  variation in, 42
Gross profit
  data, 229
  definition, 236–37
  factors in analysis, 237
  percentage, 237
Guide for a Review of a Financial Forecast, 300
"Guides for Disclosure of Projections of Future
  Economic Performance," 300
Guy, J., 11 n

H

Hamilton, M. T., 13–14
Harris, Kerr, Forster and Company, 50
Hayes, Douglas A., 8
Hayes, R., 198 n
H. J. Heinz Company case, 290
Herring, H. C., 150 n
Hickman, W. Braddock, 183 n, 190
Horrigan, James O., 191

I

Income; *see also* Earnings
   definition, 124
   distortion, 288–90
   forecasting, 296–301
   importance of nonfund items, 114
   miscellaneous, 259
   net; *see* Net income
   smoothing, 288–90
Income analysis
   objectives, 222–25
   relevant net income, 223–25
Income reporting, accounting risk, 271
Income statement, 33, 236–68
   accounting standards, 225
   administrative costs, 258–59
   advertising costs, 273–74
   amortization of tools, 254
   analysis of sales and revenues, 226
   analytical recasting and adjustments, 280–85
   bad debt expenses, 257–58
   balance sheet data, 229
   break-even analysis, 240–52
   components, 225
   for conglomerates, 226–32
   cost of sales, 236
   data, 229
   depreciation, 253
   discretionary and future-directed costs, 272–73
   earnings evaluation, 270–308
   earnings forecasting, 296–301
   earnings power concept, 301–4
   Financial Accounting Standards 14, 230–32
   financial reporting by diversified enterprises, 226–32
   gross profit, 236–40
   income tax disclosure, 259–66
   interim financial statement, 304–6
   "line of business" data, 228–29
   maintenance and repair costs, 254–55, 273
   management's discussion and analysis, 233–34
   methods of revenue recognition, 234–35
   monitoring performance and results, 304–8
   necessary data, 226–28
   net income ratio, 268
   operating ratio, 266–68
   recasting and adjusting procedure, 281–85
   revenue recognition, 234–35
   research and development costs, 274

Income statement—*Cont.*
   research studies on, 229–30
   SEC requirements, 231
   segmented earnings contribution matrix, 227–28
   selling expenses, 255–57
   significance of, 222
   stability and trend of revenues, 232–33
   tools of analysis, 225
   year-end adjustments, 305
Income taxes, 259–66
   adjustment, 174
   analysis of disclosures, 261–66
   beginning/ending balance, 264
   deferral method, 262
   effective rate, 260
   flow-through method, 262
   impact on earnings-coverage ratios, 171
   rates, 266
   SEC reporting requirements, 260–66
Index fund, 16 n
Index number analysis, 255
Index number trend series, 30
   for long-term analysis, 31–32
Indirect evidence, 26
Industrial bond rating, 186–87
Industries, specialized, 316–17
Industry ratios, 50; *see also* Ratio
Integrated Disclosure System, 115–16
Intercompany comparisons, 33–34
Interest
   average effective rate paid, 258–59
   on bonds, 171–72
   capitalized, 172
   equivalent on unrecorded pension obligations, 120, 174–75
   expensed, 172
   implicit in lease obligations, 173
   tax deductibility, 158
Interest expense, 203 n
Interest incurred, 171–72
Interim financial statements, 304–6
Interim reports
   APB Opinion 28, 306
   implications for analysis, 307–8
   SEC requirements, 306–7
Internal Revenue Service, 49
Inventories; *see also* First-in first-out inventory method *and* Last-in, first-out inventory method
   alternative methods of management, 105
   as assets, 278
   in capital structure, 153–54
   conversion period, 104–5
   as current assets, 88, 101–2
   days to sell, 103
   determining size of, 93
   interpretation of turnover ratios, 103–4
   measuring turnover, 101–5
   misstatement of, 288–89

Inventories—*Cont.*
prepaid expenses, 105
turnover ratio, 102
valuation of, 35
Investment; *see also* Return on investment
capital asset pricing model, 12–13
categories of risk, 9–11
components of unsystematic risk, 11–12
efficient market hypothesis, 13–18
portfolio theory, 9
random walk hypothesis, 13
recent development in theory, 9–18
risk-return evaluation, 9
Investment base
averaging, 202–3
defining, 199–202
depreciable assets, 200–201
equity capital, 201
and investor's cost, 202
long-term liabilities, 201
modified asset bases, 199–200
relating income to, 203–4
shareholder's equity, 201–2
total assets, 199
Investment tax credit, 262

J—K

Jacobs, F. A., 150 n
JWT Group, Inc. case, 290
Kaplan, R., 14 n
Kottler, P., 11 n

L

Labor unions, 20
Lasman, D. A., 151 n, 166 n
Last-in, first-out (LIFO) inventory method, 35,
88, 102, 105, 153, 234 n, 272, 305, 308
Lawyers, 20
Lease
capitalized, 173
financing by, 2
Lender's risk, 2–3
Lerner, E. M., 227–28, 230 n
Leverage, operating; *see* Operating leverage concept
Liabilities; *see* Contingent liabilities *and* Current liabilities
Licensed accountants, 344
Life insurance accounting, 316
LIFO; *see* Last-in, first-out inventory method
Line-of-business data, 228–29
Ling, James, 17
Lintner, John, 12
Liquidity
funds flow analysis, 121–44
index, 112
short-term; *see* Short-term liquidity
Little, I. M. D., 297
Loans; *see* Credit *and* Credit grantors

Londontown Manufacturing Company case, 288–89
Long-term cash forecasts, 130–32
Long-term credit, 2
requirements of analysis, 3
Long-term debt
as current liability, 89
definition, 163 n
equity capital ratio, 163–64
Long-term leases, 150
capitalized, 176 n
Long-term liabilities, 201
return on, 206–7
Long-term rental payments, 176
Long-term solvency, 42
earnings coverage of preferred dividends, 183
effect of capital structure, 160
evaluation of earnings coverage ratio, 183–85
funds flow coverage of fixed charges, 180–82
key elements, 146–47
Marine Supply Company, 333–35, 341–42
payment of fixed charges, 169–80
rating of debt obligations, 185–86
ratio of earnings to fixed charges, 177–80
stability of flow of funds from operations, 182
Lorie, J. H., 13–14
Losses; *see* Extraordinary gains and losses

M

McCloy Report of 1975, 359
McCormick Company case, 359
McFarland, Walter B., 230 n
McKesson and Robbins case, 359
Maintenance and repair costs, 254–55, 273
Management
advantages of monitoring data, 18–19
effect of gains or losses on, 295–96
effectiveness, 197
evaluation of, 271
objectives in financial analysis, 18–19
responsibility for financial statements, 344
role in earnings forecast, 299
Management's Discussion and Analysis of Financial Conditions and Results of Operations,
116–19, 233–34, 281, 298, 366
Marine Supply Company
aspects of financial condition, 326
asset utilization, 336–37
capital structure, 333–35, 341–42
cash from operations, 329–30
debt-equity ratio, 334–35
financial analysis, 317–43
funds flow analysis, 330–33
long-term solvency, 333–35, 341–42
operating performance, 338–39, 342
principal advantages, 318
return on investment, 320, 335–36, 342
short-term liquidity, 327–28, 341
Market measures, 40
Marketable securities, 154

Markowitz, H., 9
Mattel, Inc., 257–58, 305–6
  case, 359
Mautz, R. K., 230
May, C., 6
MDA; see Multiple discriminant analysis
Merger analysts, 19
Merwin, Charles L., 190
Miller, M., 155 n
Minimum earnings, 285
Minority interests, 152–53
  earnings from, 170–71
Modigliani, F., 155 n
Modigliani-Miller thesis, 155–56
Molodovsky, N., 6
Monte Carlo trials, 44
Moody's Investor Service, 49, 185
Multiple discriminant analysis (MDA), 191
Municipal securities rating, 188–89

N

National Association of Music Merchants, 50
National Cash Register Company, 49
National Decorating Products Association, 50
National Electrical Contractors Association, 50
National Farm and Power Equipment Dealers Association, 50
National Fuel Gas Company, 88
National Office Products Association, 50
National Retail Hardware Association, 50
National Student Marketing case, 359
Net funds flow, 182
Net income
  data, 229
  margin, 217
  measuring, 223–24
  ratio, 268
  relevant, 223–25
  variation in, 268
Net nonfund items, 114
Net tangible assets, 168
Net trade cycle, 110
Net working capital; see Working capital
New York City Moratorium, 188 n
Nonfund items, 114
Nonmarket risk; see Unsystematic risk
Nonrecurring nonoperating gains or losses, 294
Nonrecurring operating gains and losses, 292–93
Notes payable, 89

O

Occupancy-capacity analysis, 42
Off-balance sheet financing, 150–51
Oil and gas industry, 316
Operating cycle, 87
Operating leverage concept, 249–50
Operating performance, 42; see also Performance evaluation
  Marine Supply Company, 338–39, 342

Operating potential, 250
Operating ratio, 266–68

P

Penn Central Company, 89
Pension liabilities, 35
Pension obligations, interest on, 174–75
Performance evaluation, 196–268
  amortization of tools, 254
  asset utilization, 213–16
  bad debt expenses, 257–58
  break-even analysis, 240–52
  cost of sales analysis, 236, 253
  criteria, 196–97
  depreciation, 253
  diverse views, 196
  earnings, 270–308
  general administration costs, 258
  gross margin, 237–40
  gross profit, 236–37
  income statement analysis, 222–35
  income taxes, 259–66
  maintenance and repair costs, 254–55
  net income ratio, 268
  operating ratio, 266–68
  return on common stockholders' equity, 216–20
  return on investment, 197–213
  selling expenses, 255–57
Pooling of interests concept, 277
Portfolio theory of investment, 9
  capital asset pricing model, 12–13
Predictive functions of analysis, 26
Preferred dividends, 183
Preferred stock, 2, 153
  in capital structure, 166
  dividend requirements, 173
Prepaid expenses
  as current assets, 89
  definition, 105
Present value theory of common stock, 5
Price-earnings ratio, 6, 40
Principal repayment requirements, 175–76
Pro forma financial statements, 125
Professional organizations, 48–49
Profitability
  analysis, 3
  and asset turnover, 208–13
Progress payments, 90
Public accountants, 344
Public accounting profession, 344–45
Public utilities, 316

Q

Qualification of opinion, 365–66
  by auditors, 351–52
  uncertainty, 366
Quality of earnings; see Earnings quality
Quality of Earnings Report, 303
Quick ratio; see Acid-test ratio

R

Radical interest; *see* Equity interest
Randell, Cortes, 17
Random walk hypothesis, 13
Rappaport, A., 227–28, 230 n
Rate-regulated companies, 316
Rating
  of corporate bonds, 186–88
  of debt obligations, 185–86
  industrial bond issue, 186–87
  limitations, 189
  municipal securities, 188–89
Ratio
  acid-test; *see* Acid-test ratio
  current; *see* Current ratio
  definition, 34
  of depreciation to gross plant and equipment, 253
  dividend payout; *see* Dividend payout ratio
  of earnings to fixed charges, 177–80
  factors affecting, 35
  illustration of computations, 36–40
  interpretation of, 35–36
  market measures, 40
  predictors of business failure, 189–92
  price-earnings; *see* Price-earnings ratio
  sources of information, 48–50
  testing relationships, 40–42
  as tools of analysis, 34–35
Ratio analysis, 34–40
Ratio change analysis, 18–19
Recurring nonoperating gains and losses, 293–94
Regan, P. J., 151 n
Registration Statements, 27
Regulatory agencies, 20
Repair costs, 254–55, 273
Report of the Special Review Committee of the Board of Directors of Gulf Oil Corporation, 359
Research and development (R and D) costs, 274–76
Reserves, 152
  for future costs and losses, 289
Residual risk, 10
Return on common stockholders' equity (ROCSE)
  analysis of, 216–20
  components, 216–17
  equity growth rate, 217–18
  financial leverage effects, 218–20
Return on investment (ROI), 42
  ability to earn, 198
  adjusting components of, 204–13
  analysis and interpretation, 207
  averaging investment base, 202–3
  basic elements, 199–204
  book versus market values, 202
  calculation, 200–201
  defining investment base, 199–202

Return on investment (ROI)—*Cont.*
  depreciable assets, 200–201
  effect of gains or losses on, 295
  equity capital, 201
  importance of, 197
  internal decision and control tool, 198
  investors' cost/investment base, 202
  long-term liabilities, 201
  long-term liabilities plus equity capital, 206–7
  major objectives, 197–98
  management effectiveness, 197
  Marine Supply Company, 320, 335–36, 342
  measure, 197–213
  modified asset bases, 199–200
  profitability and asset turnover, 208–13
  projected earnings, 198
  relating income to investment base, 203–4
  return on modified asset bases, 206
  return on stockholders' equity, 207
  return on total assets, 206
  shareholders' equity, 201–2
Revenues
  analysis of, 226
  stability and trend of, 232–33
Revenues only data, 229
Richardson, A. P., 17
Risk
  beta index, 10
  capital asset pricing model, 12–13
  categories of, 9–11
  components of unsystematic, 11–12
  residual, 10
  systematic, 10
Risk-return evaluation, 9
Risk-reward ratio, 2–3
Robert Morris Associates, 49–50
A. H. Robins Company, 303–4
ROCSE; *see* Return on common stockholders' equity
Rohr Industries, 116
ROI; *see* Return on investment
Roll, R., 14 n
Rosenberg, B., 11 n
Rules of thumb in current ratio evaluation, 109

S

S & P; *see* Standard & Poor's Corporation
Safety margin, 248
Sales; *see also* Annualization
  cost of; *see* Cost of sales
  importance in current ratio, 111
  inflation of, 289
  seasonality, 305–6
  stability and trend of, 232–33
Sales to assets ratios, 215
Sales to cash ratio, 213–14
Sales estimates, in cash flow forecasting, 125
Sales to fixed assets ratio, 214–15
Sales to inventories ratio, 214

Sales to receivables ratio, 214
Sales and revenues analysis, 226
Sales to short-term liabilities ratio, 215
Sanzo, Richard, 50
SAS; *see Statements on Auditing Standards*
SCFP; *see* Statements of changes in financial position
Scholes, M., 11 n
Seasonality of sales, 305–6
Securities Act of 1933, 27, 271
Securities Act of 1934, 271
Securities and Exchange Commission (SEC), 49, 174, 364
  Accounting Series Release 155, 173 n
  audit requirements, 357–58
  company filings with, 27
  disclosure requirements, 164
  Form 8-K, 307
  Form 10-K, 307
  formula for ratio of earnings to fixed charges, 177, 179–80, 184
  Financial Reporting Release No. 1
    Section 203, 87, 89
    Section 204, 87, 89
    Section 301, 307
    Section 303, 307
    Section 304, 307, 357
    Section 501, 233, 234 n
    Section 503, 231
    Section 603, 358, 362
  Guides for Disclosure of Projections of Future Economic Performance, 300
  income reporting requirements, 231, 233–34
  Integrated Disclosure System, 115–16
  interim report requirements, 306–7
  Management's Discussion and Analysis of Financial Condition and Results of Operations requirements, 116–19, 233–34, 281, 298, 366
  regulation on compensating balance arrangements, 87
  regulation on fixed charges coverage ratio, 173
  Regulation S-K, 231
  Regulation S-X, 27 n
  Rule 14c-3, 27 n
Security analysis
  computer-assisted, 44–45
  investment theories, 9–18
Segmented earnings contribution matrix, 227–28
Seidler, L. J., 360 n
Seizure or destruction of property, 294
Selling expenses, 255–57
Semivariable costs, 245
Sensitivity analysis, 44–45
SFAS; *see Statements of Financial Accounting Standards*
Shareholders' equity, 201–2
Sharpe, W. F., 12
Sherwood, H. C., 189

Short-term cash forecasts, 124–30
  and long-term forecasts, 130–32
  pro forma financial statements, 125
  techniques, 125–30
Short-term credit, 2, 89
  lender's concern, 3
Short-term liquidity, 42
  acid-test ratio, 113
  analysis of, 85–119
  average accounts receivable turnover ratio, 97–101
  capacity to borrow, 115
  cash flow related measures, 114–15
  current ratio, 91–97
  financial flexibility, 115
  funds flow ratio, 113–14
  importance of nonfund items, 114
  interpretation of current ratio, 107–12
  liquidity index, 112
  management's discussion and analysis, 115–19
  Marine Supply Company, 327–29, 341
  measures of current assets, 86–105
  measures of current liabilities, 106–7
  measures of inventory turnover, 101–5
  significance, 85–86
  use of short-term cash forecasts, 124–32
  working capital, 86–91
Short-term solvency, 161
Sinking fund requirements, 180
Small Business Administration, 49
Smith, Raymond F., 190
Speagle, R. E., 301
Sprouse, Robert T., 230 n
Standard & Poor's Corporation, 44, 49, 185, 187
Standards of field work, 347–48
Standards of reporting, 348
Statements on Auditing Standards (SAS), 347–48, 366
  "Independent Auditor's Responsibility for the Detection of Errors and Irregularities," 358 n
  6, 233 n
  23, 19 n
  43, 350 n
Statements of changes in financial position (SCFP), 25–27, 228–29
  analysis of, 132–33
  evaluation, 136–39
  illustration of, 133–36
  impact of adversity, 141–43
  projection of, 139–44, 161
  recasting, 136
  value to analyst, 138
Statements of Financial Accounting Standards (SFAS)
  3, 306 n
  5, 152, 289
  6, 89
  12, 87, 280 n
  13, 150, 173, 177, 316–17

Statements of Financial Accounting Standards
   (SFAS)—*Cont.*
  14, 230–32
  16, 288 n
  34, 172, 355
  52, 280 n
  71, 316
Stock; *see* Common stock *and* Preferred stock
Stock market
  collapse of early 1970s, 16–17
  efficient market hypothesis, 13–18
  investment theories, 9–18
Stock valuation techniques, 5–9
Stockholders' equity, return on, 207, 216
Straight-line depreciation, 14
Systematic risk, 10

T

T-accounts, 262–66
Tandy Corporation, 217
Tax rate, 206
Tax ratio, 260
Tax Refund Receivable account, 262
Tax retention rate, 217 n
Taxes
  current liabilities, 89
  deferred, 149–50; *see also* Deferred tax account-
    ing
Taxes Currently Payable account, 262, 265
Thompson, R. B., 298 n
Tools, amortization of, 254
Total debt-total capital ratio, 162–63
Total debt-total equity capital ratio, 163
Total information set, 28
Trade creditors, 2
Trend analysis, 18–19
  changes over time, 108
  in comparative financial statements, 28–30
  in current ratio, 107–11
  of earnings, 303
  index-number, 30–31
Troy, Leo, 49
Turnover ratios
  sales to cash, 213–14
  sales to fixed assets, 214–15

Turnover ratios—*Cont.*
  sales to inventories, 214
  sales to receivables, 213
  sales to other assets, 215
  sales to short-term liabilities, 215

U—V

Uncertainty qualifications, 366
Unconsolidated subsidiaries, 152
Unfunded past or prior service costs, 151
  interest on, 174–75
Unfunded vested pension liability, 151
  interest on, 174–75
Union Carbide, 288
United States Department of Commerce, 49
United States Department of the Treasury, 49
United States Financial case, 359
Unrecognized pension obligation, 193
Unsystematic risk, 10
  components, 11–12
Value Line data base, 44
Variable-cost percentage, 250
Variable costs, 240–41

W—Y

Weil, R. L., 151 n, 166 n
White, G. I., 15 n
Whittaker Corporation case, 359
Williams, John B., 5
Winakor, Arthur, 190
Woolsey, Sam M., 364 n
Working assets, 90
Working capital, 86–91
  current assets, 86–89
  current liabilities, 89–90
  deferred tax accounting, 90
  definition, 86
  measure of liquidity, 90–91
  valid standards, 111
  working assets, 90
Write-down of assets, 289
Yale Express case, 359
Year-end adjustments to income statements, 305
Year-to-year change in comparative statements,
  30